Hᴏʟʟʏᴡᴏᴏᴅ'ꜱ Wᴇꜱᴛ

Film & History

The Film & History series is devoted to creative scholarly works that focus on how feature films and documentaries represent and interpret history. Books in the series explore the significant impact of motion pictures on our society and analyze films from a historical perspective. One goal of the series is to demonstrate how historical inquiry has been reinvigorated by the increased scholarly interest in the intersection of film and history. The Film & History series includes both established and emerging scholars and covers a diverse array of films.

Series Editors

Peter C. Rollins and John E. O'Connor

HOLLYWOOD'S WEST

 *The American Frontier in Film, Television, and History*

EDITED BY
PETER C. ROLLINS
JOHN E. O'CONNOR

THE UNIVERSITY PRESS OF KENTUCKY

Paperback edition 2009
Copyright © 2005 by The University Press of Kentucky

Scholarly publisher for the Commonwealth, serving Bellarmine University,
Berea College, Centre College of Kentucky, Eastern Kentucky University,
The Filson Historical Society, Georgetown College, Kentucky Historical Society,
Kentucky State University, Morehead State University, Murray State University,
Northern Kentucky University, Transylvania University, University of Kentucky,
University of Louisville, and Western Kentucky University.
All rights reserved.

Editorial and Sales Offices: The University Press of Kentucky
663 South Limestone Street, Lexington, Kentucky 40508-4008
www.kentuckypress.com

13 12 11 10 09   5 4 3 2 1

"Challenging Legends, Complicating Border Lines: The Concept of
'Frontera' in John Sayles's *Lone Star*" © 2005 by Kimberly Sultze.

The Library of Congress has cataloged the hardcover edition as follows:

Hollywood's West : The American frontier in film, television, and history / edited by
Peter C. Rollins and John E. O'Connor.
     p. cm.
   Includes bibliographical references and index.
   ISBN-10: 0-8131-2354-2 (hardcover : alk. paper)
   1. Western films—United States—History and criticism. 2. Western television
programs—United States. I. O'Connor, John E. II. Rollins, Peter C.
   PN1995.9.W4A44 2005
   791.436'278—dc22
                                    2005018026
   ISBN-13: 978-0-8131-2354-7 (hardcover: alk. paper)
   ISBN-13: 978-0-8131-9196-6 (pbk.: alk. paper)

This book is printed on acid-free recycled paper meeting
the requirements of the American National Standard
for Permanence in Paper for Printed Library Materials.

Manufactured in the United States of America.

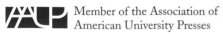

Member of the Association of
American University Presses

To two great heroes on the intellectual frontier
who have inspired the coeditors for decades:

ALAN HEIMERT (1928–1999)

Powell M. Cabot Professor of American Literature
Harvard University
and

E. JAMES FERGUSON (1917–2002)

Professor of History
Queens College and the Graduate Center of
City University of New York

CONTENTS

🖎 *Ray Merlock*

PREFACE

The Western obviously means different things to different people. To some, it conjures a sense of nostalgia, memories of Saturday afternoons at the downtown picture show, where a kid could get popcorn, a soft drink, and candy for a dime, or a quarter, or seventy-five cents (depending on the decade) and cheer Gene, Roy, Hoppy, Durango, or any number of hard-riding heroes. For others, the Western brings to mind Sunday nights with the family, watching *Bonanza* (NBC, 1959–1973) on a new color TV.

To filmmakers and production students, the Western must be cited as one of the building blocks of filmmaking, a genre possibly as old as moving pictures, cameras, screens, and projectors. *The Great Train Robbery* (1903) helped establish cinematic terminology and narrative possibility. Orson Welles, in preparation for directing *Citizen Kane* (1941), acknowledged screening John Ford's *Stagecoach* (1939) over and over (once stating he watched it more than forty times, on another occasion stating he viewed it so many times he lost count), always with different technicians enabling him to inquire how this was done or why Ford chose to do a shot or scene that way. Film schools for decades used (and still use) a documentary on editing entitled *Interpretation and Values: The Filming of a Sequence from the Television Series* Gunsmoke (28 min., 1958) to clarify the concepts of "establishing shot," "master shot," "inserts," and "cut-ins and cutaways" and the varied ways a scene can be assembled, thereby instilling in the minds of would-be filmmakers a primal connection of Westerns to filmmaking.

To discerning critics, historians, and fans, the Western undeniably includes some of the finest motion pictures ever made, remaining for decades a preferred genre for directors, producers, and stars central to American—even to world—

Clint Eastwood, frontier icon,
in *Hang 'em High.*

cinema. The American Film Institute's (AFI) List of the Top 100 American Movies of the Twentieth Century, compiled and released at the turn of the millennium, included nine Westerns—no. 33, *High Noon;* no. 50, *Butch Cassidy and the Sundance Kid;* no. 63, *Stagecoach;* no. 69, *Shane;* no. 75, *Dances with Wolves;* no. 88, *The Wild Bunch;* no. 82, *Giant;* no. 96, *The Searchers;* and no. 98, *Unforgiven*—while several others on the list (*The Treasure of the Sierra Madre, Midnight Cowboy, Star Wars, Taxi Driver,* and *Raiders of the Lost Ark*) obviously are informed by and owe debts to the iconography and themes of Westerns. And it is the Western that has been the source of introspection and insight for a considerable portion of what has become landmark film and cultural criticism, including Robert Warshow's essay "The Westerner," André Bazin's "Le Western," and the other extraordinary scholarly contributions discussed by Peter Rollins and John O'Connor in the introduction to this collection.

To other observers, though, the Western currently exists primarily as a curiosity, a once popular, once fashionable, once immensely profitable form of entertainment that wore out, exhausted its possibilities, and has, except for isolated reappearances, more or less vanished. Coinciding with (perhaps even contributing to) the appraisal of the Western as a relic are suggestions that the genre's decay and demise resulted from its manifesting (indeed, perhaps even celebrating) destructive and damaging tendencies and practices of American culture. In the documentary *Sam Peckinpah's West: Legacy of a Hollywood Renegade* (2004), when questioned about director Peckinpah's classic Western film *The Wild Bunch* (1969), Paul Schrader, an admirer, fan, and himself a screenwriter-director of violent fare, acknowledged what he felt to be Peckinpah's ultimate understanding of and approach to the Western: "I know it's an anachronism. I know it's fascist. I know it's sexist. I know it's evil and out of date. But, God help me, I love it so." What Schrader may be suggesting is that, by the late 1960s, Peckinpah was aware that commonly held models of masculinity and masculine behavior had become suspect. Peckinpah was able to appreciate how and why diverse factions, all in good conscience, could denounce or even ignore the Western. The form, however, in which he had begun his career as a writer of television Western episodes, could—at least for him—still be seen as a place for myth, legend, and political expression and, in his own words, still be described as "a universal frame within which it is possible to comment on today."

While teaching a recent course on the history of film, I included, among the works to be studied, John Ford's *The Searchers* (1956). I was a bit taken aback when several students in the class acknowledged *The Searchers* was the first Western they had ever seen. Two students admitted it was the first John Wayne film they had ever watched. Most of the African American students in the class stated they had never before viewed an entire Western. Several young women registered in the course confessed they never thought the Western had any application to them, except for a young woman who confided she had once stopped and watched part of a Clint Eastwood Western on television when she saw her father sitting and watching it. Today's students, of course, have numerous entertainment and time-passing choices. Westerns, of course, still are available for consumption—not in the quantity they once were, but perhaps located in a small section in the movie rental store, or among television reruns, or even sometimes via a new film or television programming enterprise such as HBO's 2004 series *Deadwood.* None of these developments, however, can diminish the possibility that rethinking, reimagining, and realigning the Western with contemporary issues of race, class, gender, and violence will lead to newly refined, freshly insightful critical, cultural, and historical analysis.

The perspectives and essays available in this collection resulted from the conference "The American West(s)" hosted by *Film & History: An Interdisciplinary*

Journal of Film and Television Studies (www.filmandhistory.org) in Kansas City, Missouri, in 2002. Scholars from around the world attended, all anxious to share their thoughts and convictions about Western(s), what they mean, and what they imply. It may not be necessary to love the Western (as Sam Peckinpah no doubt did, and the gathering's keynote speaker, John Cawelti, and those who participated in the conference and contributed to this volume do) in order to use and enjoy this book. The collection stands as a laudable journey west, a well-intentioned and well-presented quest to confront shifting cultural and historic frontiers and to both discover and rediscover what has thrilled, pleased, and often disturbed motion picture and television audiences for so long. Americans in particular and citizens of the world in general are likely to find studying the Western is actually a way to confront the past, face the present, and better understand themselves.

ACKNOWLEDGMENTS

Deborah Carmichael, associate editor of *Film & History*, was regularly involved in moving this project along—with her usual tact and diligence. The 2002 and 2003 CD-ROMs from *Film & History* were edited by her and contain additional articles on the West as a follow-up to our international conference on the subject in 2002. (See the *Film & History* Web site for details about the CD-ROMs: www.filmandhistory.org.)

Susan Rollins provided late-afternoon fruit snacks and Internet advice.

Paritosh Shah and Steve Smith of Instructional Technology Services, University of South Carolina Upstate, deserve thanks for scanning the Ray Merlock Collection photos and lobby cards. As a collector of such memorabilia, Ray Merlock—who also wrote the preface—has been an invaluable colleague. Steve Brown and Martha Halihan of Oklahoma State's Technology Support Center were ready with nimble software and personal service to provide working copies of pictures for the editors.

The librarians of the Oklahoma State University Edmon Low Library were most helpful in guiding us to appropriate sources to enhance this volume.

Unless otherwise indicated, all illustrations are from the Ray Merlock Collection.

John E. O'Connor and Peter C. Rollins

INTRODUCTION
The West, Westerns, and American Character

There is no more characteristic American art form than the Western film. Even when it is produced in Italy, Finland, East Germany, Hungary, Australia, or Japan, there is no mistaking the American institutions that are being represented or the distinctively American character types portrayed. Scholars have been interested in the wide variety of Western stories and representations of the West for generations. Consider *The West of the Imagination*, a 1986 PBS television series focusing on nineteenth-century painters and photographers of the frontier who "like the writers and storytellers became America's primary mythmakers" (Goetzmann x). For the eras prior to cinema, painting, works of sculpture, and literary representations conveyed the myths of the West. But in our media age, by far the most influential forces in shaping images of the American West have been entertainment films and television programs. In these visual narratives, Hollywood has interpreted America to itself.

The Western legacy has pervaded popular culture and the ordinary activities of life. Any person even vaguely familiar with the century-long history of Western movies and TV shows might reasonably assume, despite the testimony of the never-been-kissed Marshal Matt Dillon (James Arness), that the typical barmaid in a Western tavern had at least a "questionable" reputation. And everyone knows that you would not want to be the guest of honor at "a necktie party." Teenagers "ride shotgun" (on the passenger's side) while their friend drives the car; their teachers "shoot from the hip" when they ask an unexpected question on a quiz; and a deserted shopping center on a Sunday morning is like a "ghost town." These and other colloquialisms derive from the liminal persistence of Western narratives in the American mind.

Courtesy of Fred Buckner.

Monument Valley. Iconic landscape for the Western.

The West as Myth and Symbol

Indeed, throughout its history, American culture would be almost unimaginable without the West as a touchstone of national identity. The novels of James Fenimore Cooper (1789–1851) identified the basic character types for the genre and stated for all time America's apprehensions about the loss of a natural frontier—a fear embodied in the lectures of old Leatherstocking (Natty Bumppo) and most memorably stated in Cooper's third novel, *The Pioneers* (1823). At the same time Cooper was putting to paper these concerns about a vanishing frontier, the painter Thomas Cole (1801–1848), leader of the Hudson River school of painting, created a famous series entitled *The Course of Empire*. Although these paintings were placed in the age of classical Greece and Rome, their lessons were timely for an expanding America. According to Cole, great nations begin their destinies close to nature; as they progress, they move away from the values of the wild, and eventually their accomplishments are

These paintings are from Thomas Cole's *The Course of Empire* series. *Above: The Arcadian or Pastoral State* shows a civilization in balance with nature (painting 2 of 5 in the series). *Below: The Consummation of Empire* depicts a society in excess (painting 3 in the series).

overwhelmed; they suffer the inevitable "course of empire"—decadence, decay, and death. While neither Cooper nor Cole believed that the United States had reached an imbalanced relationship with nature, they joined transcendentalists Emerson and Thoreau in identifying this drift toward overdevelopment as a serious concern for the future. According to Perry Miller, the preoccupation was fundamental to our national identity: "The American, or at least the American artist, cherishes in his innermost being the impulse to reject completely the gospel of civilization, in order to guard with resolution the savagery of his heart" (216). Later in the nineteenth century and early 1900s, the paintings of Frederic Remington (1861–1909), Charles Russell (1864–1926), Albert Bierstadt (1830–1902), and others of what might be called the "Rocky Mountain school" of painters captured the sometimes Darwinian conflict between man in nature and, alas, between the expanding white civilization and the declining traces of Native Americans. Prior to World War I, an American president, Theodore Roosevelt (1901–1909), celebrated "the strenuous life" and identified it with his own struggles as a rancher on the western frontier—a struggle that may have foreshadowed later foreign policy applications as the United States launched its own Darwinian entrance into the international arena. In the recent past, the photography of Ansel Adams (1902–1984) preserved and celebrated a vision of the American landscape that inspired the creation of organizations like the Sierra Club and led to the preservation of California's Yosemite National Park and adjacent wilderness lands. Admired widely for his work and awarded the Medal of Freedom by President Jimmy Carter in 1980, Adams was a voice for the wilderness with direct access to the Oval Office. As recently as 2004, congressional debates over exploitation of huge oil reserves discovered beneath the Arctic National Wildlife Refuge (ANWAR) of Alaska were framed in terms of previous fears about a final conquest of the wild. Throughout our cultural history, Americans have been in awe of their frontier experience, and it has been rendered to comment on vital national issues, which it actually may have helped shape.

For two centuries observers have debated the extent of the influence of the frontier on American history and on the character of Americans as a people. When Hector St. John de Crèvecoeur asked in 1782, "What, then, is the American, this new man?" he expressed his belief that the vast open spaces of the New World and the opportunities they created had helped set Americans apart—though not always in a positive way, since Crèvecoeur was disturbed about frontier violence (69). More than fifty years later, when another

Courtesy of the Huntington Library.

Visionary of a "frontier thesis,"
F. J. Turner.

Frenchman, Alexis de Tocqueville, wrote *Democracy in America* (1835), he warned reactionaries in his own country that "democracy was irreversible as well as irresistible" (Mansfield xx). From the earliest colonial settlements until the Oklahoma land runs of the 1890s, there had always been a demarcation between the more or less civilized area and the frontier (see chapter 1). Whether it was the forest primeval, the danger of starvation or thirst in the American desert, or the threat of wild animals or still wilder Indians, the West was a training ground for national character.

It was exactly such challenges that inspired the imagination of the historian Frederick Jackson Turner (1861–1932). According to the "Turner thesis," the old-world aristocratic pretensions and the established cultural assumptions that immigrants brought with them were irrelevant on the frontier. For example, social status helped little when people had to hunt for or grow their own food and struggle for survival in the face of hostile elements; indeed, the "gentleman" who could not fend for himself was often worse off than the hardscrabble, but adaptable, immigrant farmer. Ethnic differences also paled on the frontier, where people survived, or failed, to on the basis of their wits and their willingness to work hard. Supported by the chronology of when individual states adopted constitutional reforms such as universal male suffrage, Turner also posited that the West was the wellspring of American democratic practice that, in addition, provided a safety valve for the rest of American society. According to Turner's famous "safety valve" corollary, when urban pressures built up in nineteenth-century America, pressures such as the labor unrest and political protest that were perplexing European cities at the same time, the availability of a frontier allowed Americans to move on, perhaps to a job in the Midwest if not to a frontier farm, relieving the overpopulation, as well as the perceived potential for unrest in industrial cities. As late as 1912, Elinore Pruitt Stewart presented herself to American readers as a living example of the safety valve thesis in her *Letters of a Woman Homesteader,* an epistolary narrative celebrating the exhilarating opportunities for homesteaders. (In 1980, the book was adapted into what might be described as a "Vietnam syndrome" film in *Heartland* [dir. Richard Pearce].)

Sensing for themselves, as Turner had argued, that the West was such a central force in American life, Hollywood producers used it as a backdrop for a myriad of dramatic relationships and situations that were characteristic of the American experience and American values—and therefore, presumably, especially appealing to American audiences. Turner's ideas, first laid out in a since-famous presentation before the American Historical Association in 1893, struck such a responsive chord at the time because experience seemed to support his view. What lay ahead if, as people could readily extrapolate from Turner's ideas, the West filled up with settlers and the frontier no longer provided the release it had in the past from proliferating urban problems and no longer continued to reinforce the egalitarian values thought so central to American civilization? Would, or could, distinctive American ideals survive? (See chapter 13.)

CLASSICS ON THE WESTERN: THE EVOLVING SCHOLARLY VISION

Many of us became interested in the study of the Western after reading Henry Nash Smith's *Virgin Land: The American West as Symbol and Myth,* first published by the Harvard University Press in 1950. As Smith explained in his preface to the twentieth-anniversary printing, "I wanted to protest against the common usage of the term 'myth' to mean simply erroneous belief, and to insist that the relationship between the imaginative constructions I was dealing with and the history of the West in the nineteenth century was a more complicated affair" (vii). The approach would attract many in the field of American culture studies.

Smith's classic began with eighteenth-century visions of the frontier and marched forward through Manifest Destiny, the works of James Fenimore Cooper, and the dime novels of Ned Buntline to the great agrarian myths embodied in the Homestead Act, the importance of a positive vision of the railroad as an agent of progress, and the efforts by John Wesley Powell and others to preserve the West by settling it on sound ecological principles. On issues such as the safety valve theory, Smith showed the disparity between ardent belief and the cruel realities of migration to an undeveloped frontier. Smith is famous for his dissection of the great historian's vision: "The idea of nature [at the frontier] suggested to Turner a poetic account of the influence of free land as rebirth, a regeneration, a rejuvenation of man and society constantly recurring where civilization came into contact with the wilderness along the frontier" (253). The general lesson of *The Virgin Land* was that America's future as a complex society in a complicated international environment would require a reevaluation of its agrarian mythology—and a rejection of it. Smith's book is so noteworthy because he was both a scholar and a visionary—an interdisciplinary student of American society who could appreciate the past on its own terms and then move forward to suggest change. The book is an enduring classic because it avoids the simplistic approach of many volumes to follow—works that are guilty of "presentism" of the first order and use the putative wisdom of the present, often Freudian theory, to excoriate the past.

Perhaps the best-known scholar of the Western genre is John G. Cawelti, who updated his earlier study with his appropriately titled *Six-Gun Mystique Sequel* in 1999. For litterateurs, Cawelti's *Six-Gun Mystique* (1971) was the intellectual progeny of Smith's classic work; written some twenty years later, it voiced an unapologetic approach to the popular arts. Where Smith evoked the curiosity of the anthropologist in his study of dime novels, newspaper articles in favor of western expansion, or magazine illustrations, Cawelti accepted such artifacts as objects for aesthetic appreciation. In many ways, Smith was still attached to "high culture" even as he studied the many manifestations of the popular. For example, the words "movie," "motion picture," and "film" never appear in the index to Smith's classic—even though the previous twenty years had seen the release of countless films directly related to Smith's themes of an expanding West: *Stagecoach* (1939), *Union Pacific* (1939),

John Cawelti urges scholars to take popular culture seriously—especially the Western.

Northwest Passage (1940), *They Died with Their Boots On* (1941), *The Ox-Bow Incident* (1943), *The Virginian* (1946), *My Darling Clementine* (1946), and *Red River* (1948) deserved study but lay outside the purview of the Harvard University dissertation writer. (One wonders whether Smith, ensconced in a carrel at the Widener Library during these decades, may have failed to notice what was showing at the Brattle Street Theatre.)

Cawelti, who admitted that he enjoyed both popular novels and films, connected the print and visual media in his study. As early as the first few pages of *The Six-Gun Mystique*, while attentive to literary manifestations of the West in American literature, Cawelti takes note of *The Great Train Robbery* (1903), *Shane* (1953), *The Wild Bunch* (1969), and even the popularity of the Western on television as reflected in the Nielsen ratings (1–6). Such a spectrum begins at the origins of the genre, touches base with the classic Western, and shows awareness of the antiheroic innovations of the Vietnam era. And none of this study is conducted with apologies; instead, Cawelti tried to promote a theory of "formula" to film study, a notion akin to the genre tradition of literary scholarship in the 1950s associated with an outgrowth of the New Critical

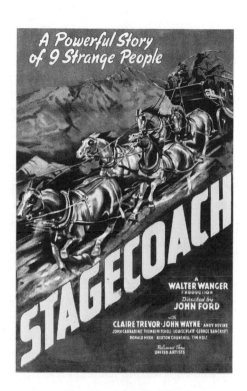

A microcosm of American society in a hostile world: *Stagecoach*.

approach promoted by popularizers of the work of Cleanth Brooks and Robert Penn Warren, especially in their textbooks *Understanding Literature* and *Understanding Poetry*. As Cawelti explained, popular arts were based on understood "conventions," and it was the work of scholars to explore how the conventions of a particular genre were applied in any particular work of literature or film: "Westerns must have a certain kind of setting, a particular cast of characters, and follow a limited number of lines of action. A Western that does not take place in the West, near the frontier, at a point in history when social order and anarchy are in tension, and that does not involve some form of pursuit, is simply not a Western" (31). In Cawelti's scheme the ideal scholar—like many authors in this collection—must be attentive to continuities and variations of such factors as setting, the complexity of characters, types of situations, and patterns of action. By extension, popular culture texts can be used as platforms from which to explore the concerns of any era (see chapters 10 and 11).

The enthusiasm and ingenuousness of *The Six-Gun Mystique* inspired hundreds of students to divert their scholarly pilgrimage down the trail of popular culture studies. Indeed, the long essay was such a fresh breeze that Ray Browne, the editor in chief of the Popular Press, in rushing it into print, forgot to put a copyright date on the book version! (Cawelti reflects on the context and writing of the book in his talk to the Film and History League on the 2003 CD-ROM Annual produced by *Film & History*.) Directly and indirectly, contributors to this collection are greatly indebted to these scholarly trailblazers.

As novelists and filmmakers continued to play upon frontier situations, other historians responded to Turner, either endorsing or questioning aspects of his interpretation. Still others built on Turner's base to develop even broader ideas about what defined America. During the Eisenhower era (1953–1961), David M. Potter argued that the open space of the frontier was merely one expression of a larger experience America had with *abundance*. In his *People of Plenty: Abundance and the American Character* (1957), Potter was quick to note that land was the most important resource in which an agricultural country could be rich. But, later in America's growth, there had also been abundant raw materials and labor to promote the development of American industry— and more jobs meant still more opportunities. In addition to exploring the mythic basis of the nation, Westerns also have had the ability to elucidate social and cultural concerns for contemporary audiences.

Confronting Modern America in the Western Film, the subtitle of John H. Lenihan's *Showdown* (1980), indicates this author's concern with analysis of the genre as comment on post–World War II social and political issues. Lenihan analyzes Westerns in relationship with American cold war anxieties, racial tensions, and a general cultural malaise producing both alienation and complacency. He contends that "the study of a single genre is especially revealing of how a particular form is modified in accordance with the constantly changing concerns and attitudes of a society" (4). Interpreting *Broken Arrow* (1950), among other films, as an argument for peaceful coexistence, he situates Indian/ cavalry negotiations in a context of cold war policy. For Lenihan the "Indian problem" also represented a means for Western films to deal with racial issues of segregation and protest, citing *Broken Arrow* and *Devil's Doorway* (1950) as but two examples (see chapter 6). By refiguring racial questions in a historic past, Western film provided a distance for reconsidering the present. Problems of racial equality served to underscore the larger discomfort of individuals within a changed society. He notes that outlaw stories like those distilled in *Jesse James* (1939) prefigured fears of alienated delinquency in cold war era

Masculinity and violence in 1958.

films such as *The Left-Handed Gun* (1958) or *One-Eyed Jacks* (1961). While acknowledging that *High Noon* (1952) is often seen as a movie underscoring the Red scare, Lenihan also sees Hadleyville as a society no longer solidly united in preserving traditional values, looking instead to maintain "appearances" for Northern investors. Unfortunately for Marshal Will Kane (Gary Cooper), capital rather than shared values motivated the community (see chapter 8). One of the strengths of Lenihan's work is his ability to trace multiple postwar themes not only within the genre but also in individual films, recognizing the underlying complexity of Westerns. For Lenihan, the frontier myth in film spoke eloquently to cultural issues of post–World War II America.

Two volumes by Patricia Nelson Limerick, *The Legacy of Conquest: The Unbroken Past of the American West* (1987) and *Something in the Soil: Legacies and Reckonings in the New West* (2000), went off in a different direction, promoting a more critical "New Western History," but one that still identified

American culture with the frontier experience. Meanwhile, Richard Slotkin's *Gunfighter Nation: The Myth of the Frontier in Twentieth-Century America* (1992) continued to argue that Turner's ideas not only had become "the basis of the dominant school of American historical interpretation" but also had provided "the historic rationale for the ideologies of both Republican progressives and Democratic liberals for much of the ensuing century" (3).

Slotkin's work, referred to frequently in this collection, applies an American studies approach to the "myth" of the West in a way that appeals to many contemporary scholars. The title of the work should give some hint to its approach, which can be interpreted as an attempt to pick up the analysis of images of the West where Henry Nash Smith left off at the end of *The Virgin Land.* At each point along the way, Slotkin places the violence of the West in continuity with various outcomes—racial hatred (vigilantes); violent masculinity (marshals, detectives, and other "killer elites"); alienation (cult of the outlaw); destruction of frontier enemies (both "good" and "bad" Indian films); and veneration of a fascist federal government (cavalry films). The overview begins with the Kennedy administration (1960–1964) and its celebration of the "New Frontier" and ends with the Vietnam conflict, which falls into place as a logical culmination of a "demoralized" national tradition of truculent expansionism and violence. The My Lai massacre figures as a logical outcome of a perverted legacy, just another trip to "Indian country" (581–91), and the later presidency of Ronald Reagan (1980–1988) is no more than "the Recrudescence of the Myth."

Like many wrongheaded books, Slotkin's *Gunfighter Nation* is nonetheless compelling; the writing is trenchant, and the intensity of vision holds any reader. Alas, the error of "presentism," the quality that often makes such a book an exciting read, is precisely the flaw that detracts from its lasting value. As an indication of the problem, an informal reviewer on Amazon.com described the book with these mixed feelings: "It makes a good point in showing how Western movies mirror the times in which they are made and how the frontier experience is still with us today. The two drawbacks of the book are its EXTREMELY long length and its Leftist ideology that pops up toward the end." These criticisms notwithstanding, many scholars in *Hollywood's West* have found Slotkin's analysis an excellent jumping-off point for their own—less hortatory—studies.

While Slotkin encompasses much, he omits important details that reveal a far more complex reality. There is room in Slotkin for the imperial Teddy Roosevelt ("The clamor of the peace faction has convinced me that this country

President Roosevelt as Cooper's Leatherstocking.

Thomas Moran's *Grand Canyon of the Yellowstone* (1872).

needs a war") but no place for Roosevelt as the greatest of our wilderness presidents. This Roosevelt camped in Yosemite with John Muir and was a decisive force in creating several of our national parks. He even went so far as to commission Thomas Moran to paint his famous *Grand Canyon of the Yellowstone* (1872) to convince Congress to acquire 1.25 million acres of one of the great natural wonders. (The initial acquisition took place in 1908 and was nearly doubled in 1975 by President Gerald Ford.)

Historians (like moviemakers) are products of the times in which they write (or film). Turner spoke within the context of his times; nineteenth-century definitions of American history were based on a white male–dominated perspective. Slotkin, attempting to make sense of the contentious Vietnam War years, reduced American history to a single essence: violence. In contrast, New West historians, working within a growing consciousness of national cultural diversity, emphasize the complexity of the American West by adding the "stories" of those peoples absent from Turner's assessment of westward expansion. Patricia Nelson Limerick, probably the best-known spokesperson for a revised history of the American West, points to absent or distorted voices in historical frontier exposition: Native Americans, Hispanics, African Americans, Asians, and women. Rather than the oversimplification of history from Turner's distant vantage point or the bilious distillation of Slotkin, Limerick builds upon the national frontier narrative through inclusion of the "messy" details of America's past—what she calls *la frontera* (see chapter 12).

The most often cited "revisionist" films about the West are *Little Big Man* (1970) and *Dances with Wolves* (1990), yet both films rework Native American history through the experiences of white protagonists. Hispanics most often retain stereotypical traces of lazy ineptitude, buffoonery, or violent banditry. Robert Redford's *Milagro Beanfield War* (1988) replaces many of the conventional Latin American portraits, but, again, the conclusion requires Anglo assistance. Film representations of African American contributions to western history generally work from the tradition of John Ford's *Sergeant Rutledge* (1960); television productions are particularly fond of the story of the buffalo soldiers, with productions in 1979, 1992, and 1997. In each case, unlike the Indians they attack, blacks have been assimilated into an expansionist mind-set; African Americans thus implicitly support the suppression of native peoples. Asians, beyond slant-eyed Stepin Fetchit–like roles or shadowy opium pushers, are almost invisible in Western films, although a massive infusion of

Racial revisionism in John Ford's *Sergeant Rutledge*.

coolic labor facilitated the completion of the transcontinental railroad, an achievement emblematic of Manifest Destiny. Jackie Chan's parody, *Shanghai Noon* (2000), humorously overturns many such derogatory genre conventions (see chapter 10).

Women, of no matter what ethnicity, now less restricted to the schoolmarm-civilizer or golden-hearted prostitute role, have earned stronger positions in Western film, but male mediation usually becomes necessary for conflict resolution. For example, Ron Howard's film *The Missing* (2003) undercuts the cinematic possibilities of a strong woman's surviving alone in the wilderness with the convenient reappearance of a long-absent father. This lack of truly revisionist Western movies demonstrates just how fundamental Turner's mythic vision remains for the film industry. As Patricia Limerick points out, "In the late *twentieth century* [and into the twenty-first], the scholarly understanding formed in the late *nineteenth* century still governs most of the public, rhetorical uses of the word 'frontier'" (*Something in the Soil* 92). Despite attempts to reinscribe American history to include traditionally marginalized stories, and in spite of any politically correct agenda for moviemakers, Western genre conventions remain entrenched in the American psyche.

Left: From book to film, Owen Wister's *The Virginian* (1902) becomes a classic film in 1929.

Below: Modern chivalry from Japan to the United States. *The Magnificent Seven* (1960).

THE CINEMATIC WEST

Textbooks and monographs are not the only, or even necessarily the best, places for observing the intimate role that the West has played in shaping American history and culture. As noted previously, representations have also appeared in novels and short stories, in oft-told and retold legends and traditional tales, even on radio, where, for example, the Lone Ranger got his start as early as 1933 (see chapter 3). Several of the earliest memorable film productions were Westerns, including, arguably, the first Edison film to tell a story, *The Great Train Robbery* (1903), and one of the earliest productions by director D. W. Griffith, *The Battle at Elderbush Gulch* (1914). One of the best-remembered early feature films of the sound era, *The Virginian* (book, 1902; film, 1929), starring Gary Cooper, was based on a popular Western novel by Owen Wister. By midcentury, Western symbols had become common in the culture, even in that most ubiquitous of American institutions, the TV commercial. How many youngsters were tempted to begin an unhealthy smoking habit by the macho image of the horseback-riding, rough-and-ready "Marlboro Man"? And how many Americans were converted to environmentalism in the 1970s

Marshal Dillon of *Gunsmoke* endorsing "smokes."

by the often-reproduced and particularly touching image of Cherokee actor Iron Eyes Cody (1914–1999) shedding a tear for his littered and polluted homeland?

The Western offered numerous opportunities for delving into social issues—in the frontier town taken over by outlaws, for example, in *The Magnificent Seven* (dir. John Sturges, 1960). Some stories, including this one, were borrowed from other cultures. Although *The Magnificent Seven* starred Hollywood regulars Yul Brynner, Steve McQueen, Charles Bronson, James Coburn, and Eli Wallach, the concept for the film was developed from the traditional Japanese warrior drama released a few years earlier as *The Seven Samurai* (dir. Akira Kurosawa, 1954). There was also the anthropological observation of Native American cultures in films such as Delmer Daves's *Broken Arrow*, which brought viewers inside Native American societies to portray their authentic beliefs about the land and about leadership styles—often surprisingly tolerant of dissent and disagreement. Westerns could offer the opportunity for family drama in TV series such as *Little House on the Prairie* (1974–1982) and *Bonanza* (1959–1973), the latter with Ben Cartwright (Lorne Green), his three sons (Pernell Roberts as Adam; Dan Blocker as "Hoss"; and Michael Landon as "Little Joe"), and Hop Sing (Victor Sen Yung), the Ponderosa's Chinese cook. Unlike these and the more recent PBS series *Frontier House* (2002), which tried to reproduce the everyday experience of ordinary settlers in 1880s Montana, earlier film productions that were promoted for their accuracy to detail, films such as *Iron Horse* (1924) and *Union Pacific* (1939), concentrated on re-creating great moments in history, such as the driving of the final spike in the transcontinental railroad, completing the connection between east and west at Promontory Point, Utah, only four years after the Civil War.

There was also the drama of the landscape itself. One contributor to the companion volume to the PBS television series *The West* (1996) described a sunset reverie he had experienced in the company of a busload of foreign tourists looking out on Monument Valley on the border between Arizona and Utah. He reflected on the many Western films that had been photographed there, including John Ford's *Stagecoach*, the first "talkie" shot on location there in 1938. Since then scores of other films, perhaps most recently *Thelma and Louise* (1991), and dozens of television commercials have made use of that dramatic landscape—a wilderness topography that has become an archetype of the American frontier experience (Ward 381–94).

Buffalo with Buffalo Bill.

"Not that long ago" in years gone by, some Westerns capitalized on a dramatic structure that based its narrative in the memory of some *anciano* who had lived through the early days. Consider the TV series *Death Valley Days* (1952–1970), which opened every program with a bearded "old-timer" setting the stage for that night's story by introducing the current host (over the twenty years of the series, the torch was passed from Stanley Andrews to Ronald Reagan, to Robert Taylor, and finally to Dale Robertson). There was Dustin Hoffman as the 121-year-old "yarn-spinner" in *Little Big Man*, remembering the Indians' struggle to defend their cultures, culminating with a satirical Native American perspective on "Custer's last stand." Another good example is *Red River*, which used the device of an on-screen book, *Early Tales of Texas*, with pages turning to retell the story of the building of a cattle empire in Texas and the opening of the Chisholm Trail (now Interstate Highway 35) needed to bring cattle to market at the new railhead in Kansas City (see chapter 5).

There is no shortage, of course, of actual historical characters to be treated in Western films. Consider the many representations of Buffalo Bill, Kit Carson, Billy the Kid, Doc Holliday, Wyatt Earp, Wild Bill Hickok, Brigham Young, and Bat Masterson. Consider also the Western stars who either played these characters or created their own Western personae: William S. Hart, Hoot Gibson, Will Rogers, John Wayne, and Clint Eastwood, to name only a few. The character of the Lone Ranger galloped from radio to television in 1949, with Jay Silverheels as Tonto and Clayton Moore as his "Kemo Sabe" (faithful friend) with his trademark silver bullets and his horse, Silver. Many of these heroes served as masculine role models for Americans—both on a personal level and in terms of a "cowboy" outlook on foreign policy. There were Western characters transported into other times and other genres, such as Dennis Weaver (Marshal Dillon's deputy from *Gunsmoke*) as a horseback-riding urban detective in television's *McCloud* (1970–1977). In another type of chronological and genre shift, the oil-rich Ewing family of *Dallas* (1978–1991) constituted the subject of a prime-time Western soap opera; in 1980, the entire world was left from one season to the next wondering "Who shot JR?"

There were women, of course, who took on leading Western roles: Judy Garland in *The Harvey Girls* (1946) and Doris Day in *Calamity Jane* (1953). There was the worldly Miss Kitty of *Gunsmoke,* and her near opposite, the innocent teenage Penny, niece of Sky King, the TV rancher of the 1951–1953 seasons, who tended his "spread" and chased desperadoes in his private plane, the *Songbird.* Other characters included Gabby Hayes, riding along with Hopalong Cassidy, and Pat Brady, Roy Rogers's sidekick, who preferred his stripped-down jeep, "Nelly-belle," to four-legged transportation—an obvious nostalgic allusion to the most beloved form of military transportation of World War II.

If Gabby Hayes and Pat Brady were poking fun at individual Western characters, another series of films made fun of the entire genre. Early efforts such as Charlie Chaplin's *Gold Rush* (1925), Buster Keaton's *The General* (1927), and Laurel and Hardy's *Way Out West* (1937) were followed in later years by Rowan and Martin's *Once upon a Horse* (1958), Lee Marvin and Jane Fonda in *Cat Ballou* (1965), Jack Palance in *City Slickers* (1991), and what many consider the best—if the most mindless—of the genre, Mel Brooks's *Blazing Saddles* (1974). As recently as 1985, *Rustlers' Rhapsody* spoofed the B Western and its conventions, with emphasis on the transvaluation in American mores from the 1940s to the Age of Aquarius; in each case a new generation has challenged and modified a traditional genre (see chapter 10).

But comedy notwithstanding, producers honored certain traditions and institutions time after time, starting with the selfless sheriff or marshal who brought law and order to the wilderness. There was the pony express; regardless

Blazing Saddles (1974): paradox and parody.

of conditions, the mail (not to mention all those tempting-to-robbers payroll chests sent by stagecoach) had to get through. There was the U.S. Cavalry (agent of federal authority), stationed at frontier posts throughout the West and ready to come to the rescue at a moment's notice. The cavalry was best memorialized in a trio of John Ford films: *Fort Apache* (1948), *She Wore a Yellow Ribbon* (1949), and *Rio Grande* (1950); later it was shamelessly parodied in the TV series *F Troop* (1965–1967; see chapter 4).

Challenged with lawlessness, settlers or townspeople in numerous Westerns invoked "Judge Lynch," taking justice into their own hands. William Wellman's *Ox-Bow Incident* was a definitive statement against lynching (released at a time when Americans were acutely aware of Nazi repression in Germany); following it came a series of Westerns that addressed liberal issues of the post–World War II period. *High Noon* has been called a left-wing Western, partly due to its association with the screenwriter Carl Foreman, who was asked to leave the set in midproduction because of producer Stanley Kramer's fear of the House Committee on Un-American Activities (HUAC). In the film, Gary

Cavalry tales: actors John Wayne, John Agar, Joanne Dru, and Henry Fonda.

Cooper's character, Marshal Will Kane, takes his stand against a just-released-from-prison criminal who had previously terrorized the town of Hadleyville, but he has to do so alone because the cowardly townspeople will not support him. Attacking community panic and conformity, Foreman suggested that his story was also about McCarthyism in Hollywood. As Michael Coyne observes, Foreman "scripted *High Noon* as a left-wing parable damning Hollywood's moral cowardice in the face of the witch-hunters" (99). (This interpretation has problems in that *High Noon* was the most-watched film in the White House between 1954 and 1986 and is evidently a film viewed by presidents whenever they feel they are leading without sufficient national support [Bravo]; see chapter 8). In what has been interpreted as a rebuttal to *High Noon,* John Wayne, in *Rio Bravo* (dir. Howard Hawks, 1959), plays a lawman who stands firm, holding accused murderers in jail despite the threats of their cohorts and *turning down* offers of assistance from the townspeople. Wayne, of course, unabashedly supported anticommunist causes in Hollywood (Wills 191–203), and the "answer" of *Rio Bravo* was that true westerners would not shirk their responsibilities but would—unlike the inhabitants of Foreman's Hadleyville—band together to oppose a common foe.

Although these Westerns certainly reflected the times in which they were made, others addressed issues of the day even more directly. Consider *Bad Day at Black Rock* (dir. John Sturges, 1955), a "contemporary Western" in which the protagonist, John McCreedy (Spencer Tracy), comes to an isolated desert town not on horseback but on a railroad liner—symbol of an urbane, post–World War II America. McCreedy is a wounded World War II combat amputee (left arm) intent on visiting a Japanese-born farmer to deliver his son's posthumously awarded Medal of Honor, but he finds that the farmer was killed early in the war, during the wave of anti-Nisei repression and internment. Tracy's character seeks justice as the locals try to thwart him in his quest. The film clearly evokes comparison with *High Noon,* but the criticism is directed against regional prejudice and the national movement to place Japanese Americans in internment camps during World War II. (In 1988, the Civil Liberties Act appropriated funds to award each internee $20,000 in reparations; an apology to the Nisei was included as part of the legislation.)

As Westerns of the 1950s reflected cold war concerns, so films of the 1960s and 1970s addressed contemporary issues. Jon Tuska sees a late-century development of what he calls "a Western without heroes," singling out *Cat Ballou,* along with *Hang 'em High* (1968), *Will Penny* (1968), and *Monte Walsh* (1970), as well as "Westerns with only villains," in which class he also places Sam Peckinpah's *Ride the High Country* (1962) and *The Wild Bunch.* With a different perspective, Michael Coyne believes that Western films of the 1960s were centered on the estrangement and alienation of traditional heroes, "lionized men who had outlived their time and stood poised at the edge of the sunset," citing "three superb elegiac Westerns" of 1962: *The Man Who Shot Liberty Valance, Lonely Are the Brave,* and *Ride the High Country* (118, 106). Westerns of the late 1960s and the early 1970s displayed an increasing cynicism and violence that reflected the national experience of war, assassination, riot, and Watergate.

The thirteen chapters in the present volume have been arranged in four chronological groups, intended to relate both to the then-current development of film art and production as well as to the social, political, and cultural concerns prevailing at the time—and therefore likely to be reflected in the works discussed. Further research is always encouraged. The bibliography provided by Jack Nachbar and Ray J. Merlock begins with a distillation of the classic writings on the Western and then focuses on more recent studies written after 1980. The filmography by John Shelton Lawrence is of infinite usefulness and, just by objectifying the chronology of the genre on paper, will suggest all kinds of research ideas to students and scholars. (We know this result based on our experiences with the filmography by Lawrence for our earlier book *Hollywood's White House* [2003].)

Early Sound Era Westerns, 1931–1939

Cimarron (1931), produced during the first decade of sound films, was based on the eponymous popular novel by Edna Ferber, an author of epic fictions noted for her detailed historical research. In chapter 1, Jennifer Smyth's perusal of the RKO production files at the Academy of Motion Picture Arts and Sciences uncovered screenwriter Howard Estabrook's annotated copy of Ferber's book; along with other documents in the file, it revealed how he had probed the historical aspects of the story, intending to bring an authentic "epic" to the screen—one that reflected Oklahoma's actual experience of settlement and growth rather than merely echoing genre conventions and clichés. In the process Estabrook and director Wesley Ruggles may have presaged our current interest in the New Western History, questioning the mythic vision of Frederick Jackson Turner by bringing forward questions of race and gender and the expropriation of tribal lands. As Smyth observes, *Cimarron* may even be said to have introduced a new "film historiography" to the screen. That the Oklahoma epic made $1.3 million during the darkest year of the Great Depression is testimony that authentic history and entertaining filmmaking were not necessarily mutually exclusive; would that Hollywood and TV filmmakers absorb that lesson.

Not all Westerns conformed to formula. As Cynthia J. Miller explains in chapter 2, Jed Buell produced films that clearly deviated from the norm. In nine of Buell's pictures, Fred Scott brought an operatic voice to the frontier in ways that elevated the "culture" of such productions but grated on the ears of typical audiences for the genre—who were looking for a singer in the style of Tex Ritter or Gene Autry, not a Caruso. Perhaps the most bizarre of Buell's alternative Westerns was *The Terror of Tiny Town* (1938), with a cast drawn entirely from a theatrical troupe of midgets. Despite a lot of "novelty-driven humor at the expense of little people," Buell also burlesqued the dominant

Harlem on the Prairie promises six-guns and swing.

1930s cinematic view of the West as "a very serious, earnest place, where American myths and values were played out on the big screen." Miller closes with a consideration of Hollywood's first black singing cowboy, Herb Jeffries, in films such as *Bronze Buckaroo* (1939) and *Harlem on the Prairie* (1939). Not until John Ford's *Sergeant Rutledge* and the Mel Brooks parody *Blazing Saddles* would a black hero stake a claim in an environment traditionally allotted for Anglo-Saxon cultural heroes.

Chapter 3 on the early sound era Westerns considers not a specific production but a well-known Western persona. The Lone Ranger got his start as a character created for radio in the 1930s; later, he made the transition into film and eventually into a long-running television series. John Shelton Lawrence analyzes how the elements of the Lone Ranger's juvenile Western image became "defining markers" for his character and those of subsequent "superheroes" in American culture. As part of Lawrence's prizewinning study of American culture, this chapter has many applications beyond the particular franchise and beyond the genre of the Western, using a landmark popular culture artifact to examine the mind-set of America's moral imagination.

The Post–World War II Western, 1945–1956

It should come as no surprise that America's World War II experience had ripple effects in motion pictures, especially Westerns. In chapter 4, Kathleen McDonough establishes as a reference point the short-lived cycle of British Empire films that preceded the war, including *Lives of a Bengal Lancer* (1935), *The Charge of the Light Brigade* (1936), and *The Light That Failed* (1939). She argues that these films—in which the Europeans sought "to bring the benefits of civilization to the colonized indigenous people as a duty, as the 'White Man's Burden'"—can be compared to John Ford's classic Westerns after the war about "taming the land and containing or exterminating savage elements, either Indians or outlaws, who threaten the well-being of the settlers." In the same way that Shirley Temple's character in the empire film *Wee Willie Winkie* (1937) is helped to understand the higher duty of "the Corps," so characters, particularly women, are initiated into the fellowship of the U.S. Cavalry in John Ford's famous martial trilogy—*Fort Apache, She Wore a Yellow Ribbon,* and *Rio Grande.* Calling them "regimental women," to distinguish them from other Western roles played by "domesticating women," McDonough finds these characters to be central to the narratives. She also discusses the reintegration of erstwhile adversaries (such as former Confederate soldiers) into cavalry units and the failure of former Native American opponents to make that same transition. According to McDonough, all these details of characterization have direct relevance as subtle commentary on the need for a strong military during the early days of the cold war.

Another film from the same notable era for the Western is addressed by John Parris Springer in chapter 5. Ostensibly, *Red River* is about the creation of an American empire in the West after the Civil War, but another key issue, men finding the right women with whom to spend their lives, pervades both the plot and the characterizations. Ironically, although Hawks's view of the feminine becomes central, it is in one of the most masculine of his films. The issues arise from both Tom Dunson's (John Wayne) and his adopted son Matthew Garth's (Montgomery Clift) relationships with women—one's opportunity lost at the outset of the film and the other's fulfilled at the end. And these are not the only important females in the film. Robert Sklar has stressed that, although Dunson owned a prize bull, the heifer brought to the partnership by Garth was essential, "the indispensable feminine" (175). In doing so, Hawks symbolized the importance of a fruitful family—not the individual—as the building block of a healthy nation.

Two films from 1950 are treated in the last two chapters in this part. Chapter 6 by Joanna Hearne focuses on the main character in Anthony Mann's *Devil's Doorway*. Played by non-Indian Robert Taylor, he is a Native American returning to Wyoming from the hazards of Civil War service duties only to find himself embroiled in a "race war." The problems faced by Indians in the post–Civil War era reflected their more general troubles in the late 1940s and early 1950s, when the government's policy was seeking to "terminate" Indian tribes as legal entities. After considerable background research, Hearne concludes that the film is "a case study of the corruption, prejudice, and greed that pushed forward an agrarian 'American dream' of homestead land and immigrant opportunity." In *Giant* (1956), based on another Edna Ferber epic novel (see chapter 1 for a critique of the screen adaptation of her *Cimarron*), director George Stevens was coming to grips with an American variant of the racism that had shocked him and many other veterans of the European theater during World War II. (Stevens would go on to make a version of *The Diary of Anne Frank* three years after his Texas epic.) As Monique Baxter reveals in chapter 7, the treatment of the Hispanic minority of the state, the "Tejanos," came under the microscope in a nation that had fought for the "Four Freedoms." Nearly half a million Tejanos had served in the war, and they demanded—and received—recognition when they returned home; because the film was released some two years after the 1954 landmark *Brown v. Board of Education* decision by the U.S. Supreme Court, the film was more of a confirmation of trends in American culture than a radical critique. While sympathetic to the position of Mexicans and critical of Jim Crow, the film portrays the solution to the problems as being in the hands of sensitive and progressive Anglos—a message that was less radical than what readers would have found in Ferber's novel.

The Cold War Western, 1950–1981

The third part of the book deals with Westerns from the 1950s through the 1970s. In chapter 8, Matthew J. Costello posits that Fred Zinnemann's *High Noon* was the progenitor of a series of "law-and-order films" to follow, films that serve as a spiritual barometer of their times: *The Tin Star* (1957), *Warlock* (1959), and *Firecreek* (1968). The central conflict of *High Noon* has a "virtuous individual, meeting the threat to community even with the potential for death that it entails," and offers a strong statement criticizing the "vital center" (a 1950s term originally coined by historian Arthur Schlesinger Jr. to represent an alliance between the nonfascist Right and the noncommunist Left) for its "lack of public virtue and its failure to support the noble, virtuous individual who risks all to defend a community unworthy of that defense." In *The Tin Star* Henry Fonda plays Morgan Hickman, an ex-sheriff who turned bounty hunter when the town refused to help him and his ailing wife in their time of need. After his wife and son die, Hickman mentors a new young sheriff (Anthony Perkins) through a crisis much like Hadleyville's in *High Noon*. Indeed, Costello argues that the entire film is an updated commentary on the earlier production, one that emphasizes the loss of personal integrity rather than *High Noon*'s broader theme of the individual's responsibility to society. The community of Edward Dmytryk's *Warlock* is a mining town terrorized by a gang of rustlers and murderers. The town hires a vigilante (again Henry Fonda) to restore order. On one level the film presents Dmytryk's allegory for the experience of HUAC and the Hollywood Ten. (Dymytryk went to jail for one year as part of the Ten but later became a "friendly witness" to the committee.) On another level it undoes the lesson of *High Noon* as the Fonda character, having tutored the town's young sheriff into a capable law man and then personally killing the town's chief desperado, decides to move on rather than face off against his protégé. Costello suggests that this development reflects a decline in confidence in liberal values. The third film, *Firecreek* (1968), released during a particularly traumatic year in American history, also casts Henry Fonda, this time as a "bad guy" in a "town of losers," and suggests that the "vital center is dead, but just doesn't realize it yet." There is no moral vision, and no one will stand up against the outlaws. Furthermore, in contrast to an enduring theme of the Western film, there is no hope for "building a civilization." Such was the mood of America in the era of the Tet offensive in Vietnam and the assassinations at home of Martin Luther King Jr. and Robert Kennedy.

In chapter 9, Winona Howe describes *The Professionals* (1966) as a man's film that also reveals a "stratification of class" and the "narrow range of choices for women of Hispanic ethnicity in the West." In the process it traces the progression of the Mexican Revolution of 1911, which, because of its radical agenda, has spawned such productions as *Viva Zapata!* (1952) and *Old Gringo* (1989). Like the Bolshevik revolution in Russia in 1917, the social uprisings in Mexico have proved to be of enduring interest to Hollywood, giving the movie colony an opportunity to explore the motives of those who oppose an exploitative society—but at a relatively safe distance of time and space. With a somewhat mixed vision in 1966, *The Professionals* evokes the contemporary concern with gender roles and vulnerabilities; as one of the critics cited by Howe explains, the film is "'the halfway house between the altruism of the Seven [i.e., *The Magnificent Seven*] and the harsh nihilism of the Bunch [i.e., *The Wild Bunch*]'" What comes through, however, is the importance of women to a viable society—a theme that Howard Hawks dramatized in *Red River*, almost twenty years earlier (see chapter 5).

Matthew Turner explains how much of the humor in Western parodies is based on a reversal of expectations built up in a presumed lifetime of viewing Westerns. In chapter 10, he introduces *Cat Ballou, Blazing Saddles, Rustlers' Rhapsody,* and *Shanghai Noon* as vehicles for such parody. In a larger sense, although its days were numbered and its vision bleak, the Western after 1968 still served as a canvas on which contemporary American issues could be engaged. Most scholars share Matthew Turner's view that parodies come during the twilight of an art form—and, indeed, many parodies have certainly emerged as a form becomes outmoded and tired. In contrast, many other scholars have discovered, in recent days, that parodies of the Western not only flourished during the supposed demise of the genre but were a contemporary echo from the earliest days. One of Will Rogers's earliest films, *Two Wagons—Both Covered* (1924), was a parody of the ambitious epic *The Covered Wagon* (1923), directed by James Cruze during an era when most Westerns sought to be paeans to America's founding myths. The parody has a long lineage in the history of Westerns—such films have delighted audiences for decades.

The Postmodernist Western, 1980–2000

The final part of the book brings us closer to the present. In chapter 11, Alexandra Keller discusses two sets of historical assumptions about the frontier: Frederick Jackson Turner's proposal of "an area of free land," the settlement of which "explains American development," and "Buffalo Bill Cody's more violent scenario in which 'the bullet is the pioneer of civilization.'" Keller contrasts *Walker* (1987) and *Dances with Wolves* (1990): in relation to the first, she stresses what she calls the "emphatic fall from heroic abolitionist to psychotic imperialist." Keller also notes historical anachronism in the "encroaching of the present tense (the 1980s) into the past of the film (the 1850s)," eventually raising questions about contemporary America's view of its Latin American neighbors in comparison to strikingly similar attitudes during the era of Manifest Destiny. She goes on to discuss questions of "material accuracy" versus "discursive accuracy," in which, for example, "historical personages may be combined to create a single character, events may be likewise conflated or compressed, but the spectator's sense of the episteme *may* in fact be stronger for doing so," and concludes her contribution with comments on John Sayles's *Lone Star* (1996). This important film closes with characters talking in a parked car at a deserted drive-in movie and suggests a liberated future for the younger generation with its concluding line, "Forget the Alamo."

Kimberly Sultze's contribution in chapter 12 focuses more closely on *Lone Star,* interpreting it as a cinematic application of Patricia Nelson Limerick's revisionist western history. The chapter shows how Sayles "strives to represent the West as a place of complexity, where people are individuals more than types, and where Chicanas/os, Anglo-Americans, African Americans, and American Indians are living intersecting lives." In the end, Sayles is seen as representing "the history of the West as a dynamic process, one in which personal history is intermixed with—and often in conflict with—'official' history." As is often the case, an independent filmmaker, in this case John Sayles, has produced a drama decades ahead of the industry in subject matter, interpretation, and technique. In many ways, *Lone Star* is a film of the 1990s that steps beyond the clichés in a way that *Cimarron* did for the early sound era Westerns (see chapter 1).

Finally, David Pierson's analysis of Turner Network Television's (TNT) made-for-TV Western films in chapter 13 concentrates on what he terms "the construction of authenticity," by which he means not only historical correctness but also a set of "standards of authenticity" that are "negotiated between producers, writers, directors, actors, fans, and the public." He then identifies a series of what he calls "authenticity markers" and finds that TNT films are primarily defined by two themes: one of "nostalgic desire for Western myths and heroes, and for mythically well-defined gender roles for men and women," and another of "cynicism concerning the effectiveness of social institutions." Explaining this seemingly incompatible combination of messages leads to some insightful observations about American society and popular culture in the age of cable. Americans yearn for the nostalgic reassurances of *Nick at Night* TV classics from the 1950s while, perhaps in the same evening of viewing, assuaging a postmodernist mind-set on cable subscription options such as *The Daily Show* with Jon Stewart on Comedy Central or reruns of HBO's *Sex in the City*.

WESTERNS AND AMERICA'S FUTURE

Popular culture in the United States presents an apparent chaos, but scholars who have taken films seriously know that movie Westerns are a touchstone to understanding the nation's concerns. At the mythic level, Westerns explore America's self-image as unique because of a proximity to nature, what Harvard scholar Perry Miller called an identity as "Nature's Nation." Contemporary politics clearly affect the construction of Westerns—witness the testimony in this collection to the pervasive significance of *High Noon* and responses to the conventions and themes of that landmark Western, both in serious form and in parodies. What has become known as "sexual politics" has been an integral part of the Western as gender representations have evolved and changed both inside and outside the theater. Even international politics and policy have a place in our study of this popular culture form—how Native Americans, Mexicans, and other minorities are treated gives clues to the pendulum swings of the nation's mood between isolationism and internationalism. The pervasive violence—indeed, the increase of it from the traditional Westerns to the balletic treatments by director Sam Peckinpah in the late 1960s to what might be called "the banality of evil" approach of HBO's *Deadwood* (2004), where a customer's head is calmly dispatched like a dirty towel to the local laundry for disposal—says volumes about the nation's declining respect for human life and perhaps its increased voyeurism in a media age.

Almost every issue in our contemporary existence surfaces in Westerns. This magnetism for American concerns and anxieties accounts for the title of John Cawelti's groundbreaking study of the Western. He called it "the six-gun mystique" to focus on a lonely hero and his quest to conquer evil—often using the antisocial option of violence. From Natty Bumppo of Cooper's novels to the Lone Ranger of the 1950s, solitary figures of integrity have stepped outside the bounds of law and order, paradoxically, for the sake of civilization. In our

Red River: building a cattle empire.

own era of terrorism, images from Westerns have often been invoked. During the cold war (1948–1989), President Ronald Reagan was labeled a "cowboy" for his solo leadership style in the 1980s, a style that led to the demise of the Soviet Union and the destruction of the Berlin Wall in 1989; after the 2003 preemptive attack on Iraq by the United States, President George W. Bush was branded as a "cowboy" in foreign affairs. In the part of the country where one of our editors lives, the cowboy label is a negative designation meaning someone who acts on his own without asking for help from others; in the part of the country where another of the editors lives, the cowboy image is a positive one denoting contact with nature by someone with a firm and clear grip on the difference between right and wrong. Perhaps neither or both are accurate descriptors. The point to be made is that issues of the frontier, the West, justice, and violence are interconnected inextricably in the American mind—even after the classic era of the Hollywood Western. Thus, the study of the evolution of the Western is not a detached, academic endeavor; it is a chance to look at the potentials of our nation as they have been explored by some of our best literary and visual artists.

WORKS CITED

Billington, Ray Allen, ed. *The Frontier Thesis: Valid Interpretation of American History?* New York: Holt Rinehart and Winston, 1966.

———. *Westward Expansion: A History of the American Frontier.* 5th ed. New York: Macmillan, 1982.

Bravo Channel's *All the Presidents' Films.* Broadcast August 8, 2003.

Brown, Dee. *The American West.* New York: Touchstone, 1994.

Buscombe, Edward, ed. *The BFI Companion to the Western.* New York: Atheneum, 1988.

Cawelti, John G. *The Six-Gun Mystique.* Bowling Green, Ohio: Bowling Green University Popular Press, 1971.

———. *The Six-Gun Mystique Sequel.* Bowling Green, Ohio: Bowling Green State University Popular Press, 1999.

Coyne, Michael. *The Crowded Prairie: American National Identity and the Hollywood Western.* London: Tauris, 1997.

Crèveceour, Hector St. John de. *Letters from an American Farmer and Sketches of Eighteenth-Century America.* Edited by Albert E. Stone. New York: Penguin, 1986.

Fagan, Herb. *The Encyclopedia of Westerns.* New York: Checkmark Books, 2003.

George-Warren, Holly. *How Hollywood Invented the Wild West: Featuring the Real West, Campfire Melodies, Matinee Idols, Four Legged Friends, Cowgirls and Lone Guns.* Pleasantville, N.Y.: Reader's Digest, 2002.

Goetzmann, William H., and William N. Goetzmann. *The West of the Imagination.* New York: Penguin, 1986.

Lenihan, John H. *Showdown: Confronting Modern America in the Western Film.* Urbana: University of Illinois Press, 1980.

Limerick, Patricia Nelson. *The Legacy of Conquest: The Unbroken Past of the American West.* New York: Norton, 1987.

———. *Something in the Soil: Legacies and Reckonings in the New West.* New York: Norton, 2000.

Mansfield, Harvey C., and Delba Winthrop, eds. Introduction to Alexis de Tocqueville, *Democracy in America.* Chicago: University of Chicago Press, 2000.

Miller, Perry. *Errand into the Wilderness.* Cambridge, Mass.: Harvard University Press, 1956.

Mitchell, Lee Clark, *Westerns: Making the Man in Fiction and in Film.* Chicago: University of Chicago Press, 1996.

Potter, David M. *People of Plenty: Abundance and the American Character.* Chicago: University of Chicago Press, 1957.

Rollins, Peter C., and John E. O'Connor, eds. *Hollywood's White House: The American Presidency in Film and History.* Lexington: University Press of Kentucky, 2003.

Schlesinger, Arthur M., Jr. *A Life in the Twentieth Century: Innocent Beginnings, 1918–1950.* New York: Houghton Mifflin, 2000.

Sklar, Robert. "Empire to the West: *Red River* (1948)." In *American History/ American Film: Interpreting the Hollywood Image,* edited by John E. O'Connor and Martin A. Jackson, 167–81. 2nd ed. New York: Ungar, 1988.

Slotkin, Richard. *Gunfighter Nation: The Myth of the Frontier in Twentieth-Century America.* New York: Atheneum, 1992.

Smith, Henry Nash. *Virgin Land: The American West as Symbol and Myth.* Cambridge, Mass.: Harvard University Press, 1950.

Stewart, Elinore Pruitt. *Letters of a Woman Homesteader.* 1912. Boston: Houghton Mifflin, 1998.

Taylor, George Rogers. *The Turner Thesis Concerning the Role of the Frontier in American History.* New York: Heath, 1956.

Turner, Frederick Jackson. *The Frontier in American History.* New York: Holt Rinehart and Winston, 1962.

———. "The Significance of the Frontier in American History." *Annual Report for the Year 1893,* 199–227. Washington, D.C.: American Historical Association, 1894.

Tuska, John. *The Filming of the West.* Garden City, N.Y.: Doubleday, 1976.

Ward, Geoffrey C. *The West: The Complete Text of the Illustrated Companion Volume to the Acclaimed PBS Television Series.* Boston: Little, Brown, 1996.

Wills, Garry. *John Wayne's America: The Politics of Celebrity.* New York: Simon and Schuster, 1997.

Wright, Will. *Six Guns and Society: A Structural Study of the Western.* Berkeley: University of California Press, 1975.

Part One

Early Sound Era Westerns
1931–1939

1 ❧ J. E. Smyth

THE NEW WESTERN HISTORY IN 1931

RKO and the Challenge of Cimarron

In early 1931, RKO Pictures released *Cimarron,* a history of an Oklahoma pioneering couple's marriage from the opening of the territory to white settlement in 1889 to the film's 1930 production year. Even before the film's completion, the Hollywood motion picture community anticipated *Cimarron* as innovative American historical cinema, and following its premiere, the studio and the trade papers presented the film as both an authoritative historical document and a landmark of American cinematic achievement.[1] At the end of the decade, filmmaker and historian Lewis Jacobs would acknowledge its profound effect on historical cinema, and as time passed, Hollywood executives and trade papers tried to justify new big-budget historical Westerns by invoking *Cimarron*'s memory (Jacobs 531; Balderston). The film became a talisman of artistic achievement for an industry traditionally credited with a short memory. Years later, Paul Rotha would remember the film as "the American cinema's one accurate study of social history" (447–48).

Yet until recently, film scholars have virtually ignored the industry's former masterpiece. *Cimarron* did not fit within the traditional critical framework for the classical Hollywood Western.[2] Its complex historical narrative, frequent text inserts, and repeated contrasts between verbal and visual historical representation seem to have made Western film historians uncomfortable. According to the critical tradition, classical Hollywood Westerns were not supposed to possess any self-conscious attitude toward history or to be capable of making their own historical arguments. Over the years, scholars have persisted in dismissing *Cimarron* as a Western myth and a frontier-glorifying epic, a passive historical artifact reflecting the fortunes of the big-budget Western during the Depression (Slotkin 278–79; Stanfield 31–40). But a closer examination of the film's production history reveals both its nuanced historical structure and active engagement with Western historiography and criticism. In 1931, *Cimarron's* screenwriter, Howard Estabrook, confronted the tradition of written history, placing the structure and rhetoric of historiography in counterpoint with the cinema's potential visual history of the West. Estabrook's redefinition of projected historical text, his rigorous engagement with a revisionist conception of western history, and his ensuing critical acclaim as a historical screenwriter succeeded in introducing a new filmic writing of American frontier history to classical Hollywood cinema.[3]

REVISIONING THE HISTORICAL FILM IN 1931

Although by 1930 a few professional historians had begun to question traditional western historiography and the eloquent eulogies to white westward settlement exemplified by the work of Frederick Jackson Turner, the criticism tended to dispute individual aspects of Turner's "frontier thesis" rather than to generate an organized alternative to the robust and self-congratulatory history expressed by Turner and popular historian Theodore Roosevelt.[4] Turner's postwar critics, historians Charles A. Beard, John C. Almach, and Carey McWilliams, contradicted Turner's proclamation of the closed frontier in 1890, deprecated his magisterial tone, and focused on his neglect of eastern values in molding the American character. Yet no accredited historian was willing or able to synthesize a developed alternative to the Turner thesis. Ironically, the first widely read "revisionist history" of the West was published by a popular American novelist, Edna Ferber. When she published *Cimarron* in early 1930, Ferber acknowledged in her foreword that while the novel was "no attempt to set down a literal history of Oklahoma," it chronicled the experience of a fictional pioneering couple from 1889 to the present day and was supported by extensive research in the state historical library in Oklahoma City. Although Ferber later claimed that *Cimarron* was a revisionist account of the American West, depicting Oklahoma's multiethnic and multiracial settlement and development, she concentrated her historical critique within her fictional protagonists, Yancey and Sabra Cravat. Ferber felt that, in creating her scathing portrait of Sabra, a bigoted pioneer woman, she was denouncing the essential materialism of mainstream American capitalist society and its sentimental view of the female pioneer (*A Peculiar Treasure* 339).

Yet academics were not willing to credit a Broadway-Hollywood success like Ferber (*Show Boat* [1929], *The Royal Family of Broadway* [1930]) with historical acumen. Writing in 1931, literary critic Percy Boynton understood the novel only as a popular reconfirmation of Turner's 1893 frontier thesis, as a culmination of twentieth-century western nostalgia (v–vi, 179). Other reviewers were more pointed in their criticism of Ferber's history. In Dorothy Van Doren's review for the *Nation*, tellingly entitled "A Pioneer Fairy Story," she concluded that, while Ferber's highly colored Western novel was poor history and trite literature, it might be the basis for an exciting film (494).[5] If Van Doren and other critics took a dim view of popular historical novelists like Ferber, their artistic expectations of motion pictures were still lower. Contemporary popular historian E. Douglas Branch was particularly anxious to separate his written historical territory from the encroachments of Holly-wood. He asserted that whereas he and other serious historians chronicled complex historical events and movements, the glorious evolution and repetition of the white frontier experience, the cinema was interested only in flashy individuals. "Calamity Jane, Simon Girty, Kit Carson, Sam Bass, make good melodrama. Billy the Kid is now in the photoplays, where, so far as I am concerned, he belongs" (v).

The Hollywood motion picture community's expectations for *Cimarron* could not have been more different. Critics anticipated that RKO would transform Edna Ferber's best-selling novel into innovative American historical cinema, not a run-of-the-mill Western or bandit biopic (*Hollywood News;* Churchill). RKO was enthusiastic, paying an unprecedented $125,000 for the story, but executives knew that they risked much to produce another expensive Western in 1930. Although Ferber's works were always screen-bankable, by late 1930 the future artistic and economic credibility of American historical cinema depended largely on *Cimarron's* national reception. The advent of sound in 1927 and its industrial takeover in 1928 had Hollywood critics and filmmakers worrying about the quality of the nation's historical cinema and especially its mainstay, the Western. This hesitancy meant that by 1930, few prestigious historical sound films had appeared.

When D. W. Griffith released his long-awaited *Abraham Lincoln* in August, most critics were appalled by its sentimentality and old-fashioned, static treatment of history. Mordaunt Hall of the *New York Times* preferred the livelier *Dramatic Life of Abraham Lincoln* (1925) and wrote that the sound film failed "to give the details of the scenes that were so ably told in the mute work." Hall complained that Griffith was guilty of "prognosticating too often in the course of scenes." Instead of portraying the events in Lincoln's life as part of a complex and evolving process, Griffith deployed Lincoln's mythic presence in order to stabilize personal and national conflicts, generating a monotonous, schoolbook narrative. The most famous, emblematic moments of Lincoln's life were strung together in a collection of tableaux and deliberately enunciated epigrams. Harry Alan Potamkin of the *New Masses* was more direct in his criticism of the sentimentalized eulogy, in his words, "a mooning idyll." According to Potamkin, Griffith's callow sense of American history portrayed "a Lincoln that any child beyond the fifth grade in school would disown." Curiously, Potamkin did not imply that the sound medium was at fault, but rather that the silent aesthetic standards Griffith had perfected years before were no longer any match for an innovative new art form. A film about Lincoln required an astute historical perspective conveyed through language and argument, not the folksy images and symbols of silent cinema, the mawkish scenes of rail-splitting and sickbed moments with Ann Rutledge. Rather than reviving the American historical cycle he had helped to create fifteen years earlier with *The Birth of a Nation* (1915), D. W. Griffith's work on *Abraham Lincoln* proved that silent techniques were no match for the historical complexities and sophistication demanded by sound-era viewers and critics.

That year, even the Western was not exempt from such criticism. A few months later, Fox Film released *The Big Trail* (1930), screenwriter Hal Evarts and director Raoul Walsh's picturization of westward expansion along the Oregon Trail. A meticulous chronicle of national expansion, the film opened with a text title that honored "the men and women who planted civilization and courage in the blood of their children." It, too, failed at the box office, but critics took its historical content more seriously. Although *Variety*'s Sime Silverman called it "a noisy *Covered Wagon*," a poor relation of the silent Western epics, he did praise *The Big Trail*'s historical aspects as the "single interesting part" (17, 27). But it was precisely the heavy history that some felt overwhelmed the flimsy romance and fictional film narrative ("*The Big Trail*" 52). There was a subtle awareness on the part of some contemporary film critics that history's multiple associations and complex narratives competed with and even counteracted the power of the traditional, clearly defined and uncomplicated screen story.

RKO had other worries. Founded only in 1928 after the financial instability of its parent companies necessitated its consolidation by the Radio Corporation

Producer William K. LeBaron, art director Max Ree, and screenwriter Howard Estabrook (far right) receive Academy Awards from presenter and U.S. Vice President Charles Curtis. (Author's collection.)

of America, Radio-Keith-Orpheum was the youngest of the major American studios (Hampton 320). It emerged with the technological revolution of sound and grew in the midst of the Depression. The studio had the fewest capital resources of all the major studios and the most invested in the as-yet-unperfected, new film form.[6] It was symbolically fitting and even more financially imperative that the young studio produce the definitive sound feature. Despite their ominous economic situation and the criticism leveled at both sound films and historical productions by leading New York and Hollywood critics, RKO executives immediately hired William K. LeBaron to oversee the production and then former stage producer and writer Howard Estabrook to create *Cimarron*'s screenplay.[7] Estabrook had a decided predilection for historical subjects and had garnered his greatest successes writing Paramount's *The Virginian* (1929) and Howard Hughes's Great War adventure, *Hell's Angels* (1930). He seemed the ideal choice to adapt *Cimarron* for the screen.

Not everyone at the studio shared this enthusiasm. RKO story editor Paul Powell still worried about his studio's great gamble with another historical epic, even after the completion of Estabrook's shooting script. "Although the characters are fictitious, this is essentially a historical novel," Powell fretted. "I believe that it is a matter of experience that historical novels have not, as a rule, proven to be good picture material, and I fear this is no exception" (5). Although *Cimarron* had sold well as a historical novel, he and others feared that the history Howard Estabrook transferred to the screen would not be palatable to a popular motion picture audience. The specter of *The Big Trail* hung over the studio. The fictional narrative codes of the cinema might again compete with the forces of history and lose; in this worst-case scenario, RKO would then sink under the cost of another historical millstone.

Yet Estabrook refused to minimize the historical elements in favor of the fictional story; like Ferber, he did extensive research on traditional texts and more recent publications in western history. While Estabrook's research bibliography included a fair share of popular histories by Walter Noble Burns and Courtney Ryley Cooper, and even Emerson Hough's historical novel *The Covered Wagon*, he was not going to pattern *Cimarron* after the triumphal chronicle of white westward expansion. Estabrook was one of the few people to read William Christie MacLeod's *American Indian Frontier* (1928), a rare view of the white settlement of America from a Native American perspective. To MacLeod, "Every frontier has two sides. . . . To understand why one side advances, we must know something of why the other side retreats." The frontiersman is no hero but the scum of the eastern settlers. Historians are to blame for romanticizing these "pioneers": "In the little red schoolhouse it is a sacrilege to intimate that the pioneers suffered from ordinary human frailties. . . . But the masses were no better than the masses of any society" (vii, 366). MacLeod's work was largely unnoticed in academic circles (Klein 146–47), but Estabrook was certainly influenced by the maverick historian's approach.

Estabrook also refused to emulate the one major Hollywood precedent for Oklahoma history, W. S. Hart's *Tumbleweeds* (1925), which had no interest in the 1893 opening of the Cherokee Strip beyond its role as a backdrop for romance. While *Tumbleweeds* ignored the Indian perspective and focused exclusively on the impending dispossession of the Strip's free-range white cowboys, Estabrook retained Ferber's revisionist picture of a multiracial and ethnic West, a dynamic space settled by Indians, mestizos, black and white southerners, Jews, and Anglo-Saxon northeasterners. But then, with the ensuing support of director Wesley Ruggles, Estabrook completely transformed and emphasized *Cimarron*'s projection of history, moving Ferber's acknowledged site of historical contention from bigoted pioneer Sabra Cravat to a broader critique of the construction of western history. The two principal filmmakers introduced the idea of re-creating the 1889 land rush (that Ferber only alluded to in her novel); of inserting historical expositions, dates, and documents within the narrative; and of introducing the film with an extensive opening title, or text foreword (Estabrook, *Cimarron* shooting script; Estabrook, *Cimarron* continuity).

Titles were an indispensable component of silent films, articulating dialogue and giving continuity to changes in time and place. But the opening titles had the greatest length and importance, particularly in silent historical films. Some of the most elaborately planned, constructed, and marketed silent histories, *The Birth of a Nation, The Covered Wagon* (1923), and *The Vanishing American* (1925), made extensive use of text prologues to lend historical authenticity and complexity to their fictional narratives. With the advent of sound, one might have expected titles to disappear, since they were merely continuity crutches for an obsolete art form. By and large, text did vanish from sound features—with one considerable exception. History films retained titles as a recognizable visual attribute, thereby self-consciously allying their narratives with the more traditional and respectable forms of written history. Filmmakers compounded the relationship, calling the opening text insert a "foreword." More than any other film in the early sound era, *Cimarron* was responsible for inaugurating this structural practice. It even went so far as to include a footnote after the credits; like Ferber's historical novel, Estabrook acknowledged a Western memoir as an invaluable resource (Sutton and MacDonald).

Howard Estabrook's vision for wedding text and image was an original component of his adaptation: an elaborate foreword and a continuous series of text inserts and documents were integrated within his first treatment and script. With Ruggles on board by August 1930, the two then superimposed a series of dates to punctuate the shooting script. Remarkably, almost all of the text and other historical iconography survived postproduction and exhibition. For *Cimarron,* text was an essential component of the historical narrative, not a postproduction afterthought used to unify a disjointed narrative like MGM's work on *The Great Meadow* (1931). The latter film, based on a historical novel by Elizabeth Madox Roberts, was a eulogy to the eighteenth-century women pioneers of Virginia and would be *Cimarron*'s historical competitor in early 1931. Like many silent epics, Charles Brabin's scripts had no interest in the historical material beyond its weak support of fictional melodrama, but late in postproduction, MGM hired dialogue writer Edith Ellis to add a historical dedication to the "women of the wilderness" and a few text inserts chronicling the stages of the grueling journey to Kentucky (Brabin; Ellis). The foreword was undoubtedly added to dress up a floundering production, but Ellis's textual inserts were modeled on *The Big Trail*. The Hal Evarts–Raoul Walsh epic used several text inserts, but only to summarize the protagonists' moods or unspecified passages of toil and time. In this sense, *The Big Trail* and *The Great Meadow*'s use of text was determined by the silent technique of elucidating the fictional narrative. In contrast, *Cimarron*'s filmmakers used text as the medium for conveying an established view of American history.

Cimarron's narrative begins with a two-shot foreword:

A NATION RISING TO GREATNESS
THROUGH THE WORK OF MEN
AND WOMEN . . . NEW COUNTRY OPENING . . .
RAW LAND BLOSSOMING . . . CRUDE
TOWNS GROWING INTO CITIES . . .
TERRITORIES BECOMING RICH STATES . . .

IN 1889, PRESIDENT HARRISON OPENED
THE VAST INDIAN OKLAHOMA LANDS
FOR WHITE SETTLEMENT . . .
2,000,000 ACRES FREE FOR THE
TAKING, POOR AND RICH POURING IN,
SWARMING THE BORDER, WAITING
FOR THE STARTING GUN, AT NOON,
APRIL 22ND.

This text expresses the dominant academic and popular view of western expansion derived from Theodore Roosevelt's five-volume *Winning of the West* and particularly Turner's essay "The Significance of the Frontier in American History." *Cimarron*'s given history stresses that the nation's progress and greatness are dependent on an organic westward expansion. It is a history of egalitarian white settlement sanctioned by the authority of the president, a panegyric to the government and the people who transformed "raw land" into a great nation. As in Turner's view, the previous occupants of the "raw land," the Indians, have been almost entirely written out of the history of the West. The "vast Indian Oklahoma lands" are opened up to white settlers by the government; there is no mention of broken treaties or territorial displacement.

Estabrook conceived *Cimarron*'s projected text titles in his preliminary draft.

The second shot of *Cimarron*'s foreword.

Courtesy of RKO Pictures.

A white merchant/pioneer tells the "red skins" to get out.

The past wars with "the weaker race" that Roosevelt documented in *The Winning of the West* have given way to triumphant settlement (Roosevelt 1:273–74). The late nineteenth-century generation descends from the "distinctive and intensely American stock who were the pioneers . . . the vanguard of the army of fighting settlers" (147–48). According to the film's prologue, as Oklahoma grows from territory to state, *Cimarron's* settlers fulfill Roosevelt's prophecy of national expansion. Inscribed within the text is Turner's belief that "American social development has been continually beginning over and over again on the frontier" and that the "true point of view in the history of the nation . . . is the Great West" (32). Turner and Roosevelt shared a faith in the western frontier as the definitive source of American national identity and history, and *Cimarron's* prologue, containing the rhetoric of progress and supplemented by presidential decree and the historical specificity of the date, April 22, 1889, appears to arrogate historical authority to the film narrative and to legitimize the established histories of Roosevelt and Turner.

Following the text prologue, *Cimarron* dissolves to shots of the settlers preparing for the land rush. Two Indians approach a tradesman's wagon. Seeing them reach for his wares, the white merchant attacks them, yelling, "Hey, drop that, red skin, and get out!" Rather than supporting the text, *Cimarron's* opening images work in counterpoint to the chauvinism of the written history and add poignancy to the unspoken dispossession and racism rampant on the frontier and all but invisible in dominant, early twentieth-century American histories. This initial contrast between text and image, between a triumphant view of American history that stresses homogeneous white settlement and the more complex reality of racism, dishonorable government policies, and brutality contained within the filmed images, is a strategy repeated throughout the film's narrative that consciously subverts traditional views of western history.[8] *Cimarron* pushes still further when it narrates Yancey Cravat's role in the land rush and his recounting the events to his southern in-laws in Wichita. Yancey may praise the expansion as "a miracle out of the Old Testament," but his rhetoric is ironic. Yancey is a mixed-blood Cherokee.

By the late 1920s, Hollywood had produced a few Westerns with Indian or mixed-blood protagonists, including *The Vanishing American* and *Red Skin* (1929), both starring Richard Dix. George Seitz's production of Zane Grey's *Vanishing American*, released to great popular and critical acclaim by Paramount, may have prepared the way for *Cimarron*. One might speculate that RKO's decision to film *Cimarron* with Dix as Yancey was evidence of a cycle of Native American Westerns and Hollywood's recognition of the Indian perspective. But while *Cimarron's* hero is not the archetypal, pure-blooded Anglo gunfighter cleansing the West of Indians, neither is he a noble, equally pure-blooded Indian condemned, like Nophaie, the "vanishing American," to extinction in a changing nation. He is not part of the binary formula of the western myth of the Indian: neither noble anachronism nor casualty of national expansion. Yancey Cravat, also known as "Cimarron," has mixed blood, and he was the first of these new heroes to dominate and adapt to historical events and change. When Estabrook first read Ferber's novel, which hinted more than once that Yancey was half Indian, he heavily underlined and annotated the passages, determined to focus on them "in dialog."[9] In his scripts, Estabrook emphasized both Yancey's ancestry and his active sympathy with his people. Yancey even has a voice in writing the history of the West; he is a news editor, and the headlines from his aptly named paper, the *Oklahoma Wigwam*, play an integral role in narrating *Cimarron's* written history of the West.

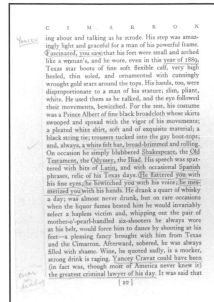

Estabrook's copy of *Cimarron* is scrawled with notes to place Yancey's Indian ancestry in the dialogue.

CIMARRON AS A COUNTERHISTORY

The film's next text insert occurs after the land rush as Yancey, Sabra (RKO's recent acquisition Irene Dunne), and son Cimarron arrive in Osage, Oklahoma. The title reads, "The boomer town of Osage—a population of 10,000 in six weeks." Again, a series of images follows which complicates the progress and optimism inherent in the town's population growth. A "half-breed" shoots a man in front of a saloon, a lawyer cheats his clients, and a pioneering husband and wife work through the night to erect their frame house. Later, after the Cravats have moved into their new house, young Cimarron is chastised by his mother for accepting a present from one of "those dirty, filthy Indians." Following this sequence, Sol Levy, the town's Jewish merchant, is abused by a group of saloon-loafing white trash. Yancey plays an ironic role in both of these scenes. Sabra's vitriolic attack on the Indians also denigrates Yancey's and young Cimarron's mixed blood and even Cimarron's name. Sol is pushed against a grain scale by one of the town bullies, and when his arms lock around the balance, he resembles a crucified Christ. Yancey saves Sol and gently extricates, or deposes, him from his cross. The film presents two scenes of violent racial hatred, the mother teaching the son to hate and an incident of anti-Semitism, which, although part of Edna Ferber's historical novel, were rarely acknowledged in the accepted history and myth of the American West.

Soon after "1890" fades in and out over a long shot of the growing town, the film introduces a new text insert: the front page of Yancey's newspaper. The headlines of the *Oklahoma Wigwam* are prominently displayed and announce former president Grover Cleveland as Harrison's possible successor, Otto von Bismarck's resignation from the German chancellery, the coming of the world's fair to Chicago, and—barely visible on the margins of the frame—Congress's decision to preserve the buffalo now that they have been slaughtered to near extinction. In spite of the seriousness of some of the articles, the male voice-overs discussing the paper only joke about the editor's note at the top of the page—Yancey and Sabra have just had a second child. The paper documents a traditional view of American expansion concurrent with European political events, while undercutting the effects of that growth with the announcement of the close annihilation of the buffalo and the public's preoccupation with trivialities. The film juxtaposes the text insert with the more critical social history revealed in the images. Soon after the glimpse of the headline news, Osage witnesses another historic event. The famous outlaw, "the Kid," a former free-range cowboy who lost his job in the wake of the developing railroad, returns to Osage. When his gang tries to rob a bank, Yancey, one of the Kid's former associates, shoots and kills him. During the battle, the townsfolk cower in their houses, and only after the Kid is killed do they emerge from their doorways. Ruggles's unusual high-angle shot transforms the citizens into vultures crowding a carcass.

Although violence was an integral part of Roosevelt's West, the bank robber, the gunfighter, and the street duel were not part of either Roosevelt's history or Turner's agrarian visions; they belonged to another past. This scene in *Cimarron* references hundreds of Hollywood Westerns since their appearance at the turn of the century, and certainly Estabrook's scripted confrontation between the Virginian and Trampas two years before. Is *Cimarron*'s gunfight merely a repetition of the ahistorical genre conventions enumerated by film theorists Will Wright, John Cawelti, Jim Kitses, and Richard Slotkin? These codifiers of the Western genre have always been uncomfortable with *Cimarron* and have quickly dismissed it as an expensive failure. The only reason *Cimarron* has ever been mentioned in Western film criticism as a historical marker is precisely because it thwarts the mythical, transhistorical structures of genre

The vulture's-eye view: after Yancey shoots his gunfighter friend, townspeople emerge from their homes.

The townspeople later decide to put the dead gunfighter on display in a storefront window.

adapted from the work of Claude Lévi-Strauss (Slotkin 233–36) and the classical narrative forms codified by David Bordwell, Kristin Thompson, and Janet Staiger in *The Classical Hollywood Cinema* (1985).

According to this critical heritage, the classical Western is composed of visual codes and themes, a recognizable iconography and a series of refined narrative structures. These genre structures have a tendency to operate transhistorically (Altman 19–29). Therefore, even though Westerns are set in the past, the discourse of the Western presents generalized images evoking frontier nostalgia. It does not question American history. Through the powerful visual symbolism of classical Hollywood genre, narrative structures dramatize the dominant cultural ideology (in this case, a triumphant endorsement of American expansion and racial progress). As with all myths, the Western is said to lack any self-reflexive relationship with its subject matter; it passively mirrors national myths rather than deliberately confronting and contesting those discourses. Yet *Cimarron*'s engagement with the text of traditional history fractures this insular genre world. This classical Hollywood Western actively engages the structure and process of history—even the archetypal scene of the shoot-out is a specific moment prefaced by a date, 1890, and a series of documented events. After Yancey has shot the Kid, the townsfolk plan to put the outlaw and his gang on display in a storefront window. Although the gunfighter may be a heroic abstraction in Western film criticism, he is documented, on view in a makeshift museum, and deliberately contained as a historical artifact in *Cimarron*'s narrative.

The next inserts occur in 1893. Again, a group of men studies the headlines, which now read, "August 17, 1893: Cherokee Strip Opening. President Cleveland Expected to Sign Proclamation on Saturday of This Week. Rush of Settlers Will Exceed 1889. Long Awaited News Stirs Country." Sabra, returning from her women's club speech, has just put Oklahoma's pioneer heritage in a safe, historical perspective. She, like Turner, views the frontier as closed and sees a new, settled era beginning. She is therefore stunned when news of further expansion inspires her husband first to criticize the government for its trickery and then to confound his criticism by cavorting off to the Strip with a group of white, gun-toting cronies. Here, *Cimarron* again challenges the Turnerian idea of a closed frontier in 1890 by showing yet another land rush about to happen in 1893. Oklahoma history proves that the frontier is still viable and that the lure of its rhetoric still blinds the nation to its own racism. But Sabra, as historian, refuses both to acknowledge her husband's need to go to the Strip and to amend her view of the past. She remains trapped in her historiography while the frontier, her husband, and the film's history rush forward.

More significantly, while the headline and documents proclaim the size and import of the expansion, Yancey's participation in that "new empire-building," that perennial last frontier, is scripted not as a national necessity but as a white man's lark and an escape from town life. The fused argument of the newspaper and Yancey's search for new territory constitutes its own critique of the impulses that drove the country to expand. Historian Gerald Nash, who would write years later that the mythic West represented an escape from the real West, viewed Hollywood cinema as an unconscious expression of this need to elude the burdens of history (206). Yet decades before Nash and other historians began to fathom the mythic undercurrents propelling the rhetoric of western history, *Cimarron* implied that the history of the West was a conscious retreat into myth. Each historically specific title in *Cimarron* is superimposed over an expanding urban landscape, and throughout the second half of the film, it is a West from which Yancey, the mythic hero, flees.

Yancey's disappearance, the passing of the Cherokee Strip, and the coming of the Spanish-American War in 1898 are united in the text of the next intertitle. The film cuts to the front page of the *Oklahoma Wigwam* (now capably run by Sabra), and male voice-overs discuss its headlines regarding the peace settlement. Yet Sol Levy and Sabra talk only of the elusive Yancey. As Sol remarks, Yancey has become "part of the history of the great Southwest." Indeed, his frontiersman type has been written into the historical record epitomized by the text inserts and Sol's projected histories. Ironically, this historicizing implies Yancey's passing as a living force while he still lives in the film diegesis. In fact, Yancey has made the transition from southwestern frontiersman to Roosevelt Rough Rider: for the past few years, he has been fighting in Cuba. The titles' institutional history makes a similar analogy, noting the end of the Cherokee Strip expansion and the coming of the Spanish-American War as if they were natural progressions in American nationhood. The headlines, which once reported the opening of the Cherokee Strip, now praise the winnings of American imperialism. In this sequence, Estabrook and Ruggles juxtaposed text and images to introduce one of the consequences of westward territorial expansion: American imperialism. With the conquest of the American West achieved, the frontier expanded beyond national borders.

Nevertheless, *Cimarron*'s structural contrast between these two events is not the straight linear progression implied by the textual inserts; rather, it is confounded by the screen images. It is important to remember what is not shown in this sequence. One never sees that other frontier. *Cimarron*'s historical narrative remains within Osage, and there is no narrative progression from the American West to Cuba and the Philippines. The diegesis circulates within the racial prejudices of Oklahoma. The actions of Sabra and Yancey Cravat also thwart any imagined narrative conflation of territorial expansion and imperialism. Although Sabra's dislike of the "lazy" Indians' neglect of the land appears to sanction a Manifest Destiny view of continental expansion, she is no advocate of imperial expansion. Yancey, as a Rough Rider, executes the letter of American imperialism in Cuba, but he is not motivated by Sabra's racial prejudice or chauvinism. It is his childish love of adventure and personal glory that motivates his expansionist acts.

Yancey's conflicting thoughts and actions, his sympathy for and kinship with the Indians and his own lust for frontier adventure, may embody what Richard Slotkin has called the ideological ambivalence of the American frontier, most vividly expressed in the mythic forms of classical Hollywood cinema (34). Yancey is the frontiersman who makes Oklahoma run, watches the town of Osage grow, and then leaves when civilization stifles him. He is the archetypal "hunter hero" who destroys the wild frontier he inhabits and embodies America's ambivalence to expansion (Slotkin 5; Stanfield 34). By killing the Kid, Yancey unwittingly condemns his world and himself to the past. He understands the Indians, but goes on the Cherokee run.

Slotkin's assertion of mythical ambivalence is misleading. In his analysis, myths disarm critical investigation (14), their narratives are simple, and the language of myth is written with no greater complexity than as a series of binary oppositions and resolutions contained within the dominant, triumphant view of American history and the bland, happy endings of Hollywood films. Yet *Cimarron*'s self-conscious historical structure proposes that traditional texts on western history present a bombastic and reductive version of the past. Yancey's exaggerated "last frontier" rhetoric and Sabra's mimed use of his words to historicize Oklahoma's early years are both parodies. At one point, as Sabra strikes a pose and mimics her husband's initial speech about Oklahoma's miraculous history (in a suitably deep voice), Yancey smiles, both genuinely amused and wistful. In Estabrook and Ruggles's film, Turner's rhetoric defining the essential national character and Roosevelt's faith in American expansion are not the foundations of another heroicized tale of the American past; they

Courtesy of RKO Pictures.

Sabra's frontier rhetoric elicits a sad smile from Yancey.

are the imperfect means by which people justify themselves. Rather than memorializing America's myths, *Cimarron* confronts them.

The next series of titles begins in 1907, announcing Oklahoma's statehood, and then cuts to a close-up of Roosevelt's grim portrait and signature on the document. This unusual series of images recalls Roosevelt as both president and historian. Both men affected Oklahoma's history. Yet Roosevelt's histories of the West endorse the industrial progress and unproblematic, racially justified expansion that Ruggles and Estabrook's film contests. Roosevelt's evolving West sanctions the eventual extinction of the Indians, the triumph of the white race, and certainly does not admit the immigration of non-European ethnic groups (Slotkin 38–42). Osage's oil-rich Indians and immigrant Chinese would not fit into Roosevelt's West. Within the film, the president's endorsement of Oklahoma's statehood makes no great changes to Osage. Roosevelt's belief that the frontier had to end as a natural step in the industrial progress of the United States is contrasted with the film's visualizing of the persistence of class and race prejudice, government corruption, and the obsolete Yancey's refusal to disappear entirely from the history of Oklahoma.

SCRIPTING MODERN AMERICAN HISTORY

By 1929, skyscrapers obliterate Osage's view of the western horizon. Yet even amid this modernity, the age has become self-consciously historical. Sabra reprints Yancey's famed 1907 editorial excoriating the government for its mistreatment of the Osage Indians. The nation, on the verge of the Great Depression and a deflation of the shibboleth of expanding national success, looks back with a distinctly sentimentalized attitude toward the past. Sabra's racism has been transformed by comfortable success into nostalgic regret. Her eulogy to her husband as a liberal man ahead of his time honors the power of an individual to influence his government's policy. As Sabra remarks proudly, they have done exactly what he wanted in the end, and the Indians are now U.S. citizens. But are the Osage Indians better off? Since oil was discovered on their land, they have become some of the state's wealthiest inhabitants. They drive around Osage in Packards and Rolls-Royces, and the women wear tribal blankets and jewelry over their Paris gowns. Are they assimilated U.S. citizens, or a self-determining Osage nation? Estabrook and Ruggles deliberately created a conflicted visual place for Indians in modern society.

In that same sequence Sabra also remembers that the last time she had any news of her husband was when a soldier recalled having seen him fighting at Château-Thierry, his hair dyed black to disguise his age. Has America's participation in the Great War (1917–1918) become an extension of the frontier in the American mythic consciousness? The border skirmishes, repossession of territory, bloody conflict, and racialized propaganda are a bitter genealogy for a mere escapist frontier myth. In 1926, Lewis Mumford drew a deliberate connection between the sterile myths of the West and the devastating realization of the new frontiers in France and Flanders. Because of the pervasiveness of the frontier idea, "one finds that the myth of the Pioneer Conquest had taken possession of even the finer and more sensitive minds: they accepted the ugliness and brutalities of pioneering, even as many of our contemporaries accepted the bestialities of war . . . in the end, the pioneer was as far from Rousseau and Wordsworth as the inventor of poison gas was from the troubadour who sang the Song of Roland" (Mumford 73). Historian David Kennedy would later connect the frontiers of the West and the Great War, alluding to Willa Cather's *One of Ours* (1922) as contemporary evidence of this feeling (Kennedy 218–19; Cather 118). Edna Ferber's decision to make Yancey a war veteran may be a reflection of Cather's frequent frontier doughboy protagonists (Tom Outland in *The Professor's House* is yet another), but the filmed *Cimarron* deliberately transforms Ferber's passing narrative mention of the Great War into dialogue between Sabra and her printer (Ferber 367). Sabra's memories of Yancey as an Indian rights crusader are immediately followed by what she has heard of his battlefront heroics. The filmmakers consciously juxtaposed these two ways of thinking about the past. The allusion to Yancey's participation in the Great War is perhaps, as far as Sabra is concerned, just another crusade of her errant husband, but it may also be an indirect critique on the part of the filmmakers of an aging frontier myth whose ideas of noble conquest locked the nation into the bitterest of wars. The bloody and ironic descent of Yancey's frontier heritage overshadows Sabra's growing historical consciousness.

The final text insert occurs in 1930, when Sabra, now a congresswoman at a political banquet, again intones Yancey's overblown expansionist rhetoric to justify the course of Oklahoma's history. However, she radicalizes her speech by emphasizing the legacy of pioneering women: "The women of Oklahoma have helped build a prairie wilderness into the state of today." This feminist tone came at a time when traditional values and the authority of the pioneer patriarch were in dispute. By 1930, the citizens of Oklahoma were some of the first Americans to experience the pinch of the Great Depression. Month by month, the reality of drought, unemployment, and poverty hardened, but Estabrook and Ruggles made no direct allusion to the Depression. Perhaps in omitting defeat, *Cimarron* ultimately resolves its conflicted early history and sanctions a comforting myth of American progress. One could also speculate that when Ferber wrote *Cimarron* in 1929, the Depression had not yet happened; Estabrook and Ruggles just stuck to the book. Yet *Cimarron's* filmmakers deliberately took the diegesis beyond the crash to 1930 and transformed the structure of the narrative. Did they believe that they were creating a usable past and a mythic narrative conclusion that would help the nation to deal with economic defeat? These are difficult questions; no conference memos exist detailing RKO's feelings about the ending. Yet the feast for Sabra is a political celebration. The fact that she was elected during the Depression may signify the country's imagined need for pioneers to lead, but it also suggests that male pioneers have failed to extricate the state from its present economic crisis. If Sabra is one of those who oversaw the growth of Oklahoma from prairie wilderness to statehood, perhaps she also is the one to rebuild the demoralized state.

Shortly after Yancey's death in an Oklahoma oil field, the film concludes at a ceremony commemorating the Oklahoma Pioneer. Naturally, the subject is a colossus of Yancey in his broad-brimmed hat and Prince Albert coat. His hand rests on the butt of his gun, and a young Indian crouches behind him, as if seeking shelter in Yancey's enormous shadow. *Cimarron's* projection of Oklahoma's elegy to the Pioneer, a mythic symbol, is ironic. Yancey, a historic figure in the film's narrative, has become an abstract hero, a larger-than-life, flawless figure embodying the society's perception of the passing of an age. The man who repeatedly dispossessed the Oklahoma Indians of their land and even denied his own mixed Indian heritage, while still acting as a friend to the oppressed, has become by the film's conclusion the savior of the weak. Popular history has written him as a hero. The final shots of the unveiled monument are not simply the filmmakers' patriotic coda; rather, Yancey's heroic statue belongs to a narrative structure that consistently draws attention to the present generation's redefinition of the past.

RKO AND THE PERILS OF SUCCESS

RKO's gamble with a sophisticated historical film paid off. Estabrook and Ruggles's production dominated every major critical poll of the year's best films (Alicoate 32); *Cimarron* would even win Academy Awards for Best Picture and Best Screenplay. If the Academy's recognition was a marker for a film's "seriousness" as an art, then surely *Cimarron* succeeded. For the next sixty years, it would be the only Western to garner such accolades, despite the genre's accelerating popularity. Although some of the film's reviewers recalled the uneasy reception of *The Big Trail*, the majority understood *Cimarron's* rigorously historical structure and content as an advance in the history of American cinema rather than as a narrative flaw. Robert E. Sherwood was ecstatic: "The excellence of *Cimarron* is further proof that the movie is the national art of America." Richard Watts Jr. introduced the idea that the film was a far better history than Ferber's historical novel or, potentially, any written history. If he had any criticism of the film, "it is only because the genuine brilliance of the production makes the slight dissatisfaction aroused by the photoplay both puzzling and worthy of careful consideration." Ferber's fictional romance and bowdlerized West, which Dorothy Van Doren pictured as ideal for a large-scale motion picture, were actually, for Watts, the least appealing qualities. For Watts,

Cimarron's complex use of western history made the film a success. It was certainly a rare moment when a film critic believed that history could take the place of the conventional fictional film narrative.

Ironically, the newest medium for representing the past, and one denigrated and resented by traditional historians, was projecting a reading of western history that challenged the ability of both traditional and revisionist written histories to synthesize the past. Carl Becker was the most prominent academic historian to question the objectivity of traditional views of the past and to recognize professional history's need to reconcile itself to a popular audience. He presented his address to the American Historical Association several months after *Cimarron*'s release: "The history that lies in unread books does no work in the world. The history that does work in the world, the history that influences the course of history, is living history, that pattern of remembered events, whether true or false, that enlarges and enriches the collective specious present, the specious present of Mr. Everyman" (Becker 16–17).

Although Becker said nothing of cinema, undoubtedly this ultimate form of popular history would be Mr. Everyman's choice. Yet with *Cimarron*, cinema had penetrated the realm of serious history and led its popular audience away from the cultural comfort of myths and into a complicated and hitherto uncharted historical territory. While contemporary academics picked away at isolated inadequacies of Turner's thesis and traditional western historiography, a popular novel and an even more popular film articulated a persuasive new way to look at the past. Curiously, the film's structure and historical concerns seem to have anticipated the so-called New Western History of the late twentieth century (White). In 1931, *Cimarron* presented a multiracial and ethnic West; it elevated minorities to positions of power within the narrative, and it gave Native Americans a voice in creating the historical record. The film also articulated a thorough and prolonged critique of the accepted historiography; it interrogated the rhetoric of traditional written history with images that counteracted and even denied the omniscience of the written word. Yet unlike much of the late twentieth-century historiography that echoed the divisive rhetoric of poststructuralism and the postmodern suspicion of narrative history, *Cimarron* managed to retain a historical complexity without sacrificing a coherent synthesis of historical change. It could tell one story with many voices, combining a critical historical viewpoint with a lucid cinematic synthesis.

Film critic Thornton Delehanty realized that *Cimarron* was exceptional, observing that the film "set a mark for pictures of its kind which, it is not hard to believe, may never be hit again." Unfortunately, Delehanty's remark would haunt American historical filmmaking. Certainly the production circumstances were unique. Estabrook and Ruggles were responsible for *Cimarron*'s unusual union of narrative coherence and historical complexity, but RKO could not afford another artistic success. In spite of the fact that *Cimarron* made $1.38 million in the worst industrial year of the Great Depression, the studio had spent $1.5 million to make it (Haver 67). Executives replaced William LeBaron with David O. Selznick (son-in-law of Metro-Goldwyn-Mayer mogul Louis B. Mayer). Wesley Ruggles left RKO to direct Mae West and Carole Lombard vehicles; it would be nine years before he made another historical Western, Columbia's *Arizona* (1940). Estabrook remained at RKO, collected his Oscar, and tried to write his next project, *The Conquerors,* without interference.

But his days as the sole author of a film script were limited. Working on *Cimarron,* Estabrook had experienced what few screenwriters had ever attained: extensive and unusual power in creating a prestigious and influential film. With *Cimarron*'s release, the press concentrated almost exclusively on Estabrook as the film's author. London's *Graphic* did an in-depth interview with him entitled "Writer's Gold in Hollywood." Estabrook wrote articles for the *Hollywood Reporter* crediting the film with generating a renewed interest in American history. "In almost every city where *Cimarron* has been exhibited," he wrote, "the interest aroused in its historical theme has been reflected in a demand for volumes dealing with this page of American history." He was suddenly the most prominent screenwriter in Hollywood, and an influential American historian with the widest public imaginable. He had become Mr. Everyman's historian. But *Cimarron* was also his nemesis. Having adapted and subtly transformed other people's work, Estabrook now wanted to write his own historical screenplay. Perhaps the deepening Depression affected him, perhaps his surge of public recognition altered his critical judgment, but Estabrook now wanted to project a message to the public. *The March of a Nation,* conceived as an episodic story of a New York financial family, focused on the country's triumphs over a series of financial crises from 1873 to 1929 (Estabrook 1932). History would now serve the needs of contemporary events. Estabrook even planned to film each episode, or historical "transition," with shots of a man perusing an enormous history book. A shot of a venerable old book with a date, such as "1873," would be followed by a close-up of a relevant engraving.

Selznick's response a week later was simply "Flat!" He hired hack writers Robert Lord and Humphrey Pearson to gut Estabrook's pet epic. Eventually, Selznick and cranky action director William Wellman revamped Estabrook's epic antidote to the Great Depression into a cheaper and more pugnacious version of *Cimarron*. Estabrook's multiracial West and hero were gone, as were the ironic text inserts and precise use of dates. Instead, the producer ordered Czech émigré and montage specialist Slavko Vorkapich to make a series of newspaper montages to cover holes in the narrative. Vorkapich, with possibly less interest in American history than Selznick, replaced as much of the projected text as possible with a series of images of rising and falling columns of money (Vorkapich). Even with Richard Dix playing the lead, the film failed. Both Selznick and the young Wellman had a rather conventional view of the West; triumphant white "Conquerors" interested them more than America's "Cimarron" past. Estabrook never recovered his former status as Hollywood's most influential western historian. Several years later he would join his friend LeBaron at Paramount, not as a writer but as an associate producer and behind-the-scenes historical script doctor.

NOTES

1. For a sampling of the major critical responses, see *Hollywood News*, August 12, 1930; Edward Churchill, *Exhibitors' Herald World*, September 13, 1930; *Variety*, January 28, 1931, 14; "Real Sabra Weeps as She Sees Film," unmarked press clipping (January 1931); Richard Watts Jr., "*Cimarron* Shows the Pioneer in the Wilds of Old Oklahoma," *New York Herald Tribune*, February 1, 1931; Howard Estabrook, "This Amusement School of Ours," *Hollywood Reporter*, May 8, 1931, Margaret Herrick Library, Academy of Motion Picture Arts and Sciences (AMPAS), Beverly Hills, California.

2. Richard Slotkin's distinction between the mythic province of cinema that reinforces broad cultural assumptions and symbols and the serious historical world of professional written history approximates the more general view within film studies regarding the discourse of classical Hollywood cinema. Although Robert A. Rosenstone (*Visions of the Past* [Cambridge, Mass.: Harvard University Press, 1995]), Natalie Zemon Davis (*Slaves on Screen* [Cambridge, Mass.: Harvard University Press, 2001]), and Janet Walker (*Westerns: Films through History* [New York: Routledge, 2001]) have challenged the assumption that American historical films and Westerns are incapable of serious historical arguments, their efforts have avoided classical Hollywood cinema and instead have concentrated on films made after the decline of the studio system and the "demystification" of genre

achieved during the postmodern era. Rosenstone and others have also insisted on a "separate but equal" status for visual history, rather than noting cinema's self-conscious engagement with the discourse of written history.

3. The contemporary scholarly consensus among film scholars and historians writing about film continues to deny the possibility of a "filmic writing of history," particularly for classical Hollywood cinema. See Marc Ferro, *Cinema and History*, trans. Naomi Green (Detroit, Mich.: Wayne State University Press, 1988), 161–63; and Robert A. Rosenstone, "Inventing Historical Truth on the Silver Screen," *Cineaste* (Spring 2004): 29–33.

4. Charles A. Beard, "The Frontier in American History," *New Republic*, February 16, 1921, 349–50; John C. Almach, "The Shibboleth of the Frontier," *Historical Outlook* 16 (May 1925): 197–202; Kerwin Lee Klein, *Frontiers of the Historical Imagination* (Berkeley: University of California Press, 1997), 21; Bernard De Voto, "Footnote on the West," *Harper's*, November 1927, 714–22; Carey McWilliams, "Myths of the West," *North American Review* 232 (November 1931): 424–32.

5. See also reviews of *Cimarron*, "In Odd Oklahoma," *Time*, March 24, 1930, 80; G. T. H., *New Republic*, April 30, 1930, 308; Stanley Vestal, *Saturday Review of Literature*, March 22, 1930, 841.

6. RKO's merger also marked the first alliance between cinema and radio companies, or film and sound.

7. *Cimarron* is a unique film in the "classical" age of American film in that it had only one screenwriter. Estabrook was the sole author of the script, a rare accomplishment in an industry that preferred assigning a number of writers to one project.

8. Early drafts of the script and notes confirm that Estabrook conceived this structural practice from the beginning (Estabrook Collection, AMPAS).

9. Estabrook's annotated copy of Ferber's *Cimarron*, Howard Estabrook Collection, AMPAS, 10–11; Estabrook, "Adaptation and Structure of Screen Play," May 22, 1930, A20; first draft, June 19, 1930, 35; shooting script, August 27, 1930, A23.

Works Cited

Alicoate, Jack, ed. *The 1931 Film Daily Year Book of Motion Pictures*. The Film Daily, 1932.

Almach, John C. "The Shibboleth of the Frontier." *Historical Outlook* 16 (May 1925): 197–202.

Altman, Rick. *Film/Genre*. London: British Film Institute, 1999.

Balderston, John. *The Last of the Mohicans* treatment. March 7, 1935. Edward Small Collection, Special Collections, University of Southern California.

Beard, Charles A. "The Frontier in American History." *New Republic* 25 (February 16, 1921): 349–50.

Becker, Carl. "Everyman His Own Historian." 1931 Address to the American Historical Association. El Paso, Tex.: Academic Reprints, 1960.

"*The Big Trail.*" *Photoplay* 38, no. 6 (November 1930): 52.

Bordwell, David, Kristin Thompson, and Janet Staiger. *The Classical Hollywood Cinema: Film Style and Mode of Production to 1960.* New York: Columbia University Press, 1985.

Boynton, Percy H. *The Rediscovery of the Frontier.* Chicago: University of Chicago Press, 1931.

Brabin, Charles. *The Great Meadow* treatment. May 26, 1930. MGM Collection, Special Collections, University of Southern California (MGM/USC).

———. *The Great Meadow* continuity. June 14, 1930. MGM/USC.

———. *The Great Meadow* shooting script. August 12, 1930. MGM/USC.

———. *The Great Meadow* dialogue and cutting continuity. December 12, 1930. MGM/USC.

Branch, E. Douglas. *Westward: The Romance of the American Frontier.* New York: Appleton, 1930.

Cather, Willa. *One of Ours.* New York: Knopf, 1922.

Cawelti, John G. *The Six-Gun Mystique.* Bowling Green, Ohio: Bowling Green University Popular Press, 1971.

Churchill, Edward. "*Cimarron.*" Review. *Exhibitors' Herald World,* September 13, 1930.

Cimarron. Production files. RKO Collection, UCLA Arts Special Collections.

"*Cimarron.*" Review. *Hollywood News,* August 12, 1930.

"*Cimarron.*" Review. *Variety,* January 28, 1931, 14.

Davis, Natalie Zemon. *Slaves on Screen.* Cambridge, Mass.: Harvard University Press, 2001.

Delehanty, Thornton. "The New Films." Review of *Cimarron. Evening Post,* January 27, 1931, 13.

De Voto, Bernard. "Footnote on the West." *Harper's,* November 1927, 714–22.

Ellis, Edith. *The Great Meadow* titles. November 5, 1930. MGM/USC.

Estabrook, Howard. *Cimarron* research bibliography. 1930. Howard Estabrook Collection, Margaret Herrick Library, Academy of Motion Picture Arts and Sciences (AMPAS).

———. *Cimarron* adaptation and structure of screen play. May 22, 1930. Howard Estabrook Collection, AMPAS.

———. *Cimarron* first draft. June 19, 1930. Howard Estabrook Collection, AMPAS.

———. *Cimarron* shooting script. August 27, 1930. Howard Estabrook Collection, AMPAS.

———. *Cimarron* continuity. January 12, 1931. Howard Estabrook Collection, AMPAS.

———. *The Conquerors* first draft. December 24, 1931. RKO Collection, Box 184. UCLA Arts Special Collections.

———. "This Amusement School of Ours." *Hollywood Reporter*, May 8, 1931.

Ferber, Edna. *Cimarron*. Garden City, N.Y.: Doubleday, 1930. Annotated by Howard Estabrook. Howard Estabrook Collection, AMPAS.

———. *A Peculiar Treasure*. New York: Doubleday, Doran, 1939.

Ferro, Marc. *Cinema and History*. Translated by Naomi Greene. Detroit, Mich.: Wayne State University Press, 1988.

Grey, Zane. *The Vanishing American*. New York: Grosset and Dunlap, 1925.

G. T. H. "*Cimarron*." Review of *Cimarron* by Edna Ferber. *New Republic*, April 30, 1930, 308.

Hall, Mordaunt. "*Abraham Lincoln*." *New York Times*, August 26, 1930, 24:1.

Hampton, Benjamin. *History of the American Film Industry from Its Beginnings to 1931*. 1931. New York: Dover, 1970.

Haver, Ronald. *David O. Selznick's Hollywood*. New York: Knopf, 1980.

"In Odd Oklahoma." Review of *Cimarron*, by Edna Ferber. *Time*, March 24, 1930, 80.

Jacobs, Lewis. *The Rise of the American Film: A Critical History*. New York: Harcourt, Brace, 1939.

Johnston, William A. "Writer's Gold in Hollywood." *Graphic*, May 2, 1931, 172.

Kennedy, David. *Over Here: The First World War and American Society*. New York: Oxford University Press, 1980.

Kitses, Jim. *Horizons West: Anthony Mann, Budd Boetticher, Sam Peckinpah: Studies of Authorship within the Western*. Bloomington: Indiana University Press, 1969.

Klein, Kerwin Lee. *Frontiers of the Historical Imagination*. Berkeley: University of California Press, 1997.

MacLeod, William Christie. *The American Indian Frontier*. New York: Knopf, 1928.

McWilliams, Carey. "Myths of the West." *North American Review* 232 (November 1931): 424-32.

Mumford, Lewis. *The Golden Day*. New York: Boni and Liveright, 1926.

Nash, Gerald. *Creating the West: Historical Interpretations, 1890–1990*. Albuquerque: University of New Mexico Press, 1991.

Potamkin, Harry Alan. "*Storm over Asia* and *Abraham Lincoln*." *New Masses*, October 1930, 16.

Powell, Paul. *Cimarron* story treatment and critique. June 28, 1930. *Cimarron* Script Collection. RKO Special Collections, UCLA Film and Television Archive.

"Real Sabra Weeps as She Sees Film." Unmarked press clipping, January 1931. AMPAS.

Roosevelt, Theodore. *The Winning of the West*. 5 vols. New York: Putnam's, 1907.

Rosenstone, Robert A. *Visions of the Past: The Challenge of Film to Our Idea of History*. Cambridge, Mass.: Harvard University Press, 1995.

———. "Inventing Historical Truth on the Silver Screen." *Cineaste* (Spring 2004): 29–33.

Rotha, Paul. *The Film Till Now*. Rev. ed. New York, 1967.

Sherwood, Robert. "The Moving Picture Album." Review of *Cimarron. Hollywood Citizen-News,* February 7, 1931.

Silverman, Sime. *"The Big Trail." Variety,* October 29, 1930, 17, 27.

Slotkin, Richard. *Gunfighter Nation: The Myth of the Frontier in Twentieth-Century America.* Norman: University of Oklahoma Press, 1992.

Stanfield, Peter. *Hollywood, Westerns and the 1930s: The Lost Trail.* University of Exeter Press, 2001.

Sutton, Fred E., and A. B. MacDonald. *Hands Up!* New York: Bobbs-Merrill, 1927.

Turner, Frederick Jackson. "The Significance of the Frontier in American History." 1893. In *Rereading Frederick Jackson Turner: "The Significance of the Frontier in American History" and Other Essays,* edited by John Mack Faragher, 31–60. New York: Henry Holt, 1994.

Tuska, John. "The American Western Cinema: 1903–Present." In *Focus on the Western,* edited by Jack Nachbar, 25–43. Englewood Cliffs, N.J.: Prentice-Hall, 1974.

Van Doren, Dorothy. "A Pioneer Fairy Story." *Nation,* April 23, 1930, 494.

Vestal, Stanley. *"Cimarron."* Review of *Cimarron,* by Edna Ferber. *Saturday Review of Literature,* March 22, 1930, 841.

Vorkapich, Slavko. Memo to David O. Selznick. Undated, 1932 [?]. *The Conquerors* Production File, Box p-40. UCLA Special Arts Collection.

Walker, Janet, ed. *Westerns: Films through History.* New York: Routledge, 2001.

Warshow, Robert. "Movie Chronicle: The Westerner." In *Focus on the Western,* edited by Jack Nachbar, 45–56. Englewood Cliffs, N.J.: Prentice-Hall, 1974.

Watts, Richard, Jr. *"Cimarron* Shows the Pioneer in the Wilds of Old Oklahoma." *New York Herald Tribune,* February 1, 1931, sec. 8, p. 3.

White, Richard. *Western History.* Washington, D.C.: American Historical Association, 1997.

Wright, Will. *Six Guns and Society: A Structural Study of the Western.* Berkeley: University of California Press, 1975.

TRADITION, PARODY, AND ADAPTATION
Jed Buell's Unconventional West

In the 1930s, a different kind of West appeared on Hollywood's "Poverty Row." It was a West animated by "little people" brawling in barrooms, a black hero singing his way into the heart of the rancher's daughter, an opera singer-turned-cowboy, and a penguin. It was Jed Buell's West. Little recognition is given to Buell for leaving his imprint on the Western musical as a genre. Credited with producing only about a dozen "singing cowboy" films, all released between 1936 and 1940, he was undoubtedly not the most active of contributors, but he may have been one of the most imaginative. Known as "quirky," a "man with the gimmick," and a producer who knew how to get box office, Buell gained a small flash of notoriety for producing the now-cult classic *The Terror of Tiny Town* (1938). And perhaps that is to be expected. His musical Westerns were cut from the same schematic cloth as the rest, observing the same tropes and traditions, utilizing the same script formulas and cinematic techniques. Most of the internal or structural analyses brought to bear on Western films in general can be applied with the same success or failure to Buell's work as to the efforts of others.

Yet the value of Buell's contribution to the genre may be found precisely in its variations on the musical Western theme. As Will Wright points out, the Western is a social phenomenon—a historically situated part of the cultural language by which America understands itself (10). Jed Buell's films were part of that understanding—sometimes a unique part. Buell's productions frequently challenged the sameness of the cinematic West—a territory where certainty reigned supreme, and cowboy heroes held steady to rural American identities and values in a time of rapid social change. That West, and the characters who

Courtesy of the Danielle Buell Collection.

Jed Buell, a producer with box-office savvy.

inhabited it, avoided confrontations with the social and moral attitudes and concerns of its audiences and reinforced shared ideas of "the way things ought to be" for mainstream America (Stanfield 98; Tuska 8–9). Jed Buell's musical Westerns used parody, gimmickry, and casts of unlikely characters to turn "the way things ought to be" on its ear. Buell's work might have been unremarkable were it not for the cultural commentary inherent in these small artifacts of moving picture industry history. While elements of all were in keeping with the Western myths and traditions of the day, the success or failure of the unique aspects of Buell's musical Western legacy—whether viewed as parody or desperation, exploitation or mutation, the result of genius or greed—speaks to the social and cinematic culture of the 1930s.

FROM COMEDY TO COWBOYS

Jed Buell began his career in the movie industry in the early 1900s, as manager of the Orpheum Theater in Denver. Seeking relief from Colorado's altitude, he moved to Hollywood in his twenties and landed a job with Mack Sennett, "the King of Comedy." Over time, Buell advanced from unit publicist to publicity director for Sennett's popular Keystone Studios—known for the antics of the Keystone Cops, risqué bathing beauties, lions on leashes, and the master of silent comedy, Charlie Chaplin. When the stock market crash of 1929 left Keystone foundering, Buell, a man known for being able to get things done financially, began his own small Poverty Row production company, Spectrum Pictures. Buell's old ties to the Keystone "family" would come into play in his copro-duction of several musical Westerns with a close friend, the actor Stan Laurel (who funded *Tiny Town*), in his casting of Fred Scott as Spectrum's premier singing cowboy, and in his choice of Al St. John (Fatty Arbuckle's nephew) to replace Fuzzy Knight as Fred Scott's comic sidekick. But perhaps most significantly, Buell took from Keystone a sense of comic timing that would resurface time and again during his production career as he teamed with notables like well-known Western director Sam Newfield (director of *Terror of Tiny Town*) and Fred Myton (the writer behind *The Mad Monster, Shadows of Death,* and other B horror flicks).

Buell has been referred to by some as the father of the "mutant Western"— a subgenre characterized by its perversion of the Western—seeking to deface its icons, obliterate its themes, and desecrate its status as a genre (Brophy 1). The mutant Western, according to Brophy, is created by a series of tensions and interactions that rework the Western's cultural, mythical, sociological, and cinematic conventions in the wackiest fashion possible for comic or political effect—the perfect foil to the assumptions and anticipated actions, stars, and symbols of the classical Western (Brophy 3, 18). It is this last aspect—that of confronting common (or classical) expectations about, and creating contrast to, the musical Western—that has some merit when considering Buell's films. Each facet of Jed Buell's West addresses and twists popular genre expectations in some way, creating hybrids that open up the West to faces and voices ordinarily repressed or relegated to other genres.

FRED SCOTT, "THE SILVERY-VOICED BUCKAROO"

The first voice to be heard in Jed Buell's West was that of Fred Scott. In the mid-1930s, the popularity of the B Western was waning, until Nat Levine's Mascot studios produced a song-infused serial, *The Phantom Empire* (1935), starring former WLS Barn Dance radio performer Gene Autry. Autry's success as a cowboy crooner, first in *Empire* (1935), then, in rapid succession that same year, *Tumbling Tumbleweeds, Melody Trail, The Sagebrush Troubadour,* and *Singing Vagabond,* sent rival studios rushing to find their own singing cowboys. Buell's Spectrum Pictures recruited Fred Scott as its new cowboy crooner, launching his film series with *Romance Rides the Range* (1936). Scott's billing, initially as the "Silvery-Voiced Baritone" and later as the "Silvery-Voiced Buckaroo," was an acknowledgment of his training as an opera singer. He had grown up captivated by the recordings of singers like Enrico Caruso and John McCormack and taught himself to sing by vocalizing along with their records. By the age of twelve, he was on stage, and throughout his teen years he acted and sang in local theatrical productions. Scott later enrolled in acting school, where he was formally trained in voice and opera. After a part in *Rio Rita* (1929) and a few comedies for Pathe and Keystone (where he met Jed Buell), Scott joined the San Francisco Opera Company in 1932. He returned to films in 1936 and after a small part as a singing cowboy in a Harry Carey–Hoot Gibson film, *The Last Outlaw* (1936), was quickly signed by Buell for a musical Western series (DeMarco 67).

Fred Scott would go on to star in more than a dozen Western musicals, nine of them for Buell—and each of the films in his series was well situated in the myth and tradition of the day. While the details of content might differ among musical Westerns—a dam here, a railroad there, ranch wars, the search for lost family—the more abstract relationships between heroes and society created in Westerns of the 1930s were fairly consistent (see Wright). Scott was an affable hero whose domestic, sentimental side was often accentuated— he befriended small children, gave care to the sick and injured, and in *Knight of the Plains* (1939) even sang "Home Sweet Home" accompanied by a little old lady on a pedal organ. In his 1939 release, *In Old Montana,* Scott topples off his horse, tangled in a clothesline. To make amends with the heroine, he helps her with her chores, crooning about the sentimental pleasures of being a "mother's helper."

The "down home" side of Fred Scott.

Scott should have been a success as a sagebrush hero. He was older than many of the other cowboy crooners—taller and more mature looking, with the added attraction of "a toothy grin so luminous that it would be the last image remaining on the screen after it had faded to black" (Stanfield 110). He was also well supported by leading ladies such as Lois January and June Allison, talented sidekicks Cliff Nazzaro and Al St. John, and, for three of his films, the production talents of the famous Stan Laurel (Lahue 208–9). Yet, by 1942, Scott and the movie industry had parted company, after sixteen musical Westerns. While Spectrum's shoestring budget was certainly at issue in audiences' lukewarm reception of Scott's pictures, it was his formal vocal training and accentless voice that led to the cowboy crooner's lack of screen success; he lacked the down-home, regional quality of Gene Autry, Tex Ritter, Eddie Dean, and others. Scott's first Buell film, *Romance Rides the Range*, attempted to bridge the divide between the star's operatic training and the audience's need for a cowboy crooner they could call their own, by setting up a city-country opposition. The film begins with Scott, a "city" opera singer,

Opera or horse opera? Fred Scott in *Romance Rides the Range.*

finishing his last curtain call for the season and arguing with his manager about what should happen next. While the manager wants his star to tour Europe, Scott insists on a vacation back to his roots—in the ranching West of his youth. Establishing this binary cultural opposition, Scott's "difference" is remedied by the fact that his roots and his heart are in the country—making him "just folks." Movie audiences ultimately disagreed, preferring to maintain the gap between popular and "high" culture, by favoring the style of Tex Ritter and Roy Rogers over Scott's unique operatic crooning.

Keystone Comedy Meets the West in
The Terror of Tiny Town

With "high culture" nowhere in sight, *The Terror of Tiny Town,* Buell's best-known, most controversial, and most baffling musical Western, was released in 1938. As with all Buell's musical Westerns, *Tiny Town* follows a standard format—a hero, a villain, two feuding families, cattle, lots of songs, and a girl. The Preston and Lawson ranches are feuding, each blaming the other for mysterious cattle disappearances. Of course, the villain, Bat Haines ("Little Billy" Rhodes), is behind the disappearances and, to make matters worse, has the sheriff in his back pocket. True to Western romance form, the hero, Buck Lawson (Billy Curtis), falls in love with Preston's niece, begins to solve the cattle mystery, and is nearly lynched for Preston's murder. After a classic fight scene with the villain in a cabin rigged with dynamite, he saves the day and gets the girl.

At this point, the similarities with more conventional musical Westerns of the day end. *The Terror of Tiny Town* draws its name from a cast composed entirely of little people. According to one magazine, the inspiration for *Tiny Town* hit Buell when an employee lamented, "If this economic dive keeps on, we'll be using midgets for actors." Before long, Buell was advertising "Big Salaries for Little People," and the project created a venue for a new kind of cowboy crooner (Medved 241): riding Shetland ponies, walking under the swinging doors of the saloon, and guzzling their booze from oversized glasses, the entire cast of *Tiny Town* was under four feet tall. Billed in the credits as "Jed Buell's Midgets," the players had all formerly been members of "Singer's Midgets"—a European theatrical novelty troupe, founded in 1914 and owned by Baron Leopold Von Singer. Throughout the 1920s and 1930s, Singer bought these little people from their families, who considered them nuisances or outcasts (Cox 9). Singer's actors traveled throughout Europe, South America, Asia, Australia, and finally the United States, playing nearly every theater on the Orpheum and Keith circuits. Prior to *Tiny Town,* one or two had been cast in films, including Laurel and Hardy's *Block-Heads* (1938) and Spencer Tracy's *They Gave Him a Gun* (1937), but the Buell film provided a springboard to stardom for several cast members. In fact, when filming for *The Terror of Tiny Town* ended, nearly the entire cast traveled directly from the set to take up residence in another tiny town—Munchkinland, in *The Wizard of Oz* (1939).

Tiny Town is often cited as a parody of musical Westerns, made at the expense of dozens of little people. Listed in nearly every "bad movie" survey ever written, it opens with an announcer proclaiming: "Ladies and gentlemen and children of all ages, we're going to present for your approval a novelty picture with an all-midget cast, the first of its kind ever to be produced. I'm told that it has everything, that it is everything that a Western should have." With this introduction, *The Terror of Tiny Town* takes on a carnivalesque feel—an air of a traveling sideshow. The hero and villain then join the emcee onstage, challenging first each other, then the unseen theater audience, in a battle of egos that thickens the air with burlesque and a kind of reflexive self-mockery completely foreign to musical Westerns of the era. *Tiny Town* draws heavily on producer Buell's and writer Myton's sense of visual comedy and harkens back to Buell's Keystone days. Early in the film, a penguin suddenly appears on a piano—just once, never to be seen again. During one of her exits, the heroine, Nancy (Yvonne Moray), runs toward a door and, instead of running around a desk, crawls under it to leave. While certain props were resized to fit the cast, others were left in their standard size, creating visual effects such as saloon patrons drinking from beer steins that look more like buckets with stems, and tiny Shetland ponies straining as they're tied to hitching posts that tower over them. Filling the traditional role of the comic sidekick is Otto, the chef (Charles Becker). Interspersed among other episodes of romance, gunslinging, and barroom brawls, the action turns periodically to the comic antics of Otto engaged in a Chaplinesque battle of wills with a reluctant duck he has planned for dinner. Otto chases the duck to and fro, around the yard, in and out of the barn, trying to outsmart the web-footed critter—with the duck nipping Otto on the behind, walking backward, and otherwise driving the poor chef to distraction. The film returns periodically to find Otto climbing into the stove, in and out of cupboards, and emerging from a pot of boiling water as the duck continues to evade capture.

If all these devices are interpreted solely as exploitive midget humor to turn a quick buck, then Buell's point may be missed. That is not to say that there was not a great deal of novelty-driven humor at the expense of little people—and at the expense of conventional singing cowboy films and African Americans, in the form of a shoeshine boy who aptly mimics the drawl and mannerisms of Stepin Fetchit (Lincoln T. Perry). But it might also be suggested that Buell was creating a new hybrid of sorts—a Western musical that was inextricably linked to the comic traditions of the Sennett era, where pratfalls, mockery, comic cops in tiny cars, and other visual oddities were the mainstays.

Author's collection.

Billy Curtis (as Buck Lawson) gets the girl in *The Terror of Tiny Town*.

Courtesy of the Danielle Buell Collection.

Jed Buell proclaimed, "Big salaries for little people" in 1938.

Author's collection.

Actor Charles Becker as comic relief in *The Terror of Tiny Town*.

The cinematic West of the 1930s was an earnest place, where American myths were played out on the big screen. In good, comic burlesque tradition, Buell created in *Tiny Town* a vehicle that laughed at the West, while the West laughed back.

BRINGING HARLEM TO THE PRAIRIE WITH HERB JEFFRIES, "THE BRONZE BUCKAROO"

Directly following *The Terror of Tiny Town* was another film that garnered Buell further criticism for exploitation, along with a few comments of praise for advancing the role of blacks in the cinematic West: *Harlem on the Prairie* (1937). The film brought the rich musical voice of Herb Jeffries to the frontier, along with a cast of black faces usually absent from the genre.

The issue of black images in the early years of film is a complex one. More than thirteen hundred African American films were produced between 1895 and 1959—feature films, both silent and sound, documentaries, soundies,

Herb Jeffries as the first African American singing
cowboy, in *Harlem on the Prairie*.

trailers and shorts, produced by sources ranging from the U.S. government to
independents to Hollywood studios (Richards 5–6). Two hundred of these
films were produced in the 1930s, and two of those are credited to Jed Buell—
Harlem on the Prairie and *The Bronze Buckaroo* (1939).

These films emerged from a social and historical context that brought
forth some of the most disturbing racist images (such as *The Birth of a Nation*
[1915] and the *Rastus* series [1910–1911]), as well as elegant and controversial
statements about African American life (such as those found in the films of
Oscar Micheaux). Mainstream cinema in the early Depression years generally

provided America with a comforting set of fantasies about the natural order of race relations in economically and politically troubled times. The actors who portrayed these images (Stepin Fetchit, Bill Robinson, Eddie Anderson, Butterfly McQueen, and Hattie McDaniels) delivered highly individualized performances and developed trademark idiosyncratic personas—cast as lazy, slow-witted, befuddled, and necrophobic, yet with timing and creativity that often stole scenes from their white counterparts (see Jerome; Kisch and Mapp; Cripps; Bogle). Mammies, porters, doormen, and sidekicks were among the only suitable roles for blacks in Hollywood—at least prior to the era of "race" movies made specifically for African American audiences. As the Depression continued, black filmmakers such as Spencer Williams (*Dirty Gertie from Harlem* [1946], *Juke Joint* [1947], *Beale Street Mama* [1947]) and George Randol and Ralph Cooper (*Dark Manhattan* [1937], *The Duke Is Tops*, with Lena Horne [1938]) produced "all-black-cast" films through independent studios for the "Chitlin' Circuit," while white studios were producing slick, glossy products for black audiences in typical Hollywood genre formats: Westerns, musicals, mysteries, gangster sagas, and crime stories.

But in the 1930s, the cinematic West was Anglo-Saxon territory. Although there had been significant African American cowboy figures in a few "race" movies, such as *A Trooper of Troop K* (1917), featuring George and Noble Johnson, and Bill Pickett's *Crimson Skull* (1921) and *The Bull-Dogger* (1923), the musical Westerns that animated the West in the "talkie" era had no black hero images. Cowboy crooners like Gene Autry, Tex Ritter, Fred Scott, Bob Baker, and others were vying for the attention of Westerns' fans, while blacks were relegated to playing dizzy comic sidekicks, loyal standbys, and stereotypes of the downtrodden. This exclusion from leading roles had a significant impact on singer Herb Jeffries. Samuel Sherman writes: "Herb Jeffries likes to tell a story about cowboys in 1937. . . . He was touring at the time with Earl 'Fatha' Hines, when he stepped out into an alley between shows. A little black child was playing cowboys with a group of white children. The little boy wanted to play his favorite cowboy, but his friends stopped him, saying 'You can't be Buck Jones. Buck Jones ain't a Negro'" (37). True enough. In the 1930s, the hundreds of small but flourishing all-black movie houses all featured an exclusively white frontier.

Jeffries lobbied independent producers to film a musical Western with a black star, until Jed Buell, aware of the market potential that fell below the radar of most Hollywood producers, agreed to take a chance on Jeffries's idea. Buell claimed that he chose a script at random from a pile on the floor, intending to adapt it for a black cast and audience, but casting would prove more difficult. Finding a competent black actor who could also sing and ride a horse eliminated all potential candidates but Jeffries, who was signed as the star of *Harlem on the Prairie* and was billed as "Black America's first singing cowboy in the movies" (Buscombe 69). Filmed on the N. B. Murray Dude Ranch, a blacks-only dude ranch in Victorville, California, Buell's production was played out in an all-black Western frontier. Jeffries went on to make two other musical Westerns with Richard Kahn of Merit Pictures between 1938 and 1939 (although Kahn received production credit for *The Bronze Buckaroo,* it was the product of a collaboration with Buell) before turning in his saddle and spurs to croon for Duke Ellington in 1939.

But black America's first singing cowboy also represented and promoted the values and class views of mainstream white society in ways identical to white musical Westerns—essentially creating yet another middle-class hero. *Harlem on the Prairie* (also released as *Bad Man of Harlem*) and *The Bronze Buckaroo,* Jeffries's two Buell-produced films, were structurally and thematically situated firmly in the traditions of musical Westerns; the stories, plot devices, and social and economic references were largely all derivative. Jeffries was the archetypal cowboy hero, complete with white hat, shining pearl-handled revolvers, a white horse, Stardusk, and a trusty sidekick, Dusty. The films conformed to the color caste conventions of the day, with Jeffries's hero, tall and light-skinned (Jeffries's skin was actually darkened with makeup because he filmed "too white"), pitted against shorter, stouter, and darker-skinned heavies and comic figures. Even the heroines—Jeffries's romantic interests—were slim, with light complexions. The "all-black-cast" Westerns contained all the expected elements of mainstream horse opera, as well as reflections of mainstream images of blacks. *The Bronze Buckaroo,* for example, finds Jeffries's sidekick (played by Lucius Brooks) little more than a wide-eyed, dim-witted stereotype that could have been found in any typical white-audience film.

Having essentially populated white films with African American actors, rather than producing work that spoke to the lives and concerns of African Americans, Buell's "all-black-cast" work received significant criticism as yet another artifact of exploitation. The two films were clearly shaped by the entertainment ideology of the day, and nothing exists to indicate that Buell was attempting to make a statement about race, equality, or African American entertainment. The fact remains, however, that with *Harlem on the Prairie*, Buell introduced a strong black hero to the musical Western, marking the first time that an African American received top billing in the genre. Both *Harlem* and *The Bronze Buckaroo* recognized black theatergoers as viable audiences, brought musical Western entertainment into black theaters, and added diversity to the roles available to African American actors at a time when other production houses were making pictures exclusively for mainstream white audiences.

A West Less Certain

Second looks like these, attempts to understand how cultural pieces came together to create the various aspects of Jed Buell's West, are revealing. The motives of audience share and profit certainly cannot be underestimated, but to view Buell's West with a single lens is limiting. Was he a man with a gimmick? The man who knew how to draw box office? Probably. But he did so in ways that shed light on cultural, social, and political issues of the time. Whether bringing to light the sharp divide between the culture of the masses and an operatic cowboy crooner, displaying the myths and traditions of the West with the kind of visual humor and self-reflexive laughter seldom found outside of vaudeville and burlesque, or creating a cinematic route to the musical West for African Americans other than as complements to white counterparts, Buell's West was an artifact of both his early career and the era in which he lived.

Buell's musical Westerns were hybrids, each in its own fashion, and their combinations of unconventional characters with the established narratives and settings of the "singing cowboy" genre served to draw attention to the traditions they inverted. The cinematic West of the 1930s was, in many ways, a place of certainty and reinforcement for mainstream American identity, and the western frontier, while perilous, was the backdrop for moral and social predictability. Western heroes did far more than refrain from smoke, drink, and rough language; they stood fast in the face of changes being wrought by the economic hardships, increasing urbanization, and rapid cultural change that characterized America in the 1930s. The singing cowboy represented a benign, respectable male identity who ascribed to and defended mainstream American values; the plots drew on a standard set of conflicts, which were ultimately resolved in culturally agreeable fashion, calming fears and fulfilling fantasies (Stanfield 4–7). The variations and whims that animated Buell's West added humor, highlighted race and class, and denied audiences a bit of that certainty and reinforcement.

Jed Buell made no more Westerns after 1939. During the 1940s, he produced five or six more films, most notably Mantan Moreland's *Lucky Ghost* (1941) and *Emergency Landing* (1941), starring Forrest Tucker. When postwar Hollywood slumped, he turned to a new medium, television, with a daytime drama, *The Kitty Gordon Story*, which fizzled out after a dispute between Buell and network executives. The golden era of the horse opera was the high point of Buell's career, and despite his role as a minor player in the Great American Musical Western, he certainly provided some of its most enigmatic moments—and threw in a penguin on a piano, for good measure.

WORKS CITED

Bogle, Donald. *Toms, Coons, Mulattoes, Mammies and Bucks: An Interpretive History of Blacks in American Films.* New York: Continuum, 2001.

Brophy, Philip. "Rewritten Westerns, Rewired Westerns." In *Stuffing No. 1, Film: Genre,* edited by Philip Brophy, Adrian Martin, and Rafaelle Caputo. Melbourne: Restuffing Publishers, 1987.

Buscombe, Edward. *The BFI Companion to the Western.* New York: Atheneum, 1988.

Cox, Stephen. *The Munchkins of Oz.* Nashville, Tenn.: Cumberland House Publishing, 1996.

Cripps, Thomas. *Slow Fade to Black: The Negro in American Film, 1900–1942.* London: Oxford University Press, 1993.

DeMarco, Mario. *Tex Ritter and Fred Scott: "The Singing Buckaroos of the Silver Screen."* N.p.: n.d.

Jerome, V. J. *The Negro in Hollywood Films.* New York: Masses and Mainstream, 1950.

Kisch, John, and Edward Mapp. *A Separate Cinema.* New York: Noonday Press, 1992.

Lahue, Kalton. *Riders of the Range: The Sagebrush Heroes of the Sound Screen.* New York: Castle Books, 1973.

Medved, Harry. *The Fifty Worst Films of All Time.* New York: Popular Library, 1978.

Richards, Larry. *African-American Films through 1959.* Jefferson, N.C.: McFarland, 1998.

Sherman, Samuel. *Legendary Singing Cowboys*. New York: Friedman/Fairfax, 1995.
Stanfield, Peter. *Horse Opera: The Strange History of the 1930s Singing Cowboy*. Chicago: University of Illinois Press, 2002.
Tuska, Jon. *The American West in Film: Critical Approaches to the Western*. Lincoln: University of Nebraska Press, 1988.
Wright, Will. *Six Guns and Society: A Structural Study of the Western*. Berkeley: University of California Press, 1975.

THE LONE RANGER
Adult Legacies of a Juvenile Western

LONE RANGER: Tonto, from this day on I'm going to devote my life to establishing law and order, to make the West a decent place to live.

TONTO: That good.

—"Enter the Lone Ranger," TV genesis episode of 1949

Born at Detroit radio station WXYZ in 1933, the Lone Ranger became a great twentieth-century mythmaking franchise. His trajectory ascended out of radio, comics, pulp novels, advertising endorsements, licensed merchandise, and fan clubs into the sphere of serialized television and the B Western. As the Ranger's commercial flare dimmed, he plummeted toward ITC/Wrather's widely scorned feature *The Legend of the Lone Ranger* (1981) and the much-derided Warner Bros. television pilot "The Lone Ranger" (February 26, 2003). In that failed two-hour resurrection, the Ranger is "Luke Hartman," a brown-hatted Harvard law student with New Age tendencies and hot springs fantasies about Tonto's sexy sister. Even the silver bullets go missing.

Yet these latter-day signs of decline should not mask the Ranger-imprinted superhero personae that still excite American screen audiences. Nor should we ignore the Lone Ranger–based metaphors that survive as terms for managerial style or the U.S. approach in foreign policy. To understand the world's cultural and political vocabulary, one must review the Ranger's calling "to make the West a decent place to live." This chapter will "return to those thrilling days of yesteryear"—the phrase so often intoned by the radio program's announcers—to sketch the Ranger's complex mythic legacy. In clarifying this cultural transmission, a pair of episodes from the radio and television series

Radio success parlayed into novels, then feature
films and television. Dust jacket from 1937 edition,
Grossett and Dunlap.

prove central in condensing the narratives, icons, and metaphors from this
franchise.

THE RANGER'S BIRTH AND EARLY LIFE

In the beginning, radio station owner George W. Trendle, writer Fran Striker,
and WXYZ drama director James Jewell[1] aimed the Lone Ranger toward a
juvenile audience. The series, which eventually drew in many voices, hands,
and faces, never wavered from its youthful focus during its greatest commercial
successes from 1933 to 1957. For children, the repetitive structure and simply

polarized moral world were appealing.[2] Each thirty-minute radio episode was bookended by Rossini's overture to *William Tell*, musical bridges from other classics, and verbal incantations that children loved to memorize, transform, and playfully toss at one another: "Come on, Kemo Sabe," "That good, Kemo Sabe," "Hi-yo Cheerios" (a witty reference to the breakfast cereal sponsorship). Each program ended with a formulaic "thanks to the Lone Ranger" or a rustically spoken question: "Who was that masked man, anyway?" each time answered by a sage voice saying, "Why, don't you know? That was the Lone Ranger!" Then the Ranger's farewell cry could be heard: "Hi-yo, Silver—aawaaay!"—with a husky intonation and an elegant stretching of the final word. These radio episodes, which ran thrice weekly for twenty-two years until 1954 (Holland 146), have achieved an immortality transcending the marketplace. First available on records, then on tape, they now circulate in noncommercial DVD sets that contain hundreds of MP3 format files. Some episodes can be downloaded from radio nostalgia sites. Along with other collectibles—cap guns, action figures, comic books, Kix Cereal's Atom Bomb Ring, the cardboard buildings of the frontier town offered as Cheerios premiums—these disks are perpetually available to bidders on eBay.

In addition to the intrinsically engaging dramas of crime and apprehension in the Old West, a significant factor in the Lone Ranger's commercial success with children was parental approval. Adults were enthusiastic about the moral content of the Ranger tales; they were happy to allow the broadcast in their homes or to place licensed Ranger merchandise in their children's hands. Illustrating just one of many commendations earned by the franchise are Senator Homer Ferguson's words of celebration for the Ranger's twentieth-anniversary radio broadcast:

> Every program came to a successful conclusion with the moral message to be learned from the Ranger's adventures. . . .
>
> George Trendle built in characteristics that would endear the Lone Ranger to the young and at the same time teach them the principles of good citizenship. In every program the Ranger illustrated the basic tenets of honesty, patriotism, fair play, tolerance, and a sympathetic understanding of people and their rights and privileges.
>
> The Lone Ranger himself is a model of American manhood. . . . The Ranger neither smokes, drinks intoxicating beverages, nor uses profanity. (quoted in Yoggy 14)

On this occasion, the script of the program itself was inserted into the *Congressional Record.*

Reflecting the spirit of idealism extolled by Senator Ferguson, the franchise strove to be a good national citizen. It founded the Lone Ranger Safety Club, in which the "Safety Scout Pledge" included commitments to "always tell the truth. . . . To be kind to birds and animals. . . . To keep myself neat and clean, To obey my father and mother." There were other ventures, such as the Lone Ranger Peace Patrol, which targeted the purchase of U.S. savings bonds (Yoggy 13–14). Few programs of the era could compete with such a patriotic aura.

THE FIRST FILMS AND TELEVISION PRODUCTIONS

Visual programming capitalized on this radio success. Serialized films from Republic studios came with *The Lone Ranger* (1938),[3] which was quickly followed by another fifteen-part compilation called *The Lone Ranger Rides Again* (1939). Exploiting George Trendle's open-ended license for the serials, Republic played loose with the character. In *The Lone Ranger* five actors acted as if they might be the Ranger, each wearing identical clothes, hats, and alternately the distinctive mask—taking it on and off. Feeling the mythic essence was diluted with this sort of guessing game and naked faces, George Trendle reasserted control of the screen franchise, stipulating that such unmasking would end (Holland 243).

Waiting a decade, Trendle authorized a Warner Bros. Lone Ranger television series that began in 1949. Overlapping the radio series for five years, it had a 221-episode run lasting through 1957 (Lentz 282–93). These visualizations of the Ranger's way of justice straightforwardly expressed the character values and vision conveyed on the radio. Yet, being budget Westerns, the television programs looked gaunt. What was cheap to convey through studio sound effects—herds of frightened animals, tribes of yelling Indians, wagon trains, and so forth—was far too expensive for weekly film shoots with budgets ranging from $12,500 in 1949 to $18,000 in 1954 (Holland 296). The Lone Ranger and Tonto's humble camp for the night, always set by the same boulder in the brushy hills, revealed the financial limits.

Yet Clayton Moore and Jay Silverheels gave excitement to the series. Their juvenile-credible acting and physical grace engaged viewers. To see them swing onto their horses in unison to exit from an admiring community was one of the TV Western's most awaited moments. This pair became the most loved of all the performers who ever played the roles for the screen. Their popularity and enthusiastic identification with their roles doubtless impaired the ability of the franchise to survive their departure. No one ever looked or sounded quite right after they were gone.

The successful Moore-Silverheels performances allowed the franchise to create three full-length films that permanently encapsulate the mythic legacy: the television compilation *Legend of the Lone Ranger* (1952), Warner Bros.' *Lone Ranger* (1956), and United Artists' *Lone Ranger and the Lost City of Gold* (1958). Even though *Legend* strung together three television episodes, it contained "Enter the Lone Ranger" from the serial's first broadcast on September 15, 1949. "Enter" successfully visualized the origins story for the Lone Ranger that had matured through years of accretion, only receiving its radio broadcast as "The Origin of the Lone Ranger" in the prior year on June 30, 1948.[4] As "Enter" worked synergistically with the often rebroadcast "Origin" on the radio, the Lone Ranger themes became succinctly and artfully established for several generations of Americans.

THE HEROIC MYTHOLOGY OF THE GENESIS

At the Lone Ranger's birth on the radio a voice announces: "This is the legend of a man who buried his identity to dedicate his life to the service of humanity and country. . . . Early settlers in the West had to be brave men and women. . . . There was danger on every side, wild beasts, savage Indians, and the Cavendish gang" ("Origin"). Butch Cavendish is an outlaw whose rogues terrorize the whole Southwest. Pursuing Cavendish, a group of six Texas Rangers led by Dan Reid, the Lone Ranger's brother, are led into an ambush, where they are trapped by rifle fire on the canyon floor at Bryant's Gap. All die except the man who becomes the Lone Ranger. The surviving Reid wakes up days later in a cave, where he has been carried by an Indian, who introduces himself as a man rescued years before when Tonto's village was attacked by renegades. Reid had even continued to wear a friendship ring given to him by Tonto when they parted as teenagers. Queried about the fate of the other Rangers, Tonto replies, "Other Texas Rangers—all dead. You only Ranger left. You lone Ranger now" ("Enter"). Thus Tonto's pidgin English creates one of the most distinctive names in American mythological history.

Together they resolve to track down the Cavendish gang, a task the Ranger sees as requiring a hidden identity. Tonto neatly cuts a mask from the brother's vest that had carried a silver Texas Ranger's star. In addition to abandoning his own badge, the Lone Ranger, through the altered vest, symbolically renounces regular law enforcement for a quasi-vigilante role. Paradoxically, he works outside the law in his efforts to aid the law. Evoking the crusading zeal of this vision, the radio narrator intones the depth of resolve: "In the Ranger's eye there was a light that must have burned in the eyes of knights in armor, a light that through the ages must have lifted the souls of strong men who fought for justice, for God!" The Ranger articulates his unconditional commitment: "Tonto, from this day on I am going to devote my life to establishing law and order, to make the West a decent place to live" ("Enter"). In one of his earliest essays on the Western genre, John Cawelti captured the peculiar outsider status of the Ranger, which became a model for Shane and many other gunfighter figures: "Though he was all good and his enemies were all bad and though he always acted as an ally of the pioneer community ... the Ranger remained curiously isolated and separated from the community." Taking the Ranger and those who followed in his mythic footsteps, Cawelti suggests that audiences "no longer preferred to see their western heroes finally integrated into the regenerated community" ("God's Country" 150).

The selfless campaign of the outsider for decency in the West is further signified by his renunciation of familial love and personal wealth. Tonto and Silver are to be his only companions. As the Ranger expressed it to Tonto in the radio program's twentieth-anniversary broadcast in 1953, "I couldn't continue without you. As long as we ride, we ride together" ("Flashback"). Although the Ranger jointly owned a silver mine with his brother, he dedicates the proceeds from his secret cache to pay the minimal expenses for his crusade and to make silver bullets, "a symbol that means justice by law. I seek the defeat by law of every criminal in the West" ("Enter").

The friendship with Tonto suggests a remarkable degree of racial reconciliation, in drastic contrast to the reality of recurring animosity between Indians and the Texas Rangers during a fifty-year struggle that lasted until 1875 (Hollon 42–45). Robert Utley's recent study of the Texas Rangers summarizes these antagonisms: "Even though Indians antedated white immigrants by centuries, Texans regarded them as interlopers, uncivilized wretches who did not know how to use the land. When the tribes that lived in

Texas behaved, they were to be tolerated. When they did not, they were to be expelled or eliminated" (294). So when Tonto says "them all good men," such symbolic harmony carries little historical truth. Tonto not only becomes the constant companion and follower of the Lone Ranger but also takes up the crusading ideology, which had played such havoc with the American Indians. He becomes the Dr. Watson in the Lone Ranger's pursuit of criminals. A more striking symbol of co-optation could scarcely be imagined, but it provides a powerful symbolic confirmation of the white man's vigilante code.

Of equal importance mythically is the Lone Ranger's taming by voice commands of the great white stallion Silver after saving him from a gory death in mythic battle with a "giant buffalo." It is part of the voluntary renunciation through which each member of the team chooses the life of moral crusade. Thus another member of the team establishes his credentials as companion fighter for justice through the status of innocent victim. Each member of the team is now a redeemed redeemer. The powerful horse responds instinctively to the sound of his name and accepts the gentle mastery of his savior. The radio narrator describes the scene:

> As the halter touched Silver, he trembled as if from a chill. Every instinct told him that he must flee at once to preserve his freedom. Yet he stood his ground. It wasn't gratitude that kept him there. It was something stronger. Some mysterious bond of friendship and understanding. He heard the man's voice and he liked it.
> "Silver, Silver, we're going to be partners!" says the Lone Ranger.
> Tonto is amazed: "Him let you use halter!"
> "Give me the saddle."
> Tonto replies, "Oh, no horse like that take saddle." ("Origin")

The Lone Ranger then states the mythic point as he places the saddle on the miracle horse that renounces freedom for service to a master: "There never was a horse like this. Now, Silver, we're going to work together" ("Origin").

The narrator reiterates the theme: "No hooves had ever beat the plains like the thundering hooves of that great horse Silver!" The opening lines of the radio program henceforth feature Silver as a full member of the redemptive team. He not only responds to his master's voice without being trained but also seems to "understand" the vigilante work in which he is engaged. The peculiar capabilities of radio sound effects make it possible to render Silver

Studio publicity shot of *The Lone Ranger*'s most popular team on the screen—
Clayton Moore, Jay Silverheels, Silver, and Scout.

virtually human, whinnying his assent to utterances of Ranger ideals. In his
moral sagacity, Silver becomes the prototype for several redeemer animals—
Lassie, Flipper, Trigger—in American popular culture.

The speed of his incomparable horse provides the Lone Ranger with a
crucial element of the superhuman: rapid mobility, the most characteristic
and coveted form of freedom in America, the ability to transcend space and
time. In the genesis episodes the need for such speed was displayed in the

Lone Ranger's inability to overtake Butch Cavendish with his former steed. "My next horse must be faster," he says, expressing his resolution to take the culprit alive and bring him to justice ("Origin"). Silver develops into a symbol of tireless endurance and strength, allowing the Ranger to accomplish miraculous feats that raise him above the merely heroic level.

While extralegal violence and personal vengeance stand central in the Ranger's ideology, there is an elaborate effort to downplay objectionable features of lynch justice historically associated with vigilantism. The masked rider is not acting as a law enforcement officer, despite wearing the black mask of cloth that had borne the star of justice. But he invariably turns his captured crooks over to the authorities for punishment. This happens despite the fact that he operates against the background of ineffective, and frequently corrupted, law enforcement. As for his inerrant guns, the radio program always begins with loud pistol shots interspersed with the overture to *William Tell*, yet the Lone Ranger never kills anyone. Tonto initially encourages him to kill Cavendish. But in the initial episode of the television series, the Ranger pledges to him, "I'm going to devote my life to establishing law and justice. . . . I'll shoot to wound, not to kill" ("Enter"). With superhuman accuracy his silver bullets strike the hands of threatening bad guys—evoking a mere "Yow!" or "My hand!" Yet their evil powers are neutralized. In an elaborate extension of the ideology of cool zeal, which relieves the vigilante of guilt in the exercise of what appears to be "hot" vengeance, the Lone Ranger's precisely calibrated power ensures minimal injury. This view resonates with the cold war's theories of nuclear deterrence, where limitless power, calmly calculated, is celebrated as the ultimate defense because it presumably will never have to be used against the vast populations who are its targets. There seems to be a message that one escapes the ambiguity of violent power through even greater power and accuracy. In such transmutation, the superhuman quality of power allows the vigilante to become the saint.

Taking together these narrative conventions and character markers for the Lone Ranger, one finds a template for the American superhero's character and environment:

1. The Bipolar Moral World: Good and evil are starkly defined, as in all melodrama (as opposed to tragedy or comedy). Even though the Ranger is part of the juvenile Western world, this bipolarity was often a feature of the adult Western and remains in the action-adventure film genre.

2. The License of Innocence/Call of Destiny: The hero acquires his special role through a profound experience of being a victim that motivates him to become an armed but selfless crusader who works solely for others. These negative experiences are presented as the call of destiny. As station owner George W. Trendle put it, the Lone Ranger would be "a guardian angel . . . the embodiment of a granted prayer" (Harmon 202). This sense of calling is eventually shared by every member of the crusading team.

3. The Supremacy of the Caucasian Male: The American superhero is a white-skinned man whose superiority is acknowledged by his constant and colonized companion, Tonto. Again, in Trendle's conception, the companion "had to be someone as free as the Ranger himself—someone who couldn't detract from the glory of the Ranger, someone who could talk little, contribute much" (Bickel 124). Properly subordinate to the white man with his perfect English, the endlessly clever Tonto never masters the pronouns "I," "we," or "he," and the perfectly spoken Ranger never bothers to help him with his English despite their life companionship. As Ted Jojola points out in his study of Native American film actors, Jay Silverheels experienced a kind of double subordination, both in the script and as the perpetually second-fiddle actor. Like Will Sampson, Dan George, and other distinguished Native American performers, the Mohawk Jay Silverheels was lucky to be on the screen at all after decades of white actors' being stained for Indian roles (14). As for women, they exist in the Ranger's world to be rescued, not as partners or interesting companions. One can see in this the juvenile version of wholesomeness, but it is a pattern stamped into much of the adult film world as well.

4. The Disguised Identity and Outsider Role: The superhero emerges in a social world of failed institutions, where laws and elected leaders cannot be relied on to provide for the community's safety; because those incompetent officials can be indifferent to the community's true needs as well as its savior, he cannot be a functioning member of that community or wear its uniform. He must normally hide behind mask, cape, horn-rimmed glasses, or some other disguising role that maintains a secret identity. This outsider status, accentuated by the serialized episodes in which he appears, precludes marriage and normal family responsibilities. Though the Lone Ranger was never tempted, the mythic conventions display the woman and her pacific values as a temptation to forsake the redemptive role. Symbolically, the rejection of women becomes the price of saving the community.

5. Super Powers, Physical and Moral: The American superhero has remarkable powers of anticipation, physical strength, and moral intuition that allow him to act effectively and nearly invincibly in confronting evil. He never starts a fight but never loses one either, just as in any shootout he can fire his weapon second and hit his target first.

6. The Calibration of Retaliatory Vengeance: The power of the American superhero is basically benign. If it hurts anyone at all, it is only the bad men, who deserve it, and only to the extent necessary to subdue them. The Ranger kills just one man, Butch Cavendish, and only when forced to do so in self-defense. Even then he does not use one of his silver bullets but engages in hand-to-hand struggle at the edge of a cliff ("Flashback").

The Ranger's constellation of mythic conventions received almost immediate acclaim as edifying fare for the nation's children, and its echoes in adult melodramas attest its continuing resonance.

This celebrated pattern in the Ranger tale is also one of the most important templates for the "American monomyth," a pervasive model in American heroic culture.[5] These mythic ingredients, though individual counterparts are widely distributed in world mythological culture, received their unique blend first with the Lone Ranger and then became normative for succeeding generations of the American superhero tradition (Lawrence and Jewett). The Ranger's spirit lives on in all those lonely heroes of popular culture who take up the burden of selflessly and disguisedly serving communities that are unworthy of their openly proclaimed identity and democratic citizenship.

These mythic seeds later germinated in comic book characters such as Batman, Superman, Captain America, and Spider-Man. In movies we have figures like Shane, multiple John Wayne personae, Buford Pusser, Rambo, Dirty Harry, Luke Skywalker, the Steven Seagal personae, the Mel Gibson action personae,[6] the Charles Bronson persona of the long-lived *Death Wish* series, *Walker: Texas Ranger,* Neo of *The Matrix,* and numerous others. These characters mutate the Lone Ranger formula in order to survive and to entertain—often through brutality—but they still reflect his legacy of selflessness, lack of initiatory aggression, and finely calibrated retaliation. As Cawelti observes in *Adventure, Mystery, and Romance,* the Lone Ranger narratives, despite the crudity of their representations, "establish themselves so completely that almost everyone in the culture has some knowledge of them and what they stand for." Their popular formula "becomes an expression of a basic pattern of meaning in the consciousness of many members of the audience" (300). Those cultural meanings possessed both negative and positive valences that retain their charge today, as one discovers in surveying the legacies of the Lone Ranger.

THE POLITICAL AND SOCIAL LEGACIES OF THE LONE RANGER

Besides his place in the culture of entertainment, the Ranger lives on in the expression of popular ideals or hopes. Jim Lichtman, a management consultant, has incorporated his book *The Lone Ranger's Code of the West: An Action-Packed Adventure in Values and Ethics with the Legendary Champion of Justice* into his practice.[7] The book recounts eight episodes from the Ranger, each followed by an imaginary interview in which Lichtman and the Ranger explore the underlying moral principles. The business writer Jeffrey Gitomer has built a sales strategy around the idea of working quietly like the Lone Ranger: "He just went about his business. Silently, doing his thing, giving value, asking for nothing, not even saying his name. That Lone Ranger was a heck of a salesperson" (24). In the field of foreign policy, Robert M. Perito paid tribute with his book *Where Is the Lone Ranger When We Need Him? America's Search for a Postconflict Stability Force*, which speaks somewhat wistfully about "the theme of all the . . . episodes. Someone was in trouble and 'the Masked Rider of the Plains' came to the rescue" (51). However, his treatise on the organization of global constabulary forces does not advise secret identity, disguises, or extralegal uses of power. There really are no "guardian angels" on the international horizon. It is merely a dream of redemption from history—or perhaps a Wilsonian vision of American order whose realization has proved so difficult.

More typically, references to "the Lone Ranger" are invoked to raise suspicions about a person who believes in magical powers or circumvents favorably regarded conventions or the rule of law. In a recent instance, Condoleezza Rice commented on national security adviser Richard Clark's testimony about the lack of urgency concerning terrorism in George W. Bush's administration by remarking, "There was no silver bullet that could have prevented the 9/11 attacks." William Safire of the *New York Times* reminded his readers that Donald Rumsfeld invoked the futility of the silver bullet fantasy just after 9/11: "In this battle against terrorism, there is no silver bullet" (28). Rumsfeld's point is surely beyond doubt.

The subjectivity of Lone Ranger accusations is manifest in the career of President Jimmy Carter. As a candidate for president he had stated, in the words of Theodore C. Sorenson, that "there would be no Kissinger-like Lone Ranger" in his administration (232). The dismissive insult had a foundation, because Kissinger himself had styled the lone cowboy image for himself in a famous interview with Oriana Fallaci. Characterizing his approach to foreign policy, he had said, "The Americans love the cowboy who comes into town all alone on his horse, and nothing else. He acts and that is enough, being in the right place at the right time, in sum a western. This romantic and surprising character suits me because being alone has always been part of my style" ("Men of the Year"). The Lone Ranger appellation, in its derisory form, would return to bite Carter, just as it stuck to Kissinger. Lance Morrow, essayist for *Time,* spoke of Carter's postpresidential career as a peacemaker, commenting that "some of his Lone Ranger work has taken him dangerously close to the neighborhood of what we used to call treason" (79). Carter's peacemaking visits to North Korea in 1994—in defiance of State Department advice against such private initiatives—conform to the pejorative associations of the Lone Ranger epithet.

The variability of application related to Jimmy Carter is multiplied when one looks into a comprehensive article collection such as Gale's InfoTrac OneFile, which yields more than three hundred titles containing "The Lone Ranger."[8] Taking a more focused look with the Boolean search string "Bush, George W. AND Lone Ranger AND Iraq" yielded ninety hits; viewpoints in the articles either accused Bush of acting like the Lone Ranger or denied the charge. Other recipients of the Ranger label included George H. W. Bush (in the run-up to the Persian Gulf War of 1991); Neil Bush (in connection with the savings and loan scandals of the 1980s); Jesse Jackson (on his run for the U.S. presidency); Oliver North Jr. (the Iran-Contra affair); Ronald Reagan (diplomacy with Gorbachev); Arthur Anderson, Inc. (in connection with its approach to auditing); Ken Lay (for his corporate leadership style); and dozens of others. The phrase "Who was that masked man?" also appears frequently. Both phrases typically evoke a man who goes against prevailing norms and risks alienation from institutional partners to achieve some goal that does not meet the approval of others.

In diplomatic language "the Lone Ranger" is a unilateralist when multilateralism seems imperative, a hot dog instead of a team player. To borrow another signifier from film culture, he is a "John Wayne." When prudent institutional players would consult, or adhere to international law and customs, the Lone Ranger bypasses them to get what he wants.[9] And what he wants is always good for community law enforcement, even though he must operate beyond its rules to assist it.

What Is the Ranger Legacy?

Like any other multigenerational mythic enterprise, the Ranger generated several legacies, ranging from a favored place in the world of collectibles and radio nostalgia to the stinging phrase expressing disapproval. To the extent that he is acknowledged at all, he represents a child phase in radio, comic books, television, and the Saturday matinee Western B movie and a style of action that is unacceptable. As John Cawelti observed, "Children can accept a Lone Ranger, but, for most adults, such a character is too pure and superheroic to serve the purposes of effective moral fantasy" (*Adventure, Mystery, and Romance* 38). Yet the pattern for his selfless heroism remains as a mythic template. While he seems utterly dead commercially, he probably slumbers. Do not be surprised if such a powerful figure of the American imagination "rides again."

Notes

1. James Jewell's name is omitted in most popular accounts of the radio series, but Dave Holland, 73, has demonstrated Jewell's centrality, including scriptwriting for the show.

2. See J. Fred MacDonald, 15–20, for a characterization of the B Western generally as having a juvenile orientation in plot and production value.

3. Republic rereleased *The Lone Ranger* in 1940 as *Hi-Yo Silver*.

4. See William C. Cline's essay "Kemo Sabe and the Cliffhangers" for an attempt to sort out the sources for different elements of the genesis story that developed at Republic Pictures and in the radio series.

5. Systematic exposition on this theme is contained in John Shelton Lawrence and Robert Jewett, *The Myth of the American Superhero;* international applications of the mythic scheme are worked out in Robert Jewett and John Shelton Lawrence, *Captain America and the Crusade against Evil.*

6. See exposition on Gibson's escapes from women in the *Lethal Weapon* series, *Braveheart,* and *The Patriot* in Lawrence and Jewett, *Myth,* 162–67.

7. Jim Lichtman was interviewed regarding the book by Alex Chadwick on National Public Radio, February 3, 1996.

8. This search was performed in Gale's InfoTrac OneFile on June 30, 2004, at the Berkeley, California, Public Library.

9. To my knowledge, a Lone Ranger is always "he," even though women can obviously behave in the ways described.

WORKS CITED

Bickel, Mary E. *George W. Trendle, Creator and Producer Of: The Lone Ranger, the Green Hornet, Sgt. Preston of the Yukon, the American Agent, and Other Successes.* New York: Exposition Press, 1971.

Cawelti, John G. *Adventure, Mystery, and Romance: Formula Stories as Art and Popular Culture.* Chicago: University of Chicago Press, 1976.

———. "God's Country, Las Vegas, and the Gunfighter." In *Mystery, Violence, and Popular Culture,* 141–51. Madison: University of Wisconsin Press, 2004.

Cline, William C. "Kemo Sabe and the Cliffhangers." In *Serials-ly Speaking,* 154–60. Jefferson, N.C.: McFarland, 1994.

"Enter the Lone Ranger" (genesis episode). September 15, 1949. *Lone Ranger Television Series.* Jack Chertok Productions.

"Flashback: The Return of Cavendish" (twentieth-anniversary radio broadcast of the Lone Ranger). January 1, 1953. ABC.

Gitomer, Jeffrey. "The Most Famous Sales Cowboy of All." *Business Record* (Des Moines), March 5, 2001, 24.

Harmon, Jim. *The Great Radio Heroes.* Garden City, N.Y.: Doubleday, 1967.

Holland, Dave. *From Out of the Past: A Pictorial History of the Lone Ranger.* Granada Hills, Calif.: Holland House, 1988.

Hollon, W. Eugene. *Frontier Violence: Another Look.* New York: Oxford University Press, 1974.

Jewett, Robert, and John Shelton Lawrence. *Captain America and the Crusade against Evil: The Dilemma of Zealous Nationalism.* Grand Rapids, Mich.: Eerdmans, 2003.

Jojola, Ted. "Absurd Reality II: Hollywood Goes to the Indians." In *Hollywood's Indian: The Portrayal of the Native American in Film,* edited by Peter C. Rollins and John E. O'Connor, 12–26. Lexington: University Press of Kentucky, 1998.

Lawrence, John Shelton, and Robert Jewett. *The Myth of the American Superhero.* Grand Rapids, Mich.: Eerdmans, 2002.

Lentz, Harris M. *Television Westerns Episode Guide: All United States Series, 1949–1996.* Jefferson, N.C.: McFarland, 1995.

Lichtman, Jim. *The Lone Ranger's Code of the West.* Santa Barbara, Calif.: Scribbler's Ink, 1996.

MacDonald, J. Fred. *Who Shot the Sheriff? The Rise and Fall of the Television Western.* New York: Praeger, 1987.

"Men of the Year: Nixon and Kissinger—Triumph and Trial." *Time,* January 1, 1973.

Morrow, Lance. "The Unfinished Presidency: Jimmy Carter's Journey beyond the White House." *Time,* May 11, 1998, 79.

"The Origin of the Lone Ranger" (origins episode for radio). June 30, 1948. Mutual Broadcasting System.

Perito, Robert M. *Where Is the Lone Ranger When We Need Him? America's Search for a Postconflict Stability Force.* Washington, D.C.: United States Institute of Peace Press, 2004.

Safire, William. "Silver Bullet." *New York Times,* April 25, 2004, 28.

Sorenson, Theodore C. "The President and the Secretary of State." *Foreign Affairs* 63 (1987–88): 231–48.

Utley, Robert M. *Lone Star Justice: The First Century of the Texas Rangers.* New York: Oxford University Press, 2002.

Yoggy, Gary A. *Riding the Video Range: The Rise and Fall of the Western on Television.* Jefferson, N.C.: McFarland, 1995.

PART TWO
THE POST–WORLD WAR II WESTERN
1945–1956

WEE WILLIE WINKIE GOES WEST
The Influence of the British Empire Genre on Ford's Cavalry Trilogy

The Shirley Temple vehicle *Wee Willie Winkie* (1937) was a curious assignment for director John Ford, whose reputation was primarily as a man's director for his skillful handling of actors like Victor McLaglen and Warren Baxter in male-oriented films such as *The Lost Patrol* (1934), *The Informer* (1935), and *Prisoner of Shark Island* (1936). Scott Eyman notes that Ford told two different stories about his reaction to this assignment, one where he said, "My face fell atop the floor," and another where he was imperturbable. "I said 'Great' and we just went out and made the picture" (181). Both stories call attention to the incongruity of pairing John Ford and America's favorite child star. However reluctant he was to take the assignment, directing a film in the British Empire genre had a profound influence on his postwar cavalry trilogy: *Fort Apache* (1948), *She Wore a Yellow Ribbon* (1949), and *Rio Grande* (1950).[1]

Wee Willie Winkie was part of a cycle of British Empire films that commenced with Paramount's hit *The Lives of a Bengal Lancer* in 1935. Other films in the cycle from Hollywood included *The Charge of the Light Brigade* (1936), *The Light That Failed* (1939), and *Gunga Din* (1939). Among the British contributions to the genre were *Sanders of the River* (1935), *Rhodes of Africa* (1936), *The Drum* (1938), and *The Four Feathers* (1939). This genre for the most part deals with military authorities in one of the far-flung outposts of the British Empire protecting the community from a native revolt. Loyalty, duty, and honor are recurrent themes that serve to glorify the British army and celebrate the esprit de corps of that tight-knit community.

The British Empire cycle was short-lived due to the outbreak of World War II. MGM's plan to film Kipling's novel *Kim* in 1942 was shelved because the U.S. Office of War Information (OWI) was concerned that it might offend

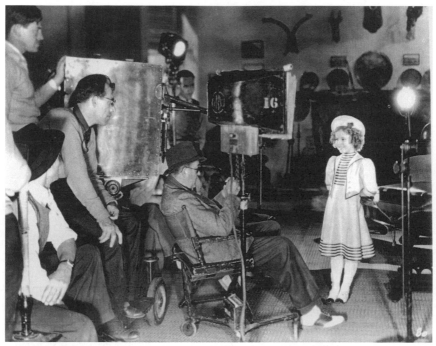

Courtesy of the Kevin Brownlow Collection.

John Ford directs Shirley Temple in *Wee Willie Winkie*. At the beginning of filming, relations were strained between the director and the child star.

India when its help was essential in the war effort. The OWI also banned a reissue of *Gunga Din* for the same reason (Richards *Visions of Yesterday* 4–5). Another reason for banning British Empire films was the fear of alienating the isolationist and anti-imperial elements in the United States when the nation was allied with Great Britain in the war.[2] Films glorifying empire seemed inappropriate at a time when the United States was engaged in a war for democracy against the fascist empires of Germany, Italy, and Japan (Richards *Age of the Dream Palace* 143).

After the war the empire genre did not recover its popularity in the United States. Instead, big-budget Westerns, which had been growing in popularity since the mid-1930s, and war films took its place as the adventure genres of choice. It is not surprising that the Western replaced the empire film because they have many elements in common. Both genres are set on frontiers in the late nineteenth century and deal with the conflict between civilization and savagery. In the 1930s and 1940s, the link was strengthened by stars moving freely between one genre and the other. The quintessential Westerner, Gary Cooper, had starred in *Lives of a Bengal Lancer,* and Errol Flynn and Olivia de Havilland, the romantic couple of English historical films like *Captain Blood* (1935), *The Adventures of Robin Hood* (1938), and *The Charge of the Light Brigade,* also made *Santa Fe Trail* (1940) and *They Died with Their Boots On* (1941) for Warner Bros.

MANIFEST DESTINY VERSUS THE WHITE MAN'S BURDEN

The conflict between civilization and savagery is handled differently in the two genres. The classic Western uses this conflict as a justification for the process of westward expansion and Manifest Destiny. In offering a definition of Manifest Destiny in 1846, William Gilpin, a soldier, politician, and promoter, asserted that "the untransacted destiny of the American people is to subdue the continent" (Smith 37). In these films, there is no overarching moral imperative other than the enrichment of the lives of the people moving west. The classic Western is concerned with taming the land and containing or exterminating savage elements, either Indians or outlaws, who threaten the well-being of the settlers. When conflict occurs, the hero's stand against lawlessness is often motivated by revenge rather than a desire to protect the community. This pattern was prevalent enough for Will Wright to classify it as the vengeance Western. His list of plot elements includes "the villains do harm *to the hero* and to the society" and "the hero defeats the villains" (69, italics added). In *Stagecoach* (1939), the Ringo Kid (John Wayne) has a shootout with the Plummer brothers because they killed his family. The murder of their youngest brother by the Clantons is the motivation for the remaining Earp brothers to clean up Tombstone in *My Darling Clementine* (1946). The benefit to the community from these shootouts is secondary.

The motivation for expansion in the empire films is to bring the benefits of civilization to the colonized indigenous people as a duty, as the "white man's burden." There are no personal motives for fighting against the forces of savagery. When noticing the preparations for war in *Wee Willie Winkie,* Priscilla (Shirley Temple) asks her grandfather, Colonel Williams (C. Aubrey Smith), why he does not like Khoda Khan (Cesar Romero), the leader of the rebellious hill tribe. He responds, "England wants to be friends with all her people. . . . It's our job to keep the big pass open so that trade can flow through it . . . and bring peace and prosperity to everybody, even to Khoda Khan."

The classic Western glorifies the individual. The hero is an outsider who often protects the community while remaining apart from it. One of the key questions in the Western is, will the hero join the community and be assimilated into the domestic sphere? Often, in the end he rides into the sunset, a symbol of freedom. In contrast, the society of the imperial film is collective. The men who protect the community are part of that community and fulfill their obligations as integral members of the group.

GLORIFYING THE COLLECTIVE

Although John Ford's cavalry trilogy was produced during the height of the big-budget Western's popularity, it does not employ the classic themes of the Western. In his chapter on the Western in *Hollywood Genres,* Thomas Schatz notes, "As a hybrid of Western and war genres, the cavalry films depict a male collective which functions as an individual unit within contested space. Its mission is to establish law and order . . . throughout the West" (71). Richard Slotkin also sees these films as "uniting the conventions and concerns of the combat films and the Westerns in a single coherent fable" (*Gunfighter Nation* 334). Instead, the cavalry trilogy is a direct transposition of the themes of the empire genre from the frontiers of Asia to the frontier of the American West. The overriding importance of the social unit of the regiment and its mission to preserve civilization as a duty is in sharp contrast to the individualism and self-interest of the Western, and unlike the exclusively male collective of war films, both the domestic and military spheres are completely integrated in empire and cavalry films.

Both Tag Gallagher and Slotkin make a connection between Ford's post–World War II Westerns and British Empire films. Gallagher calls *Wee Willie Winkie* one of Ford's most important prewar films in part "because like virtually every postwar picture it studies militarist ethos" (141). While Slotkin draws attention to formulaic similarities between *The Charge of the Light Brigade* and *Fort Apache*—the border outpost, the regiment fighting a savage foe, the dance scene, the massacre, and the fatal charge—he primarily compares *Fort Apache* to "platoon movies" because both feature initiation stories with new recruits, and both portray a melting pot ideal of American society by having different ethnicities within the ranks (*Gunfighter Nation* 336–37). He comments on the significant role of women in *Fort Apache* as "another creative possibility made plausible by the transfer of the war story to the landscape of the Western" (*Gunfighter Nation* 338). It is the presence of women both as initiates and as vital to the military community in the cavalry trilogy that suggests its closer connection to the empire genre than the platoon film.

LEARNING THE ETHOS OF THE REGIMENT THROUGH INITIATION STORIES

Initiation stories provide the plot device that stresses the collective nature of community in the cavalry trilogy and empire films. They provide the perfect opportunity to explain the workings of the social unit. As Jeffrey Richards points out, the audience is encouraged to identify with the outsiders who are undergoing initiation: "They, along with the audience, have to be taught the meaning and value of service, duty and discipline" ("Boy's Own Empire" 156). This story structure allows the expository scenes that convey the movie's message to be an organic part of the plot rather than a sermon to the audience. In *Lives of a Bengal Lancer* the outsiders are Lieutenant McGregor (Gary Cooper), a Canadian, and Lieutenant Stone (Richard Cromwell), the half-American son of the regimental commander. They are outsiders both by nationality—the rest of the regiment is from the British Isles—and by temperament. Lieutenant McGregor is individualistic and contemptuous of army regulations and traditions, while Lieutenant Stone, fresh out of Sandhurst Military Academy, is uncertain of his manhood and rebellious against the father he never knew while growing up. At the end of the film, McGregor deliberately sacrifices his life to help the regiment, and Stone earns his father's respect as a soldier. There are two initiates in *The Drum* as well. Prince Azim (Sabu) learns the value of an alliance with Great Britain and the moral superiority of the British through his friendship with Captain Caruthers (Roger Livesey). The other initiate is Elsa (Valerie Hobson), the commanding officer's niece, who marries Captain Caruthers early in the film and, by the end, accepts the responsibilities and sacrifices necessary to preserve the empire. In *Wee Willie Winkie,* the newcomers are Priscilla Williams, granddaughter of the commander Colonel Williams, and her mother, Joyce Williams (June Lange), the colonel's widowed daughter-in-law. Priscilla is befriended by Sergeant McDuff (Victor McLaglen), who transforms her into Private Winkie. Joyce Williams falls in love with Lieutenant Brandes (Michael Whalen), and their implied union signifies her acceptance of regimental life.

The initiates in Ford's cavalry trilogy include Philadelphia Thursday (Shirley Temple) and the failed initiate Colonel Thursday (Henry Fonda) in *Fort Apache;* Miss Dandridge (Joanne Dru) and Lieutenant Pennell (Harry Carey Jr.) in *She Wore a Yellow Ribbon;* and Kathleen Yorke (Maureen O'Hara), the wife of the commander, Lieutenant Colonel Kirby Yorke (John Wayne), and Jeff Yorke (Claude Jarman Jr.), the colonel's son, in *Rio Grande. Fort Apache* serves as a cautionary tale about those who do not successfully join the community, exemplified by the different fates of Colonel Thursday and his daughter. He causes the death of most of the regiment and loses his own life in an attack against the Apache because he values personal glory over a more restrained military response. Philadelphia successfully becomes part of the regiment through marriage and motherhood. Miss Dandridge is not "army" enough to winter at the fort at the beginning of *She Wore a Yellow Ribbon* and is being escorted to catch a stagecoach back to civilization. By the end of the film, she acquires the discipline and dedication to be "army" like Abby Allshard (Mildred Natwick), the commander's wife. She is no longer the willful flirt who insists on going on a picnic despite a general alarm and who toys with the affection of both Lieutenants Cohill (John Agar) and Pennell. Like Joyce Williams in *Wee Willie Winkie,* her acceptance of Lieutenant Cohill's marriage proposal symbolizes her integration into the community. Lieutenant Pennell also accepts the regimental ethos by the conclusion of the film. He no longer talks of resigning his commission and returning east. At the beginning of *Rio Grande,* Trooper Yorke's situation is similar to Lieutenant Stone's in *Lives of a Bengal Lancer.* They are both untried recruits serving under fathers they do not know. Mrs. Yorke had been separated from Lieutenant Colonel Yorke for sixteen years because he chose his duty to the army over his responsibility to protect her during the Civil War. By the end of the film, she understands and accepts her subordinate position to her only rival, the U.S. Cavalry. The son proves himself to his father and goes from being called "Trooper Yorke" to "son" by the lieutenant colonel.

Typically, both the cavalry and the empire films include a scene in which an established member of the community explains its ethos to the initiate. When, in *The Drum,* Caruthers risks his life by going to a banquet that he suspects is a trap, he tells Elsa, "A not unusual preliminary to our establishing law and order is the murder of one of our representatives." He cites the examples of Sir Lewis Cavagnari at Kabul and General Gordon at Khartoum. Mrs.

Courtesy of the Lilly Library, Indiana University, Bloomington, Indiana.

The initiate is successfully integrated into the regiment when Trooper Yorke (Claude Jarman Jr.) earns the respect of his father, Lieutenant Colonel Kirby Yorke (John Wayne) in *Rio Grande*.

Caruthers stoically allows him to depart. There are several of these expository scenes in *Wee Willie Winkie* between the colonel and his granddaughter. On one occasion he admonishes both Priscilla and her mother: "Up in those hills there are thousands of savages all waiting for the chance to sweep down the pass and ravage India. Now it's England's duty, it's my duty, dear, to see that they don't. . . . the only women we want here are those that can understand that and respect it." Priscilla takes the lesson so much to heart that she goes up into the hills alone to convince the rebels not to attack. Captain York (John Wayne) in *Fort Apache* tries to teach Colonel Thursday the code of the frontier. He protests when Thursday orders troops to trap Cochise, saying, "I gave my word to Cochise. No man is going to make a liar out of me, sir." Thursday's response, "Your word to a breech-clouted savage, an illiterate and uncivilized murderer and treaty breaker? There is no question of honor, sir, between an American officer and Cochise," illustrates his failure to adapt to the ethos of the frontier.

Another convention of the empire genre that appears in the cavalry films is the use of an inordinate amount of documentary-style footage of daily life and the rituals of the community. Like the plot device of educating the outsider, it functions as part of the audience's initiation into the collective. There are scenes of men drilling in *Lives of a Bengal Lancer, Wee Willie Winkie, Fort Apache,* and *Rio Grande;* mucking out stables in *Lives of a Bengal Lancer;* and details of going out on patrol in *She Wore a Yellow Ribbon,* where troops walk their horses every hour. Women are active in the domestic realm: setting up house (*Fort Apache*); shopping in the bazaars (*Wee Willie Winkie*); and doing laundry (*Rio Grande*). Rituals emphasize the cohesiveness of the group; they include review of the troops (*The Drum, Wee Willie Winkie, Fort Apache*); awarding decorations (*Lives of a Bengal Lancer, Rio Grande*); and regimental balls (*Fort Apache, Wee Willie Winkie, Charge of the Light Brigade, The Drum, She Wore a Yellow Ribbon*). Successful initiates choose to accept the communal nature of regimental life.

The Role of Women

It is significant that in both the imperial films and the cavalry trilogy some of the newcomers to army life are women, demonstrating their importance within the social unit. The representation of women here is different from their role in the classic Western. In the Western, one of the oppositional conflicts is between the hero's independence and his integration into the community signified by marriage. Such films draw a sharp line between the man's world and the domestic sphere. This division is apparent in *The Westerner* (1940) between the exclusively male world of the cattleman and Judge Roy Bean (Walter Brennan) and the world of the domesticated homesteader represented by the farmer's daughter Jane Ellen (Doris Davenport). The hero, Cole Hardin (Gary Cooper), eventually chooses socialization and marries the farmer's daughter. In many Westerns, this tension between independence and domestication is irresolvable, and although the hero flirts with the idea of settling down, more often than not he rides off alone into the sunset. Wyatt Earp (Henry Fonda) promises to return to Clementine (Cathy Downs) in *My Darling Clementine,* but the final shot depicts him riding away from Tombstone.

In both the empire films produced in Great Britain and the cavalry trilogy, there is no conflict over domestication. These films portray an inclusive world of both men and women, where the domestic sphere is shown to be vital to the community. The older officers and men have wives, and the young men are actively seeking mates: these regimental marriages of mutual respect include Captain and Mrs. Caruthers in *The Drum;* Captain (George O'Brien) and Mrs. Collingwood (Anna Lee), and Sergeant Major (Ward Bond) and Mrs. O'Rourke (Irene Rich), in *Fort Apache;* and Major (George O'Brien) and Mrs. Allshard in *She Wore a Yellow Ribbon*. The films feature extended scenes of courtship: balls, picnics, and rides into the countryside. It is a sign of successful integration when the woman marries into the regiment or, as in the case of the alienated Mrs. Yorke, is reconciled to her husband and his way of life.

These wives are helpmates to their men. In the empire films, the emphasis is on the physical danger and mental stress of living on the frontier. In *The Drum*, shortly after her marriage to Captain Caruthers, Elsa protects Prince Azim from assassins. When Caruthers is transferred, she insists on going with him even though she will be the only Englishwoman in Tokot. Her presence is greatly appreciated, and the residency staff drinks a toast with fine crystal to her "and all the women who come up with their men folk to lonely outposts and bring the sweetness and gentleness of the life they have left behind." In contrast to the rather opulent furnishing of the British Empire's Indian frontier, the cavalry films stress the dirt and primitive conditions of the American West. The opening sequence after the credits in *Rio Grande* shows the women and children lining the dusty road, waiting for the men to return from patrol and, upon their arrival, supporting and comforting them. There are several scenes of both officers' and enlisted men's wives washing laundry in a river. Abby Allshard, the major's wife, even helps with surgery on a wounded trooper in *She Wore a Yellow Ribbon,* and Captain Brittles pays her the ultimate compliment when he calls her "soldier."

The domesticating woman in the classic Western is frequently an obstacle to the hero's quest. This plot element is particularly common in vengeance Westerns (Wright, 68–69). These women try to force the man to act against his personal code of honor. In *The Virginian* (1929) and *High Noon* (1952), the fiancée (Mary Brian) and the new bride (Grace Kelly), respectively, deliver an ultimatum that they will end the relationship if the hero insists on fighting the villains. Typically, the hero first agrees to avoid the conflict but ultimately fights the outlaws. The women in both these films are the ones who compromise their moral code: Molly Stark, the schoolmarm, runs to and embraces the hero after the gunfight in *The Virginian,* and Amy Kane, a Quaker, shoots one of the Miller gang in *High Noon.* This pattern stresses the difference between the woman's code of conduct and the man's.

Unlike the domesticating woman of the classic Western, the regimental women understand and support the masculine code of honor. In *The Four Feathers,* Harry Faversham's (John Clements) fiancée, Ethne (June Duprez), chastises Harry for selfishly leaving the army to care for his own estates. She says, "Some people are born free. They can do as they like without concern for consequences. But you were not born free, Harry, nor was I. We were born into a tradition, a code which we must obey even if we do not believe. And we must obey it, Harry, because the pride and happiness of everyone surrounding us depends upon our obedience." Mrs. Collingwood in *Fort Apache* allows her husband to ride out with the troops to probable death rather than calling him back with the news of his appointment as an instructor at West Point because his honor is more important. She states, "Sam's no coward; he never was." As Leland Poague points out, her next comment, "I can't see him; all I can see is the flags," is prophetic of his fate, that he is going to his death and she will not see him again. The flags are not only symbols of regimental and personal honor but also part of the ritual of death and burial in the military. The aura of prophesy about Mrs. Collingwood's comment is strengthened by the concerned glances directed at her by Philadelphia and Mrs. O'Rourke (10).

THE COMMUNITY AS A MELTING POT

In John Ford's trilogy, the key aspect of assimilation into the regiment is accommodation for individuals. Classic conflicts such as East versus West and wealth/privilege versus ordinary folk find resolution. In *She Wore a Yellow Ribbon,* the rivals for Miss Dandridge's affection are opposites. Lieutenant Pennell is an easterner from a wealthy family who constantly gripes and threatens to leave the cavalry. Lieutenant Cohill is a westerner and dependent on his army pay for a living. These two rivals are reconciled after being lectured about the duties of leadership by their senior officer, and, like the other initiates, Lieutenant Pennell chooses to remain with the regiment. Ethnic conflicts are also put to rest. Much of the broad humor of the sergeants calls attention to the different nationalities and allegiances within the army. For example, in

Mrs. Collingwood (Anna Lee) protects her husband's honor by letting him ride off with the troop in *Fort Apache*. Philadelphia Thursday (Shirley Temple) and Mrs. O'Rourke (Irene Rich) look on.

Fort Apache, Sergeant Mulcahy (Victor McLaglen) promises to promote any new recruit from Ireland, and Sergeant Beaufort (Pedro Armendáriz) extends the same offer to anyone from the South. These blatant displays of favoritism are shown to be good-humored rather than divisive.

Of greater significance is the acceptance of former enemies into the community. In the empire films this assimilation is implicit, with native troops as part of the regiment who are trusted by their officers to serve against their own people. In *Rio Grande*, native scouts serve the regiment in much the same way. The reintegration of Southern soldiers from the Civil War into the ranks of the U.S. Army is a subplot in all three cavalry films, but it is most pronounced in *She Wore a Yellow Ribbon*. When a patrol finds Trooper Smith killed by Indians, Mrs. Allshard sews a Confederate flag for his burial, and his rank in the Confederate army—brigadier general—is acknowledged. Captain Brittles

The burial of Trooper Smith shows that former adversaries are accepted and honored in the regiment in *She Wore a Yellow Ribbon*. Captain Brittles (John Wayne) shows his respect while Sergeant Tyree (Ben Johnson) holds a Confederate flag.

also calls Sergeant Tyree by his Confederate rank—captain—during moments of closeness or shared danger, recognizing him as a fellow officer.

Even the natives who are in armed conflict with the community desire integration. Khoda Khan in *Wee Willie Winkie* is persuaded by Private Winkie that peace under the British is more important than independence. Cochise (Miguel Inclan) in *Fort Apache* will return to the reservation if its corrupt Indian agent is removed. Pony That Walks (Chief Big Tree) tries to preserve peace between his people and the U.S. Army but simply cannot control the young, hotheaded warriors led by Red Shirt (Noble Johnson) in *She Wore a Yellow Ribbon*. The natives in *Rio Grande* are the exception; there is no suggestion of integration. Unlike in *Fort Apache* and *She Wore a Yellow Ribbon*, there is no parley scene allowing the Apache to explain their grievances. They are more like the Indians in Westerns from the 1930s—forces of savagery and violence.

REFLECTION OF POST–WORLD WAR II CONCERNS

Many critics have discussed the role of genre films in exploring contemporary conflicts and concerns. The Hollywood-produced British Empire films of the 1930s explored America's concerns about its role in looming international struggles. Slotkin sums up the genre's function regarding America's self-image: "These movies mythologized—popularized and made intelligible in traditional terms—a major ideological shift in American politics, away from isolationism and toward preparedness for engagement in the conflicts of Europe and the Far East. . . . In the fictive landscape of Victorian Empire Hollywood movies, the British are also clearly surrogate or incipient Americans" ("Continuity of Forms" 19). The British Empire films encouraged Americans to acknowledge the benefits of colonialism through identification with characters undergoing initiation. With the stories set in a distant time and portraying a foreign colonial power, the audience could flirt with the idea of American imperialism at a safe distance when isolationism was still dominant in American political thought. The symbolic connection between British Empire films and American-style imperialism was made more concrete in *The Real Glory* (1939). It is similar to *Lives of a Bengal Lancer* in that it pairs the same director, Henry Hathaway, with the same star, Gary Cooper, in a story about a small garrison putting down a native revolt led by a fanatic, except that in *The Real Glory* the location is the Philippines in 1906 and the army is American. The reason for the U.S. Army's presence is also different from that for the British colonial forces': it is training the people for self-government after the expulsion of the Spanish. All these films tacitly advocated American intervention overseas.

Unlike the empire genre's international outlook, most Westerns explored America's domestic anxieties. The Western of the late 1930s and early 1940s revolved around the independence of a lone individual and the encroachment of civilization on his freedom. This theme reflected the changes occurring in American society in the 1930s: the failure of small farms and businesses, the mass migration of rural populations to cities, as well as New Deal policies creating a greater dependence on government assistance. These changes led to a sense of loss of independence and control over one's own destiny, the diminishing of values that were basic to America's self-image since before Horatio Alger. Postwar Westerns continued to focus on the individual, but in many of them he was a more vulnerable, alienated, and often psychologically damaged hero related to the protagonists of film noir. Referred to as "adult Westerns" because of the more complex characterizations and darker themes, they reflected society's concern with returning GIs' adjustment to civilian life. In these films, World War II was often equated with the War between the States, and Civil War veterans represented GIs suffering from what was then called "combat fatigue." As John Lenihan points out, "The lawlessness of the Jameses or Youngers, which in Westerns of the depression years was attributed to capitalist exploitation of poor farmers, becomes after World War II, a result of the violence and chaos of the Civil War" ("Classics" 37).

John Ford's cavalry trilogy addresses both domestic and international concerns of the postwar era. On the domestic level, the films reflect America's dreams of postwar adjustment rather than its fears of a difficult transition to peacetime, and they emphasize the establishment of a healthy community where families can prosper. They express the hopes of the returning GI: finding a job, taking a wife, building a home, starting a family, and belonging to a community (Pauly 257–61).

Like the British Empire films, they also explore U.S. foreign policy and its imperial aspirations. By moving the setting from British India to the American West, the symbolic connection to contemporary affairs is stronger. Herbert Jackson, commenting on this relationship in an article published in 1953, saw the appearance of good Indians in some of the postwar Westerns as a hopeful sign for the future: "Can it be that this is a genuine reflection of a greater respect for the sometimes different point of view of the rest of the world, of whom so many people are coloured? If so, it presages well for prospects of peace, which depend so largely on American patience" (190). In the parley scene between Cochise and Colonel Thursday in *Fort Apache,* Cochise is the better leader. His justification for leaving the reservation is praiseworthy, and his conditions for returning reasonable. Pony That Walks in *She Wore a Yellow Ribbon* expresses the same hope for peace, but he is shown to be ineffectual. That the Indians in *Rio Grande* are once again savages reflects the diminishing hopes for lasting peace as tensions grew throughout the world (Lenihan, *Showdown* 25–28). While *Rio Grande* was in production, relations between the United States and the Soviet Union worsened with incidents like the Berlin blockade of 1948 and the entrenchment of Soviet forces in Eastern Europe. In Asia, mainland China fell to communists, and there were numerous raids by North Korean forces into South Korea, culminating in an invasion in June 1950.

In spite of the threats to peace signified by the increasingly negative portrayal of Native Americans, the successful assimilation of various characters into the society of the army in the three films expresses a sense of optimism about the postwar world. Unlike in the adult Westerns of the 1950s, the veterans of the Confederate army in the cavalry trilogy are not stand-ins for troubled GIs but rather reintegrated and accepted former adversaries of World War II. This acceptance was mirrored in U.S. foreign policy. The purpose of the Marshall Plan, approved in 1948, was to rebuild both former Allied and Axis countries in Europe so that they could take their place as prosperous democracies in a free-market economy. It soon expanded to other countries and ultimately evolved into the Organization for Economic Cooperation and Development.

The U.S. military around the world was overseeing the rebuilding of counties destroyed in the war. If the cavalry is a symbol of U.S. forces overseas, then the final image of troops riding by and the voice-over from *She Wore a Yellow Ribbon* clearly express an imperialist ideal: "So here they are—the dog-faced soldiers, the regulars, the fifty-cents-a-day professionals, riding the outposts of a nation. From Fort Reno to Fort Apache, from Sheridan to Stark, they were all the same: men in dirty-shirt blue, and only a cold page in the history books to mark their passage. But wherever they rode, and whatever they fought for—that place became the United States." As the British Empire films of the 1930s were promoting the ideal of a Pax Britannica, so were the films of the cavalry trilogy projecting a Pax Americana.

NOTES

1. I owe a dept of gratitude to Scott Simmon for pointing out the connection between the British Empire genre and the Western subgenre of cavalry films, to Linda Brigance and Grant Kennell for reading and commenting on the manuscript, and to Lynn Downey for photographic research.

2. In *Empire: The Rise and Demise of the British World Order and the Lessons for Global Power*, Niall Ferguson cites an open letter by the editors of *Life* magazine, published in October 1942 to the people of England, revealing this anti-imperialist feeling. "One thing we are sure we are *not* fighting for is to hold the British Empire together. We don't like to put the matter so bluntly, but we don't want you to have any illusions. If your strategists are planning a war to hold the British Empire together, they will sooner or later find themselves strategizing all alone" (343).

See also Clayton R. Koppes and Gregory D. Black, "What to Show the World: The Office of War Information and Hollywood, 1942–1945," *Journal of American History* 64 (1977): 87–105, for more information about Hollywood's response to this sentiment.

WORKS CITED

Eyman, Scott. *Print the Legend: The Life and Times of John Ford.* Baltimore: Johns Hopkins University Press, 2001.

Ferguson, Niall. *Empire: The Rise and Demise of the British World Order and the Lessons for Global Power.* New York: Basic Books, 2003.

Gallagher, Tag. *John Ford: The Man and His Films.* Berkeley: University of California Press, 1986.

Jackson, Herbert L. "Cowboy, Pioneer and American Soldier." *Sight and Sound* 22 (1953): 189-90.

Lenihan, John H. "Classics and Social Commentary: Postwar Westerns, 1946–1960." *Journal of the West* 22 (1983): 34–42.

———. *Showdown: Confronting Modern America in the Western Film.* Urbana: University of Illinois Press, 1980.

Pauly, Thomas H. "The Cold War Western." *Western Humanities Review* 33 (1979): 257–72.

Poague, Leland. "'All I Can See Is the Flags': *Fort Apache* and the Visibility of History." *Cinema Journal* 27 (1988): 8–26.

Richards, Jeffrey. *The Age of the Dream Palace: Cinema and Society in Britain 1930–1939.* London: Routledge and Kegan Paul, 1984.

———. "Boy's Own Empire: Feature Films and Imperialism in the 1930s." In *Imperialism and Popular Culture,* edited by John M. Mackenzie, 140–64. Manchester: Manchester University Press, 1986.

———. *Visions of Yesterday.* London: Routledge and Kegan Paul, 1973.

Schatz, Thomas. *Hollywood Genres: Formulas, Filmmaking, and the Studio System.* New York: Random House, 1981.

Slotkin, Richard. "The Continuity of Forms: Myth and Genre in Warner Brothers' *Charge of the Light Brigade.*" *Representations* 29 (1990): 1–23.

———. *Gunfighter Nation: The Myth of the Frontier in Twentieth-Century America.* New York: HarperPerennial Library, 1993.

Smith, Henry Nash. *Virgin Land: The American West as Symbol and Myth.* Cambridge, Mass.: Harvard University Press, 1950.

Wright, Will. *Six Guns and Society: A Structural Study of the Western.* Berkeley: University of California Press, 1975.

BEYOND THE RIVER
Women and the Role of the Feminine in Howard Hawks's Red River

The films of Howard Hawks have long presented feminist critics with a paradox: they are famous for their recurrent staging of the social rituals of male bonding and camaraderie, and yet then frequently offer images of strong, independent women who undercut the authority of the male group and call its self-sufficiency into question. His action-adventure and Western films such as *The Dawn Patrol* (1930), *Only Angels Have Wings* (1939), and *Red River* (1948) are intensely masculine dramas in which tight-knit groups of men routinely face danger as part of their job, displaying a typical Hawksian code of ethics that includes an obsessive devotion to profession, a stoical resignation to hardship and adversity, a fierce loyalty and commitment to male comrades who work together in pursuit of a common goal, and the ability to exhibit what the novelist Ernest Hemingway called "grace under pressure." In films about aviators, soldiers, race car drivers, private detectives, and cowboys, Hawks offered a decidedly male point of view on the world, one that made no room for the traditionally feminine values of the maternal, the domestic, and the sentimental.

If these themes represented the full extent of Hawks's treatment of the feminine in his films, there would no doubt be little interest in him on the part of feminist critics and perhaps less interest in his work on the part of film critics generally. In fact, Hawks was a much more complex and contradictory filmmaker than a mere inventory of Hawksian themes might suggest. The most important factor complicating the sexual politics in Hawks's films is the figure of the "Hawksian woman," which he elaborated over the course of his career. She can be seen in the characters of Bonnie in *Only Angels Have Wings* and Hildy Johnson in *His Girl Friday* (1940); these are strong, independent women who are themselves professionals and equal to any man in the film.

The Hawksian woman emerges full-blown in the performances of Lauren Bacall in her first two pictures, both directed by Hawks and costarring her husband-to-be, Humphrey Bogart: *To Have and Have Not* (1944) and *The Big Sleep* (1946). Naomi Wise, in an essay entitled "The Hawksian Woman," has argued that Hawks's representation of women was a clear "exception" to the conventions that governed Hollywood's depiction of women, and such positive images of strong women as can be found in Hawks's films have led some critics to see evidence of a kind of protofeminism in his work. Wise, for example, praises the Hawksian woman for successfully synthesizing the "good girl/bad girl" polarities of Hollywood stereotypes "into a single heroic heroine, who is both sexual [because of her physical beauty] and valuable [for her intellect and ability]" (112). In fact, Wise concludes that "Hawks's heroines are, if anything, superior to the heroes," and she praises Hawks's films for containing "some of the most honest portrayals of women in any movies" (118).

One of the functions of the Hawksian woman is to lead the male character from a state of emotional aloofness to a discovery of his real feelings. Typically, Hawks's men suffer initially from a kind of emotional paralysis, displaying a reserve toward women that at times borders on overt hostility. The knowing Hawksian woman helps the central male character to discover his true feelings and resolve this psychological block, which in several cases has become, quite obviously, emotionally crippling. In doing so, as Wise points out, "Hawks's [characters] frequently show a merging of sexual roles for the benefit of both sexes—the women learn certain 'masculine' values while the men become 'feminized'" (113).

Such sexual reversals become a dominant theme in Hawks's celebrated comedies, where they often work to comically undermine rigid social and sexual differences between men and women. In films such as *Bringing Up Baby* (1938), *Gentlemen Prefer Blondes* (1952), and *I Was a Male War Bride* (1949), Hawks pushed sexual reversal to the extreme in stories that showed pliable and timid men being dominated by powerful and aggressive women. Hawks seems to have relished staging scenes of male sexual humiliation and cross-dressing in his comedies, often making the suavely masculine Cary Grant the object of such ridicule in what amounts to a running gag in their work together.

All this does suggest a somewhat complicated sexual politics at work in the films of this very traditional—even conservative—filmmaker, and herein lies the paradox of Howard Hawks for feminists. However, in light of such complexity, it is perhaps less surprising that Hawks's view of "the feminine," which is so ambivalent and contradictory in his work, as even this brief survey of his films suggests, emerges as a focal point of narrative and thematic importance in one of the most masculine of all his films: *Red River*. This was Hawks's first Western, as well as his first foray into independent filmmaking after the formation of his own company, Monterey Productions, and these circumstances ensured the complete creative attention of the filmmaker as both producer and director of the project. Shooting much of the film on location in Arizona, Hawks created a story of epic scope and high drama that would become one of the most well-known and highly celebrated Westerns of all time. In light of the canonical status of *Red River* within the Western genre, it could be argued that the film's sexual politics assume an even greater interest as indicative of larger trends and tendencies in the treatment of women and the concept of the feminine in Westerns generally. But locating *Red River* within the more limited scope of Hawks's canon most certainly helps to reveal the remarkably idiosyncratic and sustained meditation on masculinity (and, of necessity, femininity) that informed his work as a filmmaker. Among all his action/dramas, *Red River* best illuminates what Laura Mulvey has called "the central and perverse place of gender" in Hawks's films (215).

NATION-BUILDING AND SEXUAL POLITICS

From the very beginning of *Red River*, with its framing device of the expository titles and the manuscript called "Early Tales of Texas," Hawks announces a much larger historical and cultural frame for this film than is typical of his work. *Red River*, as Robert Sklar has shown, is a film about "empire, . . . about the territorial expansion of one society by the usurpation of land from others" (169); clearly, this is a theme with social and political implications. At the center of this great enterprise of nation-building—which is both a political and an economic process—are the simple biological facts of animal husbandry: the need to enlarge the herd of cattle and to populate the empty spaces of the western frontier. The settlers moving west in the wagon train at the beginning of the film try to dissuade Tom Dunson (John Wayne) from going off on his own because they fear the loss of his cow and bull: "They are needed to start up the herds when we get to California," the wagon master argues. Despite this objection, Dunson and Nadine Groot (Walter Brennan) state their intention to leave, an act of rugged, individual initiative that has unforeseen

Courtesy of Movie Goods.

A troubled icon of masculinity: John Wayne as Tom Dunson in *Red River.*

consequences when, shortly after their departure, the wagon train is attacked by Indians, and Dunson's fiancée, Fen, is killed. Fen represents another version of the settler's argument, but her appeals are pointedly erotic and familial: "You'll need me for what you've got to do," she tells Dunson. "The sun only shines for half of the day." This is a clear invitation to procreation and a life of love and work, to build a family as well as a cattle empire—larger social values than Dunson's obsessive individualism can admit—and he remains resolved in his decision to leave the wagon train. As Dunson rides away, Fen yells out to him, prophetically, "You're wrong, Tom." These words are echoed later in the film by Dunson's adopted son, Matthew Garth (Montgomery Clift), who becomes "the bearer of the feminine principle" (Sklar 175) throughout the long middle section of the film during which women are entirely absent. They are spoken a third time by Groot, Dunson's trail cook and longtime friend, who increasingly serves as a "chorus figure" in the film. Though speculation on Groot's first name might appear critical overinterpretation, there is no doubt that, along with Matt, he embodies certain "feminine" values that secure for him a moral perspective that permits a special insight into the two main characters and the problems that beset their "masculine" identities.

During the Indian attack that follows his departure from the wagon train, Dunson loses his cow, leaving him with only a bull—a state of sexual imbalance

that parallels Dunson's own situation following Fen's death. In the aftermath
of the attack, a dazed Matthew Garth—lone survivor of the wagon train—
wanders into Dunson's camp leading a cow. This encounter performs a symbolic
restoration of the feminine principle, which Dunson had renounced when he
left Fen behind: out of the union of Dunson's and Matt's livestock will grow the
prolific herds of cattle upon which the two will stake their future. At the same
time, the future of the country is also at stake, and Hawks makes it clear that
Dunson's and Matt's destinies are inextricably bound up with the larger social
and historical project of nation-building that the film explicitly addresses, both
through expository titles and through Dunson's famous speech on the eve of the
cattle drive. In this trenchant address, he directly links the success of the drive to
America's settling of the West and the expanding market for beef.

The sexual symbolism established through the union of Dunson's and
Matt's cattle is developed in several ways throughout the film. Most conspicuous is the manner in which Matt Garth is feminized through the performance
of Montgomery Clift, whose soft, boyish features and shy, sensitive manner
contrast starkly with John Wayne's more rugged look and brutal demeanor as
Dunson. There is a strong subtext at work in this film revolving around the
ambiguous sexual appeal of Clift's Garth, who also attracts the attention of
the gunfighter Cherry Valance (John Ireland). (In one notorious scene, the
two young men banter about their six-shooters with only slightly veiled sexual
double entendres.) The homoerotic subtext is quite strong in many of Hawks's
films, which often deal openly with what Hawks himself called "a love story
between two men" (McCarthy 401). Here the devotion to profession and loyalty
to an elite group of male comrades who practice a way of life defined by constant
danger and the threat of death creates a strong, often physical bond between
the characters that can be seen either as a heroic, existential link between men
or as macho posturing of the rankest sort. But in *Red River* Matt Garth
functions as an alternative to Tom Dunson's stern masculine ethos, and he
becomes the embodiment of "feminine" characteristics and values that are most
apparent in his more compassionate and humane treatment of the men on the
cattle drive.

The most conspicuous feature of *Red River's* depiction of women is their
almost complete absence from the story. Women appear only briefly at the
beginning (in the character of Fen) and then at the end with the introduction
of Tess Millay (Joanne Dru). Fen is not a character explored by Hawks in any
depth: she appears only in the opening scene, where she pleads the necessity

Generational conflict in *Red River:* John Wayne and Montgomery Clift as Tom Dunson and Matt Garth.

of women, the necessity of the feminine in the work of settling the frontier. By turning his back on her and riding away, Dunson reveals the tragic flaw that will eventually undercut his moral authority, leading to an emotional and ethical blindness brought about through his obsessive commitment to the cattle drive and to the goals of empire-building. That flaw consists of turning his back on his woman—and, by extension, the feminine principle generally—in his single-minded pursuit of the masculine goals of raising cattle and building empires.

Both Dunson and Matt represent certain problems of masculine identity: in Dunson, it is the suppression and denial of "feminine" feelings (such as compassion, tolerance, mercy) by a hyperbolic masculinity that has been deformed by emotional loss (Fen's death). For Dunson, these values must be recognized and recovered in order to reach the necessary Hawksian self-awareness. For Matt, the crisis of masculinity revolves around the struggle to integrate his latent feminine passivity with the normative values and behavior of a traditional masculine aggressiveness that must be acknowledged and confronted. The drama of that moment is underscored by Hawks's staging it as the conventional Western shoot-out that climaxes the film.

The Return of the Repressed

The key to both men's emotional self-discovery is Tess Millay. In her character, the repressed feminine principle that Dunson rejects at the beginning of the film (and which remains completely banished throughout the ensuing two-thirds of the story) suddenly erupts back into the narrative. The character of Millay in Borden Chase's original *Saturday Evening Post* serial, "The Chisholm Trail," was a prostitute and a gambler, but Motion Picture Production Code officials demanded that she be softened somewhat in the film version. Still, Millay is a powerful sexual presence in the film, despite Dru's rather limited performance in the role. It is Millay who is drawn to the virginal Matt and initiates their first romantic encounter. Later on in Abilene, she appears in Matthew's bedroom, clearly the dominant partner in their relationship. When Dunson encounters Millay for the first time, she reveals an intimate knowledge of his relationship with Matt, and the frank discussion between the two provokes a glacial thaw in Dunson's frozen emotions, as evidenced by his blunt proposition to Millay that she bear him a son. This is not a proposal of marriage, mind you, but simply a way of replacing Matt, the surrogate son he has vowed to kill, and thus it represents a desire on Dunson's part to restore the all-male group from which he has been expelled. Of course, as the inexorable logic of animal husbandry makes clear, out of such all-male groups can come no children and, thus, no future. Dunson's "proposal" to Millay has nothing to do with creating a relationship with a woman in order to produce and nurture a family; rather, it is motivated by revenge and a longing to recover the esteem and respect of other men.

It is the need to resolve the conflict between a dominant yet sterile set of masculine values and a suppressed but essentially humanizing feminine principle that is most dramatically staged in the film's conclusion. Both strands of the narrative's thematic and ideological agenda come together in the need to both deliver the cattle to Abilene (the socioeconomic premise of the film) and prepare the stage for a resolution to the conflicts between characters and the sexual imbalances and tensions that have structured their relationships up to this point. The crisis arrives in the confrontation between Dunson and Matt, which leads Tess Millay to do what no man in the film has been brave enough to attempt: intervene in the conflict. By breaking up the fight, Millay ensures, as Robert Sklar has noted, "a reconciliation between men and the

Attempting to restore the all-male group that has banished him, Dunson propositions Tess Millay (Joanne Dru).

"Masculine" conflicts are reconciled by recognizing "feminine" values in the final confrontation between Dunson and Garth in *Red River*.

promise of a normal social order" (176) based on an eventual marriage between Matt and Millay.

At the crucial moment in the conflict when Matthew Garth begins to fight Dunson, thus asserting a normative "masculine aggression," Hawks cuts to a rare close-up of Groot, who exclaims: "It's gonna be all right. For fourteen years I've been scared . . . but it's gonna be all right." It seems an inescapable conclusion to assume that what Groot has been "scared" of is the inability of these two men to resolve the different but interrelated problems of their masculine identities. Matt enters full manhood only when he is able to stand up to Dunson and resist the tyranny of the "father," shedding his "feminine" passivity for a socially sanctioned masculine aggressiveness; Dunson, on the other hand, is redeemed by his ability to show compassion and admit he was "wrong," signaled by his advice to Matt as they lie sprawled on the ground, "You better marry her." Both characters undergo an adjustment of gender roles that restores social harmony by admitting "feminine" values and insights into male relationships, though much of this recognition of true feelings and discovery of real emotions is tacit in the film. This is a Western, after all, and one directed by Howard Hawks, no less, who is famous for avoiding preachy speeches, preferring to let characters' actions and body language reveal their true thoughts and feelings.

GENERIC CONVENTIONS AND GENDER

It should be observed at this point that Millay's intervention in the conflict between Dunson and Matt and the comedic resolution that it makes possible (the film's ending in the promise of marriage) are clearly inappropriate in terms of the conventions of the Western genre, according to which one of the two men should be killed. Nor is this ending in any way commensurate with the depth of the conflict established between the two characters over the course of the film. More than one critic has complained that Millay's actions and the sudden disappearance of hostility between Dunson and Matt provide a weak and implausible ending to a story that seemed from the outset to be heading toward a much darker, more pessimistic terminus. As is, *Red River* seems to offer a typical Hollywood "happy ending." For Hawks, such compromises were understood as simply one of the necessary exigencies of commercial filmmaking. Yet such a violation of audience expectations indicates the extent to which

Hawks was willing to use the conventions of the Western genre as a mere frame for his own explorations of gender and sexual identity.

Yet such objections aside, the implications of *Red River* are clear: the sexual symbolism on which Hawks structured his story inescapably leads to a critique of the masculine values at the center of both the Western as a genre and the director's personal vision. The film suggests that men who think they can live without the companionship, guidance, and help of women who are their equals often are doomed to an obsession with work (read: "career") that isolates them from a larger community of shared human values to which women provide access. The excessively masculine ethos of Dunson (his impulse to dominate and control the all-male group, his belief in the technicalities of ownership and legal obligation) is shown to be sterile, literally a historical dead end; the "feminine" presence of Millay and, as coded in the film, Matthew Garth provides a humanizing set of values essential to nation-building, a central idea in this film and a recurrent theme within the Western genre. *Red River* is Hawks's clearest statement concerning his characteristic interest in exclusive male groups, precisely because of the way it interrogates the meaning of such a group, showing its impossibility in social and historical terms and pointing to the origins of this "all-boys club" in adolescent male fantasy and regressive wish fulfillment. *Red River* makes clear the psychic and emotional costs to men of such fantasies. In so doing, the film speaks eloquently about the need for an equilibrium between women and men, articulating an unconscious esteem for the different but equally necessary characteristics of the "feminine" and the "masculine."

Red River provides an essential key to understanding the interplay and exchange between genders that figures so prominently in Hawks's films, as well as offering a meditation on the meaning of masculinity and femininity in the Western—a genre overcrowded with stalwart male characters who are often willing to underestimate or ignore the role of women and "feminine" values in the settling of the West. It is worth noting that the title *Red River* was of Hawks's own choosing and that he insisted on it over the objections of everyone involved in the production of the film, all of whom feared it sounded too much like a "B-movie" (McCarthy 418). Hawks was right. For such a work as this, the liminal space of a river—which is like that of gender, another natural boundary to be crossed in the process of discovery—was the most appropriate emblem and title for the film.

WORKS CITED

McCarthy, Todd. *Howard Hawks: The Grey Fox of Hollywood.* New York: Grove, 1997.

Mulvey, Laura. "*Gentlemen Prefer Blondes*: Anita Loos/Howard Hawks/Marilyn Monroe." In *Howard Hawks: American Artist,* edited by Jim Hillier and Peter Wollen, 214–29. London: British Film Institute, 1996.

Sklar, Robert. "Empire to the West: *Red River* (1948)." In *American History/ American Film: Interpreting the Hollywood Image,* edited by John E. O'Connor and Martin A. Jackson, 167–81. New York: Ungar, 1979.

Wise, Naomi. "The Hawksian Woman." In *Howard Hawks: American Artist,* edited by Jim Hillier and Peter Wollen, 111–19. London: British Film Institute, 1996.

THE "ACHE FOR HOME"
Assimilation and Separatism in Anthony Mann's Devil's Doorway

In the year 1950, a postwar revival of the Western genre marked a major shift in the way Hollywood represented Native Americans, with the release of Delmer Daves's color production of *Broken Arrow* in July and Anthony Mann's first Western, *Devil's Doorway,* a few months later. Both films examine and then negate the possibility of cross-racial romance, setting that romance in the immediate post–Civil War period and featuring a male hero who is a returning Civil War veteran. Although *Devil's Doorway* has received considerably less critical attention than *Broken Arrow,* it is by far the more radical film in its depiction of frontier politics. Unlike *Broken Arrow*'s optimism about peaceful resolutions, *Devil's Doorway* confronts viewers with corruption and failure in frontier land negotiations. If *Broken Arrow* uses its Apache characters to sanction the negotiation and treaty process and to legitimate both assimilationist policies and the reservation system, *Devil's Doorway* aggressively denies these options.

Devil's Doorway functions as a drama of reintegration and subsequent disintegration, in which a returning war veteran disrupts the already uneasy balance of power in his home community, and deeply gendered representations of "home" become destabilized by racially motivated violence. The film has been discussed as an allegory for early civil rights that avoided offending conservative audiences or drawing the attention of the Hays Office and the House Committee on Un-American Activities, but it also resonates with the problems facing returning Native American veterans after World War II, including references to poor reservation conditions, chronic local prejudice, racist and outmoded government supervision, land use crises, and, most important, a federal assault on tribal lands, sovereignty, and treaty rights.[1]

Tapping the postwar assimilationist sentiment that drove the new federal Indian policy of Termination,[2] *Devil's Doorway* combines Western, film noir, and "social problem" genres to convey the contradictions inherent in the 1950s treatment of minorities, particularly coercive assimilation and segregation. The film registers public confusion and anxiety over these issues of ethnic circulation and containment, and presents Indian land—on and off reservations—as contested space, the locus of national desires for an economically bountiful "home," and simultaneously a "concentration camp" from which Indians must be released.

Although ideas about social tolerance and the United States as a liberating force in World War II deeply affected literary and media representations of Native Americans, tropes of imprisonment consistently troubled such discourses with traces of indigenous and other minority group experiences of removal, segregation, internment, and holocaust. While African Americans were vigorously segregated, Native Americans were being forced to assimilate through "relocation" to urban centers, and Japanese Americans had recently been confined in wartime "camps" that were often located on reservation lands. The liberal rhetoric in *Devil's Doorway* reflects the strong tendency during this period to substitute Indians for other minorities in Hollywood films, yet in its focus on the inadequacy of the assimilation model the film also touches on specific issues of tribal identity, sovereignty, and land rights that were central to federal Indian policy shifts in the late 1940s and early 1950s.

This tension between a generalized rhetoric of racial difference (white and Other) and the separate histories and relationships between distinct minority groups and the U.S. government emerges in critical histories of the Western as well as in cultural products of the 1950s. Steve Neale has persuasively argued that scholarly readings of cinematic representations of Indians solely as "empty signifiers" or "ethnic stand-ins" for other minorities reenact tropes of the "vanishing Indian" by "disappearing" native people from postwar America and its artistic products. The obsession with home and land at the center of *Devil's Doorway* signals a very public conflict over the status of native people, especially native veterans, as separate and sovereign peoples within the United States. Clearly, figures of Indians in Hollywood films registered changes in American perceptions of native peoples specifically, and *simultaneously* functioned as coded references to broader, multiethnic issues of racial and religious intolerance. As texts with multiple meanings, Indian Westerns are sites where traces of public discourses about African Americans, Japanese

Americans, Jewish Americans, and others mingled with and influenced the way the films addressed Native American identities and reinterpreted tribal treaty relationships with the United States.

Devil's Doorway narrates a *failure* of both negotiated agreements and the reservation system, echoing the Termination policy's implicit opposition to treaty-based tribal separatism and sovereignty. Chadwick Allen has coined the term "treaty discourse" to describe the "founding discourse on which all future U.S.-Indian relations can be legally organized" ("Hero with Two Faces" 611). Treaties construct idealized versions of Indianness and whiteness that exist in a moment of accord that is both reciprocal and hierarchical, both authentic and contained.[3] Allen invokes the definition of treaties and the reservation system articulated by legal scholar Charles F. Wilkinson: treaties, Wilkinson writes, were "intended to establish homelands for the tribes, islands of tribalism largely free from interference by non-Indians or future state governments. This separatism is measured, rather than absolute, because it contemplates supervision and support by the United States" (14). It is this "measured separatism" that the Termination policy sought to rescind as the U.S. government moved toward one result of its "heritage of colonialism," what Etienne Balibar calls "a dual movement of assimilation and exclusion of the 'natives'" (42–43). In the United States' postwar growth economy, interior colonization as expansionist policy continued with new military and industrial activity, such as uranium mining and other extractive industries, on native lands (Corkin; Limerick). As in the frontier period, the country expanded into Indian territory, and a new racism against native difference, emerging from 1950s nationalism, sought to expel the "Indianness" from the country's interior.

THE DRIFTER

Devil's Doorway tells the story of Broken Lance, or Lance Poole (Robert Taylor), a Shoshone Indian and decorated Civil War veteran who returns to his tribe's ancestral land, a valley called Sweet Meadows, only to find that unchecked prejudice and greed have come with Wyoming's territorial incorporation and the railroad. Under the Homestead Act, whites could file homestead claims but Indians could not; as a result, Lance is unable to claim ownership of Sweet Meadows though he has worked the land for years as a profitable cattle ranch. The town's most prominent lawyer, Verne Coolan (Louis Calhern), is a racist who works to destroy Lance and the other Shoshones in order to open their land for white settlement. Lance hires Orrie Masters (Paula Raymond), the only other lawyer in town, to petition on his behalf; as a woman, Orrie understands something about social prejudice. Then Coolan precipitates a fight by inviting desperate sheepherders to settle Sweet Meadows. There is a suggestion of romance between Orrie and Lance, but their relationship is also combative as they argue over whether Lance should compromise with the sheepherders. In a climactic shoot-out, Lance and a group of reservation Shoshones hiding at his ranch are surrounded by vigilantes and, later, the U.S. Cavalry; the women and children are allowed to go back to the reservation, but the Shoshone men are killed. In the final scene, Lance puts on his military uniform and marches out to salute the cavalry leader but instead falls forward in death. Orrie utters the closing line, "It would be too bad if we ever forgot . . ."

Guy Trosper's script for *Devil's Doorway*—which Mann called "the best I have ever read"[4]—went through major alterations between 1946 and 1949, from a Western that pits a drifter against a big cattleman to a reactivation of the silent era's sympathetic and reformist "Indian drama."[5] Trosper's original short story, entitled "The Drifter," emphasizes conflict between cattle barons and small-time ranchers, as well as the role of assertive women in the West. Its complex plot involves Barney, a wealthy rancher hiding from his outlaw past; his new wife, Letha, a femme fatale who enjoys conflict; and Charlotte "Charley" Carmody, a civic activist and ranch owner who challenges Barney's rule and is elected as sheriff (Dudley). The drifter of the story's title is a white ranch hand named Lance Poole, whom Letha encourages to duel with Barney. As in *Devil's Doorway*, there is a battle involving dynamite (at "Hell's Gap"), but Poole, far from defending his ancestral land, is placeless; he "comes and goes. He has no home, doesn't want one" (Trosper, "Drifter"). All the primary characters are white, and the story only touches on issues of prejudice through Charlotte's unusual role as sheriff.

In May 1948, the script reappeared with an Indian theme. Lance Poole is white but is an adopted member of a mixed-race (white-native) family. He and his adopted mixed-blood brother Ira Coffee, an outlaw, work together to defend Sweet Meadows against the invading sheepherders. The script attempts comedy at the expense of the Shoshone characters through Indian stereotypes and at the expense of lawyer Orrie, whose legalistic language makes her an object of ridicule. Lance must break with Ira and his adopted Indian family to unite with Orrie, and in the end Lance himself shoots Ira rather than let him be executed by the cavalry. Thus Ira's Indianness—a "darkness" that combines the characteristics of outlaw and victim—is purged from the narrative and from Lance and Orrie's future.

In the final version, Lance is a full-blood Shoshone Civil War veteran, and his Indian and cavalry identities divide him against himself, leading to a more complex ending in which Lance is not able simply to separate himself from his "dark" half. *Devil's Doorway* involves a Native American man and a white woman, and though their relationship is left unconsummated, the film offers a bolder depiction of cross-racial romance than does *Broken Arrow*. A near-final outline of the script (December 1948) includes a scene in which Lance threatens Orrie sexually, throwing her onto the bed in his cabin before changing his mind and letting her go (Trosper, Outline). The wavering in the script treatments of Lance—he is both sexual threat and romantic object—was intended to be titillating, but the final version steers clear of potential negative audience or Hays Office reactions to any depiction of "miscegenation" on-screen. In the film, Lance accuses Orrie of staying "on the safe side of the fence" but later merely says, "Don't cry, Orrie, a hundred years from now it might have worked." The two never kiss, despite the visual preparation of soft-focus close-ups as Orrie gazes up at Lance.[6] Their relationship, always physically and emotionally tense, ends with Lance's death before it can begin.

In fact, the release of *Devil's Doorway* was delayed because producers at MGM feared the "pro-Indian" theme would put off audiences, and the ambiguous relationship between Lance and Orrie testifies to MGM's uneasiness about delving into a new kind of Western. Only after the release and strong financial success of *Broken Arrow* (which came in seventh in the year's top-grossing movies) did MGM release Mann's film.[7] While it became clear that the public and the Production Code would tolerate "pro-Indian" Westerns and images of cross-racial romance, the delayed release led viewers and critics to assume that Mann's film was a B-grade copy of *Broken Arrow* (Basinger). The story's tragic ending and downplayed romance—in a black-and-white noir visual style—made it both more complex and less commercially successful than *Broken Arrow*, which mediated its own tragic ending by asserting that the death of the Apache character Sonseeahray "put a seal on the peace" (as I discuss later).

Reviews of Mann's first Western were mixed. Writers criticized the film's lack of authenticity: a *Cue* review read, "Dyeing Robert Taylor's face and hair, painting him up and sticking a feather in his hair doesn't make him a good, bad or even a convincing Indian . . . despite the earnestness of his portrayal." *Variety* reviewers found Taylor to be "too polished and educated for the role" and accused the studio of "a colossal piece of miscasting." A *Fortnight* reviewer wrote, "Taylor is probably no more Indian in spirit than Hepburn was Chinese in *Dragon Seed.*" Other reviewers appreciated the film's "sincerity," John Alton's strong black-and-white cinematography, and the way the story "subtly draws parallels with intolerance in our own post-war period" (*Independent Film Journal*).

The reviewers' critical preoccupation with artifice and sincerity in representations of Indians points to the continuing problem of authenticity in the Indian drama and "pro-Indian" Western. Films often presented fantasy in the narrative but realism in the surface details—artifacts and costumes.[8] In this context, the social critique inherent in revisionist Westerns attests to the paradoxical desire for integrity in a genre based on "playing Indian."[9] The same films that comment on the United States' violent expropriation of indigenous lands and cultural identities also pursue the appropriation of "Indianness" through, among other things, casting. Reviewers' negative responses to the casting in *Devil's Doorway* point again to the problem of "authenticity" as a problem of unity. The disjuncture between actor and role can be seen as one more displacement in the chain of substitutions if the film is read as allegory for general racial "intolerance": Robert Taylor "stands in" for a Shoshone who "stands in" for other racial groups. However, Taylor's embodiment of a Shoshone character can also be seen in the tradition of "mixed" or "half-breed" characters who represent not only assimilationist policy but also a cultural desire to amalgamate the "treaty discourse" "between two nations into a single body."[10] The film's character Broken Lance/Lance Poole is denied precisely this privilege of freely embodying a dual identity (Shoshone *and* American). Despite—or perhaps because of—these contradictions, both the critical and the more positive reviews suggest that audiences were deeply responsive to cinematic critiques of westward expansion, a point proved dramatically by the box-office success of *Broken Arrow*.

BROKEN ARROW'S "CLEAR TALK"

In *Broken Arrow*, Tom Jeffords (Jimmy Stewart) befriends Cochise (Jeff Chandler) and negotiates a peace between the Apaches and settlers in the 1870s. The film depicts a mixed-race couple (Jeffords and his Apache child bride, Sonseeahray, played by Debra Paget) attempting to heal social rifts through their union, but peace comes only when the bond is broken and the Native American partner is sacrificed. Although the film's successful peace talks allude to the possibility of both assimilation and cultural tolerance, dual tensions of the conformist 1950s and the breakdown in cross-cultural communication toward the end of the film, along with the end of the cross-racial marriage through the death of Sonseeahray, complicate the film's verbal pro-assimilation message.[11] In contrast to *Devil's Doorway*, the events of *Broken Arrow* act as a ceremony of purification for Jeffords, who is "sick and tired of all this killing." Through his relationship with Sonseeahray and through her death, both Jeffords and his community are reborn as a nation in harmony with itself and its conquered peoples.[12]

Several critics have addressed the relationship of voice-over and dialogue to the film's function as representation. Armando José Prats has described the way Indian Westerns—especially those of the 1950s—systematically transmute visions of Indians into an absence. The appropriative vision of the films (and their white heroes) becomes a dispossession of Indians through knowledge of them; seeing, and by extension spectatorship, becomes "a hostile act" (*Invisible Natives* 11). Prats argues further that voice-over narration in *Broken Arrow* and other pro-Indian Westerns dissociates a white man or couple from the violence of Manifest Destiny and conquest yet reiterates the story of the vanishing American. As I discuss in the final section of this chapter, my reading of *Devil's Doorway* suggests a similarly conflicted positioning of the viewer as both an instigator of genocidal frontier violence and a conscientious eyewitness, ready to intervene in the name of social justice.

In *Broken Arrow*, visual icons of communication—arrows, smoke signals, hand signals, mirror signals, maps, and the U.S. mail—become tropes for military advantage during the Indian wars and have a self-referential function in which cinematic representations of history are part of the spoils of conquest. Verbal elements in *Broken Arrow* gesture to the power of the visual—and the idea of revisionism—through the motif of eyes. The script goes to some trouble to establish the superiority of Apache vision, visual communication, and military intelligence. When Jeffords is captured by the Apaches at the beginning of the film, he is forced to watch while a gold miner is buried in the sand and left, his face rubbed with mescal, for the ants to devour. Later, as Jeffords describes his plan to visit Cochise, his friend Milt warns him, "Well don't try it, Tom, the ants'll be feedin' off your eyes." When Jeffords insists, Milt leaves the room, saying, "It's *your* eyes." Later in the film, General Howard confesses that his "eyes are getting old." In contrast to these references to the vulnerability of white men's eyes, Apaches are presented as accurate readers of both the landscape and human motives. When Jeffords and his Apache teacher Juan send smoke signals to Cochise's men, Juan says, "Enough, Apache eyes are quick"; later in the same scene, he tells Jeffords not to lie to Cochise, because "his eyes will see into your heart."

This hypervaluation of Native American military prowess—here indicated through visual acuity—was part of a long-established warrior stereotype that recirculated both during and after World War II. The U.S. absorption and appropriation of this image, harnessed for national purposes during the war, became a reified media cliché. Publicity photographs portrayed native soldiers in fighting poses wearing Plains-style feather headdresses, and Pima soldier Ira Hayes's participation in putting up the American flag at Iwo Jima made him—through his photographed image—an instant celebrity and an icon of nonwhite American patriotism available for multiple public uses.[13] Publicity for *Broken Arrow* clearly emphasized the theme of overcoming racial prejudice, and secondarily the idea of historical accuracy, but methods for promoting the film made Apaches available as visual signs by appropriating historical Apache wilderness skills to target a youth audience.[14]

Broken Arrow opens with Tom Jeffords riding through the wilderness and realizing from the gathering buzzards that "something—or somebody—was getting ready to die." The "somebody" turns out to be a wounded Apache boy, never named in the film, whom Jeffords heals and returns to his people. This opening image of impending fatality is carried through in the film with the deaths of the two prominent young Apache characters, the boy and Sonseeahray. Jeffords encounters both characters during their ritual transformation from childhood to adulthood; the boy is in his "novice time," when he "learns to be a man," while Sonseeahray is "in the holiest time of her life" during the ceremony marking her transition to womanhood and eligibility for marriage. Structurally parallel, both characters are killed by whites, the boy on an Apache raid, and Sonseeahray while protecting Jeffords during an ambush of Cochise by hostile ranchers. Their deaths suggest the film's premise that Apache numbers and power will dwindle, since their life cycles have been interrupted and neither will reach full maturity or have children of their own.

When Apache warriors come to rescue the boy, they shoot an arrow near Jeffords to indicate their presence, and then two more. There is a brief, low-angle shot of Jeffords against the sky, framed and trapped by arrows that form a barrier between him and the Apache boy. "This is clear talk—it says they can still kill!" says the boy. His speech inaugurates the arrow as a primary symbol in the film, linking the ability to "speak" through action with masculine aggression and military power.[15] Later, Cochise leads a successful ambush by maintaining a high position on a bluff where he can see the action clearly, then signal different war parties to attack at key moments by having a man shoot arrows into trees or into the sky. Just as the Apaches use networks of visual signals—arrows and mirrors—to communicate across great distances in the western landscape, they also maintain tactical advantages over the U.S. military and over Jeffords by staying above them physically. Their positioning becomes a location for Apache military signaling or "speech" that occurs simultaneously with Jeffords's voice-over (as the Apaches speak, they are spoken for and spoken over by Jeffords). Such a system equates vision with appropriation and situates the spectator in the ultimate position of superiority.

Active communication is tactical power in *Broken Arrow*, and when Cochise stops the mail from running, he hampers the settlers' abilities to fight and to maintain private and commercial ties to the East. When talking with Cochise about letting the U.S. mail go through, Jeffords asserts, "When the Indian wishes to signal his brother he does so by smoke signs. This is the white man's signal [holding out a letter]. My brother can look at this and understand my meaning. We call this mail, and the men who carry the mail are like the air that carries the Apache smoke signals." The analogy between visual Apache communicative systems and the whites' use of paper—specifically maps and the U.S. mail—is quite explicit in this speech. When Jeffords first enters Cochise's wickiup, the camera briefly cuts to the leather U.S. mail bags Cochise has taken during raids. Later in the film, through treaty negotiation, the Apaches give up their military advantage and their appropriation of U.S. communications through the mail to accept a paper treaty and map of the new reservation.

When Cochise talks to the Apache leaders about the treaty, he holds the rolled-up map of their territory in his hand, and as he concludes his speech, he exchanges the map for an arrow. Their similar shapes link the objects visually, and as Cochise "breaks the arrow" to mark his approval of the treaty with the U.S. government, he indicates an exchange of "clear talk" through martial power for a representational system on paper, one to which he has no access. He renounces his method of communication, signing over the power of self-representation with his agreement to demilitarize. The film's interpretation of this treaty moment retrospectively gives Jeffords the power to speak for the Apaches, which he does by narrating events in voice-over, and it gives the filmmakers the power to assimilate the Apaches by rendering all speech in English. The visual communicative icons in the film, especially the arrow as both a weapon and a masculine symbol, can be seen as analogous to the medium of film itself, where the Apaches become visual icons rendered on the screen for public consumption. Indigenous self-representation, symbolized here by the arrow, is characterized as a sexualized threat to white settlement that becomes over the course of the film available for appropriation, what Prats might call a metonymy for Indian absence, a fragment "at once hinting at and concealing a complete human identity." The arrow as a synecdoche in this scene signifies the Indian in order "*to suppress* him"—to render him absent from the settlers' frontier landscape (*Invisible Natives* 23, 31).[16]

Jeffords's argument that the mail is not used to carry messages against the Apache is tantamount to arguing that private and public messages do not act in concert in times of war, but over the course of the film we learn—and Jeffords learns—that private and familial relations, as well as private communication, are available for public purposes. Verbal communication between groups and individuals begins to break down as Ben Slade's boy Bob lies to Cochise and Jeffords in order to lead them into Slade's ambush. For Jeffords, communication breaks down when Sonseeahray is killed and he calls the peace treaty a lie. When Cochise speaks to him, he says, "Why do you speak to me? Speak to her [the slain Sonseeahray]. What she hears I'll hear." Yet the body of Sonseeahray—a character coded as a "bearer" of culture—becomes the visual emblem of the success of Jeffords's negotiation rather than its failure. Framed with the pile of stones that mark each day of the armistice, and which also resembles a memorial or grave, Jeffords is comforted by General Howard, who tells him, "Your very loss has brought our peoples together in the will to peace." The grave/marker that puts "a seal on the peace," like Cochise's "broken arrow," also stands for the "vanishing" of native people that leaves Arizona open for white settlement. Significantly, Sonseeahray's "gift" of her body to Jeffords sexually represents a union that is broken when she also gives her body to the treaty process through her death, "signing" herself over out of love and loyalty to Jeffords.[17] Rather than devaluing the treaty process as *Devil's Doorway* does, *Broken Arrow* maintains and misreads this site of exchange in "a (fantasy) version of the treaty story in which Indians sign over all of their rights to self-determination and ongoing, distinctive identities."[18] According to Allen, "Central to these fantasies is an available and thus knowable Indianness: an Indianness defined as racially 'pure' but organized in non-Indian terms" ("Hero with Two Faces" 612). The death of Sonseeahray enables such a "pure" exchange, undisturbed by future mixed-race children, while the "broken arrow" of the film's title connects the treaty-based reservation with compromised Apache masculinity, just as does Lance's Shoshone name, "Broken Lance," in *Devil's Doorway*.

(Dis)integrating Indian Nations

In *Devil's Doorway*, the successfully assimilated Indian is rejected by whites in power, and those Indians who have gone to the reservation are driven in desperation to leave it, saying, "We will die, but we will never go back to the reservation." This is the double bind that *Devil's Doorway* presents: Indians cannot assimilate and cannot be contained, but instead are forced into a hopeless and violent conflict with the settler community. In the film, prejudicial laws and attitudes bar Lance from participating in the "American Dream" and the frontier economy of masculinity that are so central to the traditional hero of the Western genre. Indians are prohibited from buying alcohol, owning or homesteading land, and living away from the reservation; even legal recourse is nearly beyond their means. Territorial Wyoming is no longer the egalitarian society in which the assimilated Lance can build his cattle business. *Devil's Doorway* reveals white-initiated violence and racism to be institutional as well as individual, and to stem from the land greed of a new nation that reserved homesteads for white settlers. The film's focus on the post–Civil War period provides a historical code for the time when the film was made, and the issues facing the cinematic Shoshones parallel in striking ways the struggles over civic identities of native peoples—especially World War II veterans—in the post–World War II and Termination eras.[19]

The 1950s marked a time of political upheaval for native peoples specifically linked to the social changes the United States had undergone in a time of war. Historian Alison Bernstein writes that World War II "represented the first large-scale exodus of Indian men from the reservations since the defeat of their ancestors" (40). Approximately twenty-five thousand Native Americans served in the armed forces during World War II, and another forty thousand native men and women left their homelands and reservations for war-related wage work in cities and towns (40, 68). After the war, however, native people faced conflicting public reactions to their presence outside of reservations, and a nation invested in ideas of modernity and progress turned to nineteenth-century laws to control tribal collective action.[20] The Bureau of Indian Affairs (BIA), the military, and Congress advocated integrating Native Americans into white communities while segregating African Americans, though Native American and African American populations were often deeply entwined, especially in the South. Termination policies sought the breakup of reservations and the movement of native peoples to urban areas, but unfair wages, restrictive voting laws, stereotyped representations of Indians in the media, and other discriminatory practices suggested that "mainstream" American culture would not welcome full participation of native peoples as citizens.[21]

Dillon Myer, who had been head of the War Relocation Authority in charge of interning the Japanese American population from the West Coast, took over the BIA in May 1950 and actively encouraged a view of reservations as temporary centers for detainment rather than permanent land bases for tribal communities. The Termination policies enacted during his leadership of the BIA called for the disintegration of the reservation system, with forced and voluntary integration—through the "Relocation" program—of native peoples to urban areas. Liberals already involved in the fight for desegregation and civil rights in the South, and conservatives interested in eliminating special government services to native peoples, moved for different reasons (and often with good intentions) toward the same goals during Termination: dissolving the special sovereignty status of native tribes as "domestic dependent nations."[22] Indian reservations in the late 1940s and early 1950s became once again materially and discursively contested lands, claimed by multiple interests (tribal, governmental, and private), yet represented in popular rhetoric as prisons from which Indians must be "set free."

The individualist and capitalist emphases in the postwar period, along with the truly desperate situation on the Navajo and other reservations, led both politicians and ordinary citizens to view reservations not as tribal lands but as "concentration camps" for temporary detainees, rhetoric drawn from the Jewish experience in Europe that the government—and the media—never applied to the Japanese Americans in internment camps but often used in advocating the termination of reservations.[23] *Los Angeles Examiner* coverage of a drought and food shortage crisis in the Southwest characterized the Navajo reservation as "the vast concentration camp of the desert" (quoted in Bernstein 153–54). In *America's Concentration Camps: The Facts about Our Indian Reservations Today*, a pro-assimilation book published in 1956, Carlos Embry equates assimilation with freedom and reservation tribal government with "forced communism" (210), concluding that if Congress would "close our concentration camps. . . . The Indian could hope to progress as the people of this great country have progressed. The Indian then could take pride not only in being an Indian but in being an American" (229).

Such assimilationist impulses were in place before the war, however. During the war the BIA under John Collier had recommended segregated military units for Native American soldiers, but the War Department determined that integration with white units would help to "break down tribal ties" among native soldiers, even as the department maintained segregated units for African American soldiers (Bernstein 41). Many southern states, like Virginia, recognized only "two kinds of people—whites and Negroes; anyone of 'color' fell into the latter category," and in Mississippi the draft board "drafted dark-skinned Choctaws into segregated units, while lighter-skinned Indians 'passed' into white platoons" (42).

The overdetermination of black-white racial dichotomies and the blurring of distinctions between other minority groups through tropes of containment in media and governmental rhetoric offer one explanation for the use of Indians in Hollywood films to represent ethnic "Others" (making celluloid Indians into ciphers for other minorities, such as Japanese Americans and African Americans). But these elements also work conversely to bring radically different minority experiences to bear on the way the films comment on—and audiences understand—issues of Indian policy. The films themselves become an unstable and ambivalent site for the containment and circulation of ethnic identities. In classic Westerns, the image of the "savage" Indian attacking white settlers represents an impure violence meant to contrast with the cavalry's ability to purify through violence.[24] The carefully maintained racial boundaries of the Western break down when the Indian is also the cavalry, and this blurring not only disrupts the binary stability of the system of "measured separatism" but also re-presents images of native men in uniform who were very visible indeed during and immediately after World War II.

In *Devil's Doorway*, Lance's Indian/cavalry double identity threatens the boundaries on which the (white) civilization of the Western is based, and as a returned veteran of the Civil War—a war of a nation against itself—he also represents the threat of the nation's own violence brought back upon its communities.[25] *Devil's Doorway* manifests the contradictory public views of native people that brought both liberals and conservatives to endorse Termination. It supports the idea (but not the practice) of an Indian "homeland" while rejecting the treaty and reservation system, and it presents in Broken Lance/Lance Poole an unstable Indian civic identity as Lance fluctuates between integrationist and separatist impulses. The film powerfully raises but never resolves the problem of postwar American unity and national integrity, and in doing so rejects the very idea of compromise, negotiation, and treaty. The reservation, as a form of compromise with the government, is especially unacceptable to the cinematic Shoshones because it is not located on their homeland—this disjunction between Lance as an assimilated Indian living on ancestral land and his displaced reservation tribespeople increases his sense of alienation from both Indian and white cultures. The metaphor of the Civil War further amplifies the social prejudice and inner struggle Lance experiences as an assimilated Indian who is also loyal to his Shoshone people and heritage: in a near-final script, Orrie begs Lance to "stop that war that's going on inside you" (Trosper, Script).

TERMS OF CIRCULATION

In contrast to *Broken Arrow*'s self-consciously talky style, *Devil's Doorway* tells its story primarily through visual composition, noir stylistics, and costume. Jeanine Basinger calls *Devil's Doorway* and *The Furies* (1950) Anthony Mann's "transitional" films as he moved from his noir period (*T-Men* [1947], *Raw Deal* [1948]) of the late 1940s to his Western genre decade of the 1950s. Mann directed a series of films in the late 1940s and early 1950s with startlingly similar themes involving illegal or out-of-control circulation (of money, laborers, women, and guns), racial boundaries, and masculine bonds: *T-Men* deals with undercover Treasury agents tracking a counterfeit ring; *Border Incident* (1949) with undercover Immigration and Naturalization Service agents tracking illegal immigrant papers and migrant workers; *Winchester 73* (1950) with the circulation of a much-desired rifle; *The Furies* with a rancher who pays his workers with his own currency; and *Devil's Doorway*. In *Devil's Doorway*, the term of circulation—the focus of each character's desire—is not a movable thing like guns, money, or paper but rather a place, Sweet Meadows, that each wishes to see as "home." At issue is title to the land. As in *Winchester 73,* Indians are excluded from the economy of buying and selling the object of desire, and a woman circulates as a metaphor for that object. The land is spoken of as female in the film: "She's pretty," and "our mother, Sweet Meadows." The "ache for home" in *Devil's Doorway* suggests the "yearning" for the "land-as-Mother" that Annette Kolodny terms the "American pastoral impulse" (153–54). Lance's absent mother heightens his sense of the land-as-mother and of his attachment to the land, just as Orrie's absent father justifies her occupation as a lawyer. The interracial romance between Orrie and Lance cannot take place because both the narrative logic of the film—the exclusion of the Indian character from access to woman and land—and the external logic of the Production Code prohibit it.[26] *Devil's Doorway* voices a postwar longing for an uncontested home but reveals that imagined home/land (both familial and national in scale) to be fraught with private and institutional corruption.

Each of Anthony Mann's transitional films deals with what Richard Slotkin calls the Western's "transgression of the borders," specifically in terms of racial borders between whites and Mexicans or Native Americans. In *T-Men* and *Border Incident,* undercover agents marked as ethnically Other are forced to watch their white partners killed, sacrifices that allow each sting to succeed. Unlike the classic Western in which nonwhite characters represent the "dark" forces on the frontier and in the psyche, *Devil's Doorway* also resembles film noir in its exploration of the corruption inherent in settler society, particularly white men, in the identity crisis of the protagonist, and in the uneasy feeling of a world out of balance. The film helped shape Mann's impact on the Western genre, especially on the development of the "psychological" and later "revisionist" Western. The film noir movement is often attributed to cultural anxieties about the new power of women as they entered the workforce, to the sometimes unacknowledged troubles of returned World War II veterans, and to the fragmentation of a country that previously had been unified by the war effort (Place; Krutnik). African Americans and Native Americans also entered the workforce in great numbers during the war, and they too were pushed out of many industries when white soldiers returned to claim their jobs. Perhaps the heightening of racial tensions at the end of the war—the highly publicized participation of Native Americans in the war and their return to second-class citizenship at home, for example, as well as the civil rights movement—also contributed to noir's "dark" cynicism.[27]

Several critics have noted the resemblance between noir and Western heroes in their shared outsider status, their precarious positioning between law enforcer and lawbreaker, their potentially tragic fate, and their individual codes of honor. Both figures help to maintain a social order from which they do not benefit, according to Edward Recchia, yet "there still remains that essential difference between the films themselves: underlying the Western is an indefatigable sense of optimism; underlying the detective film is a critical vein of cynicism, if not pessimism. In the Western, the frontier is still to be conquered; in the detective film, there is already the smell of a civilization in the early stages of decay" (602–3). This sense of optimism, so apparent in Westerns like *Broken Arrow*, becomes muted and darkened in such "psychological" Westerns as Zinnemann's *High Noon* (1952) and Mann's *Winchester 73*, which question the purity and goodness of both the hero and the community he protects, and later by "revisionist" Westerns, such as Peckinpah's *The Wild Bunch* (1969), Penn's *Little Big Man* (1970), and Eastwood's *High Plains Drifter* (1973). Mann's 1950s Westerns played a pivotal role in developing this more disturbing side of the genre, and *Devil's Doorway*, in particular, was ahead of its time in offering a social critique of the frontier colonization (or "civilizing") process. *Devil's Doorway* combined the noir critique of "civilization in the early stages of decay" with the very process of conquering the frontier so important to the Western. The film becomes a case study of the corruption, prejudice, and greed that pushed forward an agrarian "American Dream" of homestead land and immigrant opportunity.

It is the Homestead Act of 1862 (which arrives in Wyoming with territorial incorporation) that establishes an economy of white settlement, law, and "civilization," and that excludes Lance on the basis of his status as an Indian and a "ward of the government." Lance is barred entirely from participation in this settlement order; although he is rich, he cannot buy or own his land, and although he has worked the land for more than five years, he cannot stake a claim to it under the Homestead Act. Lance's encounter with this law suggests that his "fitness" or competence in the wilderness (a defining feature of the Western hero) *and* in the capitalist market is irrelevant, because the *system* by which territories and people are incorporated into the nation ensures the survival of hierarchy.[28] Lance is also refused the right of all (white) men in the frontier Western to buy a drink in the saloon. Although his masculinity as a fighter has been proved in the war, the laws that come with territorial incorporation are perceived in the film as emasculating.

Lance Poole/Broken Lance (Robert Taylor) meets Orrie Masters (Paula Raymond).

The very idea of a treaty or negotiation becomes associated with femininity in the film, and Orrie Masters, Lance's romantic interest, comes to represent both colonizing "master" and feminine object, both home and its invasion, both a reasonable voice of compromise and tolerance and an unstable potential for betrayal. Orrie fulfills Western and noir female roles, taking on the characteristics of both Charlotte Carmody and Letha in Guy Trosper's story "The Drifter." Although she is a powerful character in the film because she is a lawyer, Lance first finds her *dusting* her books, rather than reading them, and she seems as interested in putting iodine on a cut he received in a bar fight as in filing a homestead claim for him. This scene establishes both Orrie's femininity and her infringement on the masculine province of the law. Lance's wound, which comes from his fight with Ike in a bar where territorial law has banned the sale of liquor to Indians, suggests both Lance's fighting prowess and his ultimately tragic fate. Orrie's status as a woman enables her to cross boundaries, which she continually does as a negotiator between the town and Sweet Meadows. Like the "good woman" of the Western, Orrie is chaste, associated with "civilizing" professions like the law, and in the end allied also to the cavalry when she calls them in to stop the fighting. But this act also

Sheep and cattle crowd the streets of Medicine Bow, Wyoming.

links her to the femme fatale of film noir; by summoning the cavalry, she betrays Lance, ruins his chances of winning the fight, and breaks her promise to tell no one that reservation Shoshones are hiding on Lance's ranch at Sweet Meadows. Orrie circulates among men as she attempts to negotiate compromises between the men vying for title to the land; her loyalty is made suspect by virtue of her sex. Her failure to negotiate a peaceful settlement offers the clearest example of a breakdown of cross-cultural negotiation: in one scene, she works to convince the men of Medicine Bow to sign a petition to change the law to accommodate Indian homesteaders, but her efforts are undermined as news of the first acts of violence in the conflict reach the town.

The land itself is associated with "home" and with mothering. Sweet Meadows seems to represent both what is deeply familiar to and desired by all men, and what must be kept from "outsiders" with great violence. Orrie's mother, on hearing about Jimmy's (Lance's nephew's) Shoshone rite of passage into manhood, declares, "That boy's got a good home." Lance clearly sees Sweet Meadows, his ancestral place of origin, as home and as mother: "It's hard to explain the way an Indian feels about the Earth . . . it's the pumping of our blood, it's the love we've got to have. My father said the Earth is our Mother. I was raised in this valley; now I'm part of it, like the mountains and the hills, the deer, the pine trees and the wind. Deep in my heart I know I belong. If we lose it now, we might as well all be dead." In this speech, Lance associates relocation away from the land with disappearing. The film engages the well-used trope of the "vanishing American," but Lance's connection between losing the land and vanishing also presumes a loss of identity and land base as reservation communities were forcibly (dis)integrated.

Lance's enemy, the lawyer Verne Coolan, also wishes to see Sweet Meadows as home. When trying to provoke Lance to fight in the bar, he tells his hired gun about Sweet Meadows: "It's like the laugh of a beautiful woman," he says. "It's what all men dream of when they ache for home." Coolan's lust for land-as-female is sexual rather than familial. Later, when convincing the sheep-herders to stake a claim to Sweet Meadows, Coolan says, "Through that pass the range never dries up, the mountains keep the wind out. There's a water hole in there big enough to float a clipper ship, and the grass is belly high on a steer. Oh, it's a place for home. I'd like to live there myself." And when the Shoshones flee the reservation and ask to stay at Sweet Meadows, Lance translates their request to Orrie: "They want a place to live, they want a home." Finally, as Orrie desperately tries to convince Lance to compromise with the sheepherders, she says, "They have a right to live. It's just as terrifying for them to be without a home as it is for you."

Orrie is not the only metaphor for the land. The sheepherders, seeking a home for themselves and their livestock, are always on the move in search of permanent grazing for their starving flocks. The "reservation Shoshones" who hide at Lance's ranch are also linked to the land as "home," and they too circulate—illegally. They flee from the reservation, saying that conditions there are so terrible that "we will die, but we will never go back to the reservation." In the film, the parallel groups of displaced people—the sheepherders and Shoshones—have no inherent dislike for one another. In fact, their competing need to possess Sweet Meadows as their home suggests that they have much in common, as Orrie argues. But the scene in which the herders' sheep and Lance's cattle attempt (and fail) to share the same street in town implies that different "stock" cannot share a home, just as Orrie and Lance cannot overcome their racial differences to make a home together. To the extent that the Shoshone cattlemen and Scotch-Irish immigrant sheepmen represent nonwhite

Lance prepares to defend his ancestral home.

and white men, especially returning World War II soldiers, these scenes point to postwar anxieties over disunity and competition over resources between groups coded as racially different. How can a nation of different "kinds" come together to make a home? The use of livestock as racial metaphors is even more pronounced in earlier versions of the script. In a May 1948 version, the mixed-blood Ira Coffee explains his fear of living on a reservation: "How'd you like it? You got a red hide, so your law says get into the corral with the rest of the animals! . . . We'll turn you from a bull into an ox!" (Trosper, Script). This speech to the lawyer Orrie equates reservations with dehumanization, and confinement with castration. In a scene deleted from the final script, Lance's father points out a new, all-white Hereford bull (Herefords are red cattle with white marks on the chest and head) and claims that it will "help raise a finer breed of cattle" (Kopp).[29] The whiteness of the "red" bull clearly represents Lance's assimilated status and the possibility of racial mixture.

Mann depicts Lance's transformation from "good Indian" to "bad Indian" through the classical Hollywood technique of repetition and variation. Orrie enters Lance's cabin in parallel scenes to ask him to compromise with the sheepherders, and later with the cavalry. In each scene they stand facing one another in a two-shot framed by the window of Lance's cabin. But in the latter scene, the cabin is a shambles: fallen pieces of wood make jagged X marks across the window, and the air is full of smoke, registering visually what Lance's father says at the beginning of the film, that Indians are "doomed" because they are surrounded by whites. This scene reverses the iconography of the classical Western in which the settlers' homesteads lie in smoking ruins. In a narrative treatment that links women and the land through the image of the home, the destruction of white settlements in the Western usually provokes the male hero to violent, often vigilante, action in revenge, as it does Ethan Edwards in *The Searchers* (1956), but in *Devil's Doorway* the destruction of the Shoshone settlement puts "a seal on the peace." As Lance says, "We're all gone."

Also parallel are two bar scenes at the Big Horn Saloon in town. The film opens, as do many Westerns, with a lone rider in the desert. As Lance rides into town a dog barks at him, a codified moment in the genre that indicates the rider's threatening, outsider status (as does the dog barking at Scar in *The Searchers* [1956], and the dog that slinks away from Wilson [Jack Palance] in *Shane* [1953]). We see that the rider is wearing a cavalry uniform. The stranger turns out to be the prodigal son returned home, and the old-timers welcome him by buying him a drink. His welcome is interrupted, though, by racist comments from a shadowy figure in the foreground. The insults serve as a warning that the masculine, egalitarian spirit of the old West—and metaphorically of World War II—will give way to a hierarchical "law and order" when the lawyers and settlers come. The scene is shot from the far end of the bar; the audience sees the three men drinking in the background, and the bar dominates the screen. The figure in the foreground—the lawyer Coolan—drinks alone and watches the men. His position as spectator mirrors that of the audience and is an example of how, as Ann Kaplan has said in another context, "Even within stories about [the United States] . . . Hollywood films mimicked the 'imperial gaze' of people who traveled to cultures in different lands" (64).

Later in the film, five years have passed and Lance has become a wealthy, successful cattleman, having combined the traditionally opposing roles of cowboy, Indian, and cavalryman. On the day he deposits $18,000 in the bank and tries to buy Zeke, the sheriff and an old friend, a drink at the saloon, he encounters the territorial law forbidding sale of alcoholic beverages to Indians. The scene is shot from the same perspective: Coolan—now with Ike, a hired gunslinger—watches the drama from the foreground in the crowded bar. Ike

Courtesy of Eddie Brandt's Saturday Matinee, Los Angeles, California.

Lance fights with Ike, the gunslinger.

fires trick shots at Lance, and during the ensuing fistfight, Coolan watches with intense interest and pleasure. Low-key lighting predominates, heightened by flashes of lightning. The bar scenes are the most noir in the film, with their claustrophobic atmosphere emphasizing Lance's entrapment by Coolan and by the townspeople who crowd around to watch the fight. The scene renders an unusually strong use of the expressionist tradition in the Western through John Alton's cinematography, which gives the bar's interior an urban, tautly ominous feel. The bar itself overwhelms the scene visually as it marks foreground and background, creating oblique lines that express Lance's growing realization that the peace he fought for will not be his to enjoy.[30]

This scene is the centerpiece of the film; the destruction that is personal and intimate in the saloon becomes epic in scale as Lance fights the sheepherders over Sweet Meadows. Coolan's absorption in the spectacle of the fight is such that he leans forward and knocks over his liquor bottle. This display of waste reveals the hypocrisy of the law denying the sale of liquor to Indians and at the same time foreshadows the shot of liquor Lance will throw in the face of the vanquished Ike. The act also alludes to the waste of Lance's life at the end of the film: blood, too, will be spilled to satisfy Coolan's—and the viewer's—desire for visual pleasure. Coolan's voyeurism fetishizes the racialized masculine body, as did his hostile gaze at the film's beginning.[31] Like Letha in Guy Trosper's original short story, Coolan finds pleasure in inciting men to fight. Like the banker in *Stagecoach* (1939), he represents a self-righteous and corrupt eastern "civilization" invading the rough, democratic purity of the old West; props such as his elegant liquor glass (distinct from other men's shot glasses) mark him as a city slicker. Coolan's delight in violence-as-performance reveals his own underlying fraudulence, and indeed he lies to the sheepherders to orchestrate a conflict. His desire to witness violence—and his gratification in the processes of destruction—drives the narrative. In contrast, Lance is here indicated as "authentic": he always tells the truth, stands by his word, is unwilling to compromise. His authenticity is heightened by his status as an Indian, as much a moral barometer and symbol of the uncorrupted as a sign of menace in the film.

The film engages in an "imperial gaze" by adopting Coolan's point of view in several key scenes, including the opening bar scene and his death at Lance's hands during the vigilante attack on Sweet Meadows. At the same time, the film critiques this gaze by vilifying Coolan's avid desire for colonizing and genocidal violence against the Shoshone people. The possessive gaze itself becomes a term of circulation: First Lance gazes on Sweet Meadows when he returns from the war, but later Orrie's gaze predominates as she becomes a witness to the male contest over the land. Finally, as Lance falls forward in death and in surrender, the young cavalry leader looks toward the "Devil's Doorway" pass into Sweet Meadows, and the camera (and thus the audience) assumes his point of view as both possessor and eyewitness.[32]

Instead of seeing an assuring future for both assimilation and the reservation system, as *Broken Arrow* promises for the Apache, viewers of *Devil's Doorway* witness the costuming equivalent of the stereotyped reversion to savagery in Lance. Visually, Lance is coded as a hero by his white hat, while Coolan and Ike wear black hats, marks of villainy since the early silent Westerns; but here the racialized "colors" of the classical Western are reversed, and a "dark" man wears a white hat. He first appears in his full cavalry uniform and later wears cowboy clothes; as the film progresses, a silver belt, headband, and beaded necklace suggest that Lance has become more identified with his Shoshone culture. Even his skin color seems to darken over the course of the film. Lance's costume changes narrate the failure of assimilation visually, linking his reestablished Indian identity to a long-standing stereotype in literature and silent film that Indians educated at boarding school or in the military will go "back to the blanket" upon return to their families and tribes.[33] Such public and governmental suspicions of "false assimilation" in terms of retained ethnic difference imply parallel fears of "counterfeit" patriotism. Lance's return to the cavalry costume at his surrender is a jarring reminder that he arrived home as a cavalry soldier as well as an Indian. Had he remained assimilated and kept his allegiance to the military, abandoning the reservation Shoshones who sought refuge on his ranch, Lance would not have had to contend with the U.S. Cavalry, but the film's politics do not allow Lance to survive *as a Shoshone* or to maintain his allegiance to the tribal nation as well as the United States. In taking in the escaped Shoshones, he seals his fate. The film's title, *Devil's Doorway*—the pass into Sweet Meadows—indicates Lance's double bind; his liminal status as an assimilated Indian relegates him to a hellish no-man's-land rather than the sweet meadows of home.[34] In the penultimate scene, Lance touches his father's pipe and his old cavalry uniform, emblems of his compound identity. Both pipe and uniform metonymically invoke the treaty-making process, but as these signs *come together* in Lance they can no longer function as markers of a "measured separatism" between nations. In this film, the postwar nation ultimately cannot accommodate a man who assimilates but retains his difference, who is Indian *and* homesteader *and* cavalry.

Devil's Doorway allows us to view postwar American culture beginning to examine its history of "de-tribalization," land theft, and relocation, even as it entered a new phase of assimilationist policy. The powerful narrative combination of the returning veteran figure and the cross-racial romance in *Devil's Doorway* brings together the construction (or destruction) of both nation and family. The Indian veteran returns from a war only to try to begin a family in the midst of another war—a race war—at home. Cross-racial romance represents a desire for an integrated family, home, and nation that transcends racial and cultural differences, but the film depicts men and women whose private lives are undone by their participation in the public work of frontier colonization, and a land that is only made "pure" through sacrificial, racially marked violence. In its complex figurations of postwar America as "home" to native people, to returning war veterans, and to powerful women, *Devil's Doorway* manifests a constellation of tensions surrounding the U.S. government's contemporary reinterpretations of its relationships with minority communities and tribal nations.

NOTES

I am grateful to Susan White, Larry Evers, Barbara Babcock, Chadwick Allen, and the editors of *Film & History* for their comments on earlier drafts of this chapter, and to Barbara Hall and Ned Comstock at the Academy of Motion Picture Arts and Sciences Margaret Herrick Library and the University of Southern California's Special Collections for assistance with archival materials. I would also like to thank Claire Brandt and Eddie Brandt's Saturday Matinee in Los Angeles, California, for providing the stills.

1. See discussions of the political subtexts of "pro-Indian" Westerns in Lehman, Lenihan, Mortimer, Petlewski, and Slotkin. For example, Richard Slotkin and Paul Petlewski argue that *Devil's Doorway* uses the Western genre as a "disguise" that, although covertly and with compromises, allows the filmmakers to treat such sensitive material as American racism and anti-Semitism. Westerns of the 1950s represented both conservative cultural values and a liberal, counterculture backlash against those values. Slotkin divides 1950s cold war Westerns into two categories, the "Cult of the Cavalry," which offers masculine, military, and heroic responses to nonwhite threats to American values, and the "Cult of the Indian," which uses the Western as a site for liberal critiques of racial and social prejudice and of right-wing politics. *Devil's Doorway*'s comments on social prejudice came at a time between the American solidarity of World War II and the violent focus on domestic issues of race during the mid-1950s civil rights movement. However, the slow gains made in the civil rights movement occurred simultaneously with an erosion of rights for native peoples. The Supreme Court outlawed segregated schools in *Brown v. Board of Education* in 1954; the Montgomery bus boycott took place in 1955; and Congress passed the Civil Rights Act to address inequalities in voting rights in 1957. During the same period, legislation undermined or ended services to Indian reservations, terminated federal recognition of tribes and treaty obligations to those tribes, and shifted more tribal lands to white ownership and control. See Jacquelyn Kilpatrick's *Celluloid Indians* for a discussion of the revival of sovereignty issues in the 1960s, 1970s, and 1980s in connection with cinematic representations of Indians.

2. "Termination" is the general term for the series of resolutions and public laws enacted between 1953 and 1961 that sought to dismantle federal trust relationships with native tribes. The policy involved a complex array of legal

strategies and negotiations with specific tribal entities. The Indian Claims Commission was established in 1946 to hear claims cases, in the hope that monetary compensation for land seized in the past would both solve the moral and legal problems of broken treaties and encourage assimilation through onetime per capita payments. The House Concurrent Resolution 108 (passed in 1953 by the Republican Eighty-third Congress) was the first of many congressional actions that terminated federal recognition of tribes, services to those tribes, and supervision of tribal assets, including land. Public Law 280 (1953) initiated a trend toward transferring civil and criminal jurisdiction over Indian lands from federal to state arenas, and throughout the 1950s the Bureau of Indian Affairs ran a "Relocation" program that encouraged native individuals and families to move to urban areas. Excellent and detailed historical information on the Termination and Relocation policies is available in publications by Drinnon, Fixico, Philp, and Wilkinson. See Kilpatrick for a description of Termination policies in relation to Indian Westerns of the 1950s (56).

3. In his recent book *Blood Narrative: Indigenous Identity in American Indian and Maori Literary and Activist Texts*, Allen asserts that indigenous activist writers "re-recognize" treaty discourse, reclaiming its original colonial authority in order to assert sovereignty through the nation-to-nation positioning implicit in treaty agreements. "Indigenous minority redeployments of treaty discourse insist that the dominant powers remember the cross-cultural and cross-national agreements it forged with indigenous nations during previous eras . . . [such redeployments] reinstate and reinvigorate this colonial discourse's original powers of legal enforcement and moral suasion" (19).

4. Quoted in Simmon.

5. A plethora of short "Indian dramas" and "pro-Indian" silent Westerns played in nickelodeons in the first decades of the twentieth century, including such titles as "The Redman's View" (1909, Biograph), "Iola's Promise" (1912, Biograph), and "White Fawn's Devotion" (1910, Pathe Freres). Reform films from the 1920s included *The Last of the Mohicans* (1920, Maurice Tourneur Productions, Associated Producers), *The Vanishing American* (1925, Paramount), and *Redskin* (1929, Schertzinger).

6. See Petlewski's discussion of Lance as a sexual threat.

7. John O'Connor argues that these plot changes, which complicate the story through moral ambiguity and the theme of racial intolerance, "fit the producers' ideas of what the public would buy . . . to enhance its appeal to post-war moviegoers" (47).

8. See Gary Edgerton's discussion of "surface realism" in Michael Mann's *The Last of the Mohicans* (1992). The impulse toward documentary content in Indian Westerns is indicated by the author's foreword to the screenplay for *Broken Arrow*: "Although this is a story film and not a documentary, it would be regrettable if the film did not convey the quality of authenticity present in a documentary history. Both the style of the narration and the selection of the background detail have been directed to achieve these ends" (Maltz).

9. See Deloria's *Playing Indian* for historical case studies and a theoretical discussion of this phenomenon.

10. Chadwick Allen, private correspondence, July 12, 2004. I am much indebted to Allen for this and other insights into the political ramifications of "treaty moments" in Westerns.

11. The film was released at a high point of anticommunist sentiment in the United States. It played in theaters alongside anticommunist films and glorified an assimilationist model for native people but was written by a blacklisted screenwriter. Albert Maltz, who wrote the script for *Broken Arrow,* was one of the Hollywood Ten, who were first blacklisted and then imprisoned; Michael Blankfort acted as his front (Ceplair). In addition to seeing native cultures as deficient or somehow "un-American" in comparison to the nonnative mainstream, many nonnative people associated tribal governments and the reservation system with communism. See Philp, *Termination Revisited;* Embry; Drinnon; and Dippie.

12. Angela Aleiss has argued that *Broken Arrow* reflects the contradictory impulses of Termination policy and early 1950s politics: simultaneous valuation of individual rights and conformity, of cultural pluralism and rapid assimilation. Frank Manchel asserts that the film's distortions of history caused "cultural confusion" that powerfully affected public memory, especially since, as he notes, *Broken Arrow* was the basis for one of the first Western television series.

Many scripts for the series were drafted by none other than Sam Peckinpah, who slipped in references to "the wild bunch" and other projects of his own ("The Poisoner (or 'The Assassin')"). He also evinced strong awareness of the politics of civic identity and voice at stake in representations of Indians. In a 1957 draft of an episode entitled "The Teacher," Cochise chastises the new schoolteacher for inundating Apache youth with American patriotism. His speech resonates with indigenous sovereignty claims and the problem of voice-over in the film *Broken Arrow:* "We asked for what we need—someone to teach numbers and the books— and we get a long-tongued woman who teaches the Apache to say words that have no meaning for them. (imitating sarcastically) We, the people of the United States . . . (then proud and angry) We are not the people of the United States—we are Chiricahua Apaches. Cochise, nor his people, wish to learn the words of a nation which permits us no voice" (Peckinpah, "The Teacher").

13. German propagandists had, according to John Collier, "predicted an Indian uprising in the United States" if Indians were drafted (quoted in Holm 103), but instead Native American patriotism lent credence to the U.S. war effort and provided fodder for U.S. propagandists; according to Tom Holm, "the fact that a nonwhite minority had so unflinchingly thrown itself into the war effort gave the American cause moral legitimacy" (107). Jacquelyn Kilpatrick cites articles in *Collier's* and the *Reader's Digest* from the 1940s that describe the superior outdoor skills, endurance, and "enthusiasm for fighting" of "the red soldier" (50).

14. Angela Aleiss's research on the studio's advice to exhibitors reveals that "gimmicks ranged from teaching viewers how to interpret the various puffs of

smoke signals . . . to building huge bonfires (with the help of the Boy Scouts and Camp Fire Girls)" (62–63). Film producers taught Apache actors (many of them veterans of the armed forces, returned from World War II) how to fit this visual image of themselves. According to Aleiss, "When Daves instructed two Indians to build food coolers, fire grates, and a bough bed in the traditional Apache manner, the men were at a loss. (The problem was solved when 'The Boy Scouts' Handicraft Book' provided the proper explanation)," and "an archery expert had to teach many Apaches to use the bow and arrow" (38).

15. The other film entitled *Broken Arrow* (1996), from director John Woo, maintains the significance of the arrow as a symbol appropriated by the U.S. military: in that film, "Broken Arrow" is the military code for lost nuclear missiles. Noncinematic military terms for weapons include the Cheyenne tank and the Tomahawk missile, again appropriating images of "savage" Indians for the colonizer's military purposes.

16. Essential to my reading of the film is Prats's brilliant analysis of *Broken Arrow* in the context of other Indian Westerns in "His Master's Voice(over): Revisionist Ethos and Narrative Dependence from *Broken Arrow* (1950) to *Geronimo: An American Legend* (1993)" and *Invisible Natives: Myth and Identity in the American Western*.

17. In Elliott Arnold's novel *Blood Brother*, from which *Broken Arrow* was adapted, Sonseeahray thinks of "her body as something to give to him [Jeffords] and she was almost impersonal in her survey" of her physical qualities. She is unconcerned about modesty, as "no Apache youth would ever look at a girl bathing," but the reader can "look" as Arnold's detailed description of Sonseeahray's body unfolds during her own mental assessment (313). She later receives advice that her union with Jeffords will merge cultures: "The new thing you will make will have part of you in it and part of him, as though it were a child" (314). However, as soon as Sonseeahray becomes pregnant and unavailable to Jeffords sexually, she is killed off; no mixed-race child embodies their union.

18. Allen, private correspondence, July 12, 2004.

19. For further discussion of the post–World War II cycle of "pro-Indian" Westerns and their relationship to contemporary Native American issues and to broader issues of ethnicity in 1950s Hollywood films, see articles by Neale and Manchel.

20. Native veterans of World War II returned to find local prejudices still strong in towns bordering reservations, and old laws such as the 1802 federal regulations concerning the sale of alcohol to Indians still in force. Dillon Myer and the BIA consistently blocked tribal attempts to choose lawyers, invoking an 1872 law prohibiting any payment or barter for legal counsel for Indian land claims without BIA approval (Bernstein; Philp, *Termination Revisited*).

21. In 1950, the median income for native men on reservations was $950, compared with $2,218 for black men and $3,780 for white men, with high unemployment rates, overcrowded schools, and high infant mortality contributing

to the alarming conditions on many reservations (Bernstein 149–50). Native Americans were prohibited from voting in state elections in Arizona and New Mexico until 1948.

22. The phrase "domestic dependent nations" originates with Chief Justice Marshall's key definition of the status of native tribes in the Supreme Court's decision in *Johnson and Graham's Lessee v. William McIntosh* (1823).

23. The blurring of distinctions between camps and reservations was intensified by the fact that Japanese Americans were interned on reservation lands in several western states; the BIA had "volunteered Indian lands as sites for the 'colonization of the Japanese'" (Collier, quoted in Bernstein 82).

24. My analysis here also complements structuralist approaches to the Western. Garry Watson has applied René Girard's theories of violence to the Western, suggesting that the "Warrior's Return" at the beginning of many Westerns introduces dangerously impure and contagious violence into the community, and this figure must be sacrificed in order to found or refound the community/nation. Girard describes the figure of the returning war veteran as "the conquering hero who threatens to destroy the liberty of his homeland" through "the contagious nature of the violence encountered by the warrior in battle" (42).

25. Literature and film about native veterans of World War II and other wars frequently depict community hostility toward returning war veterans, and their potential for violence in response: Zane Grey's novel *The Vanishing American* and Seitz's film version starring Richard Dix depict returning Navajo veterans of World War I. N. Scott Momaday's *House Made of Dawn* and Leslie Marmon Silko's *Ceremony* portray traumatized World War II vets recovering through ceremonies of reintegration and renewal in their home communities. Vietnam War veterans return home to internal and external conflict in accounts that narrate wartime and postwar experiences from a native perspective, as in Apache author Leroy TeCube's memoir of his infantry service, *Year in Nam*, and in Philip H. Red Eagle's novellas, published together in the book *Red Earth: A Vietnam Warrior's Journey.*

26. Nicolas Monti, writing about turn-of-the-century photographs from Africa, notes that for white male colonizers "the seduction and conquest of the African woman became a metaphor for the seduction and conquest of Africa" (quoted in Doane 213). The opposite construct in the Americas—a liaison between a native man and white woman—might represent the "conquest and seduction" of land as well as woman. The threat of "miscegenation" in *Devil's Doorway* is one of native integration into white family structures, of native claims to property, and of native permanence rather than disappearance.

27. See Doane's "Dark Continents" for a discussion of psychoanalytic connections between female sexuality and racial difference.

28. See Stanley Corkin's detailed exploration and criticism of the way postwar Westerns (specifically *My Darling Clementine* and *Red River*) dramatize "how men who exhibit the terms of fitness, which are not acquired but appear innate, rightfully rule" (89).

29. Chadwick Allen pointed out the color significance of the reference to Hereford cattle. In a similar fashion in her novel *Ceremony,* Leslie Marmon Silko uses crossbred "spotted cattle" as a metaphor for the protagonist Tayo's mixed-blood ancestry and ability to survive in two worlds.

30. The scene would have been even more violent without the Hays Code. In fact, this is the only scene that the MPAA suggested be cut, due to its excessive brutality. In a memo to Breen in the Hays Office dated February 10, 1950, Robert Vogel claims to have cut 25 percent of the footage in this scene, including "two objectionable kicks."

31. See Willemen's discussion of the "look at the male" in Mann's films as a "fundamentally homosexual voyeurism." Willemen argues that this imaging of the male examines "the operation of classic American cinema itself as a form of spectacle" (211–12) in which images of male ordeal reflect upon themselves as spectacle and identity.

32. I would like to thank Sean Cobb for this insight into the "circulation of the gaze" at the end of the film.

33. *Devil's Doorway* avoids most of the stereotyped "Indian English" of earlier Westerns. Although Lance's father speaks in metaphors, he uses English pronouns and articles grammatically. Although Lance initially insists on speaking English with his father, he and other characters speak the Shoshone language in many scenes late in the film ("Devil's Doorway Indian Dialog").

34. In contrast to Kitses's view that Lance and the Shoshones achieve "victory through death" (44), Tuska views *Devil's Doorway* as "a far more pernicious variety of racism" for its pro-assimilationist stance. According to Tuska, the film's "strong propaganda in favor of one-settlement culture" does not allow Indian characters "cultural integrity—the right to have [their] own culture independent of the white community" (47–48).

WORKS CITED

Aleiss, Angela Maria. "Hollywood's Ideal of Postwar Assimilation: Indian/White Attitudes in 'Broken Arrow.'" M.F.A. thesis, Columbia University, 1985.

Allen, Chadwick. *Blood Narrative: Indigenous Identity in American Indian and Maori Literary and Activist Texts.* Durham, N.C.: Duke University Press, 2002.

———. "Hero with Two Faces: The Lone Ranger as Treaty Discourse." *American Literature* 68 (1996): 609–38.

Arnold, Elliott. *Blood Brother.* 1947. Lincoln: University of Nebraska Press, 1979.

"Arrow." Script file for "Broken Arrow." June 11, 1949. Margaret Herrick Library. Academy of Motion Picture Arts and Sciences, Beverly Hills, California.

Balibar, Etienne. "Racism and Nationalism." In *Race, Nation and Class: Ambiguous Identities,* by Etienne Balibar and Immanuel Wallerstein, 37–67. Translated by Chris Turner. New York: Verso, 1991.

Basinger, Jeanine. "Mann of the West." In *Anthony Mann,* 83–157. Boston: Twayne, 1979.

Berkhofer, Robert F., Jr. *The White Man's Indian: Images of the American Indian from Columbus to the Present.* New York: Vintage/Random House, 1978.

Bernstein, Alison R. *American Indians and World War II: Toward a New Era in Indian Affairs.* Norman: University of Oklahoma Press, 1991.

Brandt, Nat. *Harlem at War: The Black Experience in World War II.* Syracuse, N.Y.: Syracuse University Press, 1996.

Ceplair, Larry. "Who Wrote What??? A Tale of a Blacklisted Screenwriter and His Front." *Cineaste* 18, no. 2 (1991): 18–21.

Corkin, Stanley. "Cowboys and Free Markets: Post–World War II Westerns and U.S. Hegemony." *Cinema Journal* 39, no. 3 (2000): 66–91.

Dayley, Jon P. *Tumpisa (Panamint), Shoshone Dictionary.* University of California Publications in Linguistics, vol. 116. Berkeley: University of California Press, 1989.

Deloria, Philip J. *Playing Indian.* New Haven, Conn.: Yale University Press, 1998.

"Devil's Doorway." Review of *Devil's Doorway. Cue,* November 11, 1950. Clipping file for *Devil's Doorway.* Margaret Herrick Library. Academy of Motion Picture Arts and Sciences, Beverly Hills, California.

Review of *Devil's Doorway. Fortnight,* October 30, 1950. Clipping file for *Devil's Doorway.* Margaret Herrick Library. Academy of Motion Picture Arts and Sciences, Beverly Hills, California.

Review of *Devil's Doorway. Independent Film Journal,* May 20, 1950. Clipping file for *Devil's Doorway.* Margaret Herrick Library. Academy of Motion Picture Arts and Sciences, Beverly Hills, California.

Review of *Devil's Doorway. Variety,* May 15–17, 1950. Clipping file for *Devil's Doorway.* Margaret Herrick Library. Academy of Motion Picture Arts and Sciences, Beverly Hills, California.

"Devil's Doorway Indian Dialog." Ms. D716. MGM Collection. Margaret Herrick Library. Academy of Motion Picture Arts and Sciences, Beverly Hills, California.

Dippie, Brian W. *The Vanishing American: White Attitudes and U.S. Indian Policy.* Lawrence: University Press of Kansas, 1982.

Doane, Mary Ann. "Dark Continents: Epistemologies of Racial and Sexual Difference in Psychoanalysis and the Cinema." In *Femmes Fatales: Feminism, Film Theory, Psychoanalysis,* 209–48. New York: Routledge, 1991.

Drinnon, Richard. *Keeper of Concentration Camps: Dillon S. Myer and American Racism.* Berkeley: University of California Press, 1987.

Dudley, Marjorie. MGM reader's report for "The Drifter." November 18, 1948. MGM Collection. Margaret Herrick Library. Academy of Motion Picture Arts and Sciences, Beverly Hills, California.

Edgerton, Gary. "'A Breed Apart': Hollywood, Racial Stereotyping, and the

Promise of Revisionism in *The Last of the Mohicans.*" *Journal of American Culture* 17, no. 2 (1994): 1–17.

Embry, Carlos B. *America's Concentration Camps: The Facts about Our Indian Reservations Today.* New York: McKay, 1956.

Fixico, Donald L. *Termination and Relocation: Federal Indian Policy, 1945–1960.* Albuquerque: University of New Mexico Press, 1986.

French, Philip. "The Indian in the Western Movie." In *The Pretend Indians: Images of Native Americans in the Movies,* edited by Gretchen M. Bataille and Charles L. P. Silet, 98–111. Ames: Iowa State University Press, 1980.

Girard, René. *Violence and the Sacred.* Baltimore: Johns Hopkins University Press, 1972.

Grey, Zane. *The Vanishing American.* New York: Grosset and Dunlap, 1925.

Holm, Tom. *Strong Hearts, Wounded Souls: Native American Veterans of the Vietnam War.* Austin: University of Texas Press, 1996.

Kaplan, Ann. *Looking for the Other: Feminism, Film and the Imperial Gaze.* New York: Routledge, 1997.

Kilpatrick, Jacquelyn. *Celluloid Indians: Native Americans and Film.* Lincoln: University of Nebraska Press, 1999.

Kitses, Jim. *Horizons West: Anthony Mann, Budd Boetticher, Sam Peckinpah: Studies of Authorship within the Western.* London: Thames and Hudson, 1969.

Kolodny, Annette. *The Lay of the Land: Metaphor as Experience and History in American Life and Letters.* Chapel Hill: University of North Carolina Press, 1975.

Kopp, Francis B. Story synopsis for *Devil's Doorway.* August 11, 1949. MGM Collection. Special Collections, University of Southern California, Los Angeles.

Krutnik, Frank. *In a Lonely Street: Film Noir, Genre, Masculinity.* New York: Routledge, 1991.

Lehman, Peter. "Texas 1868 / America 1956: *The Searchers.*" In *Close Viewings: An Anthology of New Film Criticism,* edited by Peter Lehman, 387–415. Tallahassee: Florida State University Press, 1990.

Lenihan, John H. *Showdown: Confronting Modern America in the Western Film.* Urbana: University of Illinois Press, 1980.

Limerick, Patricia Nelson. *The Legacy of Conquest: The Unbroken Past of the American West.* New York: Norton, 1987.

Maltz, Albert. "Author's Forward." Script for *Broken Arrow.* Academy of Motion Picture Arts and Sciences, Beverly Hills, California.

Manchel, Frank. "Cultural Confusion: *Broken Arrow.*" In *Hollywood's Indian: The Portrayal of the Native American in Film,* edited by Peter C. Rollins and John E. O'Connor, 91–106. Lexington: University Press of Kentucky, 1998.

Momaday, N. Scott. *House Made of Dawn.* 1968. New York: HarperCollins, 1999.

Mortimer, Barbara. "The Captive's Return and the Limits of Community in *The*

Unforgiven, Two Rode Together, and *Comanche Station."* In *Hollywood's Frontier Captives: Cultural Anxiety and the Captivity Plot in American Film,* 49–76. New York: Garland, 2000.

Neale, Steve. "Vanishing Americans: Racial and Ethnic Issues in the Interpretation and Context of Post-war 'Pro-Indian' Westerns." In *Back in the Saddle Again: New Essays on the Western,* edited by Edward Buscombe and Roberta Pearson, 8–28. London: British Film Institute, 1998.

O'Connor, John E. *The Hollywood Indian: Stereotypes of Native Americans in Films.* Trenton: New Jersey State Museum, 1980.

Peckinpah, Sam. "The Poisoner (or 'The Assassin')." Teleplay draft for *Broken Arrow,* January 26, 1957. Academy of Motion Picture Arts and Sciences, Beverly Hills, California.

———. "The Teacher." Teleplay draft for *Broken Arrow,* August 9, 1957. Academy of Motion Picture Arts and Sciences, Beverly Hills, California.

Petlewski, Paul. *"Devil's Doorway* and the Use of Genre as Disguise." In *Transformations in Literature and Film,* edited by Leon Golden, 39–46. Tallahassee: University Press of Florida, 1982.

Philp, Kenneth R., ed. *Indian Self-Rule: First-Hand Accounts of Indian White Relations from Roosevelt to Reagan.* Logan: Utah State University Press, 1995.

———. *Termination Revisited: American Indians on the Trail to Self-Determination, 1933–1953.* Lincoln: University of Nebraska Press, 1999.

Place, Janey. "Women in *Film Noir."* In *Women in Film Noir,* edited by E. Ann Kaplan, 35–67. Revised and expanded edition. London: British Film Institute, 1998.

Prats, Armando José. "His Master's Voice(over): Revisionist Ethos and Narrative Dependence from *Broken Arrow* (1950) to *Geronimo: An American Legend* (1993)." *ANQ* 9, no. 3 (Summer 1996): 15–29.

———. *Invisible Natives: Myth and Identity in the American Western.* Ithaca, N.Y.: Cornell University Press, 2002.

Pye, Douglas. "The Collapse of Fantasy: Masculinity and the Westerns of Anthony Mann." In *The Book of Westerns,* edited by Douglas Pye and Ian Cameron, 167–73. New York: Continuum, 1996.

Recchia, Edward. "Film Noir and the Western." *Centennial Review* 40 (1996): 601–14.

Red Eagle, Philip H. *Red Earth: A Vietnam Warrior's Journey.* Duluth, Minn.: Holy Cow Press, 1997.

Silko, Leslie Marmon. *Ceremony.* New York: Penguin, 1977.

Simmon, Scott. Review of *Devil's Doorway.* March 1989. Clipping file for *Devil's Doorway.* Margaret Herrick Library. Academy of Motion Picture Arts and Sciences, Beverly Hills, California.

Skerry, Philip, and Brenda Berstler. "You Are What You Wear: The Role of Western Costume in Film." In *The Material World in American Popular Film,* edited by

Paul Loukides and Linda K. Fuller, 77–86. Bowling Green, Ohio: Bowling Green State University Popular Press, 1993.

Slotkin, Richard. *Gunfighter Nation: The Myth of the Frontier in Twentieth-Century America*. Norman: University of Oklahoma Press, 1998.

TeCube, Leroy. *Year in Nam: A Native American Soldier's Story*. Lincoln: University of Nebraska Press, 1999.

Trosper, Guy. "The Drifter." Ms. MGM Collection. Special Collections, University of Southern California, Los Angeles.

———. Outline for balance of *Devil's Doorway*. December 8, 1948. Ms. D711. Margaret Herrick Library. Academy of Motion Picture Arts and Sciences, Beverly Hills, California.

———. Script for *Devil's Doorway*. May 20, 1948. Ms. MGM Collection. Special Collections, University of Southern California, Los Angeles.

Tuska, John. *The American West in Film: Critical Approaches to the Western*. Lincoln: University of Nebraska Press, 1988.

Umland, Sam. "The Representation of the Native American in the Hollywood Western." *Platte Valley Review* 19 (1991). 49–70.

Vogel, Robert. Memo to Breen. February 10, 1950. MPAA file on *Devil's Doorway*. Margaret Herrick Library. Academy of Motion Picture Arts and Sciences, Beverly Hills, California.

Watson, Garry. "The Western: The Genre That Engenders a Nation." *Cineaction* 46 (1998): 3–10.

Wilkinson, Charles F. *American Indians, Time, and the Law: Native Societies in a Modern Constitutional Democracy*. New Haven, Conn.: Yale University Press, 1987.

Willemen, Paul. "Anthony Mann: Looking at the Male." In *The Western Reader*, edited by Jim Kitses and Gregg Rickman, 209–12. New York: Limelight Editions, 1998.

GIANT HELPS AMERICA RECOGNIZE THE COST OF DISCRIMINATION
A Lesson of World War II

The years during and following World War II witnessed a considerable improvement in the social status of America's minorities. Their contributions to the war effort, through military service and war-related work on the home front, proved invaluable. More than 2.5 million black men served in the military. Approximately 500,000 Mexican American troops also participated and earned medals (DeLeon 116). Other minorities served as well, while females from these diverse groups actively volunteered at home. Consequently, support for the civil rights of American minorities grew. In the war's aftermath, knowledge of the extent of Hitler's genocidal campaign intensified positive interest in the rights of minorities. This was quite a reversal of prior attitudes. Mexicans, for example, were believed to be a vastly inferior ethnic group. During congressional hearings on Mexican immigration in 1930, one eugenicist claimed that most Mexicans were promiscuous, lazy, hungry dogs who wallowed in human filth (Hendler 130).

Ever in search of new material, Hollywood could not help but notice the changing social climate. As a result, some filmmakers after the war made a conscious effort to expose racism and discrimination. Part of Hollywood's social film era, the resulting films challenged antiethnic and racist attitudes that still permeated much of American society. *Imitation of Life* (1959) is an example of such a film. Telling the story of two single mothers, one white and the other black, the film follows their friendship as their daughters grow to adulthood. Aside from the agreeable interracial friendship between the two women, what makes this picture extraordinary is its depiction of "passing for white." When the black mother's daughter attempts to pass as white, she is confronted by extreme and violent racial prejudice. However, the picture is meant not as a condemnation but as an explanation of what it was like to be "nearly" white in the 1940s and 1950s. Another film, *Sayonara* (1957), depicts the challenge faced by American soldiers and their Japanese wives when American military officers invoke a policy against interracial marriage.

Imitation of Life and *Sayonara* were just two of several post–World War II era films that focused on minority issues, including discrimination. These films provided audience members with subject matter many had never seen before. They were socially conscious films that afforded viewers the opportunity to peer into the lives of minorities—albeit from a safe distance. When a filmmaker cared enough, the minority characters depicted in his film were multidimensional and their stories explored in greater detail. This was quite a departure from early film stereotypes. Released in 1956, *Giant* was such a film. Based on Edna Ferber's novel and under the direction of George Stevens, *Giant* was historically significant because it was the first major motion picture to explore the effects of Jim Crow legislation on Mexicans in Texas. It also was a film greatly shaped by the experiences of its primary creators—Ferber and Stevens.

In her 1939 autobiography, *A Peculiar Treasure*, Pulitzer Prize–winning author Edna Ferber described various personal encounters with anti-Semitism. The daughter of a Hungarian-born Jewish shopkeeper, Ferber recalled a particularly vexing incident at a dinner party she attended as a young woman in Ironwood, Michigan. At a party held shortly after Hitler's rise to power in Germany, the American German-born host boldly declared his support of the Nazi regime. As Ferber described it, she "heard the incredible balderdash and vicious drool with which the German fanatic [Hitler] had fed his enslaved people" (Ferber 371–72). Unable to maintain silence in the face of such animosity, she announced that she was a Jew. Stated Ferber, "I saw such hatred as I never before have seen on human countenances" (372). Forty miles from the nearest railroad, she was forced to remain in the home until transportation could be provided the next morning. Quite uneasy in her situation, Ferber locked her bedroom door that night and placed a chair-back tightly under the doorknob. "In the morning they did not speak to me," added Ferber (372). Repeatedly a victim of discrimination, Ferber mirrored such encounters in her writing.

Several years after Ferber's dinner party incident, Hollywood director George Stevens confronted the effects of Hitler's anti-Semitic campaign firsthand. As a serviceman during World War II, Stevens was assigned the duty of filming the liberation of prisoners from the Dachau concentration camp. The images he encountered shocked him and permeated many of his later films. Prior to Stevens's war experiences, the bulk of his work consisted of lighthearted, romantic fare. Following the war, his films reflected the beliefs of a man much more concerned with the motives of individuals and the dark side of human nature. His change in artistic direction ultimately united Stevens with Ferber in the film production of Ferber's 1952 novel *Giant*—a fictional account of life in twentieth-century Texas, including the nonfictional problem of discrimination against the state's Mexican populace.[1]

THE NOVEL: BEGINNINGS AND CONTROVERSY

The product of thirteen years of research, including several excursions to the region, Ferber's *Giant* evolved from the writer's interest in the "larger-than-life aura of everything Texan and the lore of the West" (Hendler 115–16). During one of her trips Ferber accompanied a Corpus Christi, Texas, doctor named Hector P. Garcia on his rounds. Primarily a physician for the Mexican community, Garcia allowed Ferber to communicate with his patients about their lives and experiences. Through such dialogue and observance, Ferber gained a deeper understanding of Mexican life in Texas (Graham 59–60). By communicating on a personal level with many Mexican Texans, Ferber likely acquired abundant material detailing Mexican and Anglo conflicts. Already sensitive toward racial and ethnic discrimination on a personal level, Ferber made the plight of Mexicans in Texas a central theme of her epic novel. Simultaneously, she exposed the land devastation, racial brutality, and misogyny inherent in the American myth of nation-building (Hendler 129).

Once published in 1952, *Giant* quickly achieved bestseller status, becoming a Book-of-the-Month Club selection in October of that year. The following year Reader's Digest Condensed Books published it as an abridged edition. Readers across the nation were fascinated by Ferber's saga depicting the wealthy Benedict clan—a Texas ranching family. Many Texans, however, were less than pleased with the novel. Offering scathing criticism of the discrimination and cruel treatment of Mexicans, *Giant* was disliked by many readers in the Lone Star State. Texans "felt impugned by Ferber's descriptions of their state as a carnival of wealth for flamboyant cattle and oil barons and a seedbed of race prejudice against Mexican Americans" (Hendler 116). Her depiction of racist characters and rampant social injustice, including the manipulation of Mexican votes during elections, intensified animosity toward the novel and its author (131). "Ferber herself reported receiving hundreds of letters that ranged from choleric to vicious; some suggested she be shot or lynched for maligning their state" (116).

THE NOVEL AS A FILM?

When talk of the development of a film based on the novel began to circulate, those opposed to the idea seemed in the majority. The *Saturday Review* noted that "the book made news by irking a considerable number of Texans," and many could not see how the film version would "fail to do the same" (28). *Newsweek* predicted, "*Giant*'s racial-segregation theme will rile many a Texan and many another" (112). The opinions of Mexican Texans were negligible. After learning that a film version of the novel was in production, one Beaumont man told a Hollywood reporter, "If you make and show that damn picture, we'll shoot the screen full of holes" (Graham 60).

Rather than halting production plans, the controversy caused by the novel convinced Hollywood executives of the box-office potential of such a project. Additionally, the story's depiction of minority discrimination was timely. Two years after the publication of the novel, the Supreme Court ruled that segregation was unconstitutional in the now-infamous *Brown v. Board of Education* (1954). Although the *Brown* decision involved black students in Topeka, Kansas, it nevertheless drew attention to minority issues across the nation. *Giant*'s focus on discrimination against and ill-treatment of Mexicans was just the sort of story Hollywood was looking for after the *Brown* decision. Led by producer and director George Stevens, in consultation with Edna Ferber, film production began in 1955.

Still concerned with the negative response the novel had evoked, Stevens and crew toned down the book's most criticized material. As Don Graham noted, "By greatly softening Ferber's indictment of social and economic oppression of Mexicans, the film left its audience with a far more affectionate portrait of Texas than did the novel" (60). Indeed, following its 1956 release, *Giant* was embraced by most Texans. Movie theaters were packed to capacity for screenings, and the film made millions at the box office. *Giant*'s theme song was played at Texas high school football games, and 1961 gubernatorial candidate John Connally used the tune as his campaign anthem. By adopting a subdued approach to the novel's more controversial topics, *Giant*'s creators safeguarded their investment while ensuring that their message against discrimination reached a mass audience.

Deconstructing the Film: Themes and Dialogue

Ferber's concern with the unjust treatment of minorities, combined with that of Stevens, is clearly visible in the motion picture *Giant*. What becomes evident from the moment the film begins is that the racist attitudes expressed by characters in the film are by no means shared by the film's creators (Griffith 19). Despite the "watered-down" nature of the script, the film maintained the book's viewpoint that anti-Mexican racism was a problem in Texas. *Giant* was intended as a social critique of racism. Many films have since tried but failed to accomplish the same goals. The key to *Giant*'s success was its framework. By placing Mexicans in direct opposition to members of the wealthy, Anglo Benedict family, Stevens revealed the differences in the lives of minority and majority groups. In this manner Ferber and Stevens demonstrated that Mexicans in Texas endured years of discrimination, while families like the Benedicts prospered from the Mexicans' suffering.

Although the precise date is not specified, the Texas epic seems to begin in the mid-1920s. As the film opens, Bick Benedict (Rock Hudson) has just arrived at a Maryland family's estate to purchase a horse. Bick returns to Texas with the horse and a new wife—the estate owner's daughter Leslie (Elizabeth Taylor). Leslie is opinionated and intelligent; one of Bick's first encounters with her involves a discussion of the Mexican War (1846–1848), in which her thoughts on the matter shock Bick. Her statement, "We really stole Texas, didn't we, Mr. Benedict? I mean, away from Mexico," leaves Bick flabbergasted. He replies, "You're catching me a bit early to start joking, Miss Leslie." Leslie's questioning of the doctrine of Manifest Destiny seems almost traitorous to the native Texan and future patriarch. To Bick and many of his contemporaries, Texas and the West "functioned historically as a repository for white America's claims to a unique national identity based on rugged individualism, manifest destiny, and empire building" (Hendler 120).

After Bick and Leslie's arrival in Texas, the plot focuses on Leslie's adaptation and her attempts to bring "civilization" to Reata, the Benedicts' ranch. On Leslie's first day at the ranch, Bick is bothered by her attempts to befriend the Mexican help:

> BICK: You shouldn't behave like that—making a fuss over those people. You're a Texan now.
> LESLIE: Well, is that a state of mind? I'm still myself.
> BICK: You're my wife, honey. You're a Benedict.
> LESLIE: I still have a mind of my own. Elsewhere being gracious is acceptable.
> BICK: Well, we're gracious but . . .
> LESLIE: Fine thing, us quarreling with the rice still in our hair.

The scene ends with both Bick and Leslie backing down from a potential argument, but this issue is one they will continue to face.

Leslie is soon introduced to Bick's pugnacious sister, Luz (Mercedes McCambridge), who, in her own words, "knows how to handle Mexicans!" Ironically, after Luz is injured in a freak accident, Mexican house servants, the very people she looks down on, are shown huddled in a hallway praying for her recovery. Their prayers are unsuccessful, and after her death a new problem emerges when the Benedict clan discovers that Luz has left a portion of Benedict property to a former ranch hand, Jett Rink (James Dean). Jett also happens to be Bick's rival; Bick prefers that Texas remain a ranching state, whereas Jett believes in the promise of a developing oil industry. A conversation between Leslie and Jett reveals early twentieth-century racist attitudes:

> LESLIE: Jett, the other people around here, why don't they help themselves like you've done?
> JETT: Well, now when you say other people what do you mean?

Leslie tells him about a recent visit she has made to a nearby Mexican village, the sickness and poverty she encountered there, and the sickly baby named Angel she helped save. Jett, who resents being placed in the same category as Mexicans, responds, "Oh, that bunch of wetbacks. Well, I hope you don't go getting me mixed up with none of them. I'm just as much a Texan as Bick Benedict is. I'm no wetback." Bick shares Jett's attitude, and he threatens to leave Leslie if she interferes again.

The story then jumps forward several years to a World War II era Christmas party at the Benedict home. Bick and Leslie's three children are now in their late teens. The Mexican baby Leslie helped save, Angel (Sal Mineo), is an adult and joins the U.S. Army. At the party he is announced as the first serviceman from the Benedict ranch; this news disturbs Bick because he perceives his own son Jordy (Dennis Hopper) as somewhat weak. Unfortunately, in both the film and the novel, Angel is killed in action during the war. His heroic deeds result in a posthumous Medal of Honor. Film and novel diverge, however, on the matter of Angel's burial. Ferber boldly condemns racism in American society by incorporating a white undertaker who "refuses to handle [Angel's] burial because he is Mexican American" (Hendler 131–32). While Stevens pays homage to Mexican American military service in the war, the film does not include the undertaker or his sentiments. Stevens instead chose to concentrate more on the honor involved in Angel's service to his country—including images of his flag-draped coffin in the burial scene.

At the same Christmas party at which Angel's enlistment is announced, Jordy meets his future wife, Juana (Elsa Cárdenas), a Mexican. Their marriage leads to a host of problems for the Benedicts, including an ethnically mixed grandson they must learn to accept. Fortunately, by the film's conclusion the members of the Benedict clan realize that Texas belongs to both its Anglo and its Mexican citizens—but there is adversity along the way.

Miscegenation: A Problem or Solution?

Miscegenation was a key theme implemented in the film's depiction of discrimination. This was, by far, the most controversial subject examined by Stevens. The *New Yorker* considered the "Mexican race problem a fierce issue" for the film (178). The "problem" revolves around the marriage between Bick's son Jordy and a Mexican nurse, Juana. Although the relationship between the couple is portrayed as loving, they must overcome numerous obstacles. One of the film's strongest attacks against racism occurs when Juana enters an upscale hair salon, after having made the appointment using her married name, Benedict. The salon staff is shocked when she arrives. At first they try to ignore her, but when she begins to complain, they tell her they are merely following the orders of the salon's owner and that she "should have gone to Sanchez's across town where they do her people." Following a phone call from

The marriage ceremony of Jordy (Dennis Hopper) and Juana (Elsa Cárdenas), a merging of two vastly different cultural backgrounds.

Juana, Jordy appears at the salon and lets the staff know just what he thinks of their policy against Mexicans. A few choice words and some broken glass later, he and Juana depart. In contrast to the film, the novel raises tensions a bit more by having Jordy "shoot up" the beauty parlor in his rage.

Although *Giant* was praised by most critics for its effort to denounce racism, the film's depiction of miscegenation was often criticized for failing to step outside established boundaries. Like similar films of the era, *Giant* portrayed a relationship between a white/Anglo male and a minority group female. It was still taboo to depict a love relationship between a white/Anglo female and a minority group male. According to Linda K. Fuller and Paul Loukides, "The social unease in matters of race is reflected in the typical movie pattern of mixed couples being composed of white males and ethnic women, rather than ethnic males and white women" (4). In this respect, *Giant* did not risk violating society's conventions. However, in depicting the plight faced by an ethnically mixed couple in 1950s Texas, the film was unique.

Courtesy of Photofest.

Jordy (Dennis Hopper) confronts a beauty parlor's staff after they refuse Juana service because she is a Mexican.

STOCK CHARACTERS REINFORCE CULTURAL GAP

Several film techniques augment the story line. The use of stock characters was particularly effective. Reviewers criticized *Giant*'s creators for casting similar-looking individuals in the roles of Mexican servants. However, these characters provided a compellingly different image from that of the Anglo characters of the Benedict family. Dark-skinned and dressed in "traditional" apparel, the Mexicans in *Giant* contrasted sharply with the characters with light skin and modern clothing, a contrast that emphasized the gap between the two cultures. The Anglos' expensive attire and lighter skin, traits commonly associated with upper classes, reinforced the dominance of Anglos over Mexicans. In *Giant*, stereotypes helped accentuate the film's message condemning racism.

George Stevens directs Mexican stock characters on the set of *Giant*. The simple clothing, hairstyles, and skin color of the Mexican characters reflect their position in society.

Paternalism

Giant further explored racism through the paternal attitudes exhibited by several of its characters toward Mexicans, such as Luz's "handling" of the ranch's Mexican workers. Throughout the history of Hollywood film, Mexicans have rarely been portrayed as being able to think for or defend themselves. The Anglo hero, whether male or female, typically stepped in to solve their problems. *Giant* zealously explored paternalism's role in the relationship between Anglo and Mexican Texans. Indeed, one of the film's most dramatic moments involves Bick's defense of his Mexican daughter-in-law and grandson.

Late in the film, when Bick and his family stop off for dinner, Bick is forced to defend Juana and her son after the diner's owner denies them service;

Courtesy of Photofest.

Leslie (Elizabeth Taylor) and Juana (Elsa Cárdenas) are shocked and humiliated after Bick's (Rock Hudson) fight in a roadside diner.

at the same time, he tries to defend the right of a Mexican family to eat at the diner. The paternalistic defense depicted by this scene demonstrates "the opinion that Mexicans are inherently servile, humble, ignorant and powerless" (Trevino 14–16). The more important lesson gained from the scene, however, is that Bick Benedict, the previously stubborn, racist Texan, has become aware of the nature of prejudice and has changed because he understands its influence in a direct and personal way.

Giant's Legacy

Like the lesson learned by Bick Benedict, the film's message altered the views of many audience members. *Giant* was particularly influential among future artists, writers, and filmmakers. According to Chon A. Noriega, "In its familial construction of a new American culture—Eastern liberalism, Western capitalism, and Mexican-Americanism—*Giant* also anticipated the cultural redefinition of 'meztizaje' by Chicano and Anglo-American border artists" (Alvarado 62). After seeing the film in 1956 when he was fourteen years old, poet Tino Villanueva "found himself awakened and transfigured in some inner way by rage he encountered from the film's concluding scene in the diner." As an adult, Villanueva even dedicated a volume of poetry to the film. The book, he claimed, reflected "the impact of Hollywood and American culture on the development of Chicano artistic expression in poetry, literature and film" (63). In turn, many of these same Chicano artists, individuals such as Cheech Marin, Robert Rodriguez, and Sandra Cisneros, have contributed significantly to an improved Hispanic image in poetry, literature, and film.

CONCLUSION

For a short time in 1956, *Giant* dared to imply that discrimination against Mexicans was a true problem in Texas. On a grander scale the film served as a denouncement of racism in general. Although Ferber's novel offered a harsher indictment against discrimination, Stevens's film version broached unprecedented territory. Like no film before it, *Giant* included studies of miscegenation, paternalism, and blatant racism in its critical analysis of the social ills that plagued early to mid-twentieth-century Texans. The end result was a film that successfully identified minority discrimination as a social issue for the state's Mexican and Anglo Texan cultures.

    Giant received nine Academy Award nominations, including nominations for best actor, best actress, and best film. George Stevens won an Oscar for best director, and the film was a critical and box-office success. However, *Giant*'s most important accomplishment was that it awakened a generation of Americans to the realization that they need not accept discrimination as a fact of life. *Giant*'s author likely approved. Of her experience in Ironwood Ferber wrote, "As I drove back to my hotel . . . I realized that a poison, virulent and dreadful, was being fed into the veins of the free American people, and that unless an antitoxin was soon administered to counteract it the most dreadful convulsions might soon rack the whole body of the land" (372). Ferber's "antitoxin" flowed throughout *Giant*.

NOTE

1. For the purpose of this chapter, the term "Mexican" refers to individuals of Hispanic ancestry living in the state of Texas, regardless of legal citizenship. The popular term "Anglo" refers to persons of white ancestry.

WORKS CITED

Alvarado, Manuel, John King, and Ana M. Lopez. *Mediating Two Worlds: Cinematic Encounters in the Americas.* London: British Film Institute, 1993.

DeLeon, Arnoldo. *Mexican Americans in Texas: An Overview.* Wheeling, Ill.: Harlan Davidson, 1993.

Ferber, Edna. *A Peculiar Treasure.* New York: Doubleday, Doran, 1939.

Fuller, Linda K., and Paul Loukides. *Beyond the Stars II: Plot Conventions in American Popular Film.* Bowling Green, Ohio: Bowling Green State University Press, 1991.

Giant. Dir. George Stevens. Perf. Rock Hudson, Elizabeth Taylor, James Dean, Dennis Hopper, Elsa Cárdenas. 1956. DVD. Warner Home Video, 2003.

Review of *Giant. New Yorker,* October 20, 1956, 178.

Review of *Giant. Newsweek,* October 22, 1956, 112.

Review of *Giant. Saturday Review,* October 13, 1956, 28.

Graham, Don. *Cowboys and Cadillacs: How Hollywood Looks at Texas.* Austin: Texas Monthly Press, 1983.

Griffith, Albert J. "The Scion, the Señorita, and the Texas Ranch Epic: Hispanic Images in Film." *Bilingual Review* 16 (1991): 19.

Hendler, Jane. *Best-Sellers and Their Film Adaptations in Postwar America:* From Here to Eternity, Sayonara, Giant, Auntie Mame, Peyton Place. New York: Peter Lang, 2001.

Trevino, Jesus Salvador. "Latino Portrayals in Film and Television." *Jump Cut* 30 (1985): 14–16.

PART THREE
THE COLD WAR WESTERN
1950–1981

REWRITING *HIGH NOON*
Transformations in American Popular Political Culture during the Cold War, 1952–1968

High Noon (1952) was a landmark artifact of American popular political culture of the cold war. Screenwriter Carl Foreman intended it as a commentary on Hollywood's capitulation to the House Committee on Un-American Activities (HUAC). Director Fred Zinnemann and star Gary Cooper shared the view that the film celebrated the nobility of the individual in the face of a failed public morality (Whitfield 147–48). John Wayne, *the* film star and conservative archetype of the period, declared it un-American (Whitfield 149; Wills 273). One scholar has characterized the film as catering to ideological extremists and challenging the "vital center" (Biskind 47). The varied reactions to the film, and its critical and commercial success, spawned a subgenre of politically self-conscious Westerns—frequently referred to as "law-and-order Westerns"— treating the nature of the American community, the role of the individual within it, and the responsibilities of citizenship and of power—all within a tale of the lone lawman defending a town from a gang of cutthroats. *High Noon*, in short, became a cinematic and ideological touchstone against which other directors sought to define their visions of the proper role of the individual in American society. This chapter explores three of these films—Anthony Mann's *Tin Star* (1957), Edward Dmytryk's *Warlock* (1959), and Vincent McEveety's *Firecreek* (1968)[1]—as successive examples of the changing historical and cultural contexts of the cold war.

While the 1950s have often been characterized as an age of conformity, recent historical studies have revealed that the decade was a period of political, economic, and cultural ferment. The early cold war (1947–1963) was an era of social change, with an emerging postindustrial economy, new planned communities, and the rise of a national security state of unprecedented power and scope. Within this context of change a new politics of group interests emerged, including the civil rights movement, a politics of gender, and early signs of a youth movement.

Amid this social and political change, citizens, government, business, and cultural agents attempted desperately to cling to some form of consensus. Cast in a variety of contexts—ideological, economic, and cultural—the key element of this consensus was a vision of American moral exceptionalism, sustained by unparalleled consumer power, uniting Americans against the extremist forces of communism and fascism. It described a community of white, middle-class, two-parent families with faith in the virtue of their leaders and the moral superiority of a free market. They were united by a mission of moral progress, defined primarily as the export of America's free-market, individualist ideology. Their mission was threatened by the forces of totalitarianism, both communist and fascist (Biskind 9–21; Corkin 19–37; Maland 190–91; Whitfield 53–76). While this consensus was articulated, defended, and sought by many, if not most, there is ample evidence that it became increasingly fragmented from the early 1950s, unraveling fully by the mid-1960s.

Tom Engelhardt sees this fragmentation as intimately related to the breakdown of an American consensus he identifies with the American war story: a tale of ambush against Americans leading to a justifiable moral crusade to defeat unconditionally the attacker. He argues that the decline of the war story in the context of nuclear containment (the big fear) led elites to seek to contain the parts of society that were breaking away from the consensus, including the little fears of juvenile delinquency and communist subversives. The work of Elaine Tyler May, Jane Sherron de Hart, K. A. Courdileone, and others suggests that gender identities were also sources of fear and subjects of these "little containments." The enemy within, as either communist, delinquent, or gender defier, becomes as significant a cold war enemy as the Soviet Union, and thus a subject to be contained.

Similarly, Alan Nadel treats containment as a hegemonic narrative, claiming that it became a "rhetorical strategy" used to stifle potential dissents. Where Engelhardt sees the atomic bombing of Japan and the Vietnam War as the signal moments in the decline of the war story, Nadel points to the Bay of Pigs as the undoing of the containment narrative because "the fiasco manifested a national narrative whose singular authority depended on uncontrollable

Courtesy of National Screen Service.

Gary Cooper and Grace Kelly in *High Noon*.

doubling, a gendered narrative whose coupling depended on unstable distinctions, a historical narrative that functioned independently of events, a form of writing that undermined the authority of its referents" (6).

By the 1960s the consensus had fragmented under the weight of these contradictions, and new politically active groups emerged. With the growing realization that containing communism had made the United States appear increasingly like its enemy, with domestic surveillance, purges, and disinformation generating a credibility gap, the moral certitude of the cold war consensus faded into increasing ambiguity. This ambiguity, emergent in the 1950s and apparent to very close reading in *High Noon* and *The Tin Star*, becomes clearer by 1959 (*Warlock*) and loses all semblance of subtlety by 1968 (*Firecreek*). The articulation of these various elements—cultural consensus, government, youth, and gender—reveals in these films a growing discomfort with American cultural norms, ambiguity about moral action, and increasing doubt that moral action is possible within the American community.

High Noon and Its Legacy

The law-and-order film, of which *High Noon* is the progenitor, consists of several key elements. A central character is the town, the name of which provides the title for two of these films. Hadleyville's abandonment of Marshal Will Kane (Gary Cooper) in *High Noon* provides the central moral conflict. While several perspectives are given for the town's failure to support the marshal, including the disability of his mentor, the pacifism of his Quaker wife, and the fear of the judge who sentenced Frank Miller to death, the central point is made by the mayor (Thomas Mitchell) during an ad hoc town meeting at the church. Upstate businessmen are considering investing in Hadleyville, he argues, and a gunfight in the streets on a Sunday will drive them away. He urges Kane to leave and convinces the town not to support him. The commercial interests of the town, seeking to protect their prosperity, reject the moral certitude of a noble marshal.

The middle-class interests who fear the impending conflict are not the only faction within the town. In the saloon and the hotel there are less progressive—but equally commercial—interests who see in the return of Frank Miller the potential for increased profit. These more rapacious entrepreneurs have been subdued by Kane's taming of Miller. The film suggests that the commercial and moral progress of the town was made possible only by Will Kane's defeat of Frank Miller five years earlier. Now the same people who have benefited from Kane's law and order turn their backs on him in his hour of need.[2]

The marshal (or sheriff or deputy in some cases) is the other central character in these films. In *High Noon,* he is Will Kane. Kane has quit as marshal, has married Amy (Grace Kelly), and is ready to leave town when he hears that Frank Miller will be arriving on the noon train. Although Kane never states his reasons for staying to face Miller and his gang, frequently telling people that they would not understand, it is clear that the source of his action is moral integrity. There is a strong suggestion that the conflict between Kane and Miller has a personal side to it; Kane and Miller apparently vied for the attentions of sultry saloon keeper Helen Ramirez (Katy Jurado). But within the context of the story, these personal conflicts are subordinated to the public threat posed by Miller and the moral duty this places on Will Kane. Even when everyone has abandoned him—the town, his wife, his friends—and he is facing near-certain death, he must still confront Miller and his gang. The marshal thus represents the virtuous individual, meeting the threat to community even with the potential for death that it entails. The townspeople's failure to support him leads him to reject them, throwing his badge to the ground in disgust, but only after he has successfully fulfilled his moral duty.

Other significant elements include youth, women, and the villain. *High Noon* suggested that the relationship of adults to adolescence was paternalistic, but also that youth was unreliable, as suggested by Kane's relation with his deputy, Harvey (Lloyd Bridges). Harvey clearly wants to be Kane: he is angry because Kane did not recommend him as his replacement; he is furious when the manager of the saloon suggests he is not as brave as Kane; he is sleeping with Kane's former lover. Because Harvey represents the next generation, the film seems to suggest that the impatience and ignorance of youth undermine its ability to offer an adequate moral replacement for the generation that is passing away. Both Kane and Helen Ramirez tell Harvey that he is too young and that he does not understand the moral necessity that roots Kane to Hadleyville. The next generation seems ill prepared for responsible citizenship. The moral failings of the town have corrupted it.

There are two types of women in these films: the civilizing woman who seeks to end violence and endorse the community, and the dark woman who understands the marshal and the need for violence. In *High Noon* these are Amy, Kane's newly wedded Quaker wife, and the saloon keeper, Helen Ramirez, respectively. Helen, the former lover of Kane and Frank Miller, currently is romantically involved with Harvey. Douglas McReynolds notes that neither Amy nor Helen performs a significant ideological function: Helen represents the temptation of sexual license, a corollary to the potential authoritarian power of Kane; Amy represents the temptations of middle-class domesticity that undermine the moral fiber of the town (206).

The ostensible villain, Frank Miller, is an ominous absence through most of *High Noon;* his vicious nature and threat to Kane are revealed through reference and innuendo.[3] At one time a citizen of Hadleyville, Miller was the main obstacle to Kane's campaign to establish law and order. A faction persists in the saloon and the hotel that thinks Miller provides a potential for increased income. The other business interests in town see Miller's return as a threat, although that threat will be alleviated if Kane leaves. Within the context of the tale, Miller is an outsider, an external threat who has been repulsed once and now must be expelled (Corkin 134–35; McReynolds 205).

The interweaving of these elements in *High Noon* offer a vision of American society in which the middle class has lost the nerve to defend itself, leaving an imagined individual who retains a clear moral vision to face this threat alone. Ultimately, the threat defeated, the individual leaves the shamed community in disgust, condemned for his cowardice and weakness. Youth and women offer little hope for redemption; the civilizing female (Amy) can only endorse fleeing from responsibility and is herself converted to the need for violence by her husband's predicament. Harvey is ignorant of the moral duty of the individual and too impatient to acquire the trappings of authority. *High Noon* is thus a strong voice criticizing the cold war consensus for its lack of public virtue and its failure to support the noble, virtuous individual who risks all to defend a community unworthy of that defense.

THE TIN STAR

The consensus criticized in *High Noon* seemed dominant and unchallenged during the Eisenhower years of "peaceful coexistence" (1953–1961). That consensus, however, was still perceived as tenuous, although the source of threats had changed. While the fear of an external threat persisted, people increasingly came to believe that internal fragmentation of American society was the source of trouble. Joanne Meyerowitz notes that, after the Korean War, women's business groups increasingly argued for more opportunities and rights, in contrast to the attempt to return women to the household identified by May as common in the earlier years of the cold war. James Gilbert identifies the mid-1950s as the high point of fears of juvenile delinquency (63). In 1954, Senate hearings focusing on comic books and juvenile delinquency led to the industry's self-censoring Comics Code (Nyberg 53–128).

The Tin Star seems on the surface to support a stronger consensus by reversing the ending of *High Noon*. A sheriff disillusioned with the law-and-order position, much like Will Kane, regains his faith and returns to defend the community. Closer examination reveals that rather than a reversal, *The Tin Star* offers a different perspective, not a story of the loss of public virtue but a cautionary tale of how private bitterness and alienation can undermine the strength of consensus.

In *The Tin Star*, the disillusioned sheriff turned bounty hunter, Morg Hickman (Henry Fonda), comes to a town very similar to Hadleyville. Hickman lost his faith in his community when the town failed to help him and his sick

Courtesy of National Screen Service.

Bounty hunter Morg Hickman (Henry Fonda) tutors
Sheriff Ben Owens (Anthony Perkins) in *The Tin Star*.

wife in their time of need. Feared by the town, he mentors the young sheriff,
Ben Owens (Anthony Perkins), to confront Bart Bogardus (Neville Brand).
Through his growing affection for the woman and child who take him in,
Hickman regains his faith that the community is still worth defending and
leaves to find a town where he can again become a sheriff.

In a scene toward the end of *The Tin Star,* the town fails to support the
young sheriff as he confronts a lynch mob led by Bogardus. Unlike in *High
Noon,* the town elders offer few excuses; the judge claims that as a man of the
law he cannot participate, and the banker (who is also the mayor) tries to get
the sheriff to leave town. There is little need for excuses, since the film can
only be seen as a sequel to *High Noon,* where those excuses were already offered.
At a time when his Western films were noted for their panoramic, open, colorful
backgrounds, director Anthony Mann shot *The Tin Star* in black and white,
on a set that is a virtual replica of Hadleyville. The place is never named; it
might be termed "Hadleyville prime." The failure to restate the moral conflict,

however, alters the terms of debate. The moral tension within the film is less the public failure of the town to support its sheriff than the private conflict within the ex-sheriff.

High Noon hints that Will Kane is a man of questionable moral standing: he is portrayed as authoritarian; he has had an affair with Helen Ramirez; he is given to fits of temper. Morg Hickman in *The Tin Star* is cast in a morally ambiguous light from the moment he appears leading a packhorse with a dead body draped across its back. He rejects formal authority and wants nothing to do with law and order. He is perceived as a threat to the town, someone with whom the sheriff should not associate and for whom there is no room at the hotel (McReynolds 204). The noble individual is thus further alienated from the community than was Will Kane but is still essential to it. Throughout the film the town elders try to force Hickman to leave and threaten to remove the sheriff from office if he continues to associate with him.

While the people of this town, like those in Hadleyville, fail to support the noble individual in his time of need, *The Tin Star* does not condemn them as *High Noon* damned Hadleyville. In director Fred Zinnemann's portrayal, the return of Frank Miller threatened the breakdown of social order; the fictional community—like McCarthy-era America—should have rallied to its own defense. In *The Tin Star,* the lynch mob led by Bogardus seeks to hang the McGaffey brothers (Peter Baldwin and Lee van Cleef) because they have killed Doc McCord (John McIntire). Doc is represented throughout the film as the moral center of the town: he delivers the babies that people the families that give the town identity and purpose; his diaries, in which he records all these births, serve as the only history of the town. His murder is a stab at the town's heart and offers some justification for the desire to seek revenge against his killers.[4] Where Hadleyville failed to meet the challenge of a potential threat, this town becomes violently enraged over an actual attack; the town elders, who will fail to support the young sheriff against Bogardus's lynch mob, are eager to join the posse to catch the McGaffeys. While the mob is thus not condoned in *The Tin Star,* its motivation is more understandable than is Hadleyville's fear of Frank Miller. Bogardus represents the implied Frank Miller: a threat from within. He is a citizen of the town, the proprietor of the livery. He aspired to be sheriff, but sensing his desire was based on having a "shooting license," the town council gave the job to young Ben. The actual crime committed by the McGaffey brothers is less significant than Bogardus's attempt to lynch them.

The failure of public virtue that drove *High Noon* is, in *The Tin Star*, reduced to background to the reconversion of Morg Hickman to the law-and-order position. Director Anthony Mann takes the issue of civic virtue presented in *High Noon* and makes it secondary to the private virtues of family in *The Tin Star*. In fact, the brief failure of the town's virtue and the bravado of the young sheriff in its absence provide the epiphany Hickman needs. The moral corruption of Hadleyville that leads Will Kane to throw his badge to the ground in disgust creates the scene for a renewal of faith in Morg Hickman. This is made possible because *The Tin Star* offers an intermediate level of community that is lacking in *High Noon*. Whereas Amy represented marriage and middle-class prosperity as a temptation that would keep Will Kane from fulfilling his noble duty (McReynolds 206–7), Nona Mayfield (Betsy Palmer) and her son Kip (Michel Ray) represent family as a necessary integrating device for the maintenance of social order. Nona is the widow of an Indian. With her mixed-blood son she dwells on the outskirts of town, and she takes Hickman in when the hotel refuses.[5] The growing affection between Nona and Morg is the key to his reacceptance of duty and willingness to return to the role of sheriff, as evidenced by the scenes of the search for the McGaffey brothers. Bogardus leads a posse of angry citizens, abandoning the sheriff to his own devices, while Hickman refuses to accept a deputy's badge and rides back to the Mayfield home. Finding that young Kip has ridden after the posse, Hickman rides out to protect the boy. He meets with the sheriff, who thinks he is tracking the McGaffeys, to which Hickman replies, "I'm not looking for McGaffeys. I'm looking for a boy." Only after discovering that Kip, who is safe, has found the brothers does Hickman help the sheriff capture them. The public duty of finding the brothers takes second place to the private goal of protecting his surrogate son; only after he has achieved this private goal can he turn to the public duty.

As Hickman re-creates the family he has lost, he regains his sense of moral duty. Reincorporated into a family, he also dons the badge Ben has been trying to get him to accept throughout the film. To the prefabricated family offered by Nona and Kip is added the relationship with Ben Owens, for whom Hickman takes on the role of father. At the end of the film Hickman has been accepted into the community; the final scene, where he, Nona, and Kip ride through town on a buckboard while the townspeople call him by name and wave, erases the ominous and icy greeting he received from these same people in the first scene. When young Ben asks him to stay on as sheriff, he says no;

he and his new family will settle somewhere else that needs a sheriff because this town already has one.

The importance of the private family to the public community is also seen in the relationship between Ben Owens and his fiancée, Millie (Mary Webster), the daughter of the dead sheriff Ben replaced. She eschews violence but learns through the intervention of Doc McCord that the sheriff's role is necessary. Like Amy of *High Noon,* who takes up a gun and shoots one of Frank Miller's men, Millie comes to understand that the noble duty of the sheriff must be performed. By the end of the film, as Ben and Millie walk hand in hand, the sheriff is now incorporated into the town, his idealism bound to the community's defense. Where the domestic promise of Amy tempted Will Kane from his duty, the domestication promised by Millie assures that the duty will be performed and passed on to the next generation, as Hickman has passed his skills on to young Ben.

The Tin Star unwrites *High Noon.* The transformation of the public failure of *High Noon* into the private failings of *The Tin Star* may reflect the changed context of the film; by 1957 McCarthy and HUAC no longer dominated the political scene, and peaceful coexistence was the order of the day. The external threat of communism, which had justified the witch-hunt hysteria of the early 1950s, seemed less important than the internal threats posed by the fragmentation of the American cold war consensus. While *The Tin Star* seems to reverse the message of *High Noon,* it ultimately begs the question by altering the terms of the moral dilemma. Relocated within a family, the alienated Hickman is reincorporated into the community in a way Kane could never be; his personal life in order, he can now return to his public role of defending the community, and the community, its future secure, can concern itself with purely private matters. Like the town of *The Tin Star,* consensus America is no longer expected to defend itself, merely to offer a supportive environment for noble individuals. The personal begins to outweigh the public, and the retreat into privacy, condemned in *High Noon,* becomes virtuous in *The Tin Star.*

WARLOCK

By the end of the decade, America's position in the cold war seemed to be worsening. The potential threat of *Sputnik* and assertions of missile gaps suggested graver threats than had been perceived since the end of the Korean

War in 1953. Overt tensions between the United States and the Soviet Union had eased somewhat, and prosperity continued, but something clearly was amiss. Prosperity and anticommunism appeared insufficient to give meaning to people's lives, as evidenced by the torrent of prescriptions for the tranquilizer Miltown, the unease on the part of many women that would be popularly identified by Betty Friedan (1960), and the void at the center of American culture that was revealed by Allen Ginsberg and the beats and the stories of John Cheever and other *New Yorker* writers. It was a time to reassert American consensus, but a consensus around what?

Warlock is not even a real town but an offshoot of the larger Bright Star. It is not a commercial center like Hadleyville but a mining community surrounded by the San Pueblo ranch. The citizens are threatened by the vicious illegalities of the San Pueblo rancher Abe McQuown (Tom Drake) and his gang, who have terrorized five previous deputies, massacred Mexicans, and killed the barber in cold blood. Warlock seeks to protect itself by hiring a vigilante, Clay Blaisedell (Henry Fonda). Once McQuown is subdued, Blaisedell becomes the feared presence, and he is forced to confront the new deputy, Johnny Gannon (Richard Widmark), a former member of McQuown's gang.

Michael Coyne offers a strong reading of *Warlock* as presenting the centrist position between the Far Left (the anarchy of McQuown) and the Far Right (the authoritarianism of Blaisedell), while treating the film as an allegory for director Edward Dmytryk's experiences as the only member of the Hollywood Ten to cooperate with HUAC (84–104). In this version, Johnny Gannon becomes the avatar of Dmytryk. Originally a member of the McQuown gang, Gannon becomes disillusioned over the bloodshed and joins with the town as its deputy, protecting it from the ravages of both Blaisedell and McQuown. Coyne offers a convincing interpretation of the film, but there is a much more complex treatment of the law-and-order theme than suggested by this allegory. The potential of the young Warlock to turn into a capitalist haven à la Hadleyville is secured by the conversion of Gannon to the side of law and order; the willingness of Warlock's residents to support him in the face of the threats from McQuown and Blaisedell suggests that potential will be realized. *Warlock* thus offers a more optimistic conclusion concerning the future than does *High Noon,* one more akin to *The Tin Star*'s promise of the rise of noble heroes. But it promises more from the town than either of the previous films, hence offering less faith in the noble individual and more in the supportive community.[6] That community, however, has no identity, no face, no center.

As an unincorporated town, Warlock has no public officers of its own. Its order is provided by a deputy to the sheriff of the nearby Bright City. Similarly, its law is provided by a judge—on acceptance. He is not really a judge but functions as one as long as the town accepts him as such. Judge Holloway (Wallace Ford) is a cripple, given to bellicose outbursts in defense of the law and against the vigilantism represented by Blaisedell. The judge sees Blaisedell as representative of "anarchy, murder and violence," although Blaisedell's authority is based on the same acceptance as that of the judge. "There's something bigger than all men; that's the law," the judge tells Blaisedell. Yet this law that he represents is only valid "on acceptance." It provides no help to Gannon when he confronts McQuown or Blaisedell. It is as crippled as the judge who bears it. Likewise, there is no moral center to Blaisedell, who tells Gannon, "I remember when I first killed a man. It was clear it had to be done, though I went home afterward and puked my insides out. I remember how clear it was; afterwards nothing was ever clear again, except for one thing. That's to hold strictly to the rules. It's only the rules that matter. Hold onto them like you were walking on eggs, so you know yourself you've played it as fair and as best you could."

"The rules" for Blaisedell serve the same function as "the law" for the judge: they provide a means of existing in human communities that lack a moral center. The center does hold in Warlock, as Coyne suggests, but what holds it together has no intrinsic meaning. Rules may keep order, but they do not provide moral clarity. Thus *Warlock* may suggest greater faith in the American community's ability to come together to defend itself, but what is being defended has become increasingly undefined.

The absence of an inherent meaning to the community in *Warlock* renders the film incapable of offering a coherent meaning or stable roles for any of the characters. *Warlock* fails to grant moral certainty to the marshal as in *High Noon* and *The Tin Star*. There are, in fact, two marshals: Clay Blaisedell and Johnny Gannon. Blaisedell is hired as marshal-on-acceptance, a community-sponsored vigilante. A hired gunfighter, he supplements his income by dealing faro at the casino of his clubfooted partner, Tom Morgan (Anthony Quinn). Blaisedell recognizes that his situation is temporary; once he has defended the town, it will come to fear and reject him. This is, in fact, what happens. Rather than turn on the town, however, he, like Hickman in *The Tin Star,* finds a sense of identity through the affection of a young woman, although this identity is lost when he is forced to kill Morgan. With Morgan's death, Blaisedell realizes his inability to assimilate into the community and must either destroy it or be driven away. When he faces the sheriff, he refuses to shoot, throws his gold-handled Colts into the dust, mounts his horse, and rides away alone. The people of Warlock come together for their own defense, again unwriting *High Noon,* but the provider of law and order has lost the moral certitude that was exemplified by Kane and regained by Hickman.

Gannon, a member of McQuown's gang who is disillusioned by a massacre of Mexicans, plays the role most akin to the noble marshals of previous films. Representing legitimate authority, he stands between the villainy of McQuown and the morally ambiguous vigilantism of Blaisedell. Unlike Kane in *High Noon,* he is not adept at gunfighting; the skill is all on Blaisedell's side. Gannon, however, represents a legal order and thus has the community as a support, as seen by the willingness of the town to aid him. The authoritarian elements of Will Kane are thus expelled from Warlock, while the legal consensus is offered as the hope of the future. While Blaisedell leaves town taking the authoritarianism with him, he is not in search of another Warlock, where the center will defend itself. He is instead in search of another town in need of a vigilante; the authoritarian is not reformed as in *The Tin Star,* nor is he completely expelled. He is still traveling from town to town, stopping wherever he is permitted. The center has held, but it has not led to meaningful change. It is a vacuous center, without meaning, and thus lacking redemptive power.

The meaninglessness of the community renders social roles unstable. McQuown, a lawless killer, is the initial threat, but as he and his gang are subdued, the threat to the town begins to be posed by Blaisedell. An interesting role reversal occurs as Gannon, the former gang member, becomes deputy, forcing an ultimate face-off with the original provider of order, Blaisedell. Nor is Gannon the only gang member to change sides; Curley (DeForest Kelly) helps Gannon in the fight with McQuown, although he had been one of the staunchest of McQuown's men. Similarly, Lily Dollar (Dorothy Malone) moves from wanting Blaisedell and Morgan dead to asking Blaisedell to help Gannon, declaring that she no longer cares about their feud. By the end of the film the villain has become the hero, and the hero has been expelled as a potential (if not actual) villain.

Gender roles also become ambiguous in *Warlock.* Jessie Marlow (Dolores Michaels) plays the civilizing woman who tempts Blaisedell with domesticity. Morgan, Blaisedell's partner in the casino, is the darker woman, whose love for Blaisedell leads him to commit murder. Lily Dollar, a former bar girl and ex-lover of Morgan, also represents the dark side of woman. She has come to town to seek revenge on Morgan and Blaisedell for killing her lover, Bob Nicholson. These images are less clear than in the other two films. Lily keeps a genteel house and cooks dinner, suggesting a domestic side that is unusual in the dark woman. She falls in love with Gannon and settles down in Warlock, putting aside her hatred of Morgan and Blaisedell. Jessie, likewise, claims that she is not the good girl one expects; she plays that role, but she protests, "I hate being an angel."

Morgan also plays confused roles. Although he is portrayed as a better gunfighter than Blaisedell, he is also the domestic one. When they first see their spartan rooms over the saloon, Morgan tells Blaisedell, "I'll bring in all new stuff and fix it up real fancy." Lily notes that Morgan cares more for Blaisedell than for himself, a sentiment Morgan reinforces. "It's all been for you," he pleads when Blaisedell finds that he has murdered Bob Nicholson to protect Clay from a gunfight. When Blaisedell informs him that he will settle down in Warlock with Jessie, Morgan goes on a drunken rampage, forcing Blaisedell to kill him. Blaisedell carries the body to the saloon, where he confronts the town in his grief. Kicking the crutch out from under the crippled judge, he tells him, "Crawl for it, crawl past a real man." He then sets fire to the saloon, creating a funeral pyre for his friend. Blaisedell's grief over the death of Morgan and his threats to the town bring to the surface their implied homoerotic relationship. Having killed the uncivilized woman in his life, Blaisedell cannot settle down with a civilized woman in Warlock; instead, he must ride out of town, alone, in search of other avenues through which to express his wildness. "Maybe I need to find another Morgan," he tells Jessie when she pleads with him to stay.

Failing to identify a moral purpose or identity of the town apart from rigid adherence to law, and unable to contain either authority or gender within their traditional roles, *Warlock* ultimately undermines the consensus it seems to advocate. While reinforcing the ideological consensus through the confrontations of Blaisedell, McQuown, and Gannon, the film cannot give it meaning or define social roles within it. Women in *The Tin Star* and *High Noon* were firmly lodged in their respective realms. Millie and Amy are the conventional forces of civilization who eschew violence in favor of negotiation, who tame men to live in the domestic realm of the indoors. Helen Ramirez and Nona Mayfield may have some of that domestication within them, but by dwelling on the moral and geographic fringes of the community, they provide a female counterpart to the noble male. In *Warlock,* those roles become murky. The dark woman, Lily, can be domesticated by the town, but the light woman cannot domesticate the authoritarian individual; instead, he must be surrounded by even darker companions of questionable gender (Morgan), suggesting the crisis of masculinity that K. A. Courdileone has examined as a prevalent theme of social discourse in the late 1950s. The apparent nobility of the individual, Blaisedell, can survive only when it is linked to a perverse, crippled version of himself, lacking any semblance of nobility. The town, which needs its crippled judge, is thus equated with Blaisedell—ignoble and following only his rules— who needs the crippled Morgan. While consensus is reaffirmed ideologically in the larger vision of containing the enemy, the battles are lost in the little containments of gender, authority, and any real moral content of the crippled rules that define the consensus position.

As the 1950s come to a close, *Warlock* suggests the cold war consensus is fragmenting. In the wake of red scares, threats of missile gaps, growing disaffection with an increasingly powerful and interventionist state, and the emergence of potential dissidents, the consensus lauded earlier in the decade is harder to find. Where it does exist, it seems to lack any inherent meaning other than preventing its own dissolution. The moral vacuity and role confusion of *Warlock* mirror this changing cultural environment.

FIRECREEK

By 1968, faith in the American community seems to have been shattered. Released in the same year as the Tet offensive in Vietnam, Lyndon Johnson's decision not to run for the presidency, and the assassinations of Robert Kennedy and Martin Luther King Jr., Vincent McEveety's *Firecreek* suggests that the consensus is dead, leaving only conformity. Women and youth have become incapable of redemption, and the villains are more conscious of moral issues than the heroes. *Firecreek* represents the growing irony and self-criticism of Westerns of the Vietnam era (Corkin 2) but also a rare version of the law-and-order Western after 1959.[7] As such it presents an interesting reflection on the fate of the cold war consensus as the seeds of dissent bloom into the flowers of rebellion in the 1960s.

Firecreek is a decrepit, poorly built, and more poorly maintained "cemetery of a town." "It's barely even here," villainous Bob Larkin (Henry Fonda) says.

Sheriff Cobb (Jimmy Stewart) discovers the body of Arthur Firecreek (J. Robert Porter).

It was settled by pioneers on their way to Oregon who saw in this hardscrabble valley land for which no one would challenge them. The residents are, in the words of the storekeeper Mr. Whittier (Dean Jagger), "a town of losers." "There are a lot of old people here," part-time sheriff Johnny Cobb (James Stewart) tells Bob Larkin and his men. When Larkin and his men disrupt the night to hold a wake for a dead member of their gang, the terrified townspeople go along with it. "Look at them," Mr. Whittier tells Cobb, "they're terrified because today isn't exactly like yesterday." This is the antithesis of Hadleyville. Where Will Kane was rejected because of the fear of a disruption of commercial progress, no one in Firecreek, including Sheriff Cobb, will oppose the Larkin gang. Conforming to the sameness of each day in run-down Firecreek has left them incapable of progress, of defending themselves, of doing anything other than hoping the threat will go away. The only member of the town who sees a need to confront the Larkin gang is the half-witted teenager Arthur Firecreek (J. Robert Porter). When the gang kills Arthur, they are, in effect, murdering the town; the killing occurs while Cobb is back at his farm, and all the citizens of the town stay indoors and do nothing. When Cobb discovers the body in the morning, he walks through the main street of town calling out, "How could you let this happen?" while all the citizens of the town sit at their windows, saying and doing nothing. They have become moribund through their own fear and timidity, seeking merely to maintain sameness. This is no robust community but a set of ramshackle hovels that serve as the coffins of the walking dead. There is nothing here to defend, and no one to defend it. As the young killer Earl (Gary Lockwood) says to Larkin, "This ain't no town we got to hurry through."

Firecreek strays far from the visions of marshals provided in earlier films. Although his role is not morally ambiguous (he is a family man who attends church), Sheriff Cobb does not act from moral certitude. There are no noble individuals in the town of Firecreek, save for the young Arthur. The sheriff is a farmer who is only a part-time lawman, paid two dollars a month and sporting a homemade badge on which the word "sheriff" is misspelled. He is unwilling to confront Larkin's gang, instead asking them to keep it down and not to disturb the peace. It is only after Arthur has been killed and the town terrorized that the sheriff is willing to face the gang. The moral certitude of *High Noon*'s Marshal Kane is suggested only at this point, with both the sheriff and the town indicted for their moral weakness.

Firecreek sees youth as lost and adrift, lacking any sense of morality or focus. McEveety's film offers two trajectories. The first is suggested by the younger members of Larkin's gang, particularly Earl, and by the young girl Leah (Brooke Bundy). In an early scene Earl assaults Leah and is stopped only by the arrival of Larkin, who wants to avoid open conflict with the town they are nearing. Earl gives Leah five dollars to pay for her torn dress. This satisfies her, and the attack is forgotten. Later, when the men begin to terrorize the town in the middle of the night, Leah dresses up to attract her would-be rapist, seeing in Earl a potential beau. *Firecreek* suggests that this trajectory for lost youth—delinquency, perverse promiscuity, and moral turpitude—is one of the consequences of the lost consensus.

The other trajectory, represented by Arthur Firecreek, the simpleminded assistant to the storekeeper, is equally unredemptive. Found wandering alone by residents of the town when he was a preteen, Arthur did not even know his name. He thus took the name of the town as his own. He is the only resident who wants to face the gang and drive it out. Even the erstwhile sheriff is unwilling to face them, and he restrains Arthur from acting on several occasions.

When Arthur hears screams in the night from the house of Meli (BarBara Luna), he investigates. Finding Meli being raped by one of the gang, Arthur tries to stop him and accidentally kills him. The gang sees this as murder and demands that Arthur be jailed.

The alienation and rootlessness of youth in *Firecreek* is a major change from the 1950s. Where *High Noon* saw youth as corrupted by the immorality of the town, and *The Tin Star* saw the idealism of youth as a counter to the cynicism of a disillusioned adult world, *Firecreek* suggests that the loss of identity for youth spells disaster all around. Adolescents in this film are vicious killers and rapists, whores, or starry-eyed half-wits whose idealism is quashed by the community's apathy. Left alone, Arthur acts on noble impulses. This results in his death, because no one in the town, not even Sheriff Cobb, will support his action. In the end, it is not Arthur's idealism but his murder that brings Cobb to the defense of the town. That an innocent half-wit could be lynched angers Cobb; while he argues that he has regained a sense of virtue, that conclusion is questionable. His shoot-out with the Larkin gang seems motivated more by a desire for revenge than by moral rectitude.

The women of *Firecreek* may still serve a civilizing function, but one that has only perverse and debilitating consequences. Johnny Cobb's wife (Jacqueline Scott), pregnant and going through a painful false labor, asks him why they settled in this valley rather than continuing on to the more fertile Oregon. Here the civilizing role of woman has led to a domesticity that created a town of losers who settled for "so much less than they wanted." Beside this passively corrupt domesticity sits Dulcie (Louise Latham), Leah's mother, a man-hating, brutal woman. When she first appears, she is holding a belt in her hand, ready to beat Leah for consorting with a local boy. Dulcie is frequently said to want no men around. The domestic women of Firecreek offer no hope of building civilization; instead, they either domesticate society to the point where it cannot and will not defend itself (Mrs. Cobb) or are rendered bitter and mean because of their failure to do so (Dulcie).

The dark woman in the film is Meli, an Indian who married Cobb's brother and bore a child by him, and who now runs the restaurant. There are rumors of a possible sexual liaison between Meli and Cobb. Meli does not represent the empathy between noble men and women, as did Helen Ramirez and Nona Mayfield; instead, she is one more dark secret buried under the veneer of civilization in *Firecreek*. Evelyn (Inger Stevens), very blonde and never seen out of doors, is a closer parallel to Helen Ramirez, yet she never speaks to

Cobb during the film, conversing only with Larkin. Evelyn settled in Firecreek with her father after her husband was killed by Indians, but she seems out of place. Clearly lodged within the domestic realm but not domesticated, she is attracted to Larkin. Larkin is also attracted to Evelyn, telling her that he will return to settle down with her. She will, like Amy in *High Noon,* take up a rifle at the end of the film. Unlike Amy, though, she will shoot her potential lover, Larkin, before he kills Cobb, not in the back but sniping from a window. Since the violence of man cannot be domesticated without man's losing all dignity, the only recourse is to kill the savage.

Where Cobb continually lies to himself, Larkin is completely self-aware. He recognizes his own desire to lead, even if the group is only a band of savage marauders. He identifies the similarity between his own position and that of Cobb, with both trying to hold things together for their respective communities: "We're both holding on to a greased pig." He identifies Evelyn as different from the others in this "cemetery of a town." Where Will Kane, Morg Hickman, and Clay Blaisedell understood the situation within the communities they sought to defend, vicious killer Larkin, rather than Sheriff Cobb, is the one who truly understands Firecreek. *Firecreek* implies that nobility of purpose can no longer be found within the heroic individual, but that it is known only to the enemy, who will not act on it. Larkin follows the letter of the law, if not its spirit. Like Blaisedell in *Warlock,* he plays by the rules, although on the fringes. He and his men are hired guns riding south from the northern range wars where they had been employed. He works within the law, just as Morg Hickman claimed. But while Larkin can see some nobility in himself, his gang has none. His followers engage in two attempted rapes, disrupt a church service, terrorize the town, and hang Arthur—all in less than twenty-four hours. When Evelyn shoots Larkin to save Cobb, it is at once an act of defense of the town and a mercy killing; she has given the noble villain his only possible exit from a world where domestication means emasculation.

THE END OF CONSENSUS AND OF THE LAW-AND-ORDER WESTERN

In *The End of Victory Culture,* Tom Engelhardt offers the theories of conspiracy surrounding the death of John Kennedy as an example of how much the American public had come to distrust the establishment by the mid-1960s.

He notes that this event, the most significant cultural touchstone since Pearl Harbor, seemed "open to any interpretation except the most obvious anti-Communist one" (184). The cold war consensus could not hold in the face of a government that seemed to be engaging in many of the same practices for which it castigated the enemy. The weakening of that consensus created a space in which new voices could be heard. As those new voices of the civil rights, women's, and youth movements became increasingly audible, the consensus continued to erode. By the end of the 1960s, the cold war consensus was gone.

The trajectory of the law-and-order films, commentaries on American society and the role of the individual within it, suggests a growing ambiguity about the moral center of American society. Although the community is indicted in *High Noon* for its failure to do its moral duty in defense of the individual, there is still a clear vision of what that duty is. This vision is less clear in *The Tin Star*, where the personal tragedy of Morg Hickman's family is the source of his disillusion. *Warlock* has lost a vision of moral certitude; where Will Kane and Morg Hickman knew what was right, Clay Blaisedell has only his rules, and Johnny Gannon has only the crippled law. The center may hold in *Warlock*, but it is a vacuous center, devoid of content and purpose. It is even difficult to name the villain in *Warlock;* the identities of the villain and the hero are conditional, depending on who poses the most immediate threat. Finally, the multiple transformations of roles in the film imply an inability to contain social actors. Without the moral content known to Kane and Hickman, the residents of Warlock have no fixed identities but move in and out of roles with no clear direction; this fluidity suggests the breakdown of domestic containment and renders the consensus the film seems to advocate incapable of providing meaningful social direction.

By 1968, *Firecreek* can offer no semblance of moral certainty or any accepted rules and instead must dwell firmly in ambiguity. The identification of the sheriff with the leader of the villainous gang, the overt indictment of both the town and the sheriff, the perverse roles assigned to women, and the unredemptive power of youth leave *Firecreek* a moral morass, with nothing but survival as a goal. The lack of a moral vision and the failure to see any defenders (or potential defenders) of morality imply a loss of faith in America's mission. This ambiguity ultimately contributes to the erosion of the cold war consensus, rendering moral claims problematic. Unsurprisingly, *Firecreek* seems the last film that takes *High Noon* as its thematic and ideological predecessor. Its willingness to paint as morally questionable both American society and the individual within it suggests the exhaustion of the law-and-order Western as social commentary and serves as an overture to the symphony of carnage and disillusion that will be *Once upon a Time in the West* (1968) and *The Wild Bunch* (1969).

NOTES

1. Slotkin (402–3) identifies eight films of the 1950s and early 1960s as revisions of *High Noon* or retellings of the O.K. Corral story, which he sees as essentially the same story. These are *Law and Order* (1953), *A Man Alone* (1955), *Top Gun* (1955), *Wichita* (1955), *Gunfight at the O.K. Corral* (1957), *The Tin Star* (1957), *Rio Bravo* (1959), and *Warlock* (1959). Adding *Firecreek* (1968) to the list takes the law-and-order Western into the late 1960s, when this subgenre seems to have been exhausted. The omission of *Rio Bravo* from my study may seem unjustified. While Howard Hawks referred to the film as his *High Noon*, this may have been an afterthought (Wills 273). *Rio Bravo* retains the basic structure of the law-and-order Western, but it does not treat the thematic elements in a strongly ideological fashion. The town is almost absent from the film; thus there can be little moral conflict over who is responsible for its defense. Both the female (Angie Dickinson) and youth (Ricky Nelson) play negligible roles; the main dramatic tension is the struggle of the recovering alcoholic deputy (Dean Martin). Rather than articulate an ideological position within the law-and-order framework as do the three films discussed here, *Rio Bravo* assumes a position and never challenges it. From the standpoint of ideological analysis, this renders the film much less interesting than the other three.

2. Douglas McReynolds reads the film as an allegory of the returned serviceman lamenting that the values for which he has fought have already been lost. He suggests that Hadleyville has already sunk to this state, and that the values defended by Will Kane have "squelched the idealistic vision of [Hadleyville's] founders." This may be too strong an argument. Because Kane will defeat Miller, the mayor and his ilk will remain dominant in Hadleyville, even though they are revealed as morally bankrupt. They do not, as McReynolds suggests, "embrac[e] the very evil the system was designed to protect its citizens against" (203). Instead of embracing it, by their failure to oppose that evil, they permit its return. Hence the potential for social declension follows the evidence of moral declension, rather than vice versa as McReynolds implies.

3. It is perhaps this absence that permits Slotkin to interpret so much background to the story in his discussion of the film. See *Gunfighter Nation*, 391–95.

4. Jim Kitses, setting this film in the context of Anthony Mann's other work, sees the death of Doc McCord as evidence of "how the community brings about the death of its very soul . . . by denying the existence of evil which its own attitudes

create" (60). Had the Doc been killed by Bogardus, this position would seem more justified. Instead, the McGaffey brothers kill Doc; they are not members of the community but live well outside of town. If there is an element to the community that is responsible for Doc's death, it is the racism that is also represented by Bogardus, for the McGaffey brothers, like Kip Mayfield, are identified as part Indian and thus are objects of scorn.

5. *The Tin Star* is one of the few law-and-order films that also contain a strong pro–civil rights message. Bogardus's attacks are always against "half-breeds," such as the McGaffey brothers or the man he shoots in the saloon. Nona Mayfield is ostracized for marrying an Indian and bearing a mixed-blood son.

6. Coyne offers this vision as a product of the lessening of cold war hostilities in the late Eisenhower era (1953–1961). To the extent that Biskind's reading of *High Noon* as catering to ideological extremes is correct, *Warlock*'s endorsement of the cultural consensus unwrites *High Noon* as much as *The Tin Star*. The film goes further than just endorsing the center; it implies that when the community defends the center, it can defeat the forces of villainy and convert the forces of anarchy.

7. Slotkin identifies *Warlock* as the last law-and-order Western (403).

WORKS CITED

Biskind, Peter. *Seeing Is Believing: How Hollywood Taught Us to Stop Worrying and Love the Fifties.* New York: Owl Books, 1983.

Corkin, Stanley. *Cowboys as Cold Warriors: The Western and U.S. History.* Philadelphia: Temple University Press, 2004.

Courdileone, K. A. "Politics in an Age of Anxiety: Cold War Political Culture and the Crisis in American Masculinity, 1949–1960." *Journal of American History* 87 (2000): 515–34.

Coyne, Michael. *The Crowded Prairie: American National Identity in the Hollywood Western.* London: Taurus, 1997.

De Hart, Jane Sherron. "Containment at Home: Sexuality and National Identity in Cold War America." In *Rethinking Cold War Culture*, edited by Peter J. Kuznick and James Gilbert, 124–55. Washington, D.C.: Smithsonian Institution Press, 2001.

Engelhardt, Tom. *The End of Victory Culture.* Amherst: University of Massachusetts Press, 1995.

Friedan, Betty. *The Feminine Mystique.* New York: Dell, 1963.

Gilbert, James. *A Cycle of Outrage: America's Reaction to the Juvenile Delinquent in the 1950s.* New York: Oxford University Press, 1986.

Kitses, Jim. *Horizons West: Anthony Mann, Budd Boetticher, and Sam Peckinpah: Studies of Authorship within the Western.* Bloomington: Indiana University Press, 1969.

Maland, Charles. "*Dr. Strangelove* (1964): Nightmare Comedy and the Ideology of Liberal Consensus." In *Hollywood as Historian,* edited by Peter Rollins, 190–210. Lexington: University Press of Kentucky, 1983.

May, Elaine Tyler. "Explosive Issues: Sex, Women, and the Bomb." In *Recasting America: Culture and Politics in the Age of the Cold War,* edited by Lary May, 154–70. Chicago: University of Chicago Press, 1989.

McReynolds, Douglas. "Taking Care of Things: Evolution in the Treatment of a Western Theme, 1947–1957." *Literature/Film Quarterly* 18 (1990): 202–8.

Meyerowitz, Joanne. "Sex, Gender and the Cold War Language of Reform." In *Rethinking Cold War Culture,* edited by Peter J. Kuznick and James Gilbert, 106–23. Washington, D.C.: Smithsonian Institution Press, 2001.

Nadel, Alan. *Containment Culture: American Narratives, Postmodernism, and the Atomic Age.* Durham, N.C.: Duke University Press, 1995.

Nyberg, Amy Kiste. *Seal of Approval: The History of the Comics Code.* Jackson: University of Mississippi Press, 1998.

Slotkin, Richard. *Gunfighter Nation: The Myth of the Frontier in Twentieth-Century America.* Norman: University of Oklahoma Press, 1998.

Whitfield, Stephen. *The Culture of the Cold War.* 2nd ed. Baltimore: Johns Hopkins University Press, 1996.

Wills, Garry. *John Wayne's America: The Politics of Celebrity.* New York: Simon and Schuster, 1997.

ALMOST ANGELS, ALMOST FEMINISTS
Women in The Professionals

Lee Clark Mitchell begins his book on Westerns with the following iconic description: "The image remains unaltered in countless versions from the genre's beginning—a lone man packing a gun, astride a horse, hat pulled close to the eyes, emerging as if by magic out of a landscape from which he seems ineluctably a part" (3). Mitchell's words may cause readers to visualize the Marlboro Man; more important, they also evoke a scene from any number of Western films that everyone recognizes, a scene romanticized by virtue of both the male figure and his context. Western women, however, are a different story. Jenni Calder describes the women who went west as "wives, daughters, or nieces. They might go as adventuresses. . . . The only respectable job that could take a woman West was schoolteaching" (158). The same limitations and dichotomous roles for women that existed in real life have been even more emphasized in film. John G. Cawelti has commented on the "limits of traditional sexual roles" and the Western's disinclination to present women as an "integral part of life" (121). Sandra Schackel refers to female Western stereotypes as limited to "nurturer/civilizer" and "femme fatale/vamp" (197), noting that as "men have written and directed Western films almost exclusively, women's roles tend to reflect a male perspective . . . [which] dominates the genre in ways in which women's roles are played out in accordance with male expectations of female behavior" (196); Michael Coyne simply states that "the genre predominantly marginalized women from the outset" (4). It is not surprising, then, that women's roles in Westerns are often small and unimportant; the women in these films exist chiefly as context or object. In fact, the intersection between women and Westerns is problematic; even those writers and directors who have endeavored to move away from the stereotypical roles noted here find it difficult to do so without outraging historical accuracy or overturning audience expectations.

WOMEN AND WESTERNS

That women are often treated badly (or not at all) is a particular stereotype of the Western, and a glance at a number of Westerns illustrates why this stereotype has come to be. In *Once upon a Time in the West* (1968), an innocent young woman is gunned down along with her father and brothers. An older and more experienced woman (Claudia Cardinale) is used sexually and threatened with death until she agrees to sell her land to one of the villains. She may come out the winner in the final few frames, but that hardly undoes the impression that, for a woman in the West, life might possibly turn out all right, but only if she can manage to survive long enough. *The Magnificent Seven* (1960) is a much more lighthearted film in which women serve mostly as backdrop. As the men ride across the western landscape, hands on guns, their horses' hooves drumming out the rhythm of a catchy Elmer Bernstein score, where are the women? One of the seven acquires a girlfriend, but she is hardly a vital part of the plot; furthermore, she is awarded to the youngest, most naive member of the group. Even in the iconic film *The Searchers* (1956), where a young woman is the object of the quest that drives the entire film, she is just that—an object. Other women serve as a domestic backdrop to the important action, as in the case of Laurie Jorgensen (Vera Miles), who is set aside by Martin Pawley (Jeffrey Hunter) whenever the clarion call of the quest is heard. Even though she is willing to fight for her man, Laurie quickly learns that, no matter how close she and Marty get, the moment someone says, "I heard a white child was seen with the [fill in the blank] tribe," Marty is in the saddle and off at a gallop without a "by-your-leave," let alone a farewell kiss (unless Laurie initiates it, of course). At the conclusion of John Ford's film, it appears that Ethan Edwards (John Wayne) will be taking care of the finally recovered Debbie (Natalie Wood), leaving Marty and Laurie free to be together at last. After years of Marty's repeated abandonments of Laurie, a pattern has been established. It would not be surprising if the couple were forever stalled at a stunted stage of their joint emotional development, a stage that is both inconclusive and incomplete.

Of course there are exceptions to this stereotype of Western women.

Consider *High Noon* (1952), where intrepid lawman Will Kane (Gary Cooper) is deserted, in a time of great need, by both friends and other entities from whom he might have expected support and aid. These desertions are surprising, but Will's Quaker bride, Amy (Grace Kelly), steps forward to replace the deserters and play the role of rescuer. This plot direction is unexpected because until that moment Amy has appeared to shrink from her new home in the West and all that the word "West" conveys. Furthermore, although the act of gunning down the villain may be considered unusual for a woman, the gender issue present is somewhat complicated by Amy's obvious distaste for frontier life and its inevitable violence that is present in the western town of Hadleyville. The question of whether Amy's act is appropriate for a woman in what has been a man's arena of action is muddied by the issue of whether an easterner can appropriately adapt to the West, a basic theme in the consideration of Westerns, whether on page or screen. Another woman who is distinctly unusual is the very businesslike madam (Julie Christie) in *McCabe and Mrs. Miller* (1971), but the presentation of her character is chiefly concerned with the reversal of another stereotype: the hooker with the heart of gold. Other women in the film are without power; some are freakish in appearance and are treated in a denigrating manner by those around them. The sisterhood that emerges after Mrs. Miller takes charge is briefly considered and is seen by some critics as a feminist portrayal. Another reading is that Mrs. Miller's facilitation of a warm, family atmosphere merely demonstrates another aspect of her efficiency in business: a happy hooker works harder.[1]

The Professionals

The Professionals (1966), although women are not an obvious part of its agenda, demonstrates the difficulty of forging a new role for women in the Western; critics, in fact, view it as a men's film and have not tended to consider it when discussing the role of women.[2] Michael Coyne describes *The Professionals* as "both temporally and thematically the halfway house between the altruism of the Seven and the harsh nihilism of the Bunch" (132), while Jim Hitt suggests it "merges the Old West with the New" (245). One of the flurry of Westerns in the 1960s, *The Professionals* was directed and produced by Richard Brooks (who also wrote the screenplay, based on *A Mule for the Marquesa* by Frank

Left: The poster advertising *The Professionals* in the United States featured bandoleros, signaling that this would be an action film.

Right: A German theater card is very like the poster but has made changes in the positioning of the actors and which ones are depicted.

O'Rourke) and released in 1966.[3] The film was popular with the viewing public but received mixed critical reviews;[4] it earned Oscar nominations for director, screenplay, and cinematography. *The Professionals* does not pretend to interrogate the position of women in the West, and for much of the film, the focus is firmly on men and their world of action. The four professionals of the title—Henry "Rico" Fardan (Lee Marvin), Bill Dolworth (Burt Lancaster), Hans Ehrengard (Robert Ryan), and Jake Sharp (Woody Strode)—as well as the villains (both perceived and actual) are men.

Mitchell describes *The Professionals* as one of a group of 1960s films (the others are *The Magnificent Seven, Hang 'em High,* and *True Grit*) that feature "various misfits, loners, bullies, mavericks, and sociopaths" (225). This view of the film is both surprising and incorrect, as *The Professionals* spends a considerable amount of time focusing on issues such as friendship, loyalty, honor, and what remains for an individual when the life he understands and has been living is no longer possible.[5] Interactions among the four men regarding these issues are considered in the contexts of how the men are alike, how they are different, what in their past caused them to take the directions they have, and what values they espouse. Perhaps even more important is the question of why some of these values are flexible (and thus can vary according to circumstances) whereas others are unalterable. The exchanges that investigate these issues are well written and sometimes quite witty.[6] Some contemporary critics ignored the script, seeing *The Professionals* as nothing more than an action film;[7] others noticed, but did not approve of, the rather unusual combination of talk and action. Brian Garfield, for example, decries the "occasional pretentious intervals where the characters start talking philosophically about the meaning and nature of life and revolutions and such. There's too much of that and it's sophomoric, but it's worth putting up with for the rest" (261), a statement which seems to indicate that, even though the action is already nearly nonstop, he would welcome even more. Richard Robertson mentions that "Lancaster, dashing about and flinging sticks of dynamite, was at his athletic best in *The Professionals.* Not since *The Crimson Pirate* (1952) had he had so much fun" (174). James Parish and Michael Pitts refer to the pace and general derring-do, while also slyly referencing the age of the actors: "Only once does the action slow down, during a gun battle between Palance and Burt Lancaster, who seem to be firing off philosophical asides about the life of violence mainly because they need a rest" (277). It is this on-screen discussion that, on at least

Two of the professionals (Burt Lancaster and Lee Marvin) have a
tight grip on the woman who is worth $100,000 (Claudia Cardinale).

one level, results in a surprising amount of character development in a vigorous
action film—one that is often quite brutal and bloody.

On another level, development is limited because the men have extremely
specific roles (dictated by the professional plot as defined by critic Will Wright[8]).
Rico (Marvin) is the tough leader of the team, a soldier of fortune whose hard
exterior hides the fact that he has never recovered from the death of his wife
during the Mexican Revolution. Bill (Lancaster) is a dynamiter par excellence, a
gambler, and a lady's man. The characters of Hans (Ryan) and Jake (Strode) are
less developed. Hans is the best man in that part of the world with horses, and
good horses will be vital for the job. Jake can be depended on to track anything,
climb up the side of a mountain, and silently sneak up on the most alert foe (or
at least get close enough to dispatch him with bow and arrow).[9] Collectively,

they are "The Professionals"; each is an expert in his field, and together they are an almost unstoppable force. Up to this point, there is no reason to view *The Professionals* as anything other than the men's rough-and-tumble film that it is so often described as being; a closer inspection reveals that women are participants in the action and, to some extent, direct the outcomes.

FROM SEXUAL OBJECT TO POLITICAL ACTIVIST

The plot sounds simple, but it quickly becomes more complicated: four soldiers of fortune are hired by a wealthy rancher, Mr. Grant (Ralph Bellamy), to cross the border into Mexico and retrieve his kidnapped wife. Two members of the rescue team are initially less than enthusiastic about the job because they had earlier fought alongside the kidnapper, Jesús Raza (Jack Palance), and he is a man they respect:

> BILL: [Who's got] the woman?
>
> RICO: Raza.
>
> BILL: (*speaking in a tone of disbelief*) *Our* Raza? A kidnapper?
>
> RICO: Grant's got the ransom note to prove it.
>
> BILL: Well, I'll be damned.
>
> RICO: Most of us are.

Their current situations ensure that they will accept the job, in spite of their reservations. Scenes that appear during the opening credits establish that all four men are both unhappy with, and unsuccessful in, their lives, working at dead-end jobs (if they can keep them) for which they are overqualified.[10] The $10,000-per-man reward that Mr. Grant offers, while hardly ensuring a lifetime of financial security, at least guarantees that they will be relatively comfortable for the immediate future. Furthermore, the $100,000 ransom that the men will carry to Mexico demonstrates a belief in their integrity, which helps to restore their self-images; the ransom is so large, in fact, that it leads to Bill's first speculation on the kidnapped woman's value (a theme he revisits from time to time):

> BILL: A hundred thousand dollars for a wife. She must be a lot of woman.

RICO: Certain women have a way of changing some boys into men . . . and some men back into boys.

BILL: That's a woman worth saving.

The men cross the border into Mexico and handle their dangerous conflicts with nature (heat, thirst, etc.) and man (Mexican bandits) with the skill and flair of professionals as they progress across the desert (a progress that, although it lacks the requisite number of Dantean levels, Hitt describes as "a descent into hell" [238]). Their quick reactions, years of experience, and facility with weapons (including guns, arrows, knives, and dynamite) ensure that they reach Raza's fortified hacienda, deep within Mexico. Bill expresses pleasure as he watches Chiquita (Marie Gomez), his former lover, dancing at a campfire in the courtyard, although her presence forecasts possible complications in the rescue plan if the man who loves ladies and the woman who, in his words, "never says no" decide to renew their relationship. The woman who causes the group real problems, however, is Maria Grant herself, the object of their dangerous mission. As played by sultry Claudia Cardinale, she is not a quivering, terrified kidnap victim, living on the hope that her husband will rescue her; instead, she is the kidnapper's longtime lover who helped him plan the "kidnapping" and assisted him in writing the ransom note. The Mexican Revolution may be over, but Raza continues to fight against a corrupt government;[11] for this he needs money, and Maria is helping him procure what he needs to support his ongoing rebellion. She has no desire to be rescued.

Soon after the professionals raid Raza's hacienda, Maria demonstrates a previously unknown facet of her character as she speaks emotionally on behalf of true love and a brighter future for Mexico. Rhetoric becomes an even more important part of the plot at this point, as the men's beliefs and assumptions are interrogated by Maria, who loses no chance to present her case to (depending on the point of view) her rescuers or her captors. Of course Rico and Bill realize that the rules have changed the moment they witness Maria's loving embrace of Raza, when they had expected to see terror, tears, or anger. Maria also spells out the situation for them much more explicitly, both pleading and demanding that they set her free. She has left her husband and her life as Mrs. Grant behind and has no intention of returning to either:

MARIA: I was not kidnapped.

RICO: The old badger game.

The defiant runaway wife (Claudia Cardinale), who yearns to return to her lover (Jack Palance) and her own country (Mexico).

BILL: Shakedown partners . . . bed partners.

MARIA: Raza and I grew up together. . . . We are lovers long before Mr. Joe Grant buys the place. When my father lies dying, he says Mr. Joe Grant wants you for his wife. You will become Doña Grant, that is my wish. Here, a wish is a command. But I'm very young and very foolish. I tell Mr. Joe Grant I cannot marry to him, I love another man. Very romantic, no?

Maria's attempt at persuasion does not convince her audience—they are professionals and they have accepted money from her husband to bring her back. Because her verbal endeavor has not been successful (Rico's response includes his valuation of her as a "whoring wife"), Maria then attempts to escape; later she tries to seduce Bill, correctly gauging that he is the individual in the group who is most susceptible to feminine persuasion. Initially, she offers him money for her freedom; then she offers herself. When he says, "I might say yes now, and later no," she responds, "I trust you," even as she is groping for his gun. He responds, "I trust you, too," at the same moment that viewers see the muzzle of his pistol appear between her breasts.

Maria and Chiquita: Women and Their Choices

Women's roles are small in *The Professionals,* but they demonstrate a narrow range of choices for women of Hispanic ethnicity in the West at the same time that they reveal a stratification of class that is present and fully as active as in other, more "civilized" venues.[12] There is a huge gulf between Maria, the pampered wife of Mr. Grant, and Chiquita, a leftover freedom fighter for Pancho Villa and current supporter of Jesús Raza, a lesser jefe. Yet a subtext of the film is that of choice for these women. Do they or do they not have the freedom of decision and power over their own lives? If so, how and why do they make the choices they do, and what is the outcome, particularly for those around them? Maria, through her various forms of rhetoric (and in spite of the fact that *The Professionals* has sometimes been accused of racism toward Hispanics), demonstrates that she has choices. Although she presents herself as having been forced to marry Mr. Grant (because of her filial duty), she can elect whether to continue her life as the rich and pampered Mrs. Grant or to return to the true love of her youth. She has decided to abandon her marriage and return to Mexico, but she must also consider whether her decision is solely personal, or whether she is committed to a progressive Mexico. If the latter is true, she must support Raza as he fights against a corrupt government. Her selection of the latter option engenders a variety of strategies, including attempted escape, verbal persuasion, and the proposed exchange of sexual favors for freedom. Not surprisingly, the degree of choice is, in large part, determined by class (although Maria's earlier acquiescence can be ascribed to her youth).

Chiquita's scope of action is markedly more narrow than Maria's; it is not clear whether she has truly had choices or not. She may have wanted to leave her home to become a soldier, or perhaps she was brought along as a camp follower. She may have discovered that she enjoyed the fighting and the camaraderie, or she may have had no place to return to—in the turmoil of the revolution, her family and village may have been swept away. In any event, her current life is what she knows, and it is all she wants—to fight for the man she admires and respects, and to fight by the side of her fellow rebels. Casual sex provides relief from the pressures of fighting and death, but even in this context, there are no choices; or, rather, Chiquita ignores the selection process by accepting the sexual attentions of any man who approaches her. A brief dialogue with Bill confirms this fact:

BILL: Hey, Chiquita, how's your love life?

CHIQUITA: Why, you want some?

BILL: Don't you ever say no?

CHIQUITA: Never!

BILL: Anyone?

CHIQUITA: Everyone!

Chiquita is presented as the most basic and uncomplicated individual in *The Professionals.* She eats, drinks, sleeps, makes love, and dies, slain in what is essentially a duel with her former lover. She does not take time to think or consider or choose. She only acts, and probably would not even recognize the stresses and ambiguities felt by the other characters. Maria, for example, may loathe her captors for returning her to her hated husband, and she is quick to predict their death in the desert or at the hands of Raza; at the same time, she feels pity for the injured Hans, as she expertly bandages his injured shoulder.[13] Chiquita, given her background, personality, and position, would not understand being torn between options that choice brings; the tensions that Maria feels do not exist for her soldier sister. Because of Chiquita's lifestyle, it is not surprising that she meets an early death; indeed, if she were to decide the manner of her own death, she would undoubtedly choose to die at the business end of a gun with a man's lips on hers, for it is a moment that brings together sex and violence, the two chief motifs in her life.

A True Heroine

A third woman, almost certainly Hispanic, has a tremendous impact on the story line, despite the fact that she is nameless and classless (by virtue of neither of these details' being indicated in the film). Neither a "whoring wife" (Maria) nor a lusty soldier "who never says no" (Chiquita) can possibly aspire to the position of paragon held by Rico's late wife. She is a heroine, a true believer in the revolution who never compromised her principles—as Maria has done by marrying the rich and controlling Mr. Grant and thereby abandoning her twin loves, Raza and Mexico. Not only is the true heroine, Rico's wife, never named, she is also dead, killed by the very revolution in which she was such a strong believer. Only a small part of her story is disclosed, narrated by Bill after the professionals observe a particularly violent scene, where rebels ambush and capture a supply train guarded by government troops, hanging the officers and shooting prisoners in the back of the head. Rico is clearly upset by this sight but not, as Bill explains to a questioning Hans, by the summary nature of the executions. He is disturbed because the executed prisoners are Colorados, and seeing representatives of this group has forced him to confront painful personal memories. Bill's identification of the men who are shot and the revelation of the fate of Rico's wife are instructive: "The men on that train are Colorados. Expert marksmen. Also expert at torture. A couple of years ago they burned and looted a town of three thousand people. When they finished, forty were left. Fardan's wife was one of the lucky forty. 'Why are you a revolutionary?' they asked. 'To rid the world of scum like you,' she said. They stripped her naked, ran her through the cactus 'til her flesh was . . . The other thirty-nine rebels watched her die and did nothing, just watched." It is clear that her brutal death, combined with the evolution of the Mexican Revolution from an active battle against a brutal and oppressive regime to a new government whose ambiguous and sordid political intrigues make its leaders nearly as corrupt as their predecessors, have led to disillusionment for Rico and Bill, former fighters for freedom.

This combination of nostalgia and disenchantment with earlier ideals has led critics to liken *The Professionals* to *The Wild Bunch* (1960)—a valid comparison, but one that breaks down, particularly in the films' conclusions. *The Professionals* never displays the level of misogyny present in *The Wild Bunch*, and whereas the latter evolves into a climactic firefight, the former moves in a very different direction. Unlike *The Wild Bunch*, in which most of the characters meet their end in a hail of bullets, the professionals are able to turn back the clock on their disillusionment and, although their bodies are battered, weary, and aging, recapture some of the idealism and romanticism of years gone by. They accomplish this by acknowledging the power of love and by turning their backs on Mr. Grant's money and all it represents, the money that was going to ease their declining years. A scene between the married couple cements the professionals' recommitment to justice and personal morality:

GRANT: You're back again. Nothing else matters.
MARIA: I will run away again. That matters.

GRANT: You're my wife. You belong to me.

MARIA: I belong here.

GRANT: With him?

MARIA: With him.

GRANT: I'd rather see you dead. You're coming with me.

He struggles with Maria; the force of a blow sends her sprawling on the ground. If the professionals had any doubts about their new direction, they are erased by Grant's boorish behavior and his easy assumption that only his wishes are important; no matter how he evaluates his wife's worth, he has ordered his men to kill her lover, and he would rather see her dead than see her make her own decisions. The professionals refuse to return Maria to her husband, protect the wounded Raza from Mr. Grant's goons, and head for Mexico again, this time accompanied by their former adversaries. Presumably the entire group will now lend their support to the revolution and/or reform efforts that Mexico so badly needs. The final frames show Maria driving the wagon (containing the badly wounded Raza) as the professionals ride together behind it, providing both an escort of honor and protection from Grant and his unprincipled employees.[14] Because the professionals have repeatedly indicated their loss of idealism, and their actions throughout the film have been directed to the end of earning a monetary reward, this final twist has been criticized for its lack of "realism." The ending, hopeful and romantic though it may be, demonstrates that personal growth is always possible, that talk is not necessarily cheap, and that idealism can be recovered even after it seems irretrievably lost. This sudden reversal would not have taken place were it not for the women of *The Professionals*.

WOMEN AND INFLUENCE

The professionals' turnaround occurs for a number of reasons, two of which can be attributed to women. First, there is the dead—but hardly forgotten—Mrs. Fardan, heroine and saint of the revolution they supported, whose memory is still cherished by the two members of the group (Rico and Bill) who knew her as a friend, a revolutionary comrade, and, in Rico's case, as a wife. Although she represents one reason that they turned away from the revolution, she also symbolizes a faith that never dies. She never surrendered her beliefs; in fact, she clung to them, and they sustained her under torture. And then there is Maria Grant, who, although she shows herself to be duplicitous and untrustworthy, also demonstrates an unswerving belief in her country, as well as in the man she loves.[15] This devotion leads her in some unusual directions, but she is impervious to the professionals' criticism; when Rico calls her a whore, she responds, "If we can keep the revolution alive with guns and bullets for even one more day, then I steal and cheat . . . and whore."

The impact of Chiquita on the men is negligible. She provides a diversion for Bill, while the others smile at her zest for life but are not intrigued. None of them would change for her. She is just another soldier who just happens to be of a different gender, while Maria's scope of action makes her a far more interesting character. She is only an object, a package to be delivered, until the men discover that she is on the right side—that she treasures the same ideals they used to cherish. Still, Maria has compromised at times and is thus somewhat sullied. Only the deceased Mrs. Fardan never abandoned her beliefs but held to them until death. She made similar choices to Maria's, but they were better choices. For example, both have married Anglo men, but Rico's wife married a man whose concepts of freedom and justice were in accord with her own. He also fights for the revolution, while Mr. Grant is concerned only with his own importance and gratification.[16]

Mrs. Fardan may be dead, but her influence continues, gently urging her husband and friend in the right direction, back to the ideals they abandoned after her death, when they chose material rewards over a service ethic. She is not exactly an "angel of the house," but in her role as an example to those who remember her, she serves as a version of this Victorian phenomenon transplanted to the West. Perhaps an "angel of the desert" or an "angel of the range" would be a more fitting description of the woman who fought for the revolution, defied the Colorados, and was dragged to her death. Although it is reassuring that the professionals are able to recover their ideals, it is also somewhat disconcerting to discover that the woman these hard-bitten adventurers regard as a female paragon is dead; the fact that she functions as a more modern, Hispanic version of the etherealized women of the nineteenth century who served as inspiration and spiritual impulse for the men in their lives is even more bewildering. Although Mrs. Fardan lived and died a revolutionary, she is, in fact, as much a civilizer as that most familiar stereotype of civilizing woman in the West: the schoolteacher.

PROFESSIONAL WOMEN

Schackel, in her examination of the function of women in the Western, has concluded that "women's roles are imbued with traits traditionally considered feminine: passivity, dependence, gentleness, and sensitivity, among others. . . . [T]hey must ultimately depend on a man for their happiness and security" (196). This description does not apply to the women in *The Professionals*. All three featured in this movie are, on one level, professional women. They are not specialists in the way that the corresponding male figures are, yet they act in much the same manner, whether they are planning, plotting, rebelling, or fighting alongside men. They are not, furthermore, totally dependent on men "for their happiness and security" because they are strong in their own right and hold beliefs of their own. Chiquita fights for a cause that may well be a losing one, Maria demonstrates the strength of her convictions when she and Raza are separated, and Mrs. Fardan defies the Colorados even though Rico is not present to support her. They are strong women.

It is not, perhaps, surprising that women (even in the Western) would be granted more autonomy in the 1960s than had previously been possible. The sexual revolution was in full swing, fueled by multiple societal issues and demonstrated by the publication in 1963 of Betty Friedan's *The Feminine Mystique,* the passage of the Civil Rights Act of 1964 (which prohibited employment discrimination on the basis of sex), and the founding of the National Organization for Women in 1966 (the same year that *The Professionals* was released). Clearly, the life of American women was undergoing a change, one that could not help but be reflected in the artistic spheres of fiction and film. Therefore, it is not surprising that the women of *The Professionals* do not function merely as wives or schoolteachers. Chiquita lives a life of violence. Maria and Mrs. Fardan are women who support violence (and are willing to go to any lengths to support the revolution—"whoring"[17] for one and death for the other), yet they also function in the capacity of teachers who lead their pupils to a higher level of moral understanding and behavior. Writers and directors might wish to abandon a stereotype viewed by society as outdated, but it may be difficult to do so; this situation is evident in *The Professionals,* where the women participate in the "feminine mystique" at the same time that they rebel against it. Calder categorizes women of the Western as civilizers or spunky types who must be tamed (170), but the women in *The Professionals* are not waiting for their men either at home or at the saloon. Instead, Maria and Mrs. Fardan appear to combine these stereotypes to present a new Western woman—the Victorian angel who inspires, combined with the feminist who actively participates in a life of action. This combination may be uneasy at times, but it is a better fit for the times than the earlier, more simplified stereotype; when *The Professionals* was made, the role of women in both film and society was evolving. Friedan had stated, "The only way for a woman, as for a man, to find herself, to know herself as a person, is by creative work of her own. There is no other way" (344). An active role in revolution is probably not what she had in mind by the term "creative work," but she goes on to say that the work must be something "that she can take seriously as part of a life plan, work in which she can grow as part of society" (345). The efforts put forth by women in *The Professionals* to overthrow a corrupt government and replace it with an entity that is more concerned with justice reveal an ambitious life plan; furthermore, it is one in which women and society can grow together.

The men in this film, although they have been presented as relatively secure within their identities,[18] testify by their behavior that they are not immune to the influence of a woman who is able to guide them, demonstrating both by rhetoric and by example where their loyalties should lie and the moral direction in which they should proceed. The male professionals have learned that, even though times have changed and they may feel they have been left behind, the same qualities that they earlier cherished are still applicable. Qualities such as loyalty to a cause and support for what one feels is right are never out of season. The men make this discovery as a unit, but the issue would have gone unexamined had it not been for women who, whether dead or alive, demonstrate their ability to lead as well as follow. These women are also "professionals" who can work and fight beside men; at the same time, they possess the ability, even after death, to gently shepherd these men, directing them in the ways of justice and fostering the ideals of freedom.

NOTES

1. The films that are discussed briefly in the last two paragraphs were produced over a nineteen-year period (1952–1971). Although this sample is extremely small, it would indicate that the limited treatment and development of women in the Western is not a trend that, for example, might be ascribed to a specific decade.

2. Cawelti includes *The Professionals* with films that focus on friendship between men while "women and sex are pushed into the background" (123). On one level,

this is correct, as more time is spent on the men's backstory and interactions; however, as this chapter argues, the role that women play turns out to be a very important one.

3. Maurice Jarre wrote the musical score, which, although it is supportive rather than intrusive, features haunting chords and romantic strains similar to those used in his other scores, including those for *Lawrence of Arabia* and *Doctor Zhivago*. Conrad Hall was the cinematographer; his Oscar-nominated work on *The Professionals* produced visual effects of dust and smoke generally thought possible only when working in the medium of black-and-white film.

4. Richard Robertson states that *The Professionals* "was the second highest grossing Western of that year, after *Nevada Smith*" (173); David Pirie cites it as among the most financially successful Westerns, grossing over $8 million (208). The film was also popular in Europe, particularly Germany, as evidenced by a plethora of tie-in collectibles now available on eBay and elsewhere.

5. That this film is placed at a time of temporal shift (as stated by Coyne) is signaled by the emotional displacement of the characters; it is also illustrated by details in the areas of transportation (chiefly horses, but also trains and automobiles) and weapons (arrows, as well as rifles, machine guns, and dynamite). A similar situation, although on a much larger scale, can be seen in World War I, where some soldiers piloted planes while others drove horse-drawn wagons.

6. When Bill asks Rico what the new job is, Rico answers, "You won't lose your pants. Your life, maybe, but what's that?" Bill responds, "Hardly anything at all." This exchange is particularly ironic because when Rico bails his comrade out of jail, Bill is not wearing pants, an item of clothing recently abandoned in a lady's bedroom during a hurried exit. Bill's assessment of his life as being worth "hardly anything at all" also demonstrates the degree of disillusionment with life that the professionals feel.

7. "What *The Professionals* does is to hark back to an honorable tradition in movie making that has become rare: The straightaway, uncomplicated action film that one can relax and enjoy without strain" (*Motion Picture Herald* 625). Clearly, this observation is overly simplistic.

8. The professional plot represents a shift from the familiar Western tale of a hero who essentially operates alone. Now there is "a group of heroes, each with special fighting ability, who combine for the battle. . . . Each man possesses a special status because of his ability, and their shared status and skill become the basis for mutual respect and affection" (Wright 86). Noël Carroll points out that *The Professionals* demonstrates its debt to *The Magnificent Seven* (another film that portrays a group whose members possess specialized skills), which also begins with scenes that show how the professionals were recruited (54). Although the professional plot is much more widely used in caper films, it is occasionally present as a structural device in Westerns.

9. Michael Coyne succinctly describes the concept of Strode's character as a

"Black Chingachgook" (132), a reference to Natty Bumppo's Delaware friend and the father of Uncas in James Fenimore Cooper's *The Last of the Mohicans* (1826). Although Cooper's novels are set in a different part of the country than the Southwest setting so vitally important to many Westerns, they obviously share many similarities with the traditional Western, particularly a connection with landscape (Cawelti 25); Cooper is, in fact, widely viewed as the father of the Western, based on his frontier novels *The Pioneers* (1823) and *The Prairie* (1825).

10. Rico demonstrates machine guns to the army (for which he earns forty dollars a week), Hans breaks horses, Jake works as a bounty hunter, and Bill (who has gambling debts) must be bailed out of jail.

11. The Mexican Revolution, which began in 1910, sought to replace a dictatorship with a more democratic form of government, one that would be accompanied by many reforms. Unfortunately, although the elected government of Francisco Madero tried to implement these reforms, the attempts were ineffective; the government was overthrown by a coup, and Madero was killed. For several years, Mexico's situation was dictated by chaotic struggles among various generals and local leaders from different sections of the country (including Huerta, Carranza, Zapata, and Villa), a number of whom sought to gain (and briefly held) a great degree of personal power. In the view of many historians, the revolution was chiefly agrarian; Frank Tannenbaum adds another layer, explaining that at least some of the existing political problems were dictated by the conflicting aims of country and city—although leaders meant to respond to the desires of the people, they were, sooner or later, corrupted by their exposure to a different way of life, and they "succumb[ed] to the city," with its very different set of imperatives (Tannenbaum 127). It is this change (from supporters of the people to oppressors of the people) that Bill and Rico have found discouraging, although Raza has decided to continue fighting against any political situation that he views as wrong.

12. Although Cardinale plays the part of a Hispanic woman, her ethnicity is Italian, and she was born in Tunisia.

13. Rico ascribes her action to the fact that, if Hans lives, he will slow them down and give Raza a chance to catch up. The expression on Maria's face, however, indicates her realization of the inherent tension between her desire for freedom and her decision to perform an act of mercy.

14. It is no accident that Maria is driving the wagon, a touch that provides more insight into the role of women in *The Professionals*. Maria not only is physically stronger, at this point, than the wounded Raza but also, as she whips up the horses, is setting the pace for the whole group.

15. Raza, in turn, has the same faith in her. No matter whether they are together or apart, or what their circumstances are, they belong to each other. "That will change nothing," he expostulates, when Bill says she will soon be back with her husband.

16. In spite of Maria's mistakes, she is also presented as an important individual.

When Bill says, "[I was] just wonderin' what makes you worth a hundred thousand dollars," he is clearly suggesting that her worth is connected with sexual performance. At the end of the film, when he says he has learned what makes her worth that much, the paradigm of worth has clearly been altered. Now it is based on her unshakable love for Raza and her willingness to work toward a brighter future for Mexico no matter what the personal cost may be.

17. In spite of Rico's accusation that might imply Maria has been promiscuous and in spite of her advances toward Bill, there is no evidence that Maria has betrayed the lover of her youth by sleeping with anyone except Mr. Grant, the man to whom she is legally married.

18. The uncertainties they feel are more linked to *where* they fit into the new and revised world rather than *who* they are.

WORKS CITED

Calder, Jenni. *There Must Be a Lone Ranger.* London: Hamish Hamilton, 1974.

Carroll, Noël. "The Professional Western: South of the Border." In *Back in the Saddle Again: New Essays on the Western,* edited by Edward Buscombe and Roberta E. Pearson, 46–62. London: British Film Institute, 1998.

Cawelti, John G. *The Six-Gun Mystique Sequel.* Bowling Green, Ohio: Bowling Green State University Popular Press, 1999.

Coyne, Michael. *The Crowded Prairie: American National Identity in the Hollywood Western.* London: Tauris, 1997.

Friedan, Betty. *The Feminine Mystique.* New York: Norton, 1963.

Garfield, Brian. *Western Films: A Complete Guide.* New York: Rawson, 1982.

Hitt, Jim. *The American West from Fiction (1823–1976) into Film (1909–1986).* Jefferson, N.C.: McFarland, 1990.

McDonald, Archie P., ed. *Shooting Stars: Heroes and Heroines of Western Film.* Bloomington: Indiana University Press, 1987.

Mitchell, Lee Clark. *Westerns: Making the Man in Fiction and Film.* Chicago: University of Chicago Press, 1996.

Motion Picture Herald Product Digest, November 9, 1966, 625.

Parish, James Robert, and Michael R. Pitts. *The Great Western Pictures.* Metuchen, N.J.: Scarecrow, 1976.

Pirie, David, ed. *Anatomy of the Movies.* London: Windward, 1981.

The Professionals. Dir. Richard Brooks. Perf. Burt Lancaster and Lee Marvin. Columbia, 1966.

Robertson, Richard C. "Just Dreamin' Out Loud: The Westerns of Burt Lancaster." In *Shooting Stars: Heroes and Heroines of Western Film,* edited by Archie P. McDonald, 165–81. Bloomington: Indiana University Press, 1987.

Schackel, Sandra Kay. "Women in Western Films: The Civilizer, the Saloon Singer, and Their Modern Sister." In *Shooting Stars: Heroes and Heroines of Western Film,* edited by Archie P. McDonald, 196–215. Bloomington: Indiana University Press, 1987.

Tannenbaum, Frank. *Peace by Revolution: Mexico after 1910.* 1933. New York: Columbia University Press, 1966.

Wright, Will. *Six Guns and Society: A Structural Study of the Western.* Berkeley: University of California Press, 1975.

COWBOYS AND COMEDY

The Simultaneous Deconstruction and Reinforcement of Generic Conventions in the Western Parody

Almost as long as the Western has existed as a genre in film there has been a subgenre of Western parodies: from as far back as the 1920s with Buster Keaton, continuing down to the present with Jackie Chan, the Western has been a target of parody and a rich source for comedy. Comedy relies, to a large extent, on the reversal of expectations; because of the familiarity of the highly codified conventions of the Western, it becomes a prime target. Parodies subvert the conventions of the Western in ways that breathe new life into the genre. While the Western parody mocks established formulas of the genre, it ultimately reinforces them through its acceptance of a shared set of codes. Moreover, as a survey of representative parodies will demonstrate, Western parodies also reflect the periods in which they are made.

Most scholars agree that the Western, in its most basic definition, is set on the American frontier sometime between the mid-1800s and the early 1900s. It typically is serious, often quite somber, and involves some kind of clearly defined dramatic conflict between the forces of good and evil, man and nature, or law and anarchy. The genre is composed of a complex set of codes and images, including the lonesome hero, moral justice enforced by violence, the coming of the railroad, the shoot-out, the open prairie, hats, horses, cowboys, and guns. Even though the Western parody does not reflect the prevailing dramatic mood of the Western, it does adhere to the genre's setting and incorporates its codes and images for comedic and parodic purposes.

Right: Kid Shelleen (Lee Marvin) from *Cat Ballou*.

ORIGINS OF WESTERN PARODY

A parody is a comical imitation of a genre that uses its existing codes to examine the subject in a humorous way. Parody often exists simultaneously with satire, but it can be distinguished from satire, which is designed more specifically to point out vices, follies, or problems with conventional beliefs, whereas parody is generally more lighthearted. Despite the tendency of Western parodies to

Courtesy of Photofest.

undermine or spoof the codes of the more traditional Western, they are still situated within the genre. John Cawelti supports this idea with his argument that parodies are an inevitable part of the life cycle of any genre: "One can almost make out a life cycle characteristic of genres as they move from an initial period of articulation and discovery, through a phase of conscious self-awareness on the part of both creators and audiences, to a time when the generic patterns have become so well-known that people become tired of their predictability. It is at this point that parodic and satiric treatments proliferate and new genres gradually arise" (244). Here Cawelti suggests that as genres eventually become stale, new ones arise to take their places. Dan Harries, in a slightly different take on the subject, believes that parodies renew the genre "by breathing new life into worn-out canons without specifically burying that tradition" (123). The continued popularity of both the Western and the Western parody seems to confirm these evaluations.

To understand why parody works as comedy, it is useful to look at the incongruity theory, one of the major philosophical theories of comedy. Arthur Schopenhauer, one of the most useful proponents of the incongruity theory, describes the comedy of a situation as the tension between the conceived and the perceived, or the expected and the actual (98). When expectations differ from experience, the situation becomes humorous. This explains why the Western needed to have established generic conventions before those conventions could be parodied. For this change in the Western to have occurred, something like the life cycle that Cawelti describes must have taken place. For the Western, this progression through the cycle happened quite quickly. The first Western parodies occurred early in the history of film. Mack Sennett and Douglas Fairbanks made such parodies as early as the second decade of the twentieth century. Buster Keaton appeared in comedies with Western settings, specifically *The Paleface* (1922) and *Go West* (1925). Laurel and Hardy also got into the Western parody movement in 1937 with their film *Way Out West*. Numerous others contributed their own Western parodies, including Abbott and Costello in *Ride 'em Cowboy* (1942); Bob Hope in *Paleface* (1948), *Fancy Pants* (1950), and *Son of Paleface* (1952); and Dean Martin and Jerry Lewis in *Pardners* (1956). Most of these films focused more on the comedian(s) than on making a parody of the genre; as such, they are better described as comedies set in the West than as Western parodies, but they do point to the trend of treating the Western as a comedic subject.

The Western Parody as a Subgenre

Ironically, the Western parodies exhibit their own recycled conventions and clichés. An examination of *Go West* (Edward Buzzell, 1940), *Cat Ballou* (Elliot Silverstein, 1965), *Blazing Saddles* (Mel Brooks, 1974), *Rustlers' Rhapsody* (Hugh Wilson, 1985), and *Shanghai Noon* (Tom Dey, 2000) will illustrate the variety of Western parodies and their similarities. When these parodies are examined together, patterns begin to emerge. These patterns indicate that the Western parody is in itself a generic form. Most Western parodies, in the act of mocking Western codes, end up creating their own set of generic codes to which they more or less adhere. In the act of parodying Western clichés, these films tend to reinforce the ideas that are already present in Westerns, but they do so in a new way.

Go West

The Marx Brothers film *Go West* is important because it is a transitional Western parody. The film is focused largely on the Marx Brothers and their comic personae, but there is also evidence of a more systematic parody of the genre. The film satirizes everything from saloons to shoot-outs, even though the plot follows a fairly standard formula. It centers around a young couple whom the brothers help to protect from an unscrupulous saloon owner—who wants to strike it rich by stealing the deed to their land and selling it to the railroad. The basic comic premise of the film exploits a common conflict in Westerns— a clash that occurred when easterners came west. Typically, the easterner sticks out because his attitudes and beliefs are unsuited to the new environment. In this case, the easterners stand out even more because they are the Marx Brothers. Far from falling into the clichés of the Western, however, the brothers' parody constantly overpowers generic expectations.

The film takes place relatively late in the Marx Brothers' career and in some ways is more indicative of its time than it is of their unique style of humor. In 1940, when the film was released, the nation was still trying to recover from the Great Depression. Film, like every other industry, had taken a beating, and the Marxes' film *Duck Soup* (1933), which is today considered one of their best, fared poorly at the box office. The Marxes had subsequently gone through a significant upsurge in popularity after their association with MGM and its producer Irving Thalberg. Thalberg had revamped the brothers' pictures after *Duck Soup* to tone down their idiosyncratic humor and strengthen the story line, a tradition that continued in *Go West*. Although the film was only a modest success, it spoke to the issues of the era. The film's thin plot focused on a rags-to-riches story of a young couple who sell their land to the railroad. This dream of rapid financial turnaround was still one that would have resonated with contemporary audiences. On a more basic level, though, the underlying structure of the Marx Brothers' film humor had changed: the wild anarchic humor of the late twenties and early thirties was traded in for tamer humorous digressions from the plot. As Andrew Bergman notes of comedies during this period, they tend to be constructive as opposed to their destructive predecessors (133). The tamer humor of the Marxes in this film builds on (or at least does nothing to detract from) the desire of a nation to restore faith in its institutions.

CAT BALLOU

Elliot Silverstein's *Cat Ballou*, starring Jane Fonda and Lee Marvin, was released in 1965 and more seriously adheres to Western codes than most Western parodies. One reason that this film tends to play the genre mostly straight may be that it is an adaptation of a serious novel, *The Ballad of Cat Ballou* (1956), by Roy Chanslor. In the film, Cat Ballou's father is murdered for not selling out to the railroad, and she becomes an outlaw, forming a gang to get her revenge. The film follows a fairly conventional plot but plays up its comic possibilities. While the film is at times serious, it does not strive for gritty realism, remaining situated firmly within the comic mode. The dance scene in the film is a good example of this comic restructuring of the Western; while the scene is no doubt an homage to John Ford, the film uses the dance in a very different way. Ford's sequences tend to interrupt the main narrative in films like *My Darling Clementine* (1946), but in *Cat Ballou* the dialogue and action during the dance forward the plot and set up some important later developments (such as Cat's meeting the villainous sheriff for the first time and her enlisting the two inept outlaws to protect her father). In addition, Ford's dances underscore themes such as community, harmony, and civilization, but the dance in *Cat Ballou* ends in a brawl, with everyone, including women and children, participating in the uproar. This is a clear comic inversion of Ford's established codification of the dance and hints at the violence and unrest occurring in the 1960s.

In some ways, however, *Cat Ballou* is more of a throwback to the relative calm and tranquillity characteristic of America in the 1950s, when the nearly eponymous novel was written. The film is not controversial or shocking; indeed, it was tame enough to be one of the highest-grossing films of 1965, in competition with such popular productions as *The Sound of Music, Doctor Zhivago,* and *That Darn Cat.* Mainstream film was still largely tame and family-oriented despite changing circumstances in society. The relatively low-key portrayal of violence in this film (a central element of the Western) is an interesting indication of a view of violence in popular culture that would shortly and irreversibly change. The film hints at some of the currents of society. Cat's role as a proactive woman (and the central character of the film) who makes a rapid transition from uptight schoolmarm to sexy outlaw parallels some of the changes in the image of women during the sixties. The Native American character, Jackson (Tom Nardini), is portrayed in a positive—albeit somewhat peripheral—role, showing some of the advances that minorities were making in mainstream culture. In addition, the negative portrayal of traditional authority figures, such as the sheriff, and the role of outlaws as heroes, although not innovated by *Cat Ballou,* points to the deterioration of faith in the establishment. The comedic tone of the film keeps these ideas from becoming overbearing, but the criticism, nevertheless, is present.

BLAZING SADDLES

The Western parody that is widely considered the magnum opus of the genre is Mel Brooks's *Blazing Saddles,* a film that systematically dissects nearly all the clichés and the very premises of the form. The film follows Bart, a black man (Cleavon Little), as he is elevated from railroad worker to sheriff of Rock Ridge, a small Western town sitting along the planned route for the railroad. The townspeople have demanded a sheriff for protection from outlaws (who are really employees of the railroad company that wants their land). The villains get Bart appointed as sheriff, hoping that the racist townspeople will be further disheartened and abandon the town. For his parody, Brooks uses every gag and trick in the book and even invents some as he goes along: no conventions are sacred, and no joke too easy or too obscure. The last sequence of the film, in particular, is notable for its deconstruction of the Western. As townspeople and bandits brawl, the camera pulls back to reveal the studio lot where the film is being shot. The combatants break into sets for other genre productions and eventually, in a self-reflexive moment, the villain and the two heroes end up in a movie theater watching the film *Blazing Saddles.*

Although *Blazing Saddles* is specifically a parody of the Western, it is also a product of its time. The film's deconstructionist techniques reflect the widespread turmoil of a nation dealing with Vietnam and Watergate. Just as people were questioning the things they once thought were fixed, Brooks questions and undermines every established convention of the Western. Borders become thin and even nonexistent, as previously separate genres such as the Western and the top-hat musical literally collide in a violent encounter. The film foregrounds the racial tensions that are still prevalent in society and shows the world as a nonsensical place where nothing, not even the myth of the Western, which society has created for itself, has any real meaning. While critics have suggested that the film was the final statement on the Western myth (Rushing 22), it is evident by the number of popular and critically successful Westerns and Western parodies since *Blazing Saddles* that the genre remains viable.

RUSTLERS' RHAPSODY

Perhaps the most unduly overlooked Western parody is director Hugh Wilson's *Rustlers' Rhapsody.* The film appears to have garnered relatively little critical or popular attention when it was released in 1985 and remains insignificant in the video market even though it is a complex and well-constructed parody of the "singing cowboy" Western. There are several possible reasons for the film's relative obscurity. One may be its rather narrow focus on the singing cowboy films, films starring Gene Autry or Roy Rogers that celebrate honest living and a moral code that keeps them in the West to do good. Because *Rustlers' Rhapsody* addresses this particular (and no longer popular) subgenre, many viewers have not been able to appreciate the subtle undermining of generic conventions.

Rustlers' Rhapsody identifies itself with the singing cowboy subgenre by introducing the hero (Tom Berenger) as "Rex O'Herlihan the Singing

RR-C-1

Courtesy of Photofest.

Rex O'Herlihan (Tom Berenger) as the singing cowboy from *Rustlers' Rhapsody*.

Cowboy"; indeed, he often introduces himself in this way and even signs a letter home to his mother as "The Singing Cowboy." (The opening voice-over narration also specifically references the singing cowboy movies.) The clear-cut conventions of the singing cowboy movies are central to the film. There is no trace of the later development of the Western antihero, with his questionable morals. Rex is as squeaky-clean as any Boy Scout and adheres closely to the rules of his role laid out in the singing cowboy films and in the mythology surrounding the character such as that found in Gene Autry's "Ten Commandments of the Cowboy":

1. A cowboy never takes unfair advantage—even of an enemy.
2. A cowboy never betrays a trust.
3. A cowboy always tells the truth.
4. A cowboy is kind to small children, to old folks and to animals.
5. A cowboy is free from racial and religious prejudices.
6. A cowboy is helpful and when anyone is in trouble he lends a hand.
7. A cowboy is a good worker.

8. A cowboy is clean about his person and in thought, word and deed.

9. A cowboy respects womanhood, his parents and the laws of his country.

10. A cowboy is a patriot. (quoted in Rushing 18)

Examples of Rex's adherence to this code are numerous: He never draws first, even when his life is in danger. He shoots bad guys only in the hands. (His target practice consists of shooting wooden cutouts of hands holding guns.) He helps others, going so far as to point out to the bad guys that they could accidentally shoot each other when they surround him. He even rescues a cat from a tree. Rex is also a clean and snappy dresser who does his own washing and ironing and has a wagon that serves no other purpose but to carry his immaculately clean wardrobe. He, in short, embodies all the ideals of the singing cowboy in a highly exaggerated manner.

The hero's relationship to the villain is also simplistically portrayed, as in earlier Westerns. In the film, the forces of evil are represented by not just one but two evil colonels (Andy Griffith and Fernando Rey) who team up to defeat Rex. Rex must oppose them because good must fight evil, and in that conflict, the hero must always defeat the villain. The humor relies on the assumption that both the audience and the film's characters are aware of the generic clichés. For example, characters are introduced by type—the town drunk, the evil cattle baron, the prostitute with the heart of gold, and the like. Rex states that each western town is identical, and to prove his point he accurately predicts that they have "a very pretty, but somehow asexual schoolmarm."

Rex is not the only one aware of the conventions of the Western. The two evil colonels in *Rustlers' Rhapsody* recognize that they cannot beat Rex for the simple reason that he is "good" and they are "evil." To beat Rex, they decide to hire another "good guy," the idea being that the "goodest" good guy will win. Bob Barber (Patrick Wayne), the other "good guy," dresses in white and informs Rex, "In order to be a good guy you have to be a confident heterosexual." This encounter creates a problem for Rex because he is not confident in this area of endeavor. He still lives the code of the Western that enjoins him to protect women, but not become involved with them to the point of losing his individuality (Rushing 23). Rex suffers from a lack of confidence but is eventually able to defeat the enemy through his recognition of the conventions of the genre. (He knows that his sidekick is likely to be shot, so he protects him with a bulletproof vest.) *Rustlers' Rhapsody,* through its manipulation and reversal of the generic codes of the Western, creates a very effective and self-reflexive parody.

Released during a period of relative stability and prosperity, Wilson's 1985 film takes a complicated look at what is initially portrayed as a simpler time. *Rustlers' Rhapsody* pokes fun at the simplistic conventions during the era of Gene Autry and Roy Rogers that separate good from evil, white from black (or in 1985, by extension, white from red). While there was no doubt an attempt to portray red communists as the men in the black hats at the time, Wilson's film shows in a comedic fashion that things are never so simple. The switch of the film from black and white to color at the beginning emphasizes the increased complexity of the modern era. In addition, two seemingly good guys end up on opposite sides of the conflict; the one who is finally revealed to be the bad guy is the one serving selfish interests and not the good of the people. *Rustlers' Rhapsody* also foregrounds gender and sexuality, another major preoccupation of the 1980s. The film implies that the colonel played by Griffith is a homosexual, and it constantly calls into question Rex's sexuality through his choice of wardrobe and his somewhat ambiguous relationship with women. While these commentaries are mostly gentle, they do comment on some of the societal and cultural currents of the time.

SHANGHAI NOON

Tom Dey's film *Shanghai Noon* is an interesting departure from many of the other Western parodies. Like *Cat Ballou*, it attempts to play the story relatively straight, but it also serves as a vehicle for Jackie Chan's kung fu comedy, providing for dynamic interaction between two sets of conventions and clichés: the West and the Far East. The cultural conflict and interplay are a fresh addition to the Western parody genre.

Shanghai Noon also consciously transposes the Western by showing a markedly different landscape. While ostensibly set in the American West, it was filmed in Alberta, Canada, showcasing green, mountainous landscapes rather than John Ford's arid Monument Valley. This setting, combined with the location shooting in the Forbidden City in China, lends a very different feel to the film. The film also highlights the humorous interactions that can occur when two cultures meet; the misunderstandings and comical moments suggest a pleasant way of resolving cultural differences in a world that is increasingly internationally oriented. The eventual reconciliation and friendship between the Chinese and Western characters show an exciting, yet peaceful, outcome for a world straddling a new millennium. This film perhaps represents an evolution in the Western parody that treats the Western humorously but modifies it in a way that breathes new life into the genre by examining and incorporating the elements of another culture and tradition.

Reliance on Established Western Conventions

One of the most immediately obvious references to earlier Westerns is found in the titles of the parodies. Each of the films considered here somehow refers to an earlier Western film, often in a comedic way. *Go West,* as mentioned earlier, takes the same title as a Buster Keaton film and notably refers to Horace Greeley's famous injunction of 1853, "Go West, young man." The title *Cat Ballou* came from the book on which the film was based: *The Ballad of Cat Ballou. Blazing Saddles,* in addition to its humorous implications, is a deliberately strange juxtaposition of words from other titles. It could be referring to any of a number of earlier films, including *Blazing Arrows* (1922), *Blazing Barriers* (1937), *Blazing Six Shooters* (1940), *Blazing across the Pecos* (1948), *Hearts and Saddles* (1917), *Empty Saddles* (1936), *Songs and Saddles* (1938), or *Saddles and Sagebrush* (1943). *Rustlers' Rhapsody* harkens back to many early Western titles, three of which are particularly similar: *Rustlers' Ranch* (1926), *Rustlers' Roundup* (1933), and *Rustlers' Ransom* (1950). The title *Shanghai Noon* not only conjures up images of Fred Zinnemann's *High Noon* of 1952 but also emphasizes the cross-cultural dynamics that the film presents.

In addition to borrowing titles, Western parodies borrow settings and numerous conventions, which they appropriate and transform, often through exaggeration. Contrary to Solomon's assertion that parodies like *Blazing Saddles* are anti-Westerns (12), they actually reinforce the conventions and their presence as central elements of the Western. These conventions are necessary for the humor of the Western parody to work. The sequence from *Cat Ballou* in which Lee Marvin's character transforms himself from a drunk to a classic gunfighter provides a clear example of this: "Starting very humorously with Marvin struggling into a corset, the transformation not only alters him but brings out a response in us as piece by piece the stereotyped image appears" (Tudor 6).

Another method for parodying or satirizing conventions is to demythologize them. John Cawelti explains this process by describing how a normally romanticized situation can be suddenly invested with a sense of reality (236).

Campfire scene with Slim Pickens and Alex Karras from *Blazing Saddles*.

The campfire scene in *Blazing Saddles* becomes humorous because the Western convention of the campfire is serene, often accompanied by the lonely sound of a harmonica. Brooks's scene is a slapstick reminder that the evening meal in the real West would have probably consisted of bacon and beans. When viewers expect the typical camp scene but are greeted with the roar of gas, the situation becomes comic.

Among the most important conventions in both the Western and, consequently, the Western parody is the classic shoot-out. Violence is a central element in both types of film, and the shoot-out is the codified ritual in which conflict is resolved through violence. In the parody, however (with its exaggerated version of the invincible Western hero), the violence is typically much less threatening. The shoot-out is, of course, the climactic representation of this violence: "At a certain mystical point in the interaction between two opposing forces, the western version of the duel becomes morally acceptable; both the villain and the hero know immediately when this point comes, as they do not exist as psychological entities apart from the code—rather, they

Groucho, Harpo, and Chico Marx in *Go West*.

embody the code" (Wright 43). An examination of the Western parody's treatment of the duel will reveal how this subgenre deconstructs while simultaneously reinforcing this convention.

Go West provides Harpo, the silent Marx brother, an opportunity to enter a duel with the villain. They square off in a conventional manner, but when they pull their weapons, Harpo has a small whisk broom, which he uses to dust off his adversary. Then, with typical Marx Brothers absurdity, the brush fires off a round of ammunition. Mel Brooks also uses the shoot-out; although the death scene is played up for maximum comic effect, it still represents the victory of good over evil and determines the outcome of the film. Rex's character defeats the other "good guy" in the final shoot-out of *Rustlers' Rhapsody*. During the shoot-out, it is revealed that the other "good guy" is, in reality, a bad guy, thus confirming the expectation that the good guy always wins.

There are actually two major shoot-outs in *Shanghai Noon* between the cowboy Roy O'Bannon (Owen Wilson) and his nemesis, Marshal Nathan Van

Cleef (Xander Berkeley). The first is interrupted by Chan's character, Chon, who throws a sheriff's badge like a Chinese throwing star, wounding the marshal's hand. O'Bannon complains about this interruption of the duel because he recognizes that a code of the West has been violated. (The Chinese character's interruption of the duel emphasizes the interaction and cultural conflicts that this film tries to portray.) The second duel occurs at the end of the film. While the action leading up to this moment is also comic, the shoot-out definitively defeats the Western bad guy. (The Eastern bad guy is defeated in an extended kung fu battle, maintaining that convention as well.) In these films, although the shoot-out is parodied, it ultimately plays a crucial role in the outcome of the plot; as a result, this convention is simultaneously undercut and reinforced.

The saloon, a typical hangout and location of action, makes an appearance in each of these parodies. In every case, the hero enters as a stranger and stands out among the crowd. In *Go West,* the Marx Brothers entertain the patrons of the saloon and look and act very different from the regular clientele. Cat Ballou's gang goes into the Hole in the Wall saloon initially as outsiders, but then are welcomed when the bartender recognizes Kid Shelleen (Lee Marvin). In *Blazing Saddles,* the black sheriff stands out against all the white customers. (Interestingly, nothing is made of his race at this point in the film. He sits in the back but is not accosted by any of the patrons.) Rex, in *Rustlers' Rhapsody,* comes into the saloon and orders a glass of milk. When the bartender stares at him he asks, "Is this one of those really tough bars?" When he learns that it is, he orders a glass of warm gin with a human hair in it. It is only then that he is accepted. Jackie Chan's character in *Shanghai Noon,* dressed in traditional Chinese clothes but with Native American face paint, enters the saloon, which falls silent at his strange appearance. In addition to being a place where the hero is introduced as a stranger, the saloon is also a location for violence. In each of the films it is the site for a showdown.

The coming of the railroad (a symbol of urban sophistication and technological invasion) is an important part of the plot of each of these films. *Go West* and *Blazing Saddles* are centered around a sliver of land through which the railroad needs a right-of-way. The heroes in both *Cat Ballou* and *Shanghai Noon* are train robbers, and the final climactic scene in *Go West* is a chase involving a train. In *Rustlers' Rhapsody* one of the evil colonels is bringing the railroad to town, and the Chinese villain in *Shanghai Noon* is also a railroad baron. In all these films, the railroad is a tool for the powerful, greedy men who profit at the expense of others. These elements are typical of Westerns, and the parody uses these conventions in mostly conventional ways, reinforcing its adherence to the Western generic code.

Riding Off into the Sunset

Typically, these films end with the hero or heroes riding off into the sunset and, therefore, farther west into the frontier, the traditional exodus of the cowboy. In *Shanghai Noon*, Roy and Chon ride off into the setting sun, although there is no plot- or theme-mandated reason for this exit. The ending of *Cat Ballou* is played for its comic possibilities. Cat and her love interest, Clay (Michael Callan), snuggle together in the back of a hearse as they ride into the distance. Rex calls attention to the sunset and comments on how great it is at the end of *Rustlers' Rhapsody*. The heroes in *Blazing Saddles* are similarly motivated to leave at the end of the film. They mount their horses and ride a short distance out of town, where they are met by a limousine. This anachronistically modern vehicle then drives them out into the setting sun.

Conventions of the Western Parody

Western parodies sometimes go a great deal further than borrowing conventions from the traditional Western. To ensure authenticity or tie themselves more tightly to the genre, they often use sets, costumes, and even actors from recognizable Western films. Parts of *Cat Ballou*, for instance, were filmed on the same set as *High Noon*. *Rustlers' Rhapsody* employed a similar technique to associate the film with its Western antecedents. The film made use of one of the frontier sets built in Almeria, Spain, by Sergio Leone for his "spaghetti Westerns" (Harries 43). Both *Blazing Saddles* and *Rustlers' Rhapsody* include a character who is an imitation of Marlene Dietrich's sultry saloon girl in *Destry Rides Again* (1939), and *Rustlers' Rhapsody* clothes Rex's sidekick in the outfit that Smiley Burnett wore in the Roy Rogers film *Under Western Stars* (1938) (Harries 47).

Western parodies also tend to cast major players from the genre. Both John Carroll and Robert Barrat from *Go West* had appeared in several Westerns. Lee Marvin, Arthur Hunnicutt, and Bruce Cabot from *Cat Ballou* all had many roles in serious Westerns under their pistol belts. Slim Pickens from

Blazing Saddles was also a very familiar face. *Rustlers' Rhapsody* does some interesting things with these associations. The bad "good guy," Bob Barber, is played by John Wayne's younger son, Patrick Wayne, whose presence conjures up the memory of his father, who is synonymous with the serious Western. Jackie Chan's character in *Shanghai Noon* is named "Chon Wang," which is pronounced almost identically to "John Wayne." (His partner Roy says that this is a terrible name for a cowboy, providing a nicely ironic moment.) The name of one of the villains in *Shanghai Noon*, Marshal Nathan Van Cleef, is an homage to Lee Van Cleef, another familiar icon, appearing in films such as *High Noon* and *The Man Who Shot Liberty Valance* (1962).

Western parodies also tend to follow a convention of establishing their humorous tone very early, often during the opening credits. *Go West* opens with a title quoting Greeley's famous phrase, and the subtitle states, "This is a story of three men who made Horace Greeley sorry he said it." *Blazing Saddles* opens with the burning of the Warner Brothers logo, symbolizing how the film will destroy all Western clichés once and for all (Harries 61). The opening to *Rustlers' Rhapsody* starts in black and white during a pursuit of criminals but then changes to color in a comic turn of events when the bad guys turn around and start chasing Rex. The reversal is an opening indication of the generic reversals to take place in the film.

Most of these films also use a comic technique that makes clear their construction as films. The introduction of anachronisms (elements from outside the film's historical period) to the film or to the dialogue calls attention to the genre conventions. By introducing elements that do not belong in the historical time frame, the film establishes its nonrealistic and comic nature.

Groucho Marx in *Go West* dances in a Jazz Age style. He also makes humorous reference to the famous Hollywood disclaimer: "Any resemblance between these two characters and living persons is purely coincidental." He even refers to events in the future. "Telephone? This is 1870. Don Ameche hasn't invented the telephone yet." (This line refers to the 1939 film *The Story of Alexander Graham Bell*, which came out the previous year and starred Don Ameche as the famous inventor.) *Blazing Saddles* has numerous anachronisms. For instance, Harvey Korman's character, Hedley Lamarr (a reference to actress Hedy Lamarr, in itself an anachronism), hires a group of thugs to drive the townspeople out of Rock Ridge. Crowded with anachronisms, this group includes actors in Hell's Angels outfits and Nazi uniforms. Lamarr also makes reference to the possibility of getting an Academy Award for best supporting actor. In *Rustlers' Rhapsody*, the town Rex visits is called "Oakwood Estates," a suburban name inappropriate to the era of settlement. Rex, in an aside that calls attention to genre clichés, reminds his sidekick that he holds the copyright to his theme song. *Shanghai Noon* also uses several anachronistic expressions in the nineteenth-century dialogue, introducing newer terms such as "male-dominated society" and "punk."

The music in Western parodies is often comic and many times anachronistic. Sheriff Bart in *Blazing Saddles* has a jazz theme played on-screen by the Count Basie Orchestra in the middle of the desert; later, the townspeople, as one of their church hymns, sing commentary on the movie, complete with profanity. In *Rustlers' Rhapsody*, Rex eats a hallucinogenic root and imagines backup singers and instruments—which obligingly appear on the sound track. *Cat Ballou* includes two balladeers (Nat "King" Cole and Stubby Kaye), who, like a popular culture version of a Greek chorus, sing commentary on the action.

Closely related to the anachronisms of the films are their self-reflexive qualities. Each of the films is highly aware of the generic conventions of the Western and often openly acknowledges them. At one point in *Blazing Saddles* Harvey Korman's character states, "I hate that cliché." Sheriff Bart's plea for help by stating, "You'd do it for Randolph Scott," not only connects the film with the high-profile Western film star of *Seven Men from Now* (1956), *Comanche Station* (1960), and *Ride the High Country* (1962) but shows Bart's awareness of the expectations conditioned by the genre. Roy's statement to Chon in *Shanghai Noon*, that the sick prisoner routine has been done to death, is another self-reflexive reference. Rex in *Rustlers' Rhapsody* keeps repeating, "Believe me, I know," because he is intimately aware of genre conventions. He seems to have a sixth sense that allows him to foresee when he is going to have a showdown with the bad guys, and that sixth sense is his intimate knowledge of the genre in which he exists.

The Western parody mocks the codes and conventions of a distinctively American cinematic genre while commenting—directly and indirectly—on the cultural and social issues of its time. Nevertheless, in the act of subverting those conventions and calling attention to their constructedness, the Western parody creates its own set of conventions that are closely allied to, and often rely heavily on, the conventions of the Western itself. The Western parody admits that the paradox of a code that is arbitrary, but nevertheless binding, is inherently humorous. This parodic attitude, however, does not let it stray too much from its generic model. Whether the cowboy rides off into the sunset on a horse or in a limousine, he still rides off into the sunset.

Works Cited

Bergman, Andrew. *We're in the Money: Depression America and Its Films.* New York: Harper and Row, 1972.

Blazing Saddles. Dir. Mel Brooks. Perf. Cleavon Little, Gene Wilder, Mel Brooks, Harvey Korman, Madeline Kahn, and Slim Pickens. Videocassette. Warner, 1974.

Cat Ballou. Dir. Elliot Silverstein. Perf. Jane Fonda, Lee Marvin, Michael Callan, Dwayne Hickman, Tom Nardini, Nat King Cole, and Stubby Kaye. 1965. DVD. Columbia, 2000.

Cawelti, John G. "*Chinatown* and Generic Transformation in Recent American Films." In *Film Genre Reader II,* edited by Barry Keith Grant, 227–45. Austin: Texas University Press, 1995.

Go West. Dir. Edward Buzzell. Perf. Groucho Marx, Chico Marx, Harpo Marx, John Carroll, and Diana Lewis. Videocassette. MGM, 1940.

Harries, Dan. *Film Parody.* London: British Film Institute, 2000.

Rushing, Janice Hocker. "The Rhetoric of the American Western Myth." *Communication Monographs* 50 (1983): 14–32.

Rustlers' Rhapsody. Dir. Hugh Wilson. Perf. Patrick Wayne, Tom Berenger, G. W. Bailey, Marilu Henner, Andy Griffith, Fernando Rey, and Sela Ward. Videocassette. Paramount, 1985.

Schopenhauer, Arthur. *The World as Will and Representation.* Vol. 2. Translated by E. F. J. Payne. New York: Dover, 1958.

Shanghai Noon. Dir. Tom Dey. Perf. Jackie Chan, Owen Wilson, Lucy Liu, and Xander Berkeley. DVD. Buena Vista, 2000.

Solomon, Stanley J. *Beyond Formula: American Film Genres.* New York: Harcourt Brace Jovanovich, 1976.

Tudor, Andrew. "Genre." In *Film Genre Reader II,* edited by Barry Keith Grant, 3–10. Austin: Texas University Press, 1995.

Wright, Judith Hess. "Genre Films and the Status Quo." In *Film Genre Reader II,* edited by Barry Keith Grant, 41–49. Austin: Texas University Press, 1995.

PART FOUR
THE POSTMODERNIST WESTERN
1980–2000

11 ◯ *Alexandra Keller*

HISTORICAL DISCOURSE AND AMERICAN IDENTITY IN WESTERNS SINCE THE REAGAN ERA

Because the subject of this chapter is the variety of ways that contemporary Westerns construct historical discourse—constructions that occur even when the film claims merely to entertain, and constructions that veer from the historical "truth," even when the film claims to be getting at such veracity—it may be worth starting with a rumor and a disclaimer. The rumor: that there was a candlelit shrine to John Wayne at the Alamo. Bruce Winders, curator and archivist at the Alamo in San Antonio, Texas, offered this correction:

> To my knowledge there never was a "shrine" to John Wayne at the Alamo, with or without candles. . . . There once were several items from the film on display here—his directors guild award, his coonskin cap, and a promotional painting for the movie—but these have been in storage for some time. . . . The decision was made . . . to play down the John Wayne connection. There was a shift toward having an accurate historical interpretation. I . . . have at time[s] had to tackle the clash of popular culture and history. It is an interesting challenge. There is a whole generation that has the Wayne movie (or Disney film) firmly fixed in their minds.

"CERTAIN, VERY SMALL, LIBERTIES": HISTORY AND AUTHENTICITY

The disclaimer, from the copyright page of Dave Eggers's best-selling memoir, *A Heartbreaking Work of Staggering Genius:* "All events described herein actually happened, though on occasion the author has taken certain, very small, liberties with chronology, because that is his right as an American." The refutation of the rumor is a reminder that films "clash" with history as much as they clarify it. The disclaimer is a reminder that the "taking of liberties" is almost unavoidable even in historically responsible films, and in Westerns might be a generically and culturally specific "right."

The Western is a genre whose cultural meanings, both held and contested, coalesce as something oscillating between myth and history. Before 1980, a Western could be "affirmative" like *My Darling Clementine* (1946), *Red River* (1947), or *Shane* (1952), lauding "regeneration through violence" (cf. Slotkin, *Regeneration through Violence*), the centrality of the individual, the inevitability of progress, the virtues of capitalism, the necessity of force and law, as well as the primacy of a community of men. Or it could be "critical" like *High Noon* (1952), *Cheyenne Autumn* (1964), or *Little Big Man* (1970), condemning violence and the genocide of Native Americans and trading the simplistic hero for more complex figures. Either way, there was little questioning of the cultural utility of the Western itself.

The Western's near disappearance after the critical and financial disaster of *Heaven's Gate* in 1980 (to recall how big a catastrophe that was, one need only imagine *Titanic* in the red),[1] and its resurgence with the Oscar-winning *Dances with Wolves* in 1990 and *Unforgiven* in 1992, coincide with the seismic shifts in American culture that were the Reagan–Bush I years (1980–1992). There are specific reasons, some touching the political rhetoric of Ronald Reagan himself, some touching the "natural" generic cycles of Westerns. Reagan's political rhetoric derived much of its logic, as well as its images, from classical Westerns—and Hollywood cinematic logic in general. By 1980, the Western, having become the counter-Western (e.g., Arthur Penn's *Little Big Man* and Robert Altman's *McCabe and Mrs. Miller* [1971]) for the duration of the Vietnam War, itself was experiencing a momentary and not unusual fatigue. When Reagan left office, Westerns began to return. "As a matter of fact," wrote pop culture observers Jane and Michael Stern in 1993, "the new popularity of Westerns can be quite easily explained by the fact that Reagan is no longer president. As long as that one-time sagebrush star was in the White House, Americans didn't need westerns so much because we had a cowboy hero leading the country" (28). The Sterns were certainly tongue in cheek in their assessment, but after Reagan, one may legitimately wonder whether—and why, and how—America once again "needed" Westerns.

The Western reemerged under the controversial sign of full-blown postmodernism, the conditions of which have profound implications for historical discourse. As Hayden White (who does not use the P-word) has it, the story embedded in history is a narrative act profoundly marked by context, and neither neutral nor objective. "Far from being merely a form of discourse that can be filled with different contents, real or imaginary," writes White, historical narrative "already possesses a content prior to any given actualization of it in speech or writing" (xi). History, then, is not separate from or, in its alleged objectivity, opposed to cultural production; it *is* a cultural production.

Neither authentic details of Native American dress nor, say, the appearance of Wyatt Earp in any film bearing his name guarantees historically illuminating cinema—and obviously the excessive detail in traditional Westerns often amounts to the crudest of stereotypes and inaccuracies. But in the rhetoric of 1990s revision, one of the most important proclaimed strategies was to "set the record straight." Especially in their classical mode (from John Ford's *Stagecoach* [1939] to the breakdown of the Hollywood studio system in the early 1960s), whether or not Westerns referred to actual events and people, they claimed an affinity with authenticity through an explicit grounding in "History," not in all individual texts but in the genre as a whole. Indeed, film's capacity to represent mimetically and kinetically leads to what Robert Rosenstone calls film's slide into "false historicity." As he writes, this "myth of facticity, a mode on which Hollywood has long depended, . . . is the mistaken notion that mimesis is all, that history is in fact no more than a 'period look,' that things themselves *are* history, rather than *become* history because of what they mean to a people of a particular time and place. The baleful Hollywood corollary: as long as you get the look right, you may do whatever you want to the past to make it more interesting" (*Visions of the Past* 60, italics in original). In classical Westerns, this seamless, totalizing presentation is achieved through a realist aesthetic that naturalizes information so that it *appears* historically accurate, even if it is not.[2] Despite— indeed because of—this exterior appeal to apparently genuine detail and the monolithic, inviolate discourse of History itself, the Western is the bearer of its own seamless authenticity.

During its 1980s hiatus, a certain elegiac rhetoric pervaded criticism about Westerns. Richard Slotkin's own grim prognosis was that recent Westerns had largely failed "to creat[e] . . . the *illusion of historicity* that is so central to

Courtesy of Universal City Studios, Inc.

Walker has a radically reflexive relationship to the Western genre and to the act of historicization.

the genre. . . . If Westerns do come back, it will be because someone has been able to duplicate John Ford's achievement of connecting the special language of the Western to a story and a set of images that—with absolute economy of form—will represent for us *our true place in history*" ("Prologue" 430, italics added). The Western's relationship to history is privileged, problematic, and weirdly intimate, especially for contemporary Westerns that either portray actual historical figures or invest in historical discourse to construct their narratives. *Walker* (1987), *Dances with Wolves, Thunderheart* (1992), *The Ballad of Little Jo, Tombstone, Posse* (all 1993), *Wyatt Earp* (1994), *Wild Bill* (1995), and *Lone Star* (1996) are to varying degrees self-conscious of their historical natures, as well as their chosen modes of history. They also share a self-awareness of their own historical placement on the other side of the generic diaspora of the 1980s, when the concerns of Westerns were displaced in certain subgenres of action and science fiction films. Thus, no matter what particular aesthetic strategies any individual film employs, ranging from the aggressive punk anachronism of *Walker* to the almost retro-classical look of *Dances with Wolves,* all these films have a reflexive sense of themselves as Westerns.

DANCING VERSUS WALKING: THE NOSTALGIC, THE RADICAL, AND THE CORRECTIVE WESTERN

Three films succinctly illustrate the range of historicity in Westerns since the waning Reagan years: Kevin Costner's *Dances with Wolves,* Alex Cox's *Walker,* and *Tombstone,* starring Kurt Russell as Wyatt Earp. *Dances with Wolves* is not a movie about a real person, but it aspires to be far more than a period or genre piece. *Walker* describes the antics of real-life nineteenth-century Manifest Destiny poster boy William Walker (Ed Harris). *Tombstone* claims to rehistoricize an American story so legendary it has become American myth— which is the general problem and power of Westerns.

Dances with Wolves is the best-known and most traditionally historiographical —or, more accurately, historiophotic—of these films. By 1990 it was hardly a radical revision to the Western to suggest that Anglos did horrible things to Native American nations that did nothing to provoke them. What did appear to be new was a meticulous commitment to getting the facts about the Sioux absolutely correct. The film's rhetoric hinged much of its claim to authority on this very authenticity. Much of the dialogue was spoken in Lakota, with translations provided in subtitles. Native Americans were cast in Indian roles that in earlier Westerns had typically gone to whites. The costumes, based on the paintings of Karl Bodmer (1809–1893) and George Catlin (1796–1872), were historically accurate, as one of the studio's press releases claimed, "down to the last elk tooth decoration." The authenticity culminated in the induction of Costner, producer Jim Wilson, and costar Mary McDonnell into the Rosebud Sioux Tribal Nation at the film's premiere, a kind of ritual of naturalization as performance piece and publicity stunt.

Dances with Wolves is revisionist in content, but formally it is a *nostalgic* Western (as is Eastwood's *Unforgiven*). It is nostalgic not because it yearns for the racism of yore but because it never problematizes traditional historiophotic method. For, if what the film "remembers" is more accurate than classical Westerns, it still attempts to recuperate the category of Individual Anglos.[3] Yes, white folks were institutionally terrible, the film suggests, *but this one was okay.* The Sioux Nation's renaming of Costner's Lieutenant Dunbar as Dances with Wolves permits him to colonize their historical prerogative, to speak in place of them while seeming to speak for and even with them.

Dances with Wolves is also classical in its regard of the frontier, the essential

Dances with Wolves aspires to be far more than a period or genre piece.

element of the Western that is, as historian Edward Countryman explains, "the most powerful tool for understanding America itself" (Buscombe 124). Richard White suggests that two diametrical views of the frontier dominate its popular conception—Frederick Jackson Turner's relatively peaceful, linear proposal of "an area of free land," the settlement of which "explain[s] American development" (Turner 31), and Buffalo Bill Cody's more violent scenario in which "the bullet is the pioneer of civilization." These two versions added up to an extraordinary totality. As White asserts, "By the early twentieth century there was no way to tell stories about the West, no way to talk about an American identity, without confronting either Buffalo Bill or Turner. They had divided the narrative space of the West between them" (45). Westerns typically take the form of Turner's thesis and imbue it with Cody's content, such that the progressivism, exceptionalism, and inevitability that mark Turner's discourse narrate stories of relentless violence à la Cody.

Early in *Dances with Wolves*, Dunbar says, "I've always wanted to see the frontier before it's gone"; later he describes the anguish of the Sioux: "There was only the confusion of a people unable to predict the future." For *Dances with Wolves* the frontier is strictly a location and, given the film's status as an "eco-Western," a nonrenewable resource that can be used up. The frontier is a set on which History transpires, rather than a construction of History itself.[4] *Walker,* on the other hand, sees the frontier as a *how* rather than a *what:* a sociopolitical operation rather than a geographic location. The West in *Walker* (as its story moves from Mexico to New Orleans to San Francisco to Nicaragua to Honduras) has little to do with a compass. It is instead a potentially endless series of political maneuvers that, when faced with the geographic end point of California, Alaska, or even Mexico,[5] simply move on covertly, perpetually enacting Manifest Destiny thousands of miles from "home," as the civilian William Walker, mocking the democratic process he claims to be importing, effectively "crowns" himself president of Nicaragua. Not that Dunbar is without his own expansionist imperatives, but in his case they are constructed as personal. Walker's renunciation of his U.S. passport, a legal maneuver that allows for his illegal rule of Nicaragua, on the other hand, presents an alternative to Dunbar's classical either-or binary, though hardly a more savory one.

The oppositional historical stances of the two films are further articulated by their varied use of the voice-over. In *Dances with Wolves,* Dunbar tells his own story, as lifted from his diaries. He speaks by turns retrospectively in the past tense and (rarely) impressionistically in the imperfect. Always, however, he speaks in the first person. This first person empirically identifies Dunbar's experience—it lays claim to a set of events' having happened at all, regardless of anyone's particular interpretation of it. That the narration exists in a mutually ratifying format with the visual images contributes to its impression of accuracy, and this type of voice-over is familiar from earlier protorevisionist Westerns like John Ford's apology *Cheyenne Autumn* and is hardly exclusive to the Western genre. What Dunbar says, what is written in his diary, and what happens all correspond precisely. Moreover, it emanates from a textual product—Dunbar's diaries, replete with watercolors, sketches, and the odd verse. And rather than intensifying the subjective nature of Dunbar's point of view, the proliferation of different media all telling the same story actually renders the sum total apparently objective. If in fact Dunbar might be a reliable narrator precisely because he has a unique, often prescient, and increasingly disenfranchised perspective, *Dances with Wolves*'s particular historical model actually transforms the personal narrative into a history (almost) without authorship.

The radical historical approach of *Walker* (directed by Alex Cox and starring Ed Harris) is also marked by a reflexive use of voice-over. Walker's

Walker takes a metacritical approach to its representation of the last stand.

voice-over derives from articles, speeches, essays, and letters he actually wrote, but it is not quite in the first person, as evidenced by the film's opening. This variation on a classical trope is part of how *Walker* uses historical distance to eventually collapse history utterly into the present, insisting that the past is not a place to which one can escape but a locus where it is possible to identify the source of a number of contemporary problems and issues. History for Cox is not a safe, resolved, *completed* place, as it is for Costner, but rather a highly unstable and contested set of discourses, the form of whose remembering directly speaks to the present.[6] One sees this in *Walker* in its rehearsal of the last stand trope, which, as in *Dances with Wolves,* first occurs at the beginning of the narrative.

Walker opens with William Walker's first last stand in Sonora, which serves as an overture of sorts to the numerous other last stands in which he will engage. *Dances with Wolves* regarded the last stand as a site that itself needed to be recuperated—to be made into a first stand, the survival of which ratified Dunbar as a hero and readied him to bear witness to the last stand of the Sioux. But in a postmodern Western like *Walker,* so closely aligned with New Historicist polemics, the last stand trope can proliferate itself seemingly endlessly within a single narrative. In each one, Walker (Ed Harris) appears as an austere, puritanical version of the flamboyant General George Armstrong Custer, inciting in his men a maniacal passion for the hopeless.

In its first few shots, *Walker* takes a metacritical approach to history through a very unnostalgic pastiche. The film opens with a completely black frame and a voice-over of Walker narrating his own story in the third person. (The reflexive nature of the voice-over is, of course, not yet apparent.) "In 1853 a small group of Americans journeyed to Sonora, Mexico. Their mission was to free that territory from a corrupt dictatorship. Their leader's name was William Walker."

The first image frame has Western written all over it: a wide, blue sky, a broad ribbon of dusty green trees, and a long foreground of sun-beaten earth. Across it a line of infantry and cavalry (with no recognizable uniform) races right to left as the camera tracks it in long shot. Then an intertitle appears, square red letters on black: "THIS IS A TRUE STORY." Then back to the scene, this time in a slow motion very familiar from the Westerns of Sam Peckinpah. A quartet of shots of soldiers being blown unobtrusively apart by cannon fire follows. Then the title, also in block red letters on black: "WALKER." The typeface in both cases is apparently neutral, ahistorical, almost utterly without style as opposed to the marked "Western" title fonts (usually Playbill) of any number of films, notably Anthony Mann's *The Naked Spur* (1953), Sergio Leone's *Once upon a Time in the West* (1968), and Robert Altman's *Buffalo Bill and the Indians, or Sitting Bull's History Lesson* (1976). Certainly its simplicity is a tweak on the Western look of the first few frames of action. But already an implicit political position is being taken up here. This is the bare-bones, Marxist-inspired color scheme and typeface of Nicaragua's FSLN party, the Sandinistas.[7] Director Cox frequently and publicly voiced his support for the Sandinistas (and in 1987 such sympathetic voices were far more provocative), and he extended that graphic support to the film's music.[8] Joe Strummer, composer of *Walker*'s score, had been the lead singer and songwriter for the British punk band the Clash, with which he had, just a few years earlier, put out a musically accomplished and politically astute multialbum project entitled *Sandinista*.[9] The familiarity of the film's political position is contingent on a highly intertextual *and* interdisciplinary spectatorial knowledge of Latin American politics, popular music styles from a variety of cultures, and previous Westerns. The title frame cuts to a flat, frontal medium shot of William Walker at his desk, sternly dressed in black, his interior surroundings a range of cool blues and grays to contrast with the exterior's brighter earth yellow-browns and blood reds. He speaks out loud the very words he is also writing in his diary, though he is so quiet and so tight-lipped that it is at first difficult to see it as synchronous dialogue rather than voice-over: "Walker's forces would never slip away from here. His men would rather die first."

Walker's sense of his own historicity is remarkable when compared with that of, say, Errol Flynn's General Custer of *They Died with Their Boots On* (1941). Custer is, if not naive, certainly untroubled about his relationship as a potential great man to a larger historical firmament in which he might be hung. Walker, in contrast, has an almost Foucauldian knowledge of that great man paradigm. That is, as his highly self-conscious narration explains throughout the film, he knows History to be a discursive construct. Indeed, he knows it to be one of the master narratives of Western culture. But he also knows that *any* position is a discursive one, so, given the opportunity, he might as well construct a great man discourse for himself.[10]

And whether or not his men *would* rather die first, it is what they do. Slowly, balletically, blood dances out of musketball wounds in joyful arcs and spurts as if choreographed by the Peckinpah of *The Wild Bunch* (1969), while Strummer's neo-salsa sound track cheerfully plays on. The carnage is relentless, and Cox metes it out soldier by soldier, each with a doting close-up or a prolonged slow-motion meditation on his gushing wounds. The first extreme long shot of the film shows the Mexican cavalry, flagged and uniformed, sweep in over the low, stone walls of Walker's enclave. Captain Hornsby (Sy Richardson), an African American, booms at his white private soldiers: "You *have* to sacrifice yourselves! For freedom! For justice! For religious conviction! Stand up and fight! Fight you bastards. . . . Fiiiight!!!" But they cannot fight. They are too busy being slaughtered by men wearing nicer uniforms, too busy quoting Peckinpah's articulate bloodletting.

Walker assembles what remains of his officer corps and admits defeat, saying only an act of God can save them, which, in the form of a sandstorm, it does. A French officer tells him in a trembling, portentous voice that at least they will go down in history. Walker shrugs and blinks. "Don't be so silly, man." And he walks away, leaving the Frenchman to be shot down while trying to rescue the phalanx's flag. Discursive pragmatism: they cannot go down in history unless Walker lives to write it. Put another way, Walker will go down in history while his men simply go down.

Cox's intertextual and ironic reference to history painting in some of his compositions is decidedly postmodern.

Throughout the film's opening, Walker speaks about himself as if he were another person. Now, this *is* a sign of a developed psychosis, but it is also an accomplished understanding of the nature of historical recounting and of narrative in general.[11] Walker the man, a pre-postmodern historical figure, is postmodernized by *Walker* the movie, which recognizes Walker's split personality: producer *of* historical discourse as well as produced *by* it.[12] In *Dances with Wolves,* Dunbar's first person does just the opposite—it obscures the fact that History does not happen, it is assembled out of what did.

For Cox, the reflexive and critical framing of the subjective voice in *Walker* is not enough to keep the spectator from buying into that false historicity. He also peppers the film with historical anachronism. Simultaneous to Walker's emphatic fall from heroic abolitionist to psychotic imperialist is an encroaching of the present tense (the 1980s) into the past of the film (the 1850s). Computers appear in Cornelius Vanderbilt's office, soldiers smoke Marlboros and drink Coca-Cola, members of the nineteenth-century Nicaraguan aristocracy read *Newsweek* in their horse-drawn carriages, and the marines land by helicopter to airlift American citizens out of Nicaragua. As the end credits roll, a small television shows spliced-together news reports and Reagan's presidential press conferences, which compete with each other in revealing and denying that the United States is in any way involved in Nicaraguan affairs.

This image is not a finale but a coda, wherein the appearance of the present is meant to illuminate the way that linear historical models camouflage Manifest Destiny rather than expose it. Such camouflage reflects Michael Rogin's assessment in *Ronald Reagan, the Movie,* his analysis of Reagan's complex and powerful faith in the moving image's absolute relation to truth, that during his administration President Reagan "was replacing history by visionary myth" (xvi). It is against this visionary myth that *Walker* speaks.

THIS IS (SORT OF) HOW IT REALLY HAPPENED: *TOMBSTONE* AND PARACINEMATIC VERIFICATION

Tombstone offers yet another strategy and sense of historical discourse in Westerns by using what I call "paracinematic verification." This is the use of passages from other actual fictional narratives as if they were documentary film footage to construct a field of reference internal to the viewer's experience of the film, but not necessarily to the film's story. It can also be seen in John Wayne's last film, Don Siegel's *The Shootist* (1976), and in Philip Borsos's *The Grey Fox* (1982) and Christopher Cain's *Young Guns* (1988) (two of very few 1980s Westerns, and both "true stories"), and in a slightly different way even in George Roy Hill's *Butch Cassidy and the Sundance Kid* (1969). Typically but not always presented at the beginning of the film, these interludes indicate the film's historicity and claim authenticity. The privileged documentary status normally imparted to the photograph extends to the motion picture itself in an even more reflexive gesture. Many revisionist Westerns (e.g., *The Shootist, The Grey Fox*) open with black-and-white "documentary" footage designed to place the fiction that follows under the aegis of an alleged factual past.

Tombstone was in hot competition with *Wyatt Earp,* and each claimed to best the other in telling *the* authentic Earp story. But *Tombstone,* like many 1990s Westerns, felt a need to tell this story for an audience that might have forgotten in the intervening eighties how to watch a Western.[13] It equated authenticity with pedigree and placed itself in the genealogy of classical Westerns. But at the same time it did so in a form that also put the narrative in a genealogy of (proposed) actual Western history. *Tombstone* opens with Robert Mitchum, Western icon and (at the time) beef industry spokesman, narrating in voice-over the history of western expansion, as "primitive," black-and-white, silent images play out on a small square in the middle of the larger, rectangular screen.

Though *Tombstone* uses both real and faked silent film footage, it is almost impossible to tell the difference, especially for the young audience to whom the film was targeted. The real footage comes from such standards as Edwin S. Porter's *Great Train Robbery* of 1903 (the first Western ever, and shot in New Jersey), some of Edison's early works, and some footage from the films of early Western star Broncho Billy Anderson. What is arguably insidious about this insertion of black-and-white, scratched, and silent shots of Val Kilmer's Doc Holliday and Kurt Russell's Wyatt Earp is that it signals a desire for, if not an entirely successful return to, the naturalized historical stance of classical Westerns. The last shot in the prologue montage is the famous image from *The Great Train Robbery* of the cowboy shooting directly into the camera, which immediately cuts to the full wide-screen, color image with the film's main title spread across it. This is an extraordinary ellipsis, simultaneously encompassing and collapsing the entire history of Westerns. From the earliest image to the latest, *Tombstone* proposes itself not only as the authentic story of Wyatt Earp but also as a state-of-the-art Western.

Nevertheless, *Tombstone*'s narrative closes with a diegetic recognition that the facts of Wyatt Earp had given way to myth in his own lifetime. *Tombstone* has three reflexive points of closure. First, Earp's last visit to Doc Holliday in a Colorado sanitarium closes with Earp slipping a book he has written about Holliday into the dying Doc's hands. Second, Earp heeds Doc's call to go after his love interest and live happily ever after (this is reflexive insofar as there is at least a limited commentary on the Hollywood happy ending). Finally, the closing voice-over, delivered by Mitchum, speaks of Earp's last years in Hollywood and the pallbearers at his funeral, including Tom Mix (another, wholly different kind of Western legend), who "wept openly." At the end of *Wyatt Earp*, Wyatt and Josie (Joanna Going), on a boat bound for Alaska, encounter a young man who tells the story of his uncle, whom Wyatt Earp saved in what appears to be a very dramatic way, true to the Earp legend. When Earp admits to Josie, "Some people say it didn't happen that way," she replies, "Never mind, Wyatt. It happened that way." These are the closing lines of the film. The couple takes an active role in validating the myth. This "pro-activity," to give it the nineties twist it warrants, is also an accurate reflection of the couple's postfrontier self-mythification.

FACTS VERSUS MEANING: THE HISTORIOGRAPHICAL POTENTIAL OF WESTERNS

But to what extent does it matter if Tom Mix did or did not weep, if Wyatt Earp did or did not write a book about Doc Holliday, or if Earp did or did not save a particular person from an angry lynch mob? Here it is important to clarify the different levels on which accuracy must be considered specific to the Western: factual, or material, accuracy and discursive accuracy. First, material accuracy: it will be true or not true that Wyatt Earp used a particular kind of pistol at the O.K. Corral shoot-out. It will be true or not true that he was with Josephine Marcus at a particular moment. But, following John Mack Faragher's suggestion that "audiences don't want history's messy facts; they want its meaning" (160), the virtues and limitations of material accuracy are largely self-evident: one can dress a group of actual Sioux actors in utterly authentic period clothing and have them interact with equally authentically costumed and directed cavalry and still come up with an equally factual story that communicates almost nothing of ideological, historical, political, or even dramatic importance. Second, discursive accuracy: this may forgo factual accuracy for a stronger sense of how a certain set of events occurred and what those events meant in history. Historical personages may be combined to create a single character, events may be likewise conflated or compressed, but the spectator's sense of the episteme *may* in fact be stronger for doing so. Discursive accuracy is not merely a virtual history, in which the spectator has a sense of *what it was really like*, but offers a more general sense of how the facts in question (compressed or not) came to be organized as historical narrative. Here the illusion of history takes a backseat to the impression of history.[14]

The extent to which Westerns need not be held accountable for either form of historical accuracy has thus far been somewhat overstated. One of the most important (passively) camouflaged components of Westerns (now *and* then) is their frequent aspiration not simply to represent history but to write it. Though it often may be more of a consequence than an intention, Westerns have, often by default, posed themselves as the way things were and, depending on contemporary politics and events, the way things are, or ought to be. The Westerns most firmly lodged in the generic canon along the entire course of its development are either profoundly utopian (*Stagecoach, My Darling Clementine, Dances with Wolves*) or aggressively dystopian (*The Man Who Shot*

Liberty Valance [1962], *The Wild Bunch, Little Big Man*). But in the history of writing on Western films there has been little recognition of the idea that acts of historical theorization as well as representation occur in cinematic texts.

Dances with Wolves suggests that historical narrative is a zero-sum game: if Costner got it right, that is because he is correcting those who got it wrong. But even if a film can be either correct or erroneous on any given fact, the story those facts make up can be narrativized in any number of ways.[15] *How* the facts are made into history—or stories, in the case of most Westerns—is as important as *what* the facts themselves are.[16] And how the facts are arranged into something discursive that is also recognizable as popular entertainment amounts to more than a story line; that story is also a set of rhetorical arguments that can have weighty consequences—whether they are constructed deliberately to persuade the spectator or merely to divert her for an afternoon. The linear sense of history to which *Dances with Wolves* adheres has traditionally been one of the fundamental markers of the Western genre. John Cawelti writes that the rituals of and in the Western are "means of *affirming* basic cultural values, resolving tension and establishing a sense of continuity between present and past" (32, italics added). *Walker,* as a postmodern Western, *interrogates* basic cultural values. It questions the very act of affirmation and establishes a critical sense of how United States culture draws continuities between the present and past. *Tombstone* performs an increasingly familiar cinematic three-card monte by substituting claims to being an authentic Western for claims to being an authentic history of the West.

Into the Sunset? The Persistence of Westerns

One of the more interesting sociocinematic characteristics of the 1980s was the apparently inverse influence that the presence of Ronald Reagan, the cowboy president whose rhetoric as well as his image engendered the moniker, had on Westerns themselves. Even their 1990s resurgence did not, for some, produce the abundance of texts that would unequivocally register as generic force (film's version of safety in numbers). On the face of it, this might suggest that it is a genre whose utility to public discourse is now questionable. But on November 5, 1994, Reagan wrote a letter to the American people disclosing that he had Alzheimer's disease. Toward the missive's conclusion he noted, "I

Courtesy of the Film Archive.

Tombstone claims to rehistoricize an American myth.

now begin a journey that will lead me into the sunset of my life." This figure has extraordinary resonance, all the more so in the context of the vocabulary of images of a president who was so very image conscious. Not only does it suggest, as clearly it is meant to, that Reagan was approaching his final years. It also evokes, one last time, the set of images that were most closely associated with Reagan and his administration, those of the cowboy and the Western. The suggestion that, even as Reagan was losing vital mental capacities, he would still ride off into the sunset attests to the sustained power of those Western images and their permanent association with the man. Nearly ten years later, in June 2004, the script and production of the Great Communicator's funeral (in which he had a hand) only reinforced this impression, as well as the sustained connection between Reagan's self-image and that of the United States. After a state funeral at Washington's National Cathedral attended largely by political figures, Reagan's body was flown west, to be buried, after a more personal service, at the Ronald Reagan Library (which he habitually called not a library but a "museum") at sunset.[17] Jet travel and the time difference made this reiteration of the Westering narrative not only possible but viewable by millions on the small screen, where Reagan spent more time than the silver one. The sunset burial at the western edge of America was, as most reporters covering the event remarked, extraordinarily resonant of Reagan's own attachment to the language, visual and spoken, of Westerns. The burial was also resonant because the American public needed no interpretation by journalists to read it clearly, and be moved by it.

Reagan's letter offered an abstract temporal notion of Western finality, and his funeral offered a concrete geographic one, suggesting that if the frontier is not an arbitrary designation, it is also not a fixed one. And neither, therefore, is the Western, which founds itself on this essential figure. For the line that serves to physicalize the largely ideological category of the frontier also masks the idea that, as Richard Rodriguez puts it, "'West' is imaginary" (37). Nevertheless, the Westerns set in this imaginary West have their own history, and it is worth asking what that relationship to U.S. history might be. Starting sometime in the late sixties, which is to say that time that we think of as "The Sixties," which is to say that time recently narrativized on the NBC miniseries called *The Sixties*, Westerns became increasingly focused on a particular period of frontier history—the years following the frontier's closing. Obviously, any era can be revised. But that passage of American chronology when the fact that the frontier is officially closed according to the U.S. Census is confirmed by the fact that "everything's up to date in Kansas City," to quote *Oklahoma!*, yet simultaneously challenged by the continued abundance of "wide open spaces," to quote the Dixie Chicks, has seemed to suit the revisionist needs of Western filmmakers more than any other period (except when they are not re-creating the life of Wyatt Earp). Yet if Reagan elaborated a late-cold-war Western political rhetoric that in part stemmed from an investment in Western film narratives—in which, though fictional, he was a real actor—President George W. Bush elaborates a war-on-terrorism Western political rhetoric (in which Osama bin Laden is "wanted dead or alive," and the plan for Al Qaeda is to "smoke 'em outta their holes") that in part stems from an investment in Western film narratives—in front of which, because fictional, he is (only) a real spectator. If Westerns, whether critical or affirmative, are also, like most American film genres, largely symptomatic of the sociocultural landscape, it is wholly reasonable to anticipate yet another shift in the position of Westerns, especially when, as now, even—especially—recent U.S. history is so importantly under scrutiny.

NOTES

1. For an exemplary critical analysis of *Heaven's Gate*, see Robin Wood, "Two Films by Michael Cimino," in *Hollywood from Vietnam to Reagan . . . and Beyond* (New York: Columbia University Press, 2003), 241–286.

2. Larry Ranney notes the incorrect use of firearms in several classical Westerns that was nevertheless legible both as a highly efficient internal system of codes and as a claim to historical authority. These inaccuracies also served a narrative purpose: repeating rifles were used in stories set before their invention because they literally moved the narrative along faster than a single-action rifle would have done (Ranney, "Colt 'Peacemakers'").

3. For a related discussion of Anglos as Indians, see Robert Baird, "Going Indian: *Dances with Wolves*."

4. The opening sequences of Jim Jarmusch's *Dead Man* (1995), which illustrate the protagonist William Blake's (Johnny Depp) journey westward through his point-of-view shots of the landscape, may be regarded as a short meta-Western *and* an anti–*Dances with Wolves*. A shot of a burned-out covered wagon is followed a few shots later by one of destroyed tepees. This is a frontier of decay, not progress. Jarmusch's notations of decay are not just in the wagon and tepees. At the end of the prologue, before the opening credits, the hunters open up their windows and start shooting buffalo from the train. The train's coal man explains to an obviously frightened and disturbed Blake that, at the government's request, "last year they shot a million of 'em." Even *Dances with Wolves*, though it shows hundreds of scattered buffalo corpses, largely suggests that the doom is nigh but has not actually begun, allowing the viewer to take one last nostalgic look. After the opening credits, when Blake finally arrives in Machine, he scans the wall of a building on which are nailed countless animal skulls. On the ground beneath it are piles of human skulls, by implication Native American. This is not an elegy for the West, or even for the Western, like *The Man Who Shot Liberty Valance*. The deserts, the mountains, the Conestogas, the tepees, the buffalo, the bones, the dirt, the gore: put all these

symbols together with the minimal narrative, suggests *Dead Man*'s prologue, and it is still possible to see the history of the Western. The frontier Jarmusch presents looks devastated, and if there is an elegiac quality to the film, it is an elegy of rage.

5. See *The Naked Spur* (1953), *The Far Country* (1954), and *The Wild Bunch* (1969), respectively.

6. For further analysis of the particularly postmodern nature of *Walker*'s historical critique, see Sumiko Higashi, "*Walker* and *Mississippi Burning*: Postmodern versus Illusionist Narrative," in *Revisioning History: Film and the Construction of a New Past*, ed. Robert Rosenstone (Princeton, N.J.: Princeton University Press, 1995), 174–87; and Robert Rosenstone, "*Walker*: The Dramatic Film as (Postmodern) History," in his *Visions of the Past: The Challenge of Film to Our Idea of History* (Cambridge, Mass.: Harvard University Press, 1995), 202–13.

7. It is also very similar to the font Clint Eastwood used in *High Plains Drifter* (1973).

8. Cox's previous work included the cult film *Repo Man* (1984) and *Sid and Nancy* (1986), the biopic of the Sex Pistols' Sid Vicious and his girlfriend Nancy Spungeon, as well as the dry run for *Walker*, the contemporary Western-cum-road movie *Straight to Hell* (1987) largely populated by post-punk musicians like Elvis Costello, the Pogues, the Clash, and Courtney Love.

9. The massive project of the Clash's *Sandinista* is itself a stunning, stirring, and aggressive exercise in radical left postmodern politics. It lashes itself to the mast of late punk while tempting itself with the siren calls of consumer capitalism. Out of its resistance come songs like "Charlie Don't Surf," as much about Coppola's failure to do anything but remystify Vietnam in *Apocalypse Now* as it is about the war itself, as well as the title track, which is a revision of the folk song's use as a transmitter of oral history for the masses. With *Sandinista* as a musical intertext, it is even easier to read into *Walker* not just as a critique of U.S. foreign policy under Reagan but also as a meditation on the Iran-Contra scandal, in which the sale of arms to Iran that funded the Nicaraguan Contras completely contradicted U.S. policy, to say nothing of its illegality.

10. Certain histories of Walker imply he went through significant theoretical modulations regarding history (cf. Albert Z. Carr, *The World and William Walker* [New York: Harper and Row, 1963]). Walker as a left-wing abolitionist journalist originally held to a very proto-Althusserian social critique. After Vanderbilt puts him into circulation in the framework of colonial expansion (their meeting in Cox's film is not based in fact), he reverts to a great man approach to history and ideology.

11. Hayden White suggests that knowledge is impossible outside of some narrativized context or another—though that does not imply that the events do not exist without the narrative, merely that they remain indiscernible. To distinguish his position from Foucault's, White insists that historical writing is best understood not as neutral, quasi-scientific discourse but as literary production, and just as subject to and structured by fictive forms and tropes as literature itself. See Hayden

White, *Metahistory: The Historical Imagination in Nineteenth-Century Europe* (Baltimore: Johns Hopkins University Press, 1973).

12. In this he echoes Bill Simon and Louise Spence's observation that in *Buffalo Bill and the Indians*, Buffalo Bill "seems to be taken in by his own legend, a consumer of his own image" (Bill Simon and Louise Spence, "Cowboy Wonderland, History and Myth: It Ain't All That Different from Real Life," in *Westerns: Films through History*, ed. Janet Walker [New York: Routledge, 2001], 93). This will also be more equivocally true of Bill Hickock in *Wild Bill*.

13. Though he took great pains to show his own awareness of the history of Westerns in the visual references in *Posse,* this generational forgetting was not something that concerned Mario Van Peebles. As he said, "Everyone has seen 'Bonanza,' Leone, Eastwood, yeah, yeah. Nowadays they want you to cut to the chase. The kids, they already know what you're doing before you do it." Quoted in John Stanley, "Mario and Melvin Van Peebles Bring '90s Consciousness to 'Posse,'" *San Francisco Chronicle,* May 16, 1993, 22.

14. For a discussion of the virtues and limitations of accuracy in historical discourse in a larger cinematic context, see Robert Brent Toplin, *Reel History: In Defense of Hollywood* (Lawrence: University Press of Kansas, 2002).

15. As historian Peter Gay puts it, "The tree in the woods of the past fell in only one way, no matter how fragmentary or contradictory the reports of its fall, no matter whether there are no historians, one historian or several contentious historians in its future to record and debate it." Peter Gay, *Style in History* (New York: Basic Books, 1974), 210.

16. As White (Hayden, not Richard) suggests, "What we wish to call mythic narrative is under no obligation to keep the two orders of events, real and imaginary, distinct from one another. Narrative becomes a problem only when we wish to give real events the form of story. It is because real events do not offer themselves as stories that their narrativization is so difficult." Hayden White, *The Content of the Form: Narrative Discourse and Historical Representation* (Baltimore: Johns Hopkins University Press, 1987), 4.

17. The backward-facing boots in the stirrups of the ritual riderless horse's saddle were Reagan's own, and they were English, his preferred way of riding horses. Western style was largely reserved for films, and never as many Westerns as Reagan had hoped.

WORKS CITED

Baird, Robert. "Going Indian: *Dances with Wolves*." In *Hollywood's Indian: The Portrayal of the Native American in Film,* edited by Peter C. Rollins and John E. O'Connor, 153–69. Lexington: University Press of Kentucky, 1998.

Buscombe, Ed, ed. *The BFI Companion to the Western.* New York: 2nd ed. London: André Deutsch/BFI Publishing, 1993.

Cawelti, John G. *The Six-Gun Mystique.* Bowling Green, Ohio: Bowling Green University Popular Press, 1971.

Faragher, John Mack. "The Tale of Wyatt Earp: Seven Films." In *Past Imperfect: History According to the Movies,* edited by Marck C. Carnes. New York: Henry Holt, 1996.

Gay, Peter. *Style in History.* New York: Basic Books, 1974.

Higashi, Sumiko. "*Walker* and *Mississippi Burning:* Postmodern versus Illusionist Narrative." In *Revisioning History: Film and the Construction of a New Past,* edited by Robert Rosenstone, 174–187. Princeton, N.J.: Princeton University Press, 1995.

Ranney, Larry W. "Colt 'Peacemakers,' Winchesters and Film Narratives: An Overview of the Historically Inaccurate Use of Firearms in the Western." Paper presented at the Society for the Interdisciplinary Study of Social Imagery's "The Image of the Frontier Conference," Colorado Springs, Colorado, March 15, 1997.

Rodriguez, Richard. "True West." *Harper's,* September 1996, 37–46.

Rogin, Michael Paul. *Ronald Reagan, the Movie, and Other Episodes in Political Demonology.* Berkeley: University of California Press, 1987.

Rosenstone, Robert, ed. *Visions of the Past: The Challenge of Film to Our Idea of History.* Cambridge, Mass.: Harvard University Press, 1995.

———. "*Walker:* The Dramatic Film as (Postmodern) History." In *Visions of the Past: The Challenge of Film to Our Idea of History,* edited by Robert Rosenstone, 202–13. Cambridge, Mass.: Harvard University Press, 1995.

Simon, William G., and Louise Spence. "Cowboy Wonderland, History and Myth: 'It Ain't All That Different Than Real Life.'" In *Westerns: Films through History,* edited by Janet Walker, 89–108. New York: Routledge, 2001.

Slotkin, Richard. *Gunfighter Nation: The Myth of the Frontier in Twentieth-Century America.* New York: Harper Perennial, 1993.

———. "Prologue to a Study of Myth and Genre in American Movies." *Prospects* 9 (1984): 407–32.

———. *Regeneration through Violence: The Mythology of the American Frontier, 1600–1860.* Middletown, Conn.: Wesleyan University Press, 1973.

Stern, Jane, and Michael Stern. "Why We *So* Love Those Oaters." *Los Angeles Times,* December 5, 1993, Calendar 28.

Turner, Frederick Jackson. "The Significance of the Frontier in American History." In *Rereading Frederick Jackson Turner: "The Significance of the Frontier in American History" and Other Essays,* commentary by John Mack Faragher. New York: Henry Holt, 1994. Originally published in the *Annual Report of the American Historical Association for the Year 1893* (Washington, D.C., 1894).

White, Hayden. *The Content of the Form: Narrative Discourse and Historical Representation.* Baltimore: Johns Hopkins University Press, 1987.

White, Richard. "Frederick Jackson Turner and Buffalo Bill." In *The Frontier in American Culture,* edited by James R. Grossman. Berkeley: University of California Press, 1994.

Winders, Bruce. E-mail to Andrea Miller-Keller. March 5, 2001.

Wood, Robin. "Two Films by Michael Cimino." In *Hollywood from Vietnam to Reagan . . . and Beyond,* 241–86. New York: Columbia University Press, 2003. Originally published as *Hollywood from Vietnam to Reagan* (New York: Columbia University Press, 1986).

CHALLENGING LEGENDS, COMPLICATING BORDER LINES
The Concept of "Frontera" in John Sayles's Lone Star

The idea of the frontier is extremely well established as cultural common property. If the idea of *la frontera* had anywhere near the standing of the idea of the frontier, we would be well launched toward self-understanding, directed toward a realistic view of this nation's position in the hemisphere and in the world.

—Patricia Nelson Limerick, "The Adventures of the Frontier in the Twentieth Century"

My feeling, basically, is that I've made a lot of movies about American culture and, as far as I'm concerned, it is not revisionism to include Mexican-American culture or African-American culture or any of the many other different groups. If you're talking about the history of the United States, you're always talking about those things, from the get-go.

—John Sayles, "Borders and Boundaries"

Over the past century, the idea of the frontier as a defining place and phase in the history of the United States has taken on mythic status. During the mid-1990s, the traditional conception of the frontier in the American West was challenged from two different directions, but with similar aims and results. In published histories, Patricia Nelson Limerick argued for a revised historical conception of the West as *la frontera*—a new term for a new recognition of the different groups that populated and defined the West. At about the same time, in a depiction of the West on film, John Sayles rewrote the typical Western story to highlight the intersections among racial, ethnic, and social groups and placed it along the Rio Grande in a fictional Texas border town named Frontera.

In *Lone Star*, Sheriff Sam Deeds (Chris Cooper) investigates a murder from the past in a Texas border town called "Frontera."

Historian Limerick has written extensively about the need to redefine the concept of the frontier in professional histories—and in the public imagination. She is one of a group of historians, sometimes referred to as "the new historians of the American West" or "revisionist historians," who are critical of traditional stories of ruggedly individualistic white men taming the wilderness and bringing progress; these revisionists have attempted, through their works, to recover the diversity and complexity of the history of the West.[1] In "The Adventures of the Frontier in the Twentieth Century," Limerick argues that a better model than the frontier is la frontera, which refers to the borderlands between Mexico and the United States and, in a metaphoric sense, to the borders separating countries, peoples, and authorities.

From Limerick's work, a number of characteristics of la frontera, this reconceived and rehabilitated "frontier," can be derived.[2] These characteristics find expression in the town of Frontera in the film *Lone Star* (1996). According to Limerick, la frontera as a concept focuses on a running story, not a neatly corralled model with a clear beginning and end in time (history) or in space (geography), nor with a simple solitary direction of movement east to west. La frontera is less ethnocentric than the "frontier," acknowledging that the West was and is multicultural, or, as one scholar has expressed it, was "an intergroup contact situation."[3] In la frontera, historical situations involve cultural and moral complexity, and social, political, and economic power relationships among groups are recognized. Reductionism is avoided, as Limerick writes: "Trying to grasp the enormous human complexity of the American West is not easy under any circumstances, and the effort to reduce a tangle of many-sided encounters to a world defined by a frontier line only makes a tough task even tougher" ("Adventures of the Frontier" 73). Limerick and White, when considering representations of the American West on film, have been critical of what they argue are the reductionist and distorting dichotomies of the frontier story as it has been expressed in the classic examples of the Western film genre.

John Sayles's *Lone Star* is an example of la frontera in film. In particular, the movie is an attempt to move beyond genre conventions and renegotiate ideas about the American West. Sayles strives to represent the West as a place of complexity, where people are individuals more than types, and where Chicanas/os, Anglo-Americans, African Americans, and American Indians are living intersecting lives. Ultimately, Sayles represents the history of the West as a dynamic process, one in which personal history is intermixed with— and often in conflict with—"official" history. Frontera is a place where history, legend, diversity, and issues of American identity interact. Essentially, Sayles is exploring in film what Limerick has advocated for history.

Like Limerick, Sayles is interested in the reevaluation of legendary stories of the frontier, and he chose the Texas-Mexico border for such reexamination. During interviews, Sayles has described the idea about history that lies beneath *Lone Star:* "The germ of the idea came from seeing Fess Parker play Davy Crockett and the whole legend of the Alamo. As you get older, the legend gets more complex. Someone says it's not true, or maybe parts of it are true and that the fight for freedom maybe had some economic interests" (quoted in Stein D1). For Sayles, as for Limerick, the notion of a border line is too simplistic; it deserves interrogation: "I wanted to have these three communities, where we were basically in a part of Mexico that somebody had drawn a line underneath and made into America, but the people hadn't changed" (*Sayles on Sayles* 221). In fact, when the interviewers for *Cineaste* asked Sayles whether the vision of the United States that he presents in *Lone Star* is an attempt to

Matthew McConaughey plays the legendary lawman Buddy Deeds in *Lone Star.*

recognize that the nation is "an increasingly multicultural society," Sayles backtracked to refocus their view: "It's not increasingly multicultural; it's always been so. . . . American culture is not monolingual or monoracial. It's always been a mix" ("Borders and Boundaries" 15).

Lone Star is set in the present day. Evidence of a murder that was committed forty years ago has been discovered, and Sheriff Sam Deeds (Chris Cooper) finds himself investigating a crime in which his deceased father, Sheriff Buddy Deeds (Matthew McConaughey), may have been involved. As Sam dredges up evidence that contradicts the official, legendary story of Buddy Deeds, he also encounters the social structures that have maintained and supported the legend. Sam's investigation into his personal history and his town's history becomes a metaphor for a reexamination of American national history and identity.

This chapter examines three features of *Lone Star:* Sayles's strategies for charting out unfamiliar Western cinematic terrain, including his representation of the people who inhabit Frontera; the perspective on history that is articulated in the film; and Sayles's treatment of borders. The director uses numerous techniques to frustrate attempts to draw simple lines between two dramatically conflicting forces or groups (as in a typical Western genre film). He tells a different kind of story about the American West.

Charting Unfamiliar Cinematic Terrain

John Sayles was particularly well positioned to take on a rewriting of the Western story. Early successes with *Return of the Secaucus Seven* (1980), *The Brother from Another Planet* (1984), *Matewan* (1987), *Eight Men Out* (1988), and *City of Hope* (1991) earned Sayles a reputation as a writer and director of thought-provoking films in an industry dominated by formulas.[4] *Passion Fish* (1992) and *The Secret of Roan Inish* (1994), the two works that immediately preceded *Lone Star*, served to cement that reputation. Probably more than any other American filmmaker, Sayles deserves the labels "independent" and "auteur" because he carries credits for writing, directing, and editing on most of his productions. And, since 1983, when he worked with Paramount Pictures and had to make compromises on the final cut of *Baby It's You*, Sayles has steered clear of the studios and has retained full creative control of his films (Ryan 84–86). The results are movies that reflect the struggle of an individual creative consciousness coming to terms with the social and political issues of our times.

The choice to make films outside the Hollywood system is a calculated one; Sayles knows the values and pressures on both sides. A novelist turned filmmaker, he does not like to have the stories "enhanced" for market appeal. Sayles has said: "To make a Hollywood movie, I'd have to say, 'Here's the story I'm starting with, but it's up for grabs, folks. You add this, you add that, you put this actor in and you take this actor out.' By the time you're done, it's just another movie" (quoted in Stein D1). Sayles should know—one of the ways he raises money for his film projects is by working as a script doctor and ghostwriter within the movie colony. For example, at the time *Lone Star* was released, Sayles had recently done work on the scripts for *Apollo 13*, *Mimic*, and *The Quick and the Dead* (Howell E1).

Given Sayles's experience with Hollywood formulas, it seems important to examine the choices he makes to avoid conventions in *Lone Star*—and the implications of those choices in terms of the story of the West. Going against the common standards of movie storytelling is exactly what allows Sayles to communicate the kind of complexity and continuity Limerick emphasizes in her histories. *Lone Star* was made on a budget of only $5 million (a very modest amount compared with the budgets of most Hollywood pictures), and it earned Sayles an Academy Award nomination for best original screenplay. The film also won a Bravo Special Achievement Award for outstanding feature film from the National Council of La Raza, which recognizes outstanding portrayals of Hispanics in film and television.[5]

Lone Star contains a number of main story lines that emphasize the intersecting lives of individuals from the Anglo, Mexican, and Mexican American communities, as well as the African American and American Indian populations. Characterizations are complex rather than unidimensional, creating the impression that the West is a mosaic of lives. Sayles's films are typically about communities and involve an ensemble cast. *Lone Star* is no exception. Sayles articulates his objectives with character development and storytelling in this way: "I definitely want people to leave [my movies] thinking about their lives or the lives of their friends or what's going on in the world. . . . [In my movies] there certainly is the attempt to examine the 'us and them' kind of idea and see if there's any way to think of it more as 'we'" (quoted in Beale 38). The story lines in *Lone Star* introduce and develop a number of main characters, including the Anglo sheriff Sam Deeds; the Chicana high school history teacher, Pilar Cruz (Elizabeth Peña); Pilar's mother, Mercedes (Miriam Colon), a successful businesswoman who owns the Santa Barbara Café; African American army colonel Delmore Payne (Joe Morton); and Delmore's estranged father, Otis (Ron Canada), who owns Big O's Nightclub and also runs the Black Seminole Museum in town. A large supporting cast includes a conservative bartender, illegal immigrants, high school students, the owner of a roadside souvenir stand, army privates and sergeants, a story-hungry journalist, and a Texas football fanatic.

Sayles uses a number of strategies to frustrate the attempts of characters to draw clear lines between groups, between the United States and Mexico, and between past and present. He also frustrates viewers' abilities to do the same as they watch the film. In fact, *Lone Star* makes demands on the audience on a number of levels. It is not a thriller, or escapist. It is slow-paced. Listening is crucial because the stories are based on scene and talk—dialogue. Examining the critical reception to the film is revealing not only because reviewers gave it high praise but also because they made a point of letting their readers know that this was not a typical summer movie. One example is Lewis Beale, who wrote: "There are no digitalized special effects in *Lone Star.* Writer/director John Sayles' latest film, opening Friday, also contains no car crashes, Uzi-toting drug dealers or havoc-wreaking tornadoes. In an age when sensation rules the screen, *Lone Star* is that rarest of commodities: a tale of murder, racial politics and cross-cultural pollination in a Texas border town that uses its tabloid elements to comment on society at large. It demands both patience and attention" (38). Joe Leydon commented on the time in which the story unfolds: "At a deliberately paced 134 minutes, *Lone Star* may be too much of a good thing for some impatient viewers. But it's hard to see where Sayles could cut without diminishing the pic's overall impact" (46). Kevin Jackson, writing for the *Independent* of London, put it this way: "Some viewers may feel cheated by Sayles' wide canvas and expansive method, and be left impatient for the more single-minded narrative drive of the conventional body movie. It's true that *Lone Star* is short on cop-show thrills. . . . In just about every other regard, however, it's a feast—dense, thoughtful and idiosyncratic, with some of the most quietly accomplished acting to be found in any recent American movie" (11). Janet Maslin of the *New York Times* similarly combined high praise with an acknowledgment of *Lone Star*'s exceptionalism: "[Sayles] assures the viewer that this film's many elements will converge in ways that are meaningful and moving. Indeed, *Lone Star* exists so far outside the province of slam-bang summer movies that it seems part of a different medium and a different world" (C1).

From the outset, *Lone Star* does not present cinematically familiar terrain: the landscape is different, the use of sound is different, and so are the characterizations. According to the classic formula, a Western begins with an opening establishing shot that captures the spectacular, mythic landscape—the Monument Valley of *Stagecoach* or the Grand Tetons of *Shane*. [6] Not so in *Lone Star*. From the first shot, Sayles drops into the middle of things. The only thing that has been clearly "established" is that viewers will need to sift and sort through the details themselves to begin to make sense of it all. *Lone Star* opens with a medium shot in the middle of cactus and scrub brush. There is not even the orientation typically provided by opening credits—those will come later. After a slow movement, the camera reveals a man in a patterned polo shirt and shorts in the bushes, apparently identifying local plants out of a guidebook, mumbling to himself. There is another man in the distance with a metal detector, searching an abandoned rifle range. The men are surprised to find bones, a Masonic ring, and a Rio County sheriff's badge.

Sayles's introduction to *Lone Star* and his portrayal of the landscape are closely paralleled by Limerick's introduction to *Something in the Soil: Legacies and Reckonings in the New West* (2000). Limerick writes that an accumulation of stories is buried in the Western landscape, waiting to be unearthed: "Even though some Western landscapes practice a trickster's habit of presenting themselves to newcomers as if they were fresh, untouched, vacant spaces, nonetheless, stories have become quite literally something in the Western soil" (13). Limerick contrasts, in essence, the image of the frontier landscape that is characteristic of the Western genre film with the kind of unromanticized landscape that Sayles's characters inhabit—and that, quite literally in this first scene, they have to pick through to discover detritus of the past.

Not only the opening landscape of *Lone Star* but also the sound is unusual for a Western film. It is difficult to make out what the characters are saying, and sounds and lines of dialogue overlap in a somewhat confusing style that is reminiscent of Robert Altman productions. When characters speak in a typical Hollywood movie, there is a singularly clear audio, better than real life, and the story is shown as if it is life set to music, with extensive musical scoring that sets the tone from the beginning and continues throughout the film as a cue to viewers' emotions.[7] The opening scene of *Lone Star* includes music only for the first few seconds; in fact, throughout the film, Sayles uses hardly any music at all that is not tied directly to the action on the screen: a jukebox playing at a restaurant, music at a nightclub, songs from a car radio.[8] There is very little of the kind of commentative music that is the hallmark of Hollywood productions. Without the continuous musical signals, the burden of interpretation rests more heavily on the audience. Listening closely is a necessity.

As the opening scene progresses, the director's choices continue to chart unfamiliar cinematic territory. Expectations based on the conventions of the Western are confounded. The film opens in the middle of a confusing landscape that is anything but grand; it is difficult to make out what these men in shorts and polo shirts are saying, and when a lawman finally arrives, he is not even wearing a gun. The white hat and badge are present, but Sam Deeds is not a larger-than-life character. The camera does not look up at him worshipfully but instead angles down at him, especially as he crouches near the ground (a common pose for Deeds in the film), poking around in the dirt.

In typical Sayles fashion, the film has an unusually large number of speaking characters. In fact, more than fifty characters are given voice in this treatment of the West and are allowed to articulate their various points of view. In contrast, standard Hollywood fare would have two major leads, a few supporting roles, and the rest extras. By including and developing so many speaking characters, from different walks of life and ethnic groups, Sayles is able to accomplish the kind of rewriting of the Western story that Limerick has argued for—one that is less ethnocentric. Also in a style that is typical of Sayles, *Lone Star* has certain individuals who speak only in one or two scenes but are given pivotal moments: Chucho Montoya (Tony Amendola), Wesley Birdsong (Gordon Tootoosis), and Cody the bartender (Leo Burmester).

Limerick has pointed out that one of the reasons the frontier story has lingered is that "many Americans want the Old West to be the place in the past where we go to escape complexity" (*Something in the Soil* 21). Complexity cannot be escaped in *Lone Star*. White hats and black hats lose their conventional significance. Frontera is portrayed as a town that had been controlled by Anglo-Americans, but it is on the verge of a significant shift. The largest segment of the population is Mexican American, nineteen out of twenty residents, and after the next election the mayor and sheriff are likely to be Mexican Americans. Many of the comments made by characters express different perspectives on the political and social changes occurring in the town. These comments also provide an opportunity for Sayles to weigh in on the unrealistic expectation of having class and racial lines clearly drawn. For example, a number of characters—Fenton (Tony Frank), Cody the bartender, a group of Anglo parents—represent the perspectives of the white minority whose values, beliefs, versions of history, and political power are under threat. These characters seem to want the "lines of demarcation" between right and wrong, winners and losers, and "us" and "them" cleanly drawn. Sam Deeds, Pilar Cruz, and Otis Payne, at various points in the film, articulate an alternative point of view—one that Sayles presents sympathetically. As Sam investigates the past and the legend of his deceased father, as Pilar teaches about the collective past and learns about her personal history, and as Otis talks about the past with his living son and grandson, *Lone Star* evokes a perspective that questions these demarcations. Otis Payne puts it best when he says, "Blood only means what you let it," and "There's not like there's a borderline between the good people and the bad people—you're not on either one side or the other."[9]

HISTORY AS A PROCESS

In *Lone Star*, Sayles presents history as a process; it is embodied in the searches and transformations of different characters as they investigate personal and collective pasts. In this sense, *Lone Star* is a film not only about history but also about the uses that people assign to history.

A major plot line concerns Anglo-American Sheriff Sam Deeds and his relationship to his father, the well-loved Sheriff Buddy Deeds. On the abandoned rifle range of the opening scene, evidence of a potential murder is discovered: a human skeleton, a Rio County sheriff's badge, and a Masonic ring. Once it is determined that the remains are those of the racist Sheriff Charley Wade (Kris Kristofferson), Sam's father becomes a prime suspect. Most of the townspeople believe that Buddy ran this bad man out of town years before, but Sam believes that his father murdered Wade. Indeed, Sam has been holding a grudge against his father ever since Buddy broke up Sam's relationship with his high school sweetheart, Pilar Cruz.

The film shows Sam doing many of the things that historians do: looking at artifacts—the bones, badge, and ring—and making inferences; establishing a chronology by examining records from the sheriff's office, the county, and the hospital, as well as his father's personal correspondence; and conducting interviews with the townspeople who lived in Frontera at the time of Wade's murder. When Sam, looking for evidence, asks direct questions, he seldom receives a straight, easy answer. Mayor Hollis (Clifton James) tells him a story; Otis Payne talks about many things, but not what Sam asks about; Wesley Birdsong loads his seemingly offhand comments with isolated details and metaphors. Everyone seems to keep reminding Sam that his father is a "legend," his mother was a "saint," and he is just "Sheriff Junior." A few warn him: "You go poking around in the past, you never know what you're going to dig up."

Sam finds contradictions and conflicts of interest, and in general comes to see that the truth is more complex than he had wanted to believe. One of these complexities is embodied in his father. Sam wants to kick the pedestal out from under Buddy, and in the course of his investigations, he discovers that Buddy used the town's political machine for personal profit. Nevertheless, the townspeople liked and trusted Buddy Deeds and recognized that he was far better than his abusive and racist predecessor, Charley Wade. At Big O's Nightclub, Sam questions Otis Payne about his father, and Otis implicitly compares Buddy Deeds to Charley Wade: "I don't recall a prisoner ever died in your daddy's custody. I don't recall a man in this county—black, white, Mexican—who'd hesitate for a minute before they'd call on Buddy Deeds to solve a problem. More than that I wouldn't care to say."

History and self-definition are also explored through the characters of Pilar Cruz (a high school history teacher and Sam Deeds's former girlfriend) and her parents, Mercedes and Eladio Cruz (Gilbert R. Cuellar Jr.). Pilar never knew her father, Eladio, because he was killed by Sheriff Wade before she was born—or, as she later discovers, before she was even conceived.

Discussions involving Pilar, other teachers, and parents raise the issue of whose version of history they should be teaching and how closely the textbook should be followed. Questions here about how to tell their cultures' histories are direct and explicit. After members of the faculty discuss the winners and losers of history and who should get the bragging rights, Pilar reflects: "I've only been trying to get across part of the complexity of our situation down here—cultures coming together in both negative and positive ways." Pilar's comments put her very much in the same camp as the historians such as Limerick. In *Something in the Soil,* Limerick argues that one of the main projects of the New Western History must be to show people that "benefits often came packaged with injuries . . . the negative aspects of life wove themselves into a permanent knot with the positive aspects" (21). Limerick promotes a view of history as a paradox, as opposed to history as a moral crusade.

While Pilar Cruz seems to directly advocate reconceiving history as la frontera, her mother, Mercedes, a timeworn business owner, provides an opposing perspective. She is portrayed as a proponent of assimilation, someone who crossed the Mexican-U.S. border and has never looked back. She is a Mexican American who has "made it." A respected business owner who has no interest in visiting relatives in Mexico, Mercedes accuses the Mexican American workers at her restaurant of theft and exhorts them to "speak English." At night, sitting outside on the deck of her riverfront home, she calls the border patrol when she sees people trying to cross the border between Mexico and Texas. It is only later in the film that her hypocrisy is revealed: she actually crossed the Rio Grande in the same way many years before.

The construction of identity and its relationship to history are also explored through the story line surrounding Delmore Payne, a by-the-book African American army colonel who has just taken over command at Fort McKenzie. Delmore is a "spit and polish man" whose teenage son, Chet (Eddie Robinson), is not enthusiastic about following in his father's footsteps. Like Sam Deeds, Colonel Payne has spent much of his life trying to define himself against his father, Otis. Otis has lived in Frontera for many years and runs Big O's Nightclub, in the neighborhood formerly known as "Darktown." Delmore's son, trying to learn something about his grandfather, visits the Black Seminole Museum and finds out, among other things, that his own heritage is not only African American but also American Indian.

The American Indian presence in the film has another representative: Wesley Birdsong is the owner of a roadside souvenir stand that, as he explains it, is located "between Nowhere and Not Much Else." He is another of the film's minor but memorable characters who is given important lines. During his conversation with Sam Deeds, he provides a catalyzing piece of information: Sam's much-revered father was having an affair.

As Sam Deeds, Pilar Cruz, and Delmore Payne look into their pasts, they come to realize that the personal identities they have constructed for themselves —their moral commitments to different groups—have been based on stories they have grown up with about their families, their social groups, and their country. Over the course of the film, they all discover that they have gotten some things wrong about the lives of their parents and, in the process, have gotten some things wrong about themselves. These character transformations based on personal histories serve as metaphors for a reexamination of national identity of the kind Limerick has advocated in such works as *The Legacy of Conquest* and "The Adventures of the Frontier in the Twentieth Century." In places where the characters had been trying to draw lines to define themselves and exclude others, they instead find interconnections. The case of Sam Deeds and Pilar Cruz is illustrative. Although revelations about the past happen in small ways throughout the film, it is shocking at the end to discover that Buddy Deeds had an affair with Mercedes Cruz and is, in fact, Pilar's father. Sam's father and Pilar's mother had been so dead set on breaking up their high school romance not because of ethnic prejudices but because Sam and Pilar are of the same blood. In *Lone Star*, the lines that separate groups turn out to be very fuzzy, and everyone is far more interconnected than they had believed while they were growing up.

No Clear Lines: The Visual Treatment of Borders

Like the complicating of the lines between ethnic groups, in *Lone Star* the borders between nations and the boundaries between present and past are shown to be fluid. Sayles uses a unique visual technique, a marked deviation from Hollywood's cinematic syntax, to make this point: in flashbacks, he uses no break between present and past. Instead, the transition is accomplished within a single shot and with a moving camera (no fade-outs, dissolves, or edits).

Conventions for representing flashbacks and time transitions have changed over the course of American motion picture history, but most have involved some kind of filmic punctuation device, a break in the celluloid.[10] In earlier

Sam Deeds (Chris Cooper) and Pilar Cruz (Elizabeth Peña) reminisce about their high school romance in *Lone Star.*

eras, a flashback could be signaled when a character looked up and put a finger on the side of her head, followed by a fade-out of the present and a fade-in to a view of the past with the character's voice-over recollection. Another device made use of a similar beginning, but this was followed by a pull out of focus as the film left the present and a pull into focus in a different scene in the past. Another common strategy was a montage of flipping calendar pages. Currently, the most common device is the straight cut (a simple edit) between present and past. The straight cut, however, is a *break;* it is a discontinuity that can be perceived. In terms of traditional editing, it also means a literal splice in the filmstrip.

Because *Lone Star* is about complexity and continuities, Sayles chose an unusual technique that supports formally a point that the film is making thematically. There is no break between present and past; it is all one continuous flow. This choice parallels Limerick's ideas of redefining the frontier as la frontera, a running story with no single, definitive line marking the beginning and the end. Through this strategy, Sayles suggests that our ideas about history shape our definitions of the present. There is no perfect separation.

Sayles's unusual visual technique is used repeatedly to move the action back into the past. For example, during a scene in Mercedes's restaurant, the camera moves down from Mayor Hollis's face into a close-up of a basket of tortillas on the table. As Hollis continues to narrate his story of Buddy Deeds's standoff with Charley Wade, a hand with a Mason's ring reaches into the basket to find money hidden among the tortillas. The action has shifted into the past, forty years earlier, and now the film shows Wade and Buddy exchanging threats. To return to the present, the camera cranes right from a close-up of Buddy to find Sam, arms crossed, listening to the continuation of Hollis's story. In scenes along the banks of the Rio Grande, characters reminiscing in the present are revealed as they were in the past. A moving camera that cranes left connects the adult Sam and Pilar, who are walking along the river talking about their parents and their past romance, with the teenage Sam and Pilar in the same location discussing the same thing twenty-three years earlier.

This visual technique is also used in what is arguably the most powerful scene in the film. Sam has traveled into Mexico to question Chucho Montoya. Chucho is now the "King of Tires" in Ciudad León, but Sam's interest is in the past; he wants to know what happened on the day that Eladio Cruz was killed. Chucho is another of Sayles's minor characters who is given a pivotal commentary. Chucho gives Sam Deeds a piece of his mind just before he tells him what he saw on the border forty years ago—Eladio Cruz murdered by Charley Wade:

> CHUCHO: Down here we don't throw everything away like you gringos do. Recycling, right? We invented that. The Government doesn't have to tell people to do it. . . .
>
> SAM: You ever know a fella named Eladio Cruz?
>
> CHUCHO: You the Sheriff of Rio County, right? *Un jefe muy respetado.*
>
> (*Chucho smiles, draws a line in the dirt with a Coke bottle.*)
>
> Step across this line—
>
> (*Sam obliges.*)
>
> *Ay, qué milagro!* You're not the sheriff of nothing anymore—just some *tejano* with a lot of questions I don't have to answer.
>
> A bird flying south—you think he sees this line? Rattlesnake,

In this scene from the past in *Lone Star,* Sheriff Charley Wade (Kris Kristofferson) murders Eladio Cruz at the border.

> javelina—whatever you got—you think halfway across that line they start thinking different? Why should a man?
>
> SAM: Your government always been pretty happy to have that line. The question's just been where to draw it—
>
> CHUCHO: My government can go fuck itself, and so can yours. I'm talking about people here—men. *Mi amigo* Eladio Cruz is giving some friends of his a lift one day in the back of his *camión*—
>
> —but because they're on one side of this invisible line and not the other, they got to hide in the back *como criminales*—and because over there he's just another Mex *bracero,* any man with a badge is his *jefe.*[11]

As Chucho speaks of his "*amigo* Eladio Cruz," there is another unusual transition from present to past. Up to this point, the intercutting between shots of Chucho and Sam as they converse has served to establish the sense of space and time: the location is Chucho's tire business in Mexico in the present day. But that all changes in a single shot that begins in the present but moves seamlessly into the past. Chucho is speaking while standing in front of a yellow sign. As he continues to tell his story, the camera slowly pans left, and when it reaches the side of the sign, a different location is revealed behind it. The action is now in the past, on the road across the border bridge, with Eladio Cruz trying to fix the flat tire on his truck and Charley Wade and Deputy Hollis arriving on the scene. Through Chucho's dialogue and this visual technique, Sayles is able to reiterate points that have been made in the film about the arbitrariness of borders—and the inhumane actions that can occur on one side or the other to protect those lines.

Scenes at Big O's Nightclub also link present to past. At the end of the film, the camera floats back to reveal the crucial scene from forty years earlier when Charley Wade was killed. Even though Sam has been wanting to believe that Buddy did it, he discovers that Wade was about to kill young Otis when a hesitant Deputy Hollis stopped him by shooting him in the back. The legendary Buddy Deeds, then a deputy, arrived on the scene a bit too late.

CONCLUSION: THE FRONTIER AND LA FRONTERA COEXIST

At the end of *Lone Star,* after it has been revealed that Buddy Deeds did not kill Charley Wade, Sam, Otis, and Hollis must decide what to do. Otis comments on how the truth has been hidden over the years: "Time went on, people liked the story we told better than anything the truth might have been." Hollis remarks that if word gets out about the identity of the body that was found at the rifle range, people will believe that Buddy killed Charley Wade. Sam remarks: "Buddy's a goddam legend. He can handle it."

Lone Star is more realistic than many treatments of the West on a number of levels. Sayles acknowledges that the frontier is a multicultural place and portrays it as such, recapturing its diversity. Also, and more problematically, Sayles acknowledges that the mythic Western story, as embodied in the character of Buddy Deeds, can absorb new information, revisionist tellings, and minor discrepancies and still remain archetypal. The legendary story of the West, in short, can handle it, too.

The legendary image of steely-eyed lawman Buddy Deeds is so memorable that it may have led even the most vigorous scholar and analyst toward inaccurate plot description. In *The Six-Gun Mystique Sequel,* a work that is commendable for both its scope and the importance of the ideas expressed, John Cawelti discusses *Lone Star* and gets the action in the film wrong: "In fact, the heroic father murdered a vicious lawman who was sheriff before him, mainly because this predecessor brutally exploited and abused Chicanos and African Americans" (110). As revealed in the film, Deputy Hollis was the one who killed the vicious lawman, shooting him in the back. Buddy arrived too late to participate or interfere. The version Cawelti remembers is the one that can be so easily absorbed by Buddy the legend that Sam decides to let the story stand.

Even though *Lone Star* is a successful, nuanced portrayal of la frontera, the condition that Patricia Nelson Limerick laments in "The Adventures of the Frontier in the Twentieth Century" still looms large; the traditional story of the frontier, with its dichotomies of black and white, lingers unregenerately in our public imagination. The myth of the frontier, whether written in history or represented in film, is a formula that offers a shortcut to understanding— simple definitions, simple reasoning, simple persuasion, and simple paths of action. It has tremendous staying power, especially during eras of rapid social and political change.

There is, then, a significant remaining tension for those who are concerned about public perception of America's national identity. A more historically accurate version of the American West is not necessarily a recipe for memorability or, for that matter, commercial success. Nor is it likely to quickly or easily replace the frontier in the public imagination as a new "cultural common property." Our film and television industries are based on formula stories that have a proven audience draw and track record. Sayles was able to make a film like *Lone Star,* a depiction of la frontera that also includes a recognition of the power of the mythic frontier, precisely because he was way on the margins of the Hollywood system.

Lone Star is more "realistic" because it acknowledges not only la frontera, as Limerick describes it, but also the staying power and persistence of the common frontier myth. For Sayles, it is not an either-or choice but a sense that society is going to have to figure out how to live with both "the frontier" and la frontera—with the persistent myth and the obtrusive realities of the West. Granted, it is a perplexing duality. Some critics have lamented the ambiguity of *Lone Star*'s ending. In one scene at Big O's Nightclub, Sam Deeds decides to let Buddy's heroic legend absorb what really happened on the night Sheriff Wade was killed. But in the next scene, when Sam is at the run-down drive-in movie theater with Pilar, the two seem to agree that they will, as Pilar puts it in the last line of the film, "Forget the Alamo." A crucial idea, however, may link these two seemingly contradictory scenes: the notion that individuals should not let what happened in the past—real or legendary—define their present.

In the end, David Ansen's assessment of Sayles's *Sunshine State* (2002) could be applied equally well to *Lone Star:* "It raises more issues than it can comfortably digest. . . . But who wants to complain about an American movie that has too much on its mind?" (16). When Sayles takes on the West, conflicts are not neatly positioned with resolution coming through a formula plot. He does not give us history as a packaged product. The stories of our present—and our past—are not tidy and beautifully lit; in *Lone Star,* lines are fuzzy, and relationships and individuals are complex. Even at the end of the film, there is a sense that the final stories have not been resolved. They will continue to be played out—in the relationships among individuals, their societies, and the stories they tell themselves in histories and in movies.

Notes

1. This group includes the likes of Richard White, Jack Forbes, Howard Lamar, Leonard Thompson, and Stephen Aron. See Limerick, "The Adventures of the Frontier in the Twentieth Century," 76–78, and also Worland and Countryman, "The New Western Historiography and the Emergence of the New American Westerns," 182–96.

2. For Limerick's most direct explanation of la frontera, see "The Adventures of the Frontier in the Twentieth Century," 72–95. For related ideas on the rehabilitation of the frontier by practitioners of the New Western History, see *The Legacy of Conquest,* 17–32, and *Something in the Soil,* 13–18, where Limerick argues that the history of the American West is defined by "continuity, convergence, conquest, and complexity."

3. Jack D. Forbes, quoted in Limerick, "The Adventures of the Frontier in the Twentieth Century," 76.

4. For the most complete assessment of Sayles's career and his films up to 1997, see Ryan, *John Sayles: Filmmaker.* Also recommended is *Sayles on Sayles.*

5. The NCLR Bravo Awards were the predecessors to the ALMA (American Latino Media Arts) Awards.

6. Characteristics of the Western genre have been treated extensively in the literature. See such works as Cawelti, *The Six-Gun Mystique Sequel;* Wright, *Six Guns and Society;* Buscombe and Pearson, *Back in the Saddle Again: New Essays on the Western;* Schatz, *Hollywood Genres;* Warshow, "The Movie Chronicle: The Westerner"; and Slotkin, *Gunfighter Nation: The Myth of the Frontier in Twentieth-Century America.*

7. Film is an audiovisual medium, and too often it is easy to overlook the "audio" part and focus only on the story and how it is visualized for the screen. Musical scoring as a guide for the emotional response of viewers is well understood in Hollywood. In any given scene, the accompanying sound track promotes the "appropriate" affective response: sad, scared, expectant, exultant, titillated, nostalgic. In terms of film studies scholarship, however, the sound track is much less thoroughly observed and understood, both in how it is typically employed and in the meaning of a director's choice to follow a different style.

8. The few noteworthy exceptions are music during the short credit sequences and a few scene transitions, during the short montages of Sam Deeds examining evidence and later driving, and during the final flashback.

9. The dialogue quoted in this chapter is from the film *Lone Star.* Sayles's screenplay was published in *"Men with Guns" and "Lone Star"* (1998). The published screenplay was used as a reference, and the spelling and punctuation are from this source, but the lines have been checked against the film. Where there were differences between the screenplay and the film, the dialogue from the film was used.

10. For a solid discussion of time transitions in the history of U.S. film, see Messaris, *Visual Literacy: Image, Mind, and Reality.* Significantly, almost all the conventional devices for a flashback in U.S. motion picture history have involved breaks—that is, discontinuities perceived by the viewer and also encoded within the medium itself. To create them meant physically cutting the film.

11. It is noteworthy that Chucho Montoya draws a line in the sand in this scene. This action is an allusion to accounts of the battle at the Alamo, in which William Barret Travis supposedly drew a line in the sand and asked those who would stay to cross it.

WORKS CITED

Ansen, David. "Movies: Fresh Squeezed." *Newsweek,* June 24, 2002, 16.

Beale, Lewis. "He's the Lone Wolf behind *Lone Star." Daily News,* June 19, 1996, 38.

Buscombe, Edward, and Roberta E. Pearson, eds. *Back in the Saddle Again: New Essays on the Western.* London: British Film Institute, 1998.

Cawelti, John G. *The Six-Gun Mystique Sequel.* Bowling Green, Ohio: Bowling Green State University Popular Press, 1999.

Howell, Peter. "Gunning for an Audience, John Sayles Famous for Not Doing Things the Hollywood Way." *Toronto Star,* September 8, 1997, E1.

Jackson, Kevin. "Film: Return of a Man Called Sayles." *Independent* (London), October 13, 1996, 11.

Leydon, Joe. "Sayles 'Star' Is Rising." *Variety,* March 18, 1996, 46.

Limerick, Patricia Nelson. "The Adventures of the Frontier in the Twentieth

Century." In *The Frontier in American Culture*, edited by James R. Grossman, 67–102. Berkeley: University of California Press, 1994.

———. *The Legacy of Conquest: The Unbroken Past of the American West*. New York: Norton, 1987.

———. *Something in the Soil: Legacies and Reckonings in the New West*. New York: Norton, 2000.

Maslin, Janet. "Sleepy Texas Town with an Epic Story." *New York Times*, June 21, 1996, C1.

Messaris, Paul. *Visual Literacy: Image, Mind, and Reality*. Boulder, Colo.: Westview Press, 1994.

Ryan, Jack. *John Sayles: Filmmaker*. Jefferson, N.C.: McFarland, 1998.

Sayles, John. "Borders and Boundaries: An Interview with John Sayles." Interview with Dennis West and Joan M. West. *Cineaste* 22, no. 3 (1996): 14–18.

———. *"Men with Guns" and "Lone Star."* London: Faber and Faber, 1998.

———. *Sayles on Sayles*. Interview with Gavin Smith. Boston: Faber and Faber, 1998.

Schatz, Thomas. *Hollywood Genres*. New York: McGraw-Hill, 1981.

Slotkin, Richard. *Gunfighter Nation. The Myth of the Frontier in Twentieth Century America*. New York: Atheneum, 1992.

Stein, Ruthe. "The 'Lone Star' Movies of John Sayles." *San Francisco Chronicle*, June 20, 1996, D1.

Warshow, Robert. "The Movie Chronicle: The Westerner." In *The Immediate Experience*, 89–106. New York: Macmillan, 1962.

White, Richard. "Frederick Jackson Turner and Buffalo Bill." In *The Frontier in American Culture*, edited by James R. Grossman, 6–65. Berkeley: University of California Press, 1994.

Worland, Rick, and Edward Countryman. "The New Western Historiography and the Emergence of the New American Westerns." In *Back in the Saddle Again: New Essays on the Western*, edited by Edward Buscombe and Roberta E. Pearson, 182–96. London: British Film Institute, 1998.

Wright, Will. *Six Guns and Society: A Structural Study of the Western*. Berkeley: University of California Press, 1975.

TURNER NETWORK TELEVISION'S MADE-FOR-TV WESTERN FILMS
Engaging Audiences through Genre and Themes

Randy Smith, a member of the Western Writers of America,[1] states that "some of the best recent Westerns have been totally the provenance of the cable television industry." He asserts that while the major motion picture studios are stymied by marketing conservatism, cable networks, like Turner Network Television (TNT), have been producing Westerns that are truly representative of the "best qualities of the genre." Ted Mahar echoes Smith's claim by declaring that the network's *Monte Walsh* (2003) "is one of the best westerns of the last quarter-century" ("*Monte Walsh*" 1). These comments about the quality of TNT's Western films raise several critical questions: Why did the network begin producing Western films? How does the network attract viewers for Western films? And how do these movies engage contemporary audiences?

Genre elements and conventions, like horses, cowboy heroes, or quick-draw gunfights, serve to attract audiences to Westerns. They also define what is and, more important, what is not a Western. Just as the Hollywood film industry relies on various genre markers to identify and appeal to its diverse audiences, so do TNT productions. The cable network also taps into a wide range of existing social themes and then reworks, restructures, and reshapes them into programming that engages their particular viewerships (Gronbeck 229–30). By analyzing the dominant themes in TV movies, one will be able to begin to understand why they are so popular and meaningful to a wide range of viewers.

To address the previous questions, this chapter is organized as follows: first, it will examine TNT's institutional and economic rationale for producing Westerns; second, it will analyze how the network relies on generic markers to attract viewers for Western films; and, third, it will analyze four of the network's most popular Western movies—*The Good Old Boys* (1995), *Last Stand at Saber River* (1997), *The Virginian* (2000), and *Crossfire Trail* (2001)—to identify the presence of specific themes.

TNT and the Production of Western Films

Turner Broadcasting System introduced the TNT cable network in 1988 after achieving profitability with superstation WTBS and CNN (Cable News Network). Created as a venue for Turner's vast library of films, TNT consisted almost exclusively of theatrical and television releases. Indeed, the network's MGM/UA film library includes twenty-two hundred MGM titles, along with older Warner Bros. and RKO films. TNT debuted on October 3 in 17 million cable homes—by far the largest network launch to date in cable history (Fryman and Hudson 190–93). Turner Network Television is best described as a broad-appeal channel because it offers a mix of programming similar to that available on broadcast TV networks. TNT and CNN were both ranked as having the fifth most cable subscribers, 81.8 million each, by the National Cable Television Association's 2001 ranking of the top twenty cable TV networks ("Top 20").

Since its inception, TNT has financed or produced many large-scale original productions. The network is among the most active producer of made-for-cable films. Because of Ted Turner's strong interest in Westerns[2] and the need for Turner Broadcasting to attract press attention for its subscriber networks among cable operators and customers,[3] TNT began creating and promoting original productions. Following its strategy of adapting popular literary works, the network sought to develop stories based on established Western authors and featuring actors familiar to the genre. Turner Productions' first Westerns were *Billy the Kid* (1989), based on Gore Vidal's book, and *Montana* (1990), based on a Larry McMurtry story, starring Richard Crenna and Gena Rowlands as "a brawling Western couple" (Beale 6). The cable channel resisted producing a regular, domestic Western series, like *Bonanza* (1959–1973), *The Big Valley* (1965–1969), or *Dr. Quinn, Medicine Woman* (1993–1998), the type of series that had dominated the prime-time genre since the mid-1960s, and a genre most likely to appeal to a cross section of adult male and female viewers (MacDonald 47–81). Instead, Turner Productions sought to produce traditional-style Westerns featuring rough-edged protagonists who live by a moral code and who inevitably find them-

Courtesy of Turner Broadcasting. Photo by Erik Heinila.

Conn Conagher (Sam Elliot) with Evie Teale (Katherine Ross) in Louis L'Amour's *Conagher*.

selves drawn into a fight with lawless villains.[4] Although TNT's heroes are often softened by the love of a good-hearted woman, the violence of their conflicts owes more to the popularity of Clint Eastwood lone-gunfighter Westerns than the legacy of the television domestic Western.

One of the network's earliest successes was the 1991 film version of Louis L'Amour's *Conagher*, starring Sam Elliot and Katherine Ross. The film, which debuted as TNT's highest-rated two-hour drama, tells the parallel stories of a lonely widow trying to raise two stepchildren on an isolated homestead, and a tough, honest cowboy battling cattle rustlers. Eventually, the two stories intertwine into an unique frontier romance.

In 1995, Turner Broadcasting merged with the corporate media giant Time Warner. That year TNT produced three major efforts: *Avenging Angel*, starring Tom Berenger and Charlton Heston; a film version of Zane Grey's *Riders of the Purple Sage*,[5] starring Ed Harris and Amy Madigan; and *The Good Old Boys*, starring Tommy Lee Jones and Sissy Spacek. From a mystery-Western (*Avenging Angel*) to a comedy-drama set in the early 1900s (*The Good Old Boys*), these movies illustrated the great potential of the genre.[6]

In 1997, TNT's film version of an Elmore Leonard Western, *Last Stand at Saber River*, attracted the greatest number of viewers ever for an original movie on cable. According to an A. C. Nielsen survey, some 5.1 million Americans tuned in to the Tom Selleck vehicle. Overall, the cable movie garnered a 7.3 rating, making it the third highest for an original cable movie (Haddad).

Another reason for TNT's production of Westerns is its corporate relationship, after the AOL and Time Warner merger, with Warner Home Video. Through this association, the network distributes many of its popular made-for-TV movies to retail and rental stores across the country. Because Hollywood produces fewer Westerns every year, TNT has established a marketing niche as the primary producer of new Westerns. In 2001, Warner Home Video became the nation's leading distributor when it increased its market share of the $4.1 billion rental market from 15.6 percent to 18 percent on the strength of having seventeen of the top one hundred rental titles (Herrick, "Buy-Product" 2). Although a 2002 antitrust suit by independent retailers terminated the contract practice, Warner's long-standing revenue-sharing contract with Blockbuster, the nation's leading home video rental chain, has filled the stores with product, including TNT Westerns (Herrick, "Retailer News" 29–30).

Genre Markers in TNT Westerns

Because TNT Westerns' core audience consists of genre fans, the network takes great pains to identify its movies through publicity, promotional trailers, and press kits. This study found six genre markers used by the network to attract its audience.

The first genre marker is basing its Westerns on the works of well-known Western writers. Many of TNT's movies are adaptations of popular novels written by Louis L'Amour, Zane Grey, and Elmore Leonard. TNT has even produced a cable film adaptation of the literary work that initially presented the archetypal Western hero—Owen Wister's novel *The Virginian* (1902). Of course, the practice of adapting and producing Westerns from earlier publications is hardly a new one. *The Virginian* was adapted to film first in 1929 and again in 1946: it later became a long-running television series, which aired from 1962 to 1971 (Brooks and Marsh 831–32). Turner Productions, through its promotional campaigns, communicates that its Westerns are true adaptations of these popular stories, for example, that it is presenting the first "faithful" adaptation of Wister's classic novel ("TNT: *The Virginian*").

Tom Selleck, in an interview, expresses the anxiety he felt producing a television adaptation of *Crossfire Trail*, a popular novel by Louis L'Amour, "a very dear and close friend." Selleck states that, though L'Amour passed away many years ago, he has "left behind some ump-teen-dozen-million fans all around the world that hold a keen interest in who-does-what to the revered author's work." The actor-producer says he also experienced pressure from the author's family, which is dedicated to preserving and protecting his memory. "Because, as you know, the L'Amour family doesn't exactly release this stuff to just anybody," notes Selleck (Fogarty, "Selleck and Westerns").

Another genre marker is that the network's productions feature a familiar Western cast. The two most prolific leading actors in TNT Westerns are Tom Selleck and Sam Elliot. Selleck's long-standing association with Turner Productions has led to three Westerns for the network: *Last Stand at Saber River, Crossfire Trail*, and *Monte Walsh*. Elliot has starred in *Conagher, The Desperate Trail* (1995), and *You Know My Name* (1999). Both actors also served as executive producers of their films.

A third generic sign employed by the network is to emphasize the genre's close association with American history and with familiar western symbolism. Indeed, the influential frontier thesis of Frederick Jackson Turner argues that the development of American democracy, its novel attitudes, and its social institutions are inextricably linked to the country's westward expansion (Turner 1–22). Henry Nash Smith points out that underscoring Turner's notions and the movement and cultivation of the West is the "myth of the garden," the idea of a place of continuous "rebirth, a regeneration, a rejuvenation of man and society constantly recurring where civilization came into contact with the wilderness along the frontier" (253). Historically, the Western is set at a critical moment in the formation of America as a nation, "namely at that point when savagery and lawlessness are in decline before the advancing wave of law and order, but are still strong enough to pose a local and momentarily significant challenge" (Cawelti 65). This moment reflects a deep-seated, ideological tension in American culture between the desires for unfettered individualism and for the values associated with a developing community. The fictional world of the Western provides a narrative space by which audiences can contemplate the passing of the frontier and the transition to social and cultural structures linked to the present (Cawelti 100). This domain provides a rich cross section of character types (e.g., farmer, banker, schoolmarm, prostitute) that can easily be revived within modern stories that represent ongoing social and ideological struggles taking place in contemporary American society (Cook 65).

TNT's Westerns are placed within the historical period most closely associated with the genre—the period between 1865 and the 1890s. There are, of course, a few exceptions, such as *The Good Old Boys* and *You Know My Name*, both of which take place in the early part of the twentieth century, but the mythology and character of the Old West resonate throughout these films' stories. In *You Know My Name*, for example, Bill Tilghman (Sam Elliot), a retired lawman who had captured many legendary outlaws, is called upon once again to wear a badge to rid a rowdy 1920s Oklahoma town of Jazz Age criminals. Several of the network's Westerns feature characters and narratives based on actual historical persons and events in the West, such as Bill Tilghman (1854–1924), Brigham Young (1801–1877) in *Avenging Angel*, and Sam Houston (1793–1863) and the Alamo in *Two for Texas* (1998).

Mimi White argues that from television docudramas to made-for-TV movies, television relies on history as a programming "hook" to bring in audiences and validate their viewing experiences (282–84). Verisimilitude to historical events adds dramatic intensity to both fictional and nonfictional programs; in this way, history serves as a prime legitimator for audiences to invest their viewing time. Historical references are often present in the network's promotional trailers. TNT also offers educational links for teachers and students, along with historical time lines giving perspective on the period, on many of its promotional Web sites.[7]

A fourth genre sign is the use of western scenery in TNT productions. John Cawelti asserts that "the western landscape is uniquely adaptable to certain kinds of strong contrasts of light and shadow characteristic of an arid climate together with the topographical contrasts of plain and mountain, rocky outcrops and flat deserts, steep bare canyons and forested plateaus" (70). The openness of the terrain, coupled with its topographic contrasts, visually expresses the thematic conflicts "between man and nature, and wilderness and civilization"

(Cawelti 69–70). In recent productions, the genre has come to be centered on the isolated town, ranch, or fort surrounded by a great expanse of open prairie or desert with weak ties back to civilization. The territory is a rough place, with a harsh terrain and climate, where an individual must possess and master skills to survive. Jane Tompkins asserts that the Western hero not only has these requisite skills but also reflects the toughness and hardness of this land in his very physicality and austere demeanor (69–87). To capture and express this scenery, TNT Westerns are shot on location in the High Plains, mountains, and desert regions of the western United States and Canada. The fifth genre marker is that TNT's Western narratives tend to be centered on the actions of a rugged, individualistic male protagonist. He is a man who lives close to death and whose moral character is best expressed through violent action against lawless antagonists. The heroic but violent nature of the Western hero is best expressed in a TNT promotional for its *Crossfire Trail:* "A hero is measured by the enemies he makes." Even when he works as a lawman, a rancher, a cowboy, or a mercenary, he appears to be a man with plenty of leisure time on his hands—which makes it easier for him to be drawn into local conflicts or to help a woman or a less powerful ally (Warshow 471–73). In *Crossfire Trail,* for example, Selleck plays a restless wanderer bound by a promise to look after a dying friend's widow and ranch. Harris, in *Riders of the Purple Sage,* plays a mysterious gunman who helps a proud homesteader maintain her ranch against the threats of hostile neighbors.

Sometimes, more than one protagonist is involved in the conflict. In *Two for Texas,* a pair of escaped convicts who join Sam Houston's Texas Volunteer Army to hide from authorities suddenly find themselves in the Battle of San Jacinto facing Santa Anna's army. Although TNT's heroes have rougher edges than the classic Western hero, the protagonists follow the outlines laid down by Robert Warshow. Warshow describes the hero as essentially a loner with a touch of melancholy, which derives not from his temperament but from his recognition that life is inevitably solemn. This hero is chivalrous in combat, fighting for justice and order and, most important, to preserve his sense of honor (Warshow 470–74). TNT Westerns, for the most part, present a traditional, hard-edged, mythic hero rather than the ironic, self-conscious hero who began to emerge in film and television Westerns from the late 1950s to the 1970s (*Maverick* [1957–1962], *Butch Cassidy and the Sundance Kid* [1969]). Neither are they part of the historical revisionism of the period since the late 1960s (*Little Big Man* [1970], *Buffalo Bill and the Indians* [1976], *Dances with*

Jim Lassiter (Ed Harris) rides to the rescue in *Riders of the Purple Sage.*

Wolves [1990]). Despite the presence of a few strong-willed women in these films, TNT Westerns tend to reinforce traditional notions of masculinity.

The sixth generic marker is the iconography, including horses, cattle, six-guns, Winchester rifles, barrooms, cowboy boots, and wide-brimmed hats, which crowds the promotional press kits and materials for these films. For instance, Selleck, in the pictorial promotional for *Last Stand at Saber River,* points a six-gun directly toward the camera, while dressed in classic frontier garb (*"Last Stand"*).[8] The picture not only communicates that the film is a Western but also hints at the violent nature of the film's "last stand." In a promotional still for *Buffalo Soldiers* (1997), Danny Glover is seen from a heroic, low camera angle, dressed as a Union soldier with a revolver in hand and framed by a set of clouds ("TNT: *Buffalo Soldiers*"). This image functions to place the film and the buffalo soldiers within the context of a heroic frontier legend.

Clothing is a crucial genre element in TNT Westerns. The hero, outlaw, and Native American are dressed in a more distinctive and utilitarian manner than the townspeople, who wear the standard street clothing (e.g., suits, long dresses) of the nineteenth century. The cowboy character typically wears practical clothing to mark his adaptation to nature, which usually includes "his cowboy's boots, tight-fitting pants or chaps, his heavy shirt and bandana, his gun and finally his ten-gallon hat" (Cawelti 72). Turner Productions relies heavily on these complex sets of iconic codes to structure and make its fictional and nonfictional Western characters accessible and credible to its audience.

TNT WESTERNS AND CONTEMPORARY AUDIENCES

This study found two main themes in four popular TNT Westerns (*Last Stand at Saber River, The Good Old Boys, The Virginian, Crossfire Trail*)—those of nostalgia and a cynicism regarding social institutions. These themes are effective in engaging audiences primarily because they are already part of their everyday lives. For example, a nostalgia for Western myths and heroes is prevalent in Western novels, Hollywood films, paintings, country-and-western songs, and other popular cultural forms. These topics have undeniable ideological and cultural implications.

Nostalgia

TNT productions evoke a deep-seated, nostalgic desire for Western myths and heroes, and for mythically well-defined gender roles for men and women. The Western male heroes still adhere to the same "Cowboy Code" used by Gene Autry to describe television's Western heroes in the early 1950s:

1. A cowboy never takes unfair advantage, even of an enemy.
2. A cowboy never betrays a trust.
3. A cowboy always tells the truth.
4. A cowboy is kind to small children, to old folks, and to animals.
5. A cowboy is free from racial and religious prejudice.
6. A cowboy is always helpful, and when anyone's in trouble, he lends a hand.
7. A cowboy is a good worker.
8. A cowboy is clean about his person, and in thoughts, word, and deed.
9. A cowboy respects womanhood, his parents, and the laws of his country.
10. A cowboy is a patriot. (Reeves 1826)

The traditional nature of the network's protagonists is expressed in the

Paul Cable (Tom Selleck) in
Last Stand at Saber River.

films analyzed for this study. In *Crossfire Trail,* for example, Rafe Covington (Tom Selleck) is referred to by his enemies as a "dinosaur" for honoring his promise to a dying friend to protect his ranch and wife. In *The Virginian,* the Virginian (Bill Pullman) follows the draconian code of the land and hangs his best friend, Steve (John Savage), for stealing cattle. When his fiancée, Molly Stark (Diane Lane), does not understand his adherence to such a brutal tradition, he tells her that he must be "true to himself." Paul Cable (Tom Selleck again) in *Last Stand* is a former Confederate officer who keeps his promise to his wife and family by securing their homestead in the Arizona Territory by fighting off a host of vengeful ex–Union soldiers. Despite his penchant for telling tall tales, Hewey Calloway (Tommy Lee Jones) in *The Good Old Boys* keeps his promise to save his brother's farm and ranch. Perhaps because contemporary life requires so many personal and professional compromises, TNT's audiences appreciate the traditional values expressed by these male leads.

The network's Westerns also express a nostalgia for open spaces away from the constraints of civilization. This attitude actually dates back to the popularity of traveling Wild West shows and Western dime novels in the middle to late nineteenth century. The open frontier was more than a geographic location—it symbolically expressed the still "open" opportunities and possibilities available to individuals before the West was finally closed off by the progression of modern communities. At the beginning of the twenty-first century, for middle-class Americans hoping to move to the suburbs or the countryside to temporarily escape the traffic congestion and stress of the cities, Westerns evoke a nostalgia for a mythic time and place where many possibilities were still open to people. This nostalgia is often expressed by the heroes in

TNT's Westerns. Rafe remarks to his friends in *Crossfire Trail* that the buffalo will disappear in twenty years. The great wild buffalo herds, which once freely roamed the West, enabled rugged frontiersmen and Native American tribes to live off the land. The vanishing of the grand herds represented a loss of the wildness and extravagant abundance of the wilderness.

Although several of the women in *The Virginian* condemn the Wyoming Territory for its lack of eastern "culture," the Virginian fondly refers to the rolling, nearly treeless land as the "Great Unknown" and proudly proclaims to his sweetheart, Molly, that he cannot live without it. In *The Good Old Boys*, Hewey, an aging cowboy, has spent so much time living off the land that he is uncomfortable in any interior space—except a saloon. His hunger for the youthful adventures played out in open spaces leads him to accept an invitation from a longtime friend to go on a cattle drive in Mexico rather than settling down and marrying.

TNT Westerns also represent a nostalgia for traditional gender roles for men and women. Despite the perceived restrictive nature of such roles, many male and female audience members may be briefly comforted by the nostalgic representation of men and women in a historical period,[9] like the Western, which figuratively characterizes men and women in patriarchal relationships. In these movies, for example, the male lead is represented as a skilled provider for women, children, and those in need. The hero lives close to the possibility of death and stands ready to use lethal force if challenged. While women usually do not understand the hero's violence, the character instinctively knows that certain situations demand it. The Virginian explains this perspective to Molly when he tells her that "sometimes, all a man can do is shoot." Cawelti affirms that "the cowboy hero does not seek out combat for its own sake and he typically shows an aversion to the wanton shedding of blood" (87). In *Crossfire Trail*, despite every attempt to tell the angry brother of a man he had to kill to heed his warnings and walk away, Rafe reluctantly shoots and kills the man.

TNT's Western male protagonist is invariably a man of few words and by nature suspicious and distrustful of language. This contrasts with the genre's women characters, who freely express their emotional states and feelings, in part because these women often serve as teachers of language and culture within their small communities. The hero knows that words can easily reveal too much information to one's enemies, and therefore he is naturally reserved and guarded about his identity and actions (Tompkins 47–67). In *Last Stand*, when Cable and his family are confronted by a band of former Union soldiers, he steadfastly refuses to divulge his identity or explain where his family is headed. Rafe, in *Crossfire Trail*, also declines to reveal his identity to a host of strangers, perceiving that they may soon become his mortal enemies. Rafe relaxes and opens up only in the company of men he knows he can trust. In fact, Rafe is so mysterious in his demeanor that Ann Rodney (Virginia Madsen) ventures out on horseback to talk to him and to gauge his true motivations for honoring her husband's promise to protect her and the ranch.

The villain in these movies is usually a cultured man who hides his vicious schemes and actions behind a steady barrage of words. The villain stands in marked contrast to the Western hero, who measures his every word and who knows that the villain's rhetoric conceals his intentions. Examples of this type of villain include Sam Balaam's (Dennis Weaver) unscrupulous ranch baron in *The Virginian* and Bruce Barkow's (Mark Harmon) duplicitous banker in *Crossfire Trail.*

Unlike family melodramas, these movies present a multiplicity of dramatic, fictional spaces dominated by the presence of men. These include open ranges, campfires, saloons, bunkhouses, ranch houses, and horse stables. These places provide plenty of male bonding and camaraderie, which tends to reinforce patriarchal, individualistic values and ideas over values generally attached to community spaces inhabited by women and children (Warshow 471). Each of the previously mentioned films includes an ample number of male-dominated areas. Literary critics have pointed out that the ascendance of the male-oriented Western novel in the early twentieth century was in part a reaction to feminized parlor room novels of the nineteenth century (Tompkins 28–45). These early Western novelists include Owen Wister (*The Virginian*, 1902), Andy Adams (*The Log of a Cowboy*, 1903), Zane Grey (*Betty Zane*, 1904; *The Spirit of the Border*, 1905; *Riders of the Purple Sage*, 1910), and Eugene Manlove Rhodes (*Good Men and True*, 1910; *West Is West*, 1917) (Cawelti 121–22). Women in these Westerns are chiefly confined to domestic and community spaces such as general stores, parlor rooms, schoolhouses, and churches.

The women are primarily shown in nurturing roles and professions. Each main female character in *Last Stand, The Good Old Boys, The Virginian*, and *Crossfire Trail* serves as a schoolteacher for her community. Molly in *The Virginian* gives her young students a basic civics lesson by having them recite the Declaration of Independence. She even lends the Virginian a book of Shakespeare to enlighten him. As local educators, these women are associated

The Virginian (Bill Pullman) enjoys a game of poker with his fellow cowhands.

with the advent of civilized culture. Cawelti points out that it was probably the presence of the schoolmarm more than the businessman that served as a true indicator of the final closing of the western wilderness (74).

Although TNT's Western female leads usually have prescribed social roles, they are not necessarily weak-willed or passive. Unlike Warshow's contention that Westerns present worlds where men are figuratively the adults and women children, in these films the women tend to be active and often can shoot as well as men (471). Martha Cable (Suzy Amis), in *Last Stand*, protects her husband against an ambush by shooting two of the assailants. In *Crossfire Trail*, Ann shoots Barkow in the back before he can put a final bullet in Rafe, echoing the final gunfight in *High Noon* (1952).

However, these movies also illustrate that a woman can be perceived as a threat to male characters. Eve Calloway, wife of Hewey's brother in *The Good Old Boys*, is a woman whose strength has kept her husband and her two sons focused on constructive tasks. Eve perceives Hewey as a corruptive influence on her family. While Eve's strength has helped maintain the family's farm and ranch, her dominance threatens to smother the aspirations of her older son. Reluctantly, she agrees to Hewey's request that the boy be allowed to leave home to pursue his own interests.

In traditional Westerns, the male protagonists ultimately reject marriage and family as represented by women in favor of a solitary life of unfettered freedom and self-reliance. Women are the central symbols of domesticity and civilization in the Western (Cawelti 74). With the exception of *The Good Old Boys*, most Western male heroes gradually accept the legitimate social role of women and marriage. In these movies men and women believe that each has a social role and that these positions are complementary.

Cable and his wife in *Last Stand* acknowledge each other's inner pain—his for being unable to stop a massacre of Union prisoners during the war and hers for losing their daughter to a sudden illness. In *The Virginian*, after Molly returns home, the Virginian travels east to mend their dispute and to declare his love for her; he realizes that he needs to compromise in order to have a life with her. Molly responds that since they have different backgrounds and life experiences, each has knowledge that the other does not. This promise of mutual understanding motivates Molly to return to the Wyoming Territory, marry the Virginian, and raise their family. With the preponderance of post-1960s social movements, the decline of high-paying manufacturing jobs that once enabled working-class men to assume the primary breadwinner role, and the rise of the two-income family, TNT Westerns address a yearning for a time and place where women stayed home and men were in the marketplace.

Cynicism toward Social Institutions

The popularity of Westerns in the post–World War II period can be partly attributed to their nostalgic vision for a time when individuals and personal values mattered more than institutional directives. Today, when national institutions and global corporations structure much of modern life, many Westerns express a general cynicism concerning the effectiveness of social institutions. Following the partisan discord of the Vietnam War and political scandals such as Watergate, many viewers probably share this cynicism.

Paul Cable, for example, returns home from the Civil War as an embittered veteran. Tired of war and causes, he has shifted his personal moral emphasis to his family. His bitterness comes from his inability to prevent a massacre of prisoners at a Union prison camp. The character's personal journey from patriot-warrior to alienated veteran reflects the similar experiences of the Vietnam War portrayed in Hollywood films such as *The Deer Hunter* (1978). The film's chief antagonist is not one of the former Union soldiers who try to retake Cable's former ranch but a zealous, Confederate gun smuggler who refuses to accept Southern defeat.

Rafe, in *Crossfire Trail,* confesses to Ann that he was educated by the Jesuits and that his mother had hoped he would become a priest. When she asks him what happened, he simply shrugs his shoulders and tells her that he had problems learning to "turn the other cheek." Although Rafe's formal education enables him to appreciate many fine cultural works, from Beethoven piano sonatas to poems by Keats, he has chosen the life of a cowboy because it provides him the individual freedom he craves—a life unencumbered by social institutions.

TNT's *The Virginian* and *The Good Old Boys* share a skeptical view of law enforcement. In *The Virginian,* after Judge Henry (Harris Yulin), the Virginian's boss, discovers that Trampas and Balaam are behind the region's rash of cattle rustling, he brings in federal agents; unfortunately, these inexperienced outsiders are ambushed. Ultimately, it is the Virginian, with his frontier experience and shooting skills, who must confront Trampas in individual combat.

In *The Good Old Boys,* when Hewey stops to water his horse and listen to the melodious singing voices of a choir coming from a church, the city marshal brusquely orders him to leave at once; when Hewey resists, the marshal draws a gun. A fight ensues in which Hewey knocks out the marshal and disposes of his gun in the water trough. Modern law enforcement is represented in this film as an institution more concerned with preserving the community's pristine, middle-class image than with arresting dangerous criminals. *The Good Old Boys* features another representative of law enforcement in the character of the Texas county sheriff. The sheriff is a familiar Western character who knows that the prerogatives of the law must be carefully balanced with the rights of individuals; in many ways, this judicious lawman is just as much an anachronism as Hewey.

While this study has highlighted the role of genre elements and themes in attracting audiences to TNT productions, there are, of course, numerous other appeals at work in these Westerns. The network's writers and directors, for the most part, understand the relationships among the ingredients (e.g., character, setting, narrative situation) within the Western formula and are skillful at constructing dramatic stories, which evoke intense emotions and resonate with their audiences. Although there is a strong dramatic unity of elements within the genre, TNT Westerns are not a single narrative but rather a diversity of stories featuring gunfighters, cowboys, widows, lawmen, outlaws, ranch barons, and settlers, as well as other characters. The Western's dramatic structure, with its inherent conflict between civilization and nature, has enabled countless creators to link contemporary conflicts and concerns to "a vision of the American past" (Cawelti 101). Simon Wincer, director of *Lonesome Dove, Crossfire Trail,* and *Monte Walsh,* in commenting on the universal appeal of Westerns, quotes Thomas King Whipple, from the preface of Larry McMurtry's *Lonesome Dove:* "What they dreamed, we live, and what they lived, we dream" (Horn 76). For harried, present-day audiences, Westerns present a romantic, vanished way of life—a journey by horseback, riding on a cattle drive, sleeping under the stars, and sitting at night by a quiet fire. While Hollywood continues to produce a declining number of Westerns each year, the sustained success of TNT's Westerns indicates that the genre is still very much alive and flourishing on cable television.

NOTES

1. Western Writers of America is a nonprofit organization "founded in 1953 to promote the literature of the American West and to bestow the Spur Awards for distinguished writing in the western field." The Spur Awards have broadened over the years to include awards for the best TV or motion picture drama and best TV or motion picture documentary. The organization has more than five hundred members, who write everything from traditional Western fiction to local history ("Western Writers").

2. According to Ted Mahar, Ted Turner is a big fan of John Ford's films, especially his Westerns, and of John Wayne, the actor most closely associated with Ford's Westerns ("John Ford Westerns" C.04).

3. Jay Newell, who served as director of on-air promotions for TNT from 1989 to 1998, states that "when TNT was launched, the majority of the revenue for the network was derived from cable subscriber fees," not advertising, and that "these fees were the highest among all cable channels." These fees had to be justified by greater press attention to TNT, and the network's original movies were considered key vehicles in attracting this attention. Newell maintains that the Westerns, with their scenic scope and familiar stars, were particularly distinctive competition against contemporary thrillers and detective-dramas offered by other cable networks.

4. TNT Productions also produced several films about Native Americans, including *Geronimo* (1993), *The Broken Chain* (1993), *Crazy Horse* (1996), and *Lakota Woman: Siege at Wounded Knee* (1994). While these films have not garnered

the same high ratings as TNT's traditional Westerns, they should be applauded for raising awareness of the often-overlooked historical and cultural role of Native Americans.

5. Although produced in 1995, *Riders of the Purple Sage* was originally broadcast on January 21, 1996, on TNT.

6. TNT has even produced nontraditional Westerns, which expand the Western formula. These include the gothic Western *Purgatory* (1999), starring Sam Shepard and Eric Roberts, and *King of Texas* (2002), a Western based on *King Lear,* starring Patrick Stewart and Marcia Gay Harden. These films did not produce the same high ratings as TNT's traditional Westerns, but they did provide evidence of the network's interest in expanding generic boundaries.

7. For instance, TNT's promotional Web site for *The Virginian* includes a link to an "Educator's Guide" for secondary school teachers with suggestions for using *The Virginian* in the classroom and other information ("TNT: *The Virginian*"). The Web site for TNT's *Buffalo Soldiers* also includes links to an educational guide and to "Learn More about the Buffalo Soldiers" ("TNT: *Buffalo Soldiers*"). TNT's Web site for *Last Stand at Saber River* includes a historical time line, along with information on "The Role of Women in the West" and "The Civil War in the American West" ("*Last Stand at Saber River*").

8. This shot of Selleck in *Last Stand at Saber River* repeats the final shot in Edwin S. Porter's *Great Train Robbery* (1903). The earlier film closes with a medium close-up of the outlaws' leader (actor George Barnes) pointing and shooting his revolver point-blank, directly into the camera (and, of course, the audience). This shot apparently caused a great sensation at the time with audiences. Because the shot was irrelevant to the film's plot, theater managers could choose to place it at the beginning of the film or at its end (*Great Train Robbery*). I would like to thank Peter Rollins, editor in chief of *Film & History,* for this particular insight.

9. Stephanie Coontz asserts that "visions of past family life exert a powerful emotional pull on most Americans, and with good reason, given the fragility of modern commitments" (4). She argues that these visions are an "amalgam of structures, values, and behaviors that never existed in the same time and place" (5). These dramatized and imagined images of traditional families appear not only in popular TV situation comedies (*Father Knows Best, The Cosby Show*), but also in other genres—including made-for-TV movie Westerns.

WORKS CITED

Beale, Lewis. "The Western Rides Again." *New York Daily News,* January 21, 2001, 6.

Brooks, Tim, and Earle Marsh. *The Complete Directory to Prime Time Network TV Shows, 1946–Present.* 4th ed. New York: Ballantine, 1988.

Cawelti, John. *The Six-Gun Mystique.* 2nd ed. Bowling Green, Ohio: Bowling Green State University Popular Press, 1984.

Cook, Pam, ed. *The Cinema Book.* New York: Pantheon, 1985.

Coontz, Stephanie. *The Way We Never Were: American Families and the Nostalgia Trap.* New York: Basic Books, 1992.

"Crossfire Trail." *TNT–We Know Drama–TNT Originals.* 2000. http://alt.tnt.tv/movies/tntoriginals/crossfiretrail.html (accessed July 15, 2002).

Fogarty, Taylor. "Selleck and Westerns: Speaking Well for Man." *American Western Magazine,* January 2001. http://www.readthewest.com/tomselleck.html (accessed June 2002).

Fryman, John E., and Jerry Hudson. "Turner Network Television (TNT)." In *The Cable Networks Handbook,* edited by Robert G. Picard, 190–96. Riverside, Calif.: Carpelan Publishing, 1993.

The Great Train Robbery (1903). *Greatest Films.* http://www.filmsite.org/grea2.html (accessed July 15, 2004).

Gronbeck, Bruce. "Narrative, Enactment, and Television Programming." *Southern Speech Communication Journal* 48 (1983): 229–43.

Haddad, Charles. "Turner Channels' Original Programs Make Ratings Dent." *Atlantic Journal-Constitution,* January 26, 1997. http://80proquest.umi.com.ezproxy.libraries.psu.edu/pqdweb?.

Herrick, Scott. "Buy-Product of 2001 Rentals: Ups and Downs." *Video Business,* July 16, 2001, 1–2.

———. "Retailer News." *DSN Retailing Today,* October 1, 2001, 29–30.

Horn, John. "Westerns Appeal to Aussie Director." *Chicago Sun-Times,* November 8, 1990, 76.

"Last Stand at Saber River." *TNT–We Know Drama–TNT Originals.* 2001. http://alt.tnt.tv/movies/tntoriginals/saber_river/index1.html (accessed July 15, 2002).

MacDonald, Fred J. *Who Shot the Sheriff? The Rise and Fall of the Television Western.* New York: Praeger, 1987.

Mahar, Ted. "John Ford Westerns Will Gallop into Roseway." *Oregonian,* January 21, 1993, C.04.

———. "*Monte Walsh*: A Terrific Tale at the End of the Trail." *Newhouse News Service,* January 13, 2003.

Newell, Jay. E-mail correspondence with David Pierson. January 13, 2004.

Reeves, Jimmie L. "Westerns." In *Museum of Broadcast Communications, Encyclopedia of Television.* Vol. 3. Edited by Horace Newcomb. Chicago: Fitzroy Dearborn, 1997.

Smith, Henry Nash. *Virgin Land: The American West as Symbol and Myth.* Cambridge, Mass.: Harvard University Press, 1950.

Smith, Randy D. "Keeping Western Films Alive." *American Western Magazine,* March 2001. http://readthewest.com/westernfilms.html (accessed June 2002).

"TNT: *Buffalo Soldiers.*" *TNT–We Know Drama–TNT Originals.* 1997. http://alt.tnt.tv/movies/tntoriginals/buffalo/home2.html (accessed July 13, 2002).

"TNT: *Riders of the Purple Sage.*" *TNT–We Know Drama–TNT Originals.* 2002. http://www.tnt.tv/Title/Display/0,5918,304616,00.html (accessed July 15, 2002).

"TNT: *The Virginian.*" *TNT–We Know Drama–TNT Originals.* 2001. http://alt.tnt.tv/movies/tntoriginals/virginian/info.html (accessed July 13, 2002).

Tompkins, Jane. *West of Everything: The Inner Life of Westerns.* New York: Oxford University Press, 1992.

"Top 20 Cable TV Networks, 2001." *World Almanac and Book of Facts.* 2002. http://web2.epnet.com:80/c (accessed July 30, 2002).

Turner, Frederick Jackson. *The Frontier in American History.* New York: Henry Holt, 1947.

Warshow, Robert. "Movie Chronicle: The Westerner." In *Film Theory and Criticism,* edited by Gerald Mast and Marshall Cohen, 469–87. 2nd ed. New York: Oxford University Press, 1979.

"Western Writers of America." *Western Writers of America.* 2004. http://www.westernwriters.org/about_wwa.htm (accessed May 29, 2004).

White, Mimi. "Television—A Narrative, a History." *Cultural Studies* 35 (1990): 282–300.

FILMOGRAPHY

Genre history describes and interprets the settings, plots, characters, actors, and auteurs for a family of films. In *The Filming of the West* (1976), Jon Tuska relates that he watched more than eight thousand Westerns in a decade of writing his book. Michael R. Pitts's *Western Movies: A TV and Video Guide to 4200 Genre Films* (1986) consumes 621 pages with its paragraph-scale entries. Such compilations lie beyond the frontier of this scholarly volume.

The condensed listing here reflects three sources. From John Cawelti's widely recognized genre study *The Six-Gun Mystique Sequel* (1999) we have taken the "Selected Western Films by Subject," borrowing and expanding somewhat upon his subgenre categories (211–15). In addition, principal films discussed by this volume's contributors appear with titles in bold and corresponding chapter numbers. Finally, the nine Westerns identified in the American Film Institute's Greatest 100 Movies of the twentieth century are listed. This selectivity means that readers will miss some films they regard as the best or the most popular Westerns.

A reader can still learn much from this list. To mention just one example, notice that the first spoof of the Western had appeared by 1918 with Fatty Arbuckle's *Out West*. Western parodies appeared steadily in every decade, with notable comedians such as Bob Hope, W. C. Fields, Mae West, the Stooges, Laurel and Hardy, and Abbot and Costello. If the Western was killed by *Blazing Saddles* (1974), it had certainly already been weakened by generations of laughter about its plot and character conventions. Again thinking of the Western's death, notice the series of TNT productions discussed by Matthew Turner. Although they appear in cable distribution, they reach large audiences that dwarf the theatrical audiences for some of the more critically acclaimed

Westerns of the 1950s and 1960s. If the Western could speak for itself, as Mark Twain did in 1897 after the Associated Press reported his death, it would complain of the "exaggeration."

These easily recognized subgenre categories, most derived from Cawelti, appear in the chronological listings; abbreviations used in the table are bracketed here:

Anti-Western

Border Culture/Minorities/Ethnic
  Conflict [Border]

Cavalry

Comedy and Parody

Cowboys and Cattle Kings

Eco-Western (themes of resource
  scarcity, conservation, equity)

Feminist

Gunmen

Historical (emphasis on historical
  accuracy and documents)

Marshal (sheriff)

Modern West

Musical

Native Americans

Outlaws

Pioneers and Settlers

Railroad Construction [Railroad]

Singing Cowboy

Individual films sometimes blend several subgenres.

Readers will also find initial reviews of the films in *Variety* and the *New York Times*. These important historical sources give one a sense of the initial reception of the films. Over the years, both publications issued retrospective volumes and indexes, which means that readers can find them in most research libraries. *Variety*'s reviews extend back to 1907 in the indexed paper volumes, which terminate in 1996. Page numbers for *Variety* are provided when they are available. The *Times* reviews are now available (also electronically) from the present back to 1913.

To conserve space in the tabular listings, the following abbreviations are employed for the film production and distribution companies:

20th Century-Fox Films   20CFox

Allied Artists Productions   AlliedA

Associated Features   AssocF

Argosy Pictures   Argosy

Avco Embassy   Avco

Columbia Pictures   Columbia

Edison Manufacturing Company   Edison

Famous Players-Laskey	FP-L
Metro-Goldwyn-Mayer	MGM
Monogram Pictures	MonoG
National General	NatGen
Paramount Pictures	PP
Republic Studios	Republic
RKO Radio Pictures	RKO
Sack Amusement Enterprises	Sack
Screen Guild	S. Guild
Turner Network Television	TNT
United Artists	UA
Universal International Pictures	UIP
Universal Pictures Studios	UP
Warner Bros. Pictures	WB

Year	Movie Title	Director	Studio	Format and Length
1903	*The Great Train Robbery*	Edwin S. Porter	Edison	black and white 1 reel
1906	*The Life of a Cowboy*	Edwin S. Porter	Edison	black and white 13 minutes
1914	*The Battle at Elderbush Gulch*	D. W. Griffith	Biograph	black and white 40 minutes
1917	*Bucking Broadway*	Jack (John) Ford	Universal	black and white 5 reels
1918	*Out West*	Roscoe "Fatty" Arbuckle	Comique Film Corp.	black and white 25 minutes
1923	*The Covered Wagon*	James Cruze	FP-L/PP	black and white 10 reels
1924	*The Iron Horse*	John Ford	Fox Film	black and white 12 reels
1925	*The Vanishing American*	George B. Seitz	FP-L	black and white 10 reels

In dealing with independent production companies, differing reference sources often give conflicting names. Many of the films were rereleased with alternate titles, but space does not permit their listing here. In dealing with such issues, this filmography—without any guarantee of correctness—most often relies on the American Film Institute's *Catalog of Feature Films, 1893–1970,* as the final authority. This source is available in many libraries as six printed volumes detailing more than forty-five thousand films. AFI has recently developed its contents for the Internet, available in university libraries and to the public at its Web site, http://www.afi.com.

This compilation required help. Special thanks for assistance go to several people: John Cawelti granted permission to use his list and to adapt his subgenre categories; he also made suggestions about additional categories. Chapter authors provided detailed information about their films. Ray Merlock and Jack Nachbar, with their vast knowledge based on viewing and collecting, helped with plot descriptions.

Subgenre	*NY Times*	*Variety*	Plot Summary
Outlaws	——	——	Crooks subdue station agent, rob train, flee, are pursued, caught, and killed—all in eleven minutes; the first American narrative film.
Cowboys	——	19 Jan. 1907	Quick sequence through mining camp, barroom, stagecoach ride, lariat twirling, and abduction and rescue of a girl.
Native American	——	——	Cavalry rescues settler community after conflict with Indians over the kidnapping of pets and consumption of dog meat.
Modern West	——	7 Dec. 1917: 47	Ranch foreman competes with stockbroker for ranch owner's daughter; she leaves for the city, discovers truth about stockbroker, and returns.
Comedy/ Parody	——	25 Jan. 1918	Sendup of conventions regarding frontier towns and melodramatic battles with bad men; Buster Keaton owns saloon and Fatty Arbuckle bartends.
Pioneers	17 Mar. 1923: 9	22 Mar. 1923: 28	Two wagon trains make their way to Oregon and California, encountering skulduggery and Indian attacks but finding romance.
Railroad	29 Aug. 1924: 6	3 Sept. 1924: 23	Post–Civil War railroad development layered with romance involving construction manager's daughter; theme of labor versus capital.
Native American	16 Oct. 1925: 18	21 Oct. 1925: 34	Based on Zane Grey novel and stories, film depicts interracial romance and Native American destitution; rare, early Native American protagonist.

1930	*The Big Trail*	Raoul Walsh	Fox Film	black and white 125 minutes
1931	**Cimarron** (chap. 1)	Wesley Ruggles	RKO	black and white 131 minutes
1931	**The Great Meadow** (chap. 1)	Charles Brabin	MGM	black and white 75 minutes
1936	**Romance Rides the Range** (chap. 2)	Harry Frasier	Spectrum	black and white 59 minutes
1936	*Three on the Trail*	Howard Bretherton	PP	black and white 67 minutes
1937	**Harlem on the Prairie** (chap. 2)	Sam Newfield	AssocF	black and white 54 minutes
1937	*Way Out West*	James W. Horne	Hal Roach/ Loew's	black and white 64 minutes
1938	*The Cowboy and the Lady*	H. C. Potter	Samuel Goldwyn/UA	black and white 90 minutes
1938	**The Terror of Tiny Town** (chap. 2)	Sam Newfield	Astor/Columbia	black and white 62 minutes
1939	**The Bronze Buckaroo** (chap. 2)	Richard Kahn	Hollywood Prods./Sack	black and white 57 minutes
1939	*Destry Rides Again*	George Marshall	Universal	black and white 94 minutes
1939	*Drums along the Mohawk*	John Ford	20CFox	color 130 minutes
1939	*Rovin' Tumbleweeds*	George Sherman	Republic	black and white 60 minutes
1939	*Stagecoach*	John Ford	Walter Wanger Prods.	black and white 130 minutes
1939	*Union Pacific*	Cecil B. DeMille	PP	black and white 133 minutes
1940	*Brigham Young, Frontiersman*	Henry Hathaway	20CFox	black and white 114 minutes
1940	*Buck Benny Rides Again*	Mark Sandrich	PP	black and white 82 minutes

Pioneers	25 Oct. 1930: 20	29 Oct. 1930: 17, 27	Wagon train scout (John Wayne) leads group on Oregon Trail in saga that includes romance, Indian fighting, and bad men with guns.
Pioneers/ Historical	27 Jan. 1931: 20	28 Jan. 1931: 14	Forty-year Oklahoma saga beginning with 1889 land rush on the Cherokee Strip; was the first Western film to receive an Academy Award.
Pioneers	15 Mar. 1931: 6	18 Mar. 1931: 14	Plucky settlers fight their way from Virginia to Kentucky in 1775; film displays hard physical labor, hunger, struggles with Native Americans.
Musical/ Cowboys & Cattle Kings	—	23 Dec. 1936: 62	Land fraud is set to right by opera singer/ranch owner (Fred Scott). This is the first of thirteen singing Westerns made by Scott.
Gunmen	5 May 1936: 26	—	Early Hopalong Cassidy film—one of sixty-six Cassidy films made by William Boyd; thwarts crooked small-town sheriff and gang.
Musical/ Cowboys & Cattle Kings	—	9 Feb. 1938: 14	All-black cast with singing cowboy (Herb Jeffries) helps heroine find lost gold. This film was aimed at "blacks only" theater outlets.
Comedy/ Parody	4 May 1937: 29	5 May 1937: 16	A Laurel and Hardy caper involving the delivery of gold mine certificate to daughter of a friend; the plot constantly turns on their gullibility.
Modern West	25 Nov. 1938: 19	9 Nov. 1938: 16	Romance between bored urban girl (Merle Oberon) from Florida and a Montana cowboy (Gary Cooper) whom she meets at a rodeo.
Comedy/ Parody; Musical	—	—	Western town populated by very small people (under four feet tall) is menaced by a villain, saved by hero (Billy Curtis).
Musical/ Cowboys & Cattle Kings	—	—	A rancher is held captive to pressure his sister into selling their land; singing Herb Jeffries with all-black cast.
Comedy/ Parody	30 Nov. 1939: 25	6 Dec. 1939: 14	Town with corrupt law enforcement is saved by figure who first tries moralistic maxims and then rallies everyone with his guns.
Native Americans	4 Nov. 1939: 11	8 Nov. 1939: 14	A pioneer family (Henry Fonda, Claudette Colbert) in revolutionary America steadily battle Indian attacks on their farm.
Singing Cowboy/ Eco-Western	—	10 Jan. 1940: 16	Singing cowboy story in which Gene Autry gets elected to Congress to save ranching valley from floods; fights bureaucracy in Washington.
Native Americans	3 Mar. 1939: 21	8 Feb. 1939: 17	Group of eight passengers on Overland Stage from Tonto to Lordsburgh face dangers and find redemption in new relationships.
Railroad	11 May 1939: 31	3 May 1939: 16	Central Pacific and Union Pacific race to reach Utah first amid sabotage based in politics, Indian attacks, and romance.
Pioneers	17 Sept. 1940	28 Aug. 1940	Historical recasting of Brigham Young's westward journey with Mormons to escape persecution; features bad weather and bugs.
Comedy/ Parody	25 Apr. 1940: 28	17 Apr. 1940: 13	Jack Benny, assisted by his radio crew, tries to convince ingenue that he is a real cowboy; the cast of Benny's radio show is included.

1940	*Geronimo*	Paul Sloane	PP	black and white 89 minutes
1940	**Go West** (chap. 10)	Edward Buzzell	MGM	black and white 79 minutes
1940	*Kit Carson*	George B. Seitz	Edward Small/ UA	black and white 97 minutes
1940	*My Little Chickadee*	Edward F. Cline	Universal	black and white 83 minutes
1940	*The Return of Frank James*	Fritz Lang	20CFox	color 92 minutes
1941	*They Died with Their Boots On*	Raoul Walsh	WB	black and white 140 minutes
1942	*Ride 'Em Cowboy*	Arthur Lubin	Universal	black and white 84 minutes
1943	*King of the Cowboys*	Joseph Kane	Republic	black and white 67 minutes
1943	*A Lady Takes a Chance*	William A. Seiter	RKO	black and white 85 minutes
1946	*Badman's Territory*	Tim Whelan	RKO	black and white 97 minutes
1946	*The Harvey Girls*	George Sidney	MGM	color 101 minutes
1947	*California*	John Farrow	PP	color 97 minutes
1947	*Duel in the Sun*	King Vidor	Vanguard/ Selznick	color 138 minutes
1948	**Fort Apache** (chap. 4)	John Ford	Argosy Pictures/ RKO	black and white 127 minutes
1948	*The Paleface*	Norman Z. McLeod	PP	color 91 minutes
1948	**Red River** (chap. 5)	Howard Hawks	Monterrey/UA	black and white 126 minutes
1948	*The Treasure of the Sierra Madre*	John Huston	WB	black and white 126 minutes
1949	*Bad Men of Tombstone*	Kurt Neumann	AlliedA/ MonoG	black and white 74 minutes
1949	*Canadian Pacific*	Edwin L. Marin	20CFox	color 94 minutes

Native Americans	8 Feb. 1940: 18	22 Nov. 1939: 14	Action melodrama depicting campaign to capture Indian chief Geronimo; complicated by father-son feud within the U.S. Army.
Comedy/ Parody	21 Feb. 1941: 16	18 Dec. 1940: 16	Marx Brothers help foil an evil saloon owner in a plot involving a gold mine deed, a railroad contract, and a pretty girl (Diana Lewis).
Pioneers	15 Nov. 1940: 25	28 Aug. 1940: 16	Kit Carson (Jon Hall) fights Indians and leads group to California in journey that includes Captain John Fremont (Dana Andrews).
Comedy/ Parody	16 Mar. 1940: 8	14 Feb. 1940: 18	A quip-filled variant of *Stagecoach* (1939) with W. C. Fields and Mae West as romantic antagonists in a pretend marriage.
Outlaws	18 Aug. 1940: 3	14 Aug. 1940: 14	Revenge tale about retribution of Frank (Henry Fonda) against Jesse's released killer, Bob Ford (John Carradine).
Cavalry	21 Nov. 1941: 23	19 Nov. 1949: 9	Historical romance with career of Custer (Errol Flynn) from West Point to Civil War and Little Big Horn.
Comedy/ Parody	5 Mar. 1942: 27	11 Feb. 1942: 8	Abbot and Costello, vendors at a New York rodeo show, are transported to dude ranch in West; comic stereotypes of Native Americans.
Modern West/ Gunmen	——	7 Apr. 1943: 8	Wartime singing cowboy picture for Roy Rogers, who uses circus company as cover to arrest saboteurs while singing seven songs.
Modern West	16 Sept. 1943: 25	18 Aug. 1943: 10	Eastern girl (Jean Arthur) escaping suitors falls for horse-smitten cowboy and rodeo performer (John Wayne) out West.
Outlaws/ Sheriff	31 May 1946: 27	17 Apr. 1946: 32	Bandits in southwestern locale make life difficult for the sheriff (Randolph Scott), who finally triumphs and gets a bride (Ann Richards).
Musical	25 Jan. 1946: 26	2 Jan. 1946: 8	Singing girls at Harvey House (railroad hotel chain) domesticate and romance the West; very apparent promotion of Harvey enterprise.
Pioneers/ Musical	15 Jan. 1947: 31	18 Dec. 1946: 14	Squabbles arise in disorderly 1846 California as it looks forward to statehood.
Cowboys & Cattle Kings	8 May 1947: 30	1 Jan. 1947: 14	An operatic tale of self-destructive eroticism set among cattle barons and Native Americans.
Cavalry/Native Americans	25 June 1948: A26	10 Mar. 1948: 10	Demoted general (Henry Fonda) sent to outpost where subordinate (John Wayne) fails to stop Custer-like attack against Apaches.
Comedy	16 Dec. 1948: 41	20 Oct. 1948: 11	Romantic comedy in which bumbling dentist Peter Potter (Bob Hope) pairs up with Calamity Jane (Jane Russell) to halt gun trading with Indians.
Cowboys & Cattle Kings	1 Oct. 1948: 31	14 July 1948: 12	Conflicts develop between stern cattle baron (John Wayne) and his son (Montgomery Clift), resulting in tense, threat-filled cattle drive.
Modern West	26 Jan. 1948: 88	7 Jan. 1948: 56	Character study of three men (Humphrey Bogart, Walter Huston, Tim Holt) and their greed for gold; set in the Mexican wilderness.
Outlaws	5 Mar. 1949: 10	9 Mar. 1949: 6	Bad guys during gold rush era steal, hide in the mountains, and get killed by the sheriff.
Railroad	20 May 1949: 32	9 Mar. 1949: 6	A tale of railroad expansion involving romances, opposition by Indians and others.

1949	*Colorado Territory*	Raoul Walsh	WB	black and white 94 minutes
1949	*The Dalton Gang*	Ford Beebe	Lippert./ S. Guild	black and white 58 minutes
1949	*I Shot Jesse James*	Sam Fuller	Lippert./ S. Guild	black and white 81 minutes
1949	*The Kissing Bandit*	Laslo Benedek	MGM	black and white 99 minutes
1949	**She Wore a Yellow Ribbon** (chap. 4)	John Ford	Argosy/RKO	color 103 minutes
1949	*The Younger Brothers*	Edwin L. Marin	WB	color 76 minutes
1950	*Annie Get Your Gun*	George Sidney	MGM	color 107 minutes
1950	**Broken Arrow** (chap. 6)	Delmer Daves	20CFox	color 93 minutes
1950	**The Devil's Doorway** (chap. 6)	Anthony Mann	MGM	black and white 84 minutes
1950	*The Gunfighter*	Henry King	20CFox	black and white 84 minutes
1950	**Rio Grande** (chap. 4)	John Ford	Argosy/RKO	black and white 105 minutes
1950	*Wagon Master*	John Ford	Argosy/RKO	black and white 86 minutes
1951	*Across the Wide Missouri*	William Wellman	MGM	color 78 minutes
1951	*Cavalry Scout*	Lesley Selander	MonoG	color 78 minutes
1951	*Jim Thorpe, All American*	Michael Curtiz	WB	black and white 107 minutes
1951	*Santa Fe*	Irving Pichel	Columbia	color 85 minutes
1951	*The Stooges Go West*	Edward Bernds	B. Glasser/UA	black and white 56 minutes
1952	*Bronco Buster*	Bud Boetticher	Universal	color 80 minutes
1952	*Bugles in the Afternoon*	Roy Rowland	Cagney Prods./ WB	color 84 minutes
1952	*Denver and Rio Grande*	Byron Haskin	PP	color 89 minutes

Native Americans	25 June 1949: II, 8	18 May 1949: 8	Complex interweaving of banditry and romance that ends in death for the principals; film emphasizes the artistry of the camera.
Outlaws	25 Nov. 1949: 27	30 Nov. 1949: 6	Tale of a gang in New Mexico that swindles a Navaho tribe and seeks to have blame for murder assigned to them.
Outlaws	2 Apr. 1949: 12	2 Feb. 1949: 12	A story of decline for Bob Ford after his killing of Jesse James for reward money; he becomes a stage re-enactor of the murder.
Musical	19 Nov. 1948: 35	17 Nov. 1948: 13	Set in 1830 when California was still controlled by Spain, this is a tale of comic banditry and romance punctuated by songs.
Cavalry/Native Americans	18 Nov. 1949: 35	27 July 1949: 12	Soon-to-retire cavalry officer averts impending war with Arapahos and Cheyennes; setting is 1876, when tensions are high because of Custer's defeat at Little Big Horn.
Outlaws	28 May 1949: 11	4 May 1949: 11	Sympathetic depiction of Younger brothers' attempts to obtain pardons for their James gang crimes so they can farm again.
Musical	18 May 1950: 37	12 Apr. 1950: 8	Rodgers and Hammerstein tale of Annie Oakley (Betty Hutton) and her rise from rural shooting to fame with Buffalo Bill's Wild West.
Native Americans	21 July 1950. 76	14 June 1950: 8	Tom Jeffords (Jimmy Stewart) coordinates peace talks between the Apache and the U.S. government.
Native Americans	10 Nov. 1950: P35	17 May 1950: 6	Shoshone Civil War veteran Lance Poole (Robert Taylor) fights to keep his ancestral lands; early depiction of civil rights issues.
Gunfighter	24 June 1950: 7	26 Apr. 1950: 8	Gunfighter (Gregory Peck), worn out with way of life, attempts to return to wife and child in the East so that he can lead a normal existence.
Cavalry	20 Nov. 1950: 21	8 Nov. 1950: 6	Cavalry officer (John Wayne) leads pursuit of Apaches across Rio Grande while managing family tensions with wife (Maureen O'Hara).
Pioneers	19 June 1950: 17	12 Apr. 1950: 22	Mormon wagon train joins up with medicine show people and Native Americans as they face threats from thieves.
Native Americans	7 Nov. 1951: 35	19 Sept. 1951: 6	Trapper (Clark Gable) makes opportunistic marriage to Indian woman, a chief's daughter, to gain access to hunting grounds.
Cavalry	8 June 1951: 32	18 Apr. 1951: 24	Civilian scout (Rod Cameron) tracks the theft of Gatling guns from army post and their transmission to Indian fighters.
Modern West/Native Americans	25 Aug. 1951: 7	20 June 1951: 6	Biopic of Jim Thorpe (Burt Lancaster), the notable Indian athlete cultivated by Pop Warner; focuses on assimilation outside the reservation.
Railroad	4 May 1951: 7	25 Apr. 1951: 14	Four brothers in post–Civil War period go west, one going to the railroad while others become outlaws who rob trains.
Comedy/Parody	____	18 June 1951: 6	Stooges, playing traveling peddlers, get recruited as security helpers attempting to prevent gold theft in very quickly shot film.
Modern West	____	16 Apr. 1952: 6	Older rodeo rider takes apprentice and ends up competing with him.
Cavalry	5 Mar. 1952: 32	6 Feb. 1952: 6	A story of feuding between cavalrymen for the affection of a woman; includes Custer's fatal battle with the Sioux.
Railroad	17 May 1952: 22	26 Mar. 1952: 16	Story of competition between rail companies, fights among treacherous, hotheaded men, and romance.

1952	*High Noon* (chap. 8)	Fred Zinnemann	UA	black and white 84 minutes
1952	*The Legend of the Lone Ranger* (chap. 3)	George B. Seitz	Jack Chertok	black and white 74 minutes
1952	*The Lusty Men*	Nicholas Ray	RKO/Radio	black and white 113 minutes
1952	*Rancho Notorious*	Fritz Lang	Fidelity Pictures/ RKO	color 89 minutes
1952	*Return of the Texan*	Delmer Daves	20CFox	black and white 88 minutes
1952	*Rodeo*	William Beaudine	MonoG	color 70 minutes
1952	*The Savage*	George Marshall	PP	color 95 minutes
1952	*Son of Paleface*	Frank Tashlin	PP	color 95 minutes
1953	*Calamity Jane*	David Butler	WB	color 100 minutes
1953	*Escape from Fort Bravo*	John Sturges	MGM	color 98 minutes
1953	*Hondo*	John Farrow	Wayne-Fellows/ WB	color 93 minutes
1953	*Kansas Pacific*	Ray Nazarro	AlliedA	color 73 minutes
1953	*Shane*	George Stevens	PP	color 118 minutes
1954	*Apache*	Robert Aldrich	Hecht-Lan-caster/UA	color 91 minutes
1954	*Red Garters*	George Marshall	PP	color 91 minutes
1954	*Seven Brides for Seven Brothers*	Stanley Donen	MGM	color 102 minutes
1954	*Sitting Bull*	Sidney Salkow	W.R. Frank/UA	color 105 minutes
1954	*Taza, Son of Cochise*	Douglas Sirk	UIP	color 79 minutes

Marshal	25 July 1952: 14	30 Apr. 1952: 6	Kane (Gary Cooper) pleads with Hadleyville to confront vicious gang, but only his Quaker fiancée (Grace Kelly) helps.
Gunmen/ Native Americans	2 Oct. 1949: X9	——	Television compilation with first three episodes from 1949: "Enter the Lone Ranger" (genesis), "The Lone Ranger Fights On," and "The Lone Ranger Triumphs."
Modern West	25 Oct. 1952: 12	1 Oct. 1952: 6	Poetic exploration of the itinerant world of rodeo performers with their strained domestic relationships, physical injuries, and death.
Outlaws	5 May 1952: 39	6 Feb. 1952: 6	Cowhand whose girlfriend is raped and murdered tracks the killer to a haven for outlaws managed by a woman (Marlene Dietrich).
Modern West	13 Feb. 1952: 35	13 Feb. 1952: 6	Widower returns to Texas with his young sons and becomes involved in disputes with neighboring rancher as well as romance.
Modern West	——	5 Mar. 1952: 6	A drifting rodeo group fails to pay its feed debts and is taken over by a woman with business smarts and a reluctant love for one of the performers.
Native Americans	2 Jan. 1953: 11	14 Jan. 1953: 6	White man raised as Sioux (Charlton Heston) is compelled to clarify his loyalties in wars among the Indians and with the U.S. Army.
Comedy/ Parody	2 Oct. 1952: 32	16 July 1952: 6	Bumbler (Bob Hope) goes west in search of fortune; his failure leads him to seek buxom but crooked wife (Jane Russell).
Musical	5 Nov. 1953: 40	21 Oct. 1953: 6	Historical rendition of cross-dressing sharpshooter is a comic vehicle for the wholesome charm of Doris Day.
Cavalry	23 Jan. 1954: 11	11 Nov. 1953	Imprisoned Confederate soldiers who escape during Civil War are recaptured by U.S. Cavalry, then face Indian attack together.
Native Americans	27 Nov. 1953: 99	25 Nov. 1953: 6	Louis L'Amour story with John Wayne as gunfighter Hondo Lane, who takes up with ranch woman and protects her in war with Indians.
Railroad	——	25 Mar. 1953: 24	Portrayal of railroad extension prior to the Civil War that highlights affirmative Northern interests and obstructive Southern efforts.
Gunmen	24 Apr. 1953: 30	15 Apr. 1953: 6	Buckskinned loner (Alan Ladd) trying to escape past as gunman must shoot again to save homesteaders from hired killer of cattle baron.
Native Americans	10 July 1954: 7	30 June 1954: 6	Sympathetic portrait of a Native American, Massai (Burt Lancaster), who fights relentlessly against the white man.
Comedy/ Parody	27 Mar. 1954: 13	3 Feb. 1954: 6	Complicated musical parody featuring Calaveras Kate (Rosemary Clooney) in a plot with strangers, murder, revenge, and romance.
Musical	23 July 1954: 8	2 June 1954: 6	Oregon brothers seek wives through scheme involving kidnapping, which is complicated by a snowstorm; caper is inspired by Plutarch's account of the rape of the Sabine women.
Native Americans	26 Nov. 1954: 24	15 Sept. 1954: 6	Historical fantasy about peacemaking between whites and Indians frustrated by Custer's recklessness in confronting the Sioux.
Native Americans	——	20 Jan. 1954: 6	Historical fantasy about Taza (Rock Hudson), a good, peaceful son, who struggles with a brother and with Geronimo over the issue of war with the U.S. Cavalry.

1955	*Chief Crazy Horse*	George Sherman	UIP	color 86 minutes
1955	*Indian Fighter*	Andre de Toth	Bryna Prods./ UA	color 88 minutes
1955	*The Last Frontier*	Anthony Mann	Columbia	color 97 minutes
1955	*Man from Laramie*	Anthony Mann	William Goetz/ CP	color 102 minutes
1955	*Man without a Star*	King Vidor	UIP	color 89 minutes
1955	*Oklahoma!*	Fred Zinnemann	RKO	color 145 minutes
1955	*The Second Greatest Sex*	George Marshall	UIP	color 87 minutes
1955	*Wichita*	Jacques Tourneur	AlliedA	color 80 minutes
1956	*Fastest Gun Alive*	Russell Rouse	MGM	black and white 89 minutes
1956	**Giant** (chap. 7)	George Stevens	WB	color 197 minutes
1956	*Jubal*	Delmer Daves	Columbia	color 101 minutes
1956	*The Last Wagon*	Delmer Daves	20CFox	color 99 minutes
1956	*Pardners*	Norman Taurog	PP	color 90 minutes
1956	*Pillars of the Sky*	George Marshall	UIP	color 91 minutes
1956	*The Searchers*	John Ford	C.V. Whitney/ WB	color 117 minutes
1956	*Tribute to a Bad Man*	Robert Wise	MGM	color 95 minutes
1957	*3:10 to Yuma*	Delmer Daves	Columbia	black and white 92 minutes
1957	*Pawnee*	George Waggner	Republic	color 79 minutes
1957	*Run of the Arrow*	Samuel Fuller	Universal	color 86 minutes
1957	**The Tin Star** (chap. 8)	Anthony Mann	Perlsea/PP	black and white 92 minutes

Native Americans	28 Apr. 1955: 25	23 Feb. 1955: 8	Efforts of Chief Crazy Horse (Victor Mature) to preserve Lakota Sioux land against the treachery of broken treaties and the attacks of the U.S. Cavalry.
Cavalry	22 Dec. 1955: 20	21 Dec. 1955: 6	Confederate frontier scout (Kirk Douglas) returns to Sioux territory and becomes involved in struggle to protect their gold.
Cavalry	8 Dec. 1955: 45	14 Dec. 1955: 6	Trapper (Victor Mature) who wants to wear uniform saves fort and prevents massacre but has troubled with rules of civilization.
Cowboys & Cattle Kings	1 Sept. 1955: 20	29 June 1955: 6	Revenge tale with man (James Stewart) seeking those who sold guns to Indians that were used to kill his brother.
Cowboys & Cattle Kings	25 Mar. 1955: 19	2 Mar. 1955: 8	Dempsey (Kirk Douglas) is a loner who comes to a situation of struggle between large and small ranchers and helps resolve it.
Musical	11 Oct. 1955: 49	12 Oct. 1955: 6	Rodgers and Hammerstein stage musical depicts cowboy–farm girl romance darkened by interference of jealous farm hand.
Musical	11 Feb. 1956: 12	5 Oct. 1955: 6	Remake of *Lysistrata* in which frontier women protest obstinate men's fighting over court records; they lock themselves away from sex until feud is over.
Sheriff	——	29 June 1955: 6	Wyatt Earp (Joel McCrea) is hired to quell lawlessness and takes guns away from citizens in 1870s Wichita.
Gunmen	20 June 1956: 6	13 July 1956: 23	Storekeeper (Glenn Ford) strives to avoid his father's mantle as gunfighter despite provocations.
Modern West	11 Oct. 1956: 51	10 Oct. 1956: 6	Saga of three-generation Texas family confronting twentieth-century transitions and interracial culture; notable stars include James Dean, Elizabeth Taylor, and Rock Hudson.
Cowboys & Cattle Kings	25 Apr. 1956: 39	4 Apr. 1956	A ranch *Othello* tale with Iago figure (Rod Steiger) turning rancher (Ernest Borgnine) against wife and hand (Glenn Ford).
Pioneers/ Native Americans	22 Sept. 1956: 14	29 Aug. 1956: 6	Todd (Richard Widmark) is a murderer who redeems himself by fighting Apache.
Comedy/ Parody	26 July 1956: 20	27 June 1956	Dean Martin and Jerry Lewis spoof of the western ranch that must fight villains.
Native Americans	13 Oct. 1956: 13, 15	8 Aug. 1956	Cavalry officer (Jeff Chandler) romancing woman (Dorothy Malone) while fighting Indians.
Native Americans	31 May 1956: 21	14 Mar. 1956: 6	Ethan (John Wayne) and Martin (Jeffrey Hunter) spend five years searching for their sister (Natalie Wood), who is fully assimilated in Comanche tribe.
Outlaws	31 Mar. 1956: 13	21 Mar. 1956	Ruthless land baron (James Cagney) deals with rustlers and woman he loves (Irene Pappas).
Outlaws	29 Aug. 1957: 22	14 Aug. 1957: 6	Farmer suffering from drought resorts to arresting and holding a robber to earn money; echoes of *High Noon*.
Native Americans	——	7 July 1957	Story of white man raised as Indian who finds himself in situation where he must fight former tribe members.
Native Americans	3 Aug. 1957: 8	29 May 1957	In post–Civil War setting, vengeful Confederate joins Sioux to continue fight against United States.
Sheriff	24 Oct. 1957: 37	16 Oct. 1957	Marshal turned bounty hunter (Henry Fonda) helps inexperienced sheriff (Anthony Perkins) in confronting gunfighter.

1957	*The True Story of Jesse James*	Nicholas Ray	20CFox	color 92 minutes
1958	*Buchanan Rides Alone*	Bud Boetticher	Columbia	color 89 minutes
1958	*The Gunman's Walk*	Phil Karlson	Columbia	color 95 minutes
1958	*The Last of the Fast Guns*	George Sherman	Universal	color 82 minutes
1958	*The Left-Handed Gun*	Arthur Penn	Fred Coe/WB	black and white 87 minutes
1958	*Saddle the Wind*	Robert Parrish	MGM	color 84 minutes
1958	*The Sheepman*	George Marshall	Edmund Grainger/ MGM	color 86 minutes
1958	*These Thousand Hills*	Richard Fleischer	20CFox	color 96 minutes
1959	*Alias Jesse James*	Norman Z. McLeod	Hope Enterprise/ MGM	color 92 minutes
1959	*Rio Bravo*	Howard Hawks	WB	color 141 minutes
1959	**Warlock** (chap. 8)	Edward Dmytryk	20CFox	color 122 minutes
1960	*Sergeant Rutledge*	John Ford	WB	color 111 minutes
1960	*The Unforgiven*	John Huston	James Prods/ MGM	color 125 minutes
1961	*The Misfits*	John Huston	7 Arts Prods./ UA	black and white 124 minutes
1961	*A Thunder of Drums*	Joseph Newman	Robert Enders/ MGM	color 97 minutes
1961	*Two Rode Together*	John Ford	John Ford Prods./Columbia	color 108 minutes
1962	*Geronimo*	Arnold Laven	Bedford/MGM-UA	color 101 minutes
1962	*Ride the High Country*	Sam Peckinpah	Richard E. Lyons/MGM	color 94 minutes
1963	*How the West Was Won*	Ford, Hathaway, and Marshall	MGM	color 165 minutes

Outlaws	23 Mar. 1957: 17	20 Feb. 1957	Jesse rendered a misunderstood youth in a kind of prequel to 1939 *Jesse James*; film includes episodes with Quantrill's Raiders.
Gunmen/ Border Culture	—	6 Aug. 1958: 7	Buchanan (Randolph Scott) lands in jail for defending an accused murderer and ends up cleverly purging the town.
Gunmen	—	18 June 1958: 6	Aging ex-gunman (Van Heflin) with two sons fights with son who wants to follow his path.
Gunmen	—	25 June 1958	Gunman is hired to find a man's missing brother, making discoveries about the future of his profession in the search.
Outlaws	8 May 1958: 36	30 Apr. 1958	Billy the Kid (Paul Newman) portrayed as sensitive, misunderstood teenage rebel; based on teleplay by Gore Vidal.
Gunmen	—	5 Mar. 1958	Ex-gunfighter (Robert Taylor), leading peaceful existence, spirals into violence when troublesome younger brother shows up.
Cattle Kings	8 May 1958: 36	23 Apr. 1958	Spoof involving cattle king (Leslie Nielsen) versus sheep rancher (Glenn Ford) that involves rivalry for a woman (Shirley MacLaine).
Cowboys & Cattle Kings	7 May 1959: 36	28 Jan. 1959	Ambitious cowboy (Don Murray) uses two women to climb ladder of success.
Comedy/ Parody	18 May 1959: 31	18 Mar. 1959	Extended gags from character (Bob Hope) who has sold a life insurance policy—failing to grasp the risks.
Sheriff	19 Mar. 1959: 40	18 Feb. 1959: 6	Sheriff (John Wayne) struggles to hold prisoner in jail while dealing with complex relationships; cast includes Dean Martin and Ricky Nelson.
Marshal	1 May 1959: 4	1 Apr. 1959	Town of Warlock hires gunman Blaisedell (Henry Fonda) to confront a gang, then supports deputy (Richard Widmark) in driving away Blaisedell.
Cavalry	26 May 1960: 37	13 Apr. 1960	Rutledge (Woody Strode), who was a black soldier in the Union army, is charged and tried for the rape and murder of a white woman.
Native Americans	7 Apr. 1960: 46	30 Mar. 1960	Frontier whites confront Kiowas in Texas Panhandle; Rachel (Audrey Hepburn), wife of Ben (Burt Lancaster), discovers that she is Native American herself, complicating the wars.
Modern West	2 Feb. 1961: 24	1 Feb. 1961: 6	Drifting cowboys (Clark Gable, Montgomery Clift) in scheme to round up wild mustangs ("misfits") to sell for dog food, are dissuaded by the horrified woman (Marilyn Monroe) they all love.
Cavalry	14 Sept. 1961: 35	30 Aug. 1961	Soldiers at outpost in Arizona compete for love and make war against Apaches; dismal picture of life on the frontier.
Pioneers	—	21 June 1961	Two white men (James Stewart, Richard Widmark) search for settlers captured by Indians ten years earlier.
Native Americans	—	25 Apr. 1962	Geronimo (Chuck Connors) and Apaches surrender to United States, are tricked, and fight again for their survival.
Marshal	21 June 1962: 26	9 May 1962: 7	Retired lawmen (Joel McCrea, Randoph Scott) accept gold delivery assignment and disagree about whether to steal it.
Pioneers	1 Apr. 1963: 54	7 Nov. 1962: 6	Saga of two nineteenth-century families who make perilous journey to the West in search of opportunity and adventure; film distinguished by large number of directors, cast, and shooting sites.

1963	*Hud*	Martin Ritt	Salem Prods.	black and white 112 minutes
1964	*Cheyenne Autumn*	John Ford	Ford-Bernard Smith	color 159 minutes
1964	*A Distant Trumpet*	Raoul Walsh	WB	color 117 minutes
1964	*Invitation to a Gunfighter*	Richard Wilson	UA	black and white 91 minutes
1965	**Cat Ballou** (chap. 10)	Elliot Silverstein	Columbia	color 96 minutes
1965	*Major Dundee*	Sam Peckinpah	Jerry Bresler/ Columbia	color 120 minutes
1965	*The Rounders*	Burt Kennedy	MGM	color 85 minutes
1966	*Carry On, Cowboy*	Gerald Thomas	Anglo Amal- gamated	color 94 minutes
1966	**The Professionals** (chap. 9)	Richard Brooks	Columbia	color 116 minutes
1967	*El Dorado*	Howard Hawks	Laurel Prods./ PP	color 126 minutes
1967	*Hombre*	Martin Ritt	20CFox	color 111 minutes
1968	**Firecreek** (chap. 8)	Vincent McEveety	WB	color 104 minutes
1968	*The Stalking Moon*	Robert Mulligan	Pakula Prods./ NatGen	color 109 minutes
1969	*Butch Cassidy and the Sundance Kid*	George Roy Hill	20CFox	color 110 minutes
1969	*Paint Your Wagon*	Joshua Logan	Alan Jay Lerner Prods./PP	color 166 minutes
1969	*Support Your Local Sheriff*	Bud Yorkin	UA	color 96 minutes
1969	*True Grit*	Henry Hathaway	PP	color 128 minutes

Modern West	29 May 1963: 36	8 May 1963	Hud (Paul Newman) has declined from his father's standard of honor and moves toward fraud and rape.
Native Americans	24 Dec. 1964: 8	7 Oct. 1964: 6	Using the Cheyenne march from Oklahoma to Yellowstone in 1877, film explores racism, genocide, and "civilization" of Native Americans.
Cavalry	28 May 1964: 40	27 May 1964	U.S. Cavalry officer comes to Arizona to fight, and then negotiate with, hostile Chief War Eagle, saving his reservation land.
Gunmen	——	21 Oct. 1964	Pathological killer (Yul Brynner) is hired to kill Confederate veteran who returns home to find his wife and property taken by Unionists.
Comedy/ Parody/ Feminist	25 June 1965: 36	12 May 1965: 6	Catherine Ballou (Jane Fonda) turns outlaw to stop the railroad from taking her ranch.
Cavalry	8 Apr. 1965: 45	17 Mar. 1965: 7	Set in Civil War, film reflects on that war's violence and on the conflict with Apache Indians over captives; Charlton Heston in title role.
Modern West	29 Apr. 1965: 40	13 Jan. 1965	Two horse wranglers get bored with life and attempt to change it.
Comedy/ Parody	——	6 Apr. 1966	British-made slapstick Western that applies the Carry On series treatment by spoofing cowboys, sheriffs, gunmen, etc.
Modern West/ Feminist	3 Nov. 1966: 45	2 Nov. 1966: 6	Caper film with professional team (Burt Lancaster, Lee Marvin, Robert Ryan, Woody Strode) tricked into kidnapping a reluctant female captive (Claudia Cardinale) from her lover (Jack Palance).
Cowboys & Cattle Kings	29 July 1967: 32	14 June 1967	Thornton (John Wayne) helps alcoholic sheriff Harrah (Robert Mitchum) stop range war.
Native Americans	22 Mar. 1967: II, 41	15 Mar. 1967: 6	Alienated hero John Russell (Paul Newman) takes a stagecoach journey that reveals the corruption of the passengers, undercutting myth of the Old West full of ordinary, decent people.
Marshal	22 Feb. 1968: 36	24 Jan. 1968: 6	Town of Firecreek fails to defend itself against gang of Larkin (Henry Fonda), which is ultimately defeated by farmer and part-time sheriff (James Stewart).
Native Americans	23 Jan. 1969: 57	18 Dec. 1968: 26	Indian agent (Gregory Peck) takes in escaped captives from Indians and then confronts the former husband of the woman (Eva Marie Saint).
Outlaws	25 Sept. 1969: 54	10 Sept. 1969: 36	Outdated outlaws Cassidy (Paul Newman) and Sundance Kid (Robert Redford) outrun luck in United States; notable musical score by Burt Bacharach.
Musical	16 Oct. 1969: 56	15 Oct. 1969: 15	Lerner and Loewe musical about mining town in gold rush with starring roles for Clint Eastwood, Lee Marvin, and Jean Seeberg.
Comedy/ Parody	9 Apr. 1969: 55	26 Feb. 1969: 6	Comic sendup of several conventions of the classic Western— mysterious stranger, helpless community, brave woman.
Comedy/ Parody	4 July 1969: 9	21 May 1969: 6	Comic tale with aging Rooster Cogburn (John Wayne) becoming mentor to unshaped Mattie (Kim Darby), whose father's death is avenged.

1969	*The Wild Bunch*	Sam Peckinpah	Minor-Seven Arts	color 148 minutes
1970	*Little Big Man*	Arthur Penn	Hiller-Stockbridge/ NatGen	color 150 minutes
1970	*A Man Called Horse*	Elliot Silverstein	NatGen	color 115 minutes
1970	*Soldier Blue*	Ralph Nelson	Katzka-Loeb/ Avco	color 112 minutes
1972	*Ulzana's Raid*	Robert Aldrich	Carter De Haven/Universal	color 103 minutes
1973	*Jeremiah Johnson*	Sydney Pollack	WB	color 108 minutes
1973	*Pat Garrett and Billy the Kid*	Sam Peckinpah	G. Carroll-Peckinpah/MGM	color 106 minutes
1974	**Blazing Saddles** (chap. 10)	Mel Brooks	Michael Hertzberg/WB	color 93 minutes
1976	*The Outlaw Josey Wales*	Clint Eastwood	Robert Daley/ WB	color 135 minutes
1979	*The Electric Horseman*	Sydney Pollack	Stark-Wildwood/ Columbia	color 120 minutes
1980	*Bronco Billy*	Clint Eastwood	Hackin & Dobrofsky/WB	color 119 minutes
1980	*Urban Cowboy*	James Bridges	PP	color 135 minutes
1985	**Rustlers' Rhapsody** (chap. 10)	Hugh Wilson	PP	black and white/ color 88 minutes
1987	**Walker** (chap. 11)	Alex Cox	UP	color 94 minutes
1988	*Die Hard*	John McTiernan	20CFox	color 127 minutes
1990	**Dances with Wolves** (chap. 11)	Kevin Costner	Tig Prods./ Orion	color 181 minutes
1991	*Son of the Morning Star*	Mike Robe	Republic Television	color 187 minutes
1992	*The Last of the Mohicans*	Michael Mann	Morgan Creek/ 20CFox	color 110 minutes

Outlaws	26 June 1969: 45	18 June 1969: 6	Actions of a gang and their pursuers establish end of the Old West and its myth of heroic violence that saves suffering communities.
Native Americans/ Anti-Western	15 Dec. 1970: 53	16 Dec. 1970: 17	Tall tales from Jack Crabb (Dustin Hoffman), 121-year-old survivor of Little Big Horn; allegorical treatment of American imperialism and the Vietnam War.
Native Americans	30 Apr. 1970: 46	29 Apr. 1970: 18	White John Morgan (Richard Harris), raised in captivity as an Indian, becomes a leader among them.
Native Americans	13 Aug. 1970: 29	12 Aug. 1970: 15	White man and woman survive Indian attack and struggle to get to army post; incident leads to Sand Creek Massacre (1864); echoes of the 1968 My Lai massacre in Vietnam.
Native Americans	16 Nov. 1972: 58	18 Oct. 1972: 18	Anglo and Native American scouting party search for attackers terrorizing settlers; Burt Lancaster is crusty scout in one of the last Indian wars.
Native Americans	22 Dec. 1972: 23	10 May 1972: 21	Mountain man (Robert Redford) retreats from civilization, struggles with and becomes Native American.
Outlaws	24 May 1973: 53	30 May 1973: 13	Diverging friendship between Sheriff Garrett (James Coburn) and Billy the Kid (Kris Kristofferson).
Comedy/ Parody	8 Feb. 1974: 21	13 Feb. 1974: 18	A black sheriff saves a town he was sent to ruin; the slapstick comedy is relentless—alternately scatological, racial, ethnic, and physical.
Outlaws	5 Aug. 1976: 26	30 June 1976: 20	Violent everyman revenge tale in Civil War setting leavened by existential quest and romance.
Modern West/ Comedy	21 Dec. 1979: C10	5 Dec. 1979: 22	Retired rodeo star (Robert Redford) discovers horse abuse associated with a breakfast cereal promotion and faces TV journalist (Jane Fonda).
Modern West	11 June 1980: C24	11 June 1980: 20	The versatile Bronco Billy (Clint Eastwood) owns a Wild West show and needs a female target (Sondra Locke) for his knife-throwing act.
Modern West	11 June 1980: 21	4 June 1980: 20	Oil field laborer (John Travolta) plays out cowboy fantasy at nightclub; struggles with wife (Debra Winger) over gender roles.
Comedy/ Parody	5 May 1985: C29	15 May 1985: 30	Singing cowboy spoof that pits hero (Tom Berenger) against the other good guy; also offers sendup of the spaghetti Western.
Anti-Western/ Historical	4 Dec. 1987: C36	2 Dec. 1987: 6	Loose biopic of Willam Walker, nineteenth-century American who was briefly president of Nicaragua after helping overthrow its government; film wavers between historical purpose and comedy.
Modern West	31 June 1988: B19	13 July 1988: 12	East Coast cop visits Los Angeles, thwarts hostage taking when local authorities fail to respond; reverses some East-West stereotypes.
Native Americans/ Eco-Western	9 Nov. 1990: B1	5 Nov. 1990: 2	Former Civil War officer (Kevin Costner) becomes member of Lakota Sioux tribe in South Dakota.
Native Americans	27 Jan. 1991: H29	28 Aug. 1991: 73	Miniseries on Custer and the path leading to his final battle; develops both Custer and Crazy Horse with sympathy.
Native Americans	29 Sept. 1992: B2	31 Aug. 1992: 60	Adaptation of Cooper novel featuring romance between Hawkeye (Daniel Day-Lewis) and Cora (Madeline Stowe).

1992	*Unforgiven*	Clint Eastwood	Malposo/WB	color 131 minutes
1993	*Geronimo, an American Legend*	Walter Hill	Cinergi/ Hollywood	color 115 minutes
1993	**Tombstone** (chap. 11)	George Cosmatos	Cinergi/ Hollywood	color 130 minutes
1994	*Wyatt Earp*	Lawrence Kasdan	WB	color 191 minutes
1995	**The Good Old Boys** (chap. 13)	Tommy Lee Jones	TNT	color 130 minutes
1996	**Lone Star** (chap. 12)	John Sayles	Rio Dulce & Castle Rock/ Sony	color 135 minutes
1997	**Last Stand at Saber River** (chap. 13)	Dick Lowry	TNT	color 100 minutes
1999	**You Know My Name** (chap. 13)	John Kent Harrison	TNT	color 94 minutes
2000	**Shanghai Noon** (chap. 10)	Tom Dey	Chan/Buena Vista	color 110 minutes
2000	**The Virginian** (chap. 13)	Bill Pullman	TNT	color 95 minutes
2001	**Crossfire Trail** (chap. 13)	Simon Wincer	TNT	color 90 minutes
2003	**Monte Walsh** (chap. 13)	Simon Wincer	TNT	color 95 minutes

Outlaws	7 Aug. 1992: B1	31 July 1992: 2	Reformed, domesticated gunman Will Munny (Clint Eastwood) is summoned to purge a corrupted, tyrannized town.
Native Americans/ Cavalry	10 Dec. 1993: 36	13 Dec. 1993: 36-37	Geronimo (Wes Studi) as warrior who fights against Americans and Mexicans; revisionist perspective grants respect to him.
Marshal/ Gunmen	24 June 1993: B2	3 Jan. 1994: 53	Version of Wyatt Earp story in which he unsuccessfully attempts quiet retirement.
Sheriff	18 Nov. 1994: B9	20 June 1994: 41	Leisurely life story approach to life of Earp (Kevin Costner), showing his life as a child and as aspiring lawyer.
Cowboys/ Modern West	3 Mar. 1995: B5	27 Feb. 1995: 55	Aging cowboy (Tommy Lee Jones) struggles with conflict between free lifestyle and preservation of family.
Modern West/ Border Culture	21 June 1996: C1	18 Mar. 1996: 46	Sheriff investigates murder in multiethnic border town, revealing personal and social history; considerable attention to the way diverse groups live together at present.
Pioneers & Settlers	18 Jan. 1997: 16	13 Jan. 1997: 98	Bitter ex-Confederate soldier (Tom Selleck) returns to find Union sympathizers on his homestead.
Marshal	——	1 Feb. 1999: 56	Legendary lawman Bill Tilghman comes out of retirement to battle outlaws and a corrupt federal agent in rowdy 1920s Oklahoma town.
Comedy/ Parody	6 Oct. 2000: E30	29 May 2000: 75	East meets West when imperial Chinese guard (Jackie Chan) rescues princess (Lucy Liu) in the Old West.
Cowboys & Cattle Kings	——	——	Cowboy betrayed by best friend must choose between protecting the ranch and the territorial code of justice and the pretty schoolmarm he loves.
Cowboys & Cattle Kings	24 Jan. 2001: E8	——	In this Louis L'Amour story, a cowboy drifter, to keep promise to a dying friend for the protection of his family and ranch, stands up to enemies.
Cowboys/ Modern West	17 Jan. 2003: B36	17 Jan. 2003: 12	Cowboy in 1890s Wyoming Territory must choose between traditional work and steady job as trick rider-roper in Wild West show.

○ *Jack Nachbar and Ray Merlock*

BIBLIOGRAPHY: TRAIL DUST
Books about Western Movies: Selected Classics and Works since 1980

Well, Pards, Western movies of late have been desperately looking for a decent watering hole. The stock needs fresh water. Research about these movies, on the other hand, continues to drink from clear springs and fatten up on fresh grass. There have been more books published about Westerns during the last quarter century than during the first seventy-five years when the Western was America's favorite media entertainment.

Special thanks to Camille McCutcheon, reference librarian at the University of South Carolina Upstate, for her help with this project.

BOOKS PUBLISHED BEFORE 1980

The following is a highly selected list of important books published during the first three-quarters of a century of Westerns. Readers needing a more complete listing should consult the two bibliographical volumes by Jack Nachbar.

Adams, Les, and Buck Rainey. *Shoot-Em-Ups*. New Rochelle, N.Y.: Arlington House, 1978. Credits of thirty-three hundred Westerns.

Anobile, Richard, ed. *John Ford's* Stagecoach *Starring John Wayne*. New York: Avon, 1975. A shot-by-shot, pictorial re-creation of the film.

Autry, Gene, and Mickey Herskowitz. *Back in the Saddle Again*. New York: Doubleday, 1978. Autry's autobiography.

Balshofer, Fred J., and Arthur C. Miller. *One Reel a Week*. Berkeley: University of California Press, 1967. Memoirs of two early filmmakers who made Westerns.

Barbour, Alan. *The Thrill of It All*. New York: Collier Books, 1971. Pictorial evocation of B Westerns.

Actors John Wayne and Coleen Gray in *Red River*.

Basinger, Jeanine. *Anthony Mann.* Boston: Twayne, 1979. A basic study of Mann's films.

Baxter, John. *The Cinema of John Ford.* New York: Barnes, 1971.

Bogdanovich, Peter. *Allan Dwan: The Last Pioneer.* New York: Praeger, 1971.

———. *John Ford.* Berkeley: University of California Press, 1968. Includes one of the best Ford interviews.

Brauer, Ralph, and Donna Brauer. *The Horse, the Gun, the Piece of Property: The Television Western.* Bowling Green, Ohio: Bowling Green Popular Press, 1975. A cultural analysis of the evolving structure of TV Westerns.

Brownlow, Kevin. *The War, the West and the Wilderness.* New York: Knopf, 1979. Details a number of silent Westerns rarely discussed elsewhere.

Butler, Terence. *Crucified Heroes: The Films of Sam Peckinpah.* London: Gordon Fraser, 1979.

Canham, Kingsley. *The Hollywood Professionals: Michael Curtiz, Raoul Walsh, Henry Hathaway.* New York: Barnes, 1973. Profiles the films of three directors well known for their Westerns.

Cary, Diana Serra. *The Hollywood Posse.* Boston: Houghton Mifflin, 1975. Anecdotal history of Western bit players.

On John Ford's frontier: John Wayne and Ben Johnson in *She Wore a Yellow Ribbon*.

Cawelti, John G. *Adventure, Mystery, and Romance: Formula Stories as Art and Popular Culture.* Chicago: University of Chicago Press, 1976. The section on Westerns includes insightful comments on movies.

———. *The Six-Gun Mystique.* Bowling Green, Ohio: Bowling Green Popular Press, 1971. Influential description of the classic Western story formula.

Canutt, Yakima, with Oliver Drake. *The Stuntman: Autobiography of Yakima Canutt with Oliver Drake.* New York: Walker, 1979.

Clapham, Walter. *Western Movies: The Story of the West on Screen.* London: Octopus Books, 1974.

Dickens, Homer. *The Films of Gary Cooper.* Secaucus, N.J.: Citadel, 1970. A detailed filmography with numerous photos.

Evans, Max. *Sam Peckinpah, Master of Violence.* Vermillion, S.D.: Dakota Press, 1972. Details the making of *The Ballad of Cable Hogue* (1970).

Fenin, George N., and William K. Everson. *The Western: From Silents to Cinerama.* New York: Orion Press, 1962. First book-length history of the genre in English. Revised as *The Western: From Silents to the Seventies.* New York: Grossman, 1973.

Ford, Dan. *The Life of John Ford.* Englewood Cliffs, N.J.: Prentice-Hall, 1979.

Ford, John, and Dudley Nichols. Stagecoach: *A Film by John Ford and Dudley Nichols.* New York: Simon and Schuster, 1971. The screenplay.

French, Philip. *Westerns.* New York: Viking, 1973. "Ruminations" about Westerns since 1950. Updated and published by Oxford University Press in 1977.

Friar, Ralph, and Natasha Friar. *The Only Good Indian . . . The Hollywood Gospel.* New York: Drama Book Publishers, 1972. Condemns negative stereotyping of Native American cultures in the movies, mostly Westerns.

Hanna, David. *Four Giants of the West: Stewart, Fonda, Wayne, Cooper.* New York: Belmont Tower Books, 1976.

Hart, William S. *My Life East and West.* Boston: Houghton Mifflin, 1929. Reissued by Benjamin Bloom, 1966. Hart's romanticized autobiography.

Horn, Maurice. *Comics of the American West.* New York: Winchester Press, 1977. Includes information on movie and TV comic book heroes and adaptations of Western movies into comics.

Horwitz, James. *They Went Thataway.* New York: Dutton, 1976. What happened to his childhood cowboy heroes.

Hurst, Richard Maurice. *Republic Studios: Between Poverty Row and the Majors.* Metuchen, N.J.: Scarecrow, 1979.

Jodorowsky, Alexandro. *El Topo.* Ed. Ross Firestone. New York: Douglas, 1971. The screenplay of the surreal Western and an interview with the director.

Kirkley, Donald H., Jr. *A Descriptive Study of the Network Television Western during the Seasons 1955–1956—1962–1963.* New York: Arno, 1979.

Kitses, Jim. *Horizons West.* Bloomington: Indiana University Press, 1969. A structuralist description of the Western formula and chapters on the Westerns of Anthony Mann, Budd Boetticher, and Sam Peckinpah.

Lahue, Kalton C. *Riders of the Range: The Sagebrush Heroes of the Sound Screen.* New York: Barnes, 1973. Career profiles of Western screen heroes.

————. *Winners of the West: The Sagebrush Heroes of the Silent Screen.* New York: Barnes, 1970.

MacDonald, J. Fred. *Don't Touch That Dial: Radio Programming in American Life from 1920 to 1960.* Chicago: Nelson-Hall, 1979. Includes a detailed chapter on radio Westerns.

Manchel, Frank. *Cameras West.* Englewood Cliffs, N.J.: Prentice-Hall, 1971. A brief history of Westerns.

McBride, Joseph, and Michael Wilmington. *John Ford.* New York: Da Capo, 1975. Serious film analyses of Ford's work.

McClure, Arthur, and Ken D. Jones. *Heroes, Heavies and Sagebrush.* New York: Barnes, 1972. Biographical sketches of B Western performers.

McCoy, Tim, with Ronald McCoy. *Tim McCoy Remembers the West.* Garden City, N.Y.: Doubleday, 1977. McCoy's autobiography.

McKinney, Doug. *Sam Peckinpah.* Boston: Twayne, 1979.

Meyer, William R. *The Making of the Great Westerns.* New Rochelle, N.Y.: Arlington House, 1979. Production histories of thirty Westerns.

Nachbar, Jack, ed. *Focus on the Western.* Englewood Cliffs, N.J.: Prentice-Hall, 1974. Fifteen academic essays on Western movies with filmography and bibliography.

————. *Western Films: An Annotated Critical Bibliography.* New York: Garland, 1975. Includes books and articles to 1974.

Niver, Kemp R. *The Battle at Elderbush Gulch.* Ed. Bebe Bergsten. Los Angeles: Locare Research Group, 1972. Detailed study of D. W. Griffith's best-known Western (1913).

Parish, James Robert. *Great Western Stars.* New York: Ace Books, 1976.

Parish, James Robert, and Michael R. Pitts. *The Great Western Pictures.* Metuchen, N.J.: Scarecrow, 1976. Information about two hundred Westerns.

Parkinson, Michael, and Clyde Jeavons. *A Pictorial History of Westerns.* New York: Hamlyn, 1972. Includes both color and black-and-white photos as well as commentary.

Place, J. A. *The Western Films of John Ford.* Seacaucus, N.J.: Citadel, 1974. Substantive commentary on each of Ford's Westerns with numerous photos.

Pilkington, William, and Don Graham, eds. *Western Movies.* Albuquerque: University of New Mexico Press, 1979. Twelve academic essays, each on a specific Western.

Rainey, Buck. *The Fabulous Holts: A Tribute to a Favorite Movie Family.* Nashville, Tenn.: Western Film Collectors Press, 1976.

Ricci, Mark, Boris Zmijewsky, and Steve Zmijewsky. *The Films of John Wayne.* Secaucus, N.J.: Citadel, 1970. A detailed filmography with numerous photos.

Rogers, Roy, and Dale Evans, with Carlton Stowers. *Happy Trails.* Waco, Tex.: Word Books, 1979. Autobiography of the Western's most famous married couple.

Rothel, David. *The Singing Cowboys.* New York: Barnes, 1978. Career profiles.

Sarris, Andrew. *The John Ford Movie Mystery.* Bloomington: Indiana University Press, 1975. Thematic analyses of Ford's films.

Swann, Thomas Burnett. *The Heroine or the Horse: Leading Ladies in Republic Films.* New York: Barnes, 1977. Profiles of actresses in Republic's B Westerns.

Thomas, Tony. *The Films of Kirk Douglas.* Secaucus, N.J.: Citadel, 1972. A detailed filmography with numerous photos.

Thomas, Tony, Rudy Behlmer, and Cliff McCarty. *The Films of Errol Flynn.* Secaucus, N.J.: Citadel, 1969. A detailed filmography with numerous photos, including Flynn's eleven Westerns.

Tuska, Jon. *The Filming of the West.* Garden City, N.Y.: Doubleday, 1976. Still the most comprehensive history of B Western series stars.

Tuska, Jon, Vicki Piekarski, and Karl Theide, eds. *Close-Up: The Contract Director.* Metuchen, N.J.: Scarecrow, 1976. Career overviews of ten directors, nine of whom worked in Westerns.

Wald, Malvin, and Michael Werner, eds. *Three Major Screenplays.* New York: Globe, 1972. Includes scripts of *The Ox-Bow Incident* (1943) and *High Noon* (1952).

Walsh, Raoul. *Each Man in His Time: The Life Story of a Director.* New York: Farrar, Straus and Giroux, 1974. Anecdotal autobiography.

The Searchers—for subsequent generations, a scholarly treasure trove.

Weiss, Ken, and Ed Goodgold. *To Be Continued . . .* New York: Crown, 1972. A description of movie serials.

Willis, Donald C. *The Films of Howard Hawks.* Metuchen, N.J.: Scarecrow, 1975.

Wood, Robin. *Howard Hawks.* Garden City, N.Y.: Doubleday, 1969. In-depth study of themes in Hawks's films.

Wright, Will. *Six Guns and Society: A Structural Study of the Western.* Berkeley: University of California Press, 1975.

Zinman, David. *Saturday Afternoon at the Bijou.* New York: Arlington House, 1973. Describes four B Western series: *Cisco Kid, Gene Autry, Hopalong Cassidy,* and *The Three Mesquiteers.*

HISTORY/THEORY

Aquila, Richard, ed. *Wanted Dead or Alive: The American West in Popular Culture.* Urbana: University of Illinois Press, 1996. Includes three essays on film and television Westerns.

Barbour, Alan G. *Saturday Afternoon at the Movies: 3 Volumes in 1.* New York: Bonanza Books, 1986.

Bataille, Gretchen M., and Charles L. P. Silet. *Images of American Indians on Film: An Annotated Bibliography.* New York: Garland, 1985.

————, eds. *The Pretend Indians: Images of Native Americans in the Movies.* Ames: Iowa State University Press, 1980. Articles and selected film reviews.

Buscombe, Edward, ed. *The BFI Companion to the Western.* New York: Atheneum, 1988. A short history of Westerns, a historical dictionary, a filmography, a dictionary of filmmakers, and a videography of TV Westerns.

Buscombe, Edward, and Roberta E. Pearson, eds. *Back in the Saddle Again: New Essays on the Western.* London: British Film Institute, 1998. Academic essays, some about Western movies.

Byman, Jeremy. *Showdown at* High Noon: *Witch Hunts, Critics, and the End of the Western.* Lanham, Md.: Scarecrow, 2004.

Cameron, Ian, and Douglas Pye, eds. *The Book of Westerns.* New York: Continuum, 1996. Twenty-nine scholarly essays, mostly on directors and specific films.

Canfield, J. Douglas. *Mavericks on the Border: The Early Southwest in Historical Fiction and Film.* Lexington: University Press of Kentucky, 2001.

Cassidy, John M. *Civil War Cinema: A Pictorial History of Hollywood and the War between the States.* Missoula, Mont.: Pictorial Histories, 1986. Includes a section titled "The War in the West."

Cawelti, John G. *The Six-Gun Mystique Sequel.* Bowling Green, Ohio: Bowling Green State University Popular Press, 1999. A rethinking of the ideas in his 1971 book about the Western story formula. Excellent bibliography.

Churchill, Ward. *Fantasies of the Master Race: Literature, Cinema, and the Colonization of American Indians.* 2nd ed. San Francisco: City Lights, 1998.

Cocchi, John. *Second Features: The Best of the "B" Films.* New York: Carol, 1991. Includes a chapter on the B Western.

Copeland, Bobby J. *Trail Talk.* Madison, N.C.: Empire, 1996. Miscellaneous B Western information. Meant primarily for fans.

Corkin, Stanley. *Cowboys as Cold Warriors: The Western and U.S. History.* Philadelphia: Temple University Press, 2004. The ideological content of a dozen Westerns made between 1946 and 1962.

Crow, J. Brim, III, and Jack H. Smith. *The Cowboy and the Kid.* Irving, Tex.: Wind River, 1988. Photos and nostalgia about attending B movies.

Coyne, Michael. *The Crowded Prairie: American National Identity in the Hollywood Western.* New York: St. Martin's Press, 1997. Academic study of the ideology of Westerns from the Depression to 1976.

Cusic, Don. *Cowboys of the Wild West: An A–Z Guide from the Chisholm Trail to the Silver Screen.* New York: Facts on File, 1995.

Dixon, Wheeler W., ed. *Producers Releasing Corporation: A Comprehensive Filmography and History.* Jefferson, N.C.: McFarland, 1986. Information about a studio that made low-budget Westerns.

Doyle, Michael V. *The American West on Film: The Agrarian Frontier.* Dubuque, Iowa: Kendall/Hunt, 1990.

Everson, William K. *The Hollywood Western: 90 Years of Cowboys and Indians, Train Robbers, Sheriffs and Gunslingers, and Assorted Heroes and Desperadoes.* Rev. ed. Secaucus, N.J.: Citadel, 1992. A pictorial history.

Frayling, Christopher. *Spaghetti Westerns: Cowboys and Europeans from Karl May to Sergio Leone.* London: Routledge and Kegan Paul, 1981. Rev. ed., New York: St. Martin's Press, 2000. A highly respected academic analysis.

French, Peter A. *Cowboy Metaphysics: Ethics and Death in Westerns.* Lanham, Md.: Rowman and Littlefield, 1997. Compares ethical values in Westerns with those in Christianity and other value systems.

George-Warren, Holly. *How Hollywood Invented the Wild West: Featuring the Real West, Campfire Melodies, Matinee Idols, Four Legged Friends, Cowgirls, and Lone Guns.* Pleasantville, N.Y.: Reader's Digest, 2001. A lavishly illustrated history.

Graham, Don. *Cowboys and Cadillacs: How Hollywood Looks at Texas.* Austin: Texas Monthly Press, 1983.

Green, Douglas. *Singing in the Saddle: The History of the Singing Cowboy.* Nashville, Tenn.: Vanderbilt University Press, 2002. The history of singing cowboys in all media.

Guttmacher, Peter. *Legendary Westerns.* New York: Metro Books, 1995. A brief survey of the genre.

Hafling, Barrie. *Westerns and the Trail of Tradition: A Year-by-Year History, 1929–1962.* Jefferson, N.C.: McFarland, 2001. How changes in the film industry affected Westerns.

Hilger, Michael. *The American Indian in Film.* Metuchen, N.J.: Scarecrow, 1986. An annotated filmography.

———. *From Savage to Nobleman: Images of Native Americans in Film.* Lanham, Md.: Scarecrow, 1995.

Hitt, Jim. *The American West from Fiction (1823–1976) into Film (1909–1986).* Jefferson, N.C.: McFarland, 1990.

Hoffman, Henryk. *Western Film Highlights: The Best of the West, 1914–2001.* Jefferson, N.C.: McFarland, 2003. Names the best Westerns of each year.

Hulse, Ed. *Zane Grey and the Movies.* Burbank, Calif.: Riverwood Press, 1994.

Hyams, Jay. *The Life and Times of the Western Movie.* New York: Gallery Book, 1983. A brief history, mostly photos.

Jacobs, Del. *Revisioning Film Traditions: The Pseudo-Documentary and the NeoWestern.* Lewiston, N.Y.: Mellen Press, 2000.

Kane, Jim. *Western Movie Quotations.* Jefferson, N.C.: McFarland, 1999. This book contains six thousand quotes from one thousand Westerns from the 1920s to 1998.

Kiehn, David. *Broncho Billy and the Essanay Film Company.* Berkeley: Farwell Books, 2003. A history of an early maker of Westerns.

Kilpatrick, Jacquelyn. *Celluloid Indians: Native Americans and Film.* Lincoln: University of Nebraska Press, 1999.

Kitses, Jim, and Gregg Rickman, eds. *The Western Reader.* New York: Limelight Editions, 1998. Twenty-nine essays with an overall emphasis on postmodernism.

Lachman, Ron. *Women of the Western Frontier in Fact and Fiction and Film.* Jefferson, N.C.: McFarland, 1997.

Lenihan, John H. *Showdown: Confronting Modern America in the Western Film.* Urbana: University of Illinois Press, 1980. The evolving ideology of Westerns, 1946–1979.

Lentz, Harris M., III. *Western and Frontier Film and Television Credits, 1903–1995.* Jefferson, N.C.: McFarland, 1996. A mammoth reference guide.

Loy, R. Philip. *Westerns and American Culture, 1930–1955.* Jefferson, N.C.: McFarland, 2001. How B Westerns reflect the beliefs and values of their audiences.

————. *Westerns in a Changing America, 1955–2000.* Jefferson, N.C.: McFarland, 2004. How Westerns reflect sociopolitical changes in the United States during the last half of the twentieth century.

Lusted, David. *The Western.* New York: Pearson/Longman, 2003.

Magers, Boyd. *So You Wanna See Cowboy Stuff?* Madison, N.C.: Empire, 2003. Miscellaneous materials on Westerns, mostly for fans.

Martin, Len D. *The Republic Pictures Checklist: Features, Serials, Cartoons, Short Subjects and Training Films of Republic Pictures Corporation, 1935–1959.* Jefferson, N.C.: McFarland, 1998.

Matthews, Leonard. *A History of Western Movies.* London: Royce, 1984.

Matuzak, David F. *The Cowboy's Trail Guide to Westerns.* Rev. ed. Redlands, Calif.: Pacific Sunset, 2002. Miscellaneous information on more than twenty-one hundred Westerns.

Miller, Don. *Don Miller's Hollywood Corral: A Comprehensive B-Western Roundup.* Burbank, Calif.: Riverwood Press, 1993.

Mitchell, Lee Clark. *Westerns: Making the Man in Fiction and Film.* Chicago: University of Chicago Press, 1996. Maleness and male bodies in Westerns.

Newman, Kim. *Wild West Movies: How the West Was Found, Won, Lost, Lied About, Filmed and Forgotten.* London: Bloombury, 1990. The central themes of and tensions within the genre.

O'Connor, John E. *The Hollywood Indian: Stereotypes of Native Americans in Films.* Trenton: New Jersey State Museum, 1980. Discusses ten Westerns from silents to 1970.

Okuda, Ted. *The Monogram Checklist: The Films of Monogram Pictures Corporation, 1931–1952.* Jefferson, N.C.: McFarland, 1999. Entries on 727 Monogram releases, including Westerns.

O'Meare, Doc. *The Guns of the Gunfighters: Lawmen, Outlaws, and Hollywood Cowboys.* Iola, Wis.: Krause, 2003. Half of the book describes guns used by movie and TV cowboys.

Parks, Rita. *The Western Hero in Film and Television.* Ann Arbor, Mich.: UMI Research Press, 1982. The history of Westerns as a genre and within the media in general.

Pettit, Arthur C. *Images of the Mexican American in Fiction and Film.* College Station: Texas A&M University Press, 1980.

Prats, Armando José. *Invisible Natives: Myth and Identity in the American Western.* Ithaca, N.Y.: Cornell University Press, 2002.

Rainey, Buck. *The Reel Cowboy: Essays on the Myth in Movies and Literature.* Jefferson, N.C.: McFarland, 1996.

————. *Western Gunslingers in Fact and on Film: Hollywood's Famous Lawmen and Outlaws.* Jefferson, N.C.: McFarland, 1998. A history/movie comparison of seven famous westerners.

Rollins, Peter C., and John E. O'Connor, eds. *Hollywood's Indian: The Portrayal of the Native American in Film.* Lexington: University Press of Kentucky, 1998. Academic essays. Most are critiques of individual films.

Rothel, David. *An Ambush of Ghosts: A Personal Guide to Favorite Western Film Locations.* Madison, N.C.: Empire, 1991.

Sadoux, Jean-Jacques. *Racism in the Western.* New York: Revisionist Press, 1980.

Sarf, Wayne Michael. *God Bless You, Buffalo Bill.* New York: Fairleigh Dickinson University Press, 1983. A comparison between historical westerners and their movie portrayals.

Saunders, John. *The Western Genre: From Lordsburg to Big Whiskey.* London: Wallflower Press, 2001. Thematic analyses of twelve Westerns.

Sherman, Robert G. *Quiet on the Set! Motion Picture History at the Iverson Movie Location Ranch.* Chatsworth, Calif.: Sherway, 1984.

Simmon, Scott. *The Invention of the Western Film: A Cultural History of the Genre's First Half Century.* Cambridge: Cambridge University Press, 2003. Includes sections on Native Americans in silent Westerns, John Wayne and the 1930s, and John Ford and film noir.

Slotkin, Richard. *Gunfighter Nation: The Myth of the Frontier in Twentieth-Century America.* New York: Atheneum, 1992. How Westerns reflect American ideology, especially attitudes toward race and U.S. foreign policy. The third volume of a trilogy exploring "the myth of the frontier."

Smith, Andrew Brodie. *Shooting Cowboys and Indians: Silent Western Films, American Culture and the Birth of Hollywood.* Boulder: University Press of Colorado, 2003.

Smith, Leon. *Movie and Television Locations: 113 Famous Sites.* Jefferson, N.C.: McFarland, 2000. Includes a section on ranches.

Snuggs, Ann. *Riding the Silver Screen Range: The Ultimate Western Movie Trivia Book.* Madison, N.C.: Empire, 1999.

Stanfield, Peter. *Hollywood Westerns and the 1930s: The Lost Trail.* Exeter, U. K.: University of Exeter Press, 2001. Examines both A and B Westerns of the decade.

————. *Horse Opera: The Strange History of the 1930s Singing Cowboy.* Urbana: University of Illinois Press, 2002. Singing cowboy movies as reflections of American culture during the Depression.

Tatum, Stephen. *Inventing Billy the Kid: Visions of the Outlaw in America, 1881–1981*. Albuquerque: University of New Mexico Press, 1982. Includes detailed discussions of Billy the Kid movies.

Thompson, Frank. *Alamo Movies*. Plano, Tex.: Wordmore, 1991. Includes silent and sound movies about the Alamo.

Thompson, Peggy. *Tall in the Saddle: Great Lines from Classic Westerns*. San Francisco: Chronicle Books, 1998. Contains 350 quotations from 150 movies, with photos.

Tompkins, Jane. *West of Everything: The Inner Life of Westerns*. New York: Oxford University Press, 1992. Argues that Westerns in all media were a male reaction to nineteenth-century domestic fiction.

Turner, Ralph Lamar, and Robert J. Higgs. *The Cowboy Way: The Western Leader in Film, 1945–1995*. Westport, Conn.: Greenwood Press, 1999. Traditional leadership theories as reflected in twenty-five Westerns.

Tuska, Jon. *The American West in Film: Critical Approaches to the Western*. Westport, Conn.: Greenwood Press, 1985. Revisionist interpretations.

———. *The Vanishing Legion: A History of Mascot Pictures, 1927–1935*. Jefferson, N.C.: McFarland, 1982.

Walker, Janet, ed. *Westerns: Films through History*. New York: Routledge, 2001. Essays on how Westerns have reflected and distorted history.

Whetmore, Edward J., and Jerry Harrison. *100 Years of the Hollywood Western*. Los Angeles: General Publishing Group, 1995.

Individual Films

Adams, Les, and Buck Rainey. *Shoot-Em-Ups*. New Rochelle, N.Y.: Arlington House, 1978. Reissued by Scarecrow Press in 1985. Credits of over thirty-three hundred Westerns through 1977.

Andreychuk, Ed. *The Golden Corral: A Roundup of Magnificent Western Films*. Jefferson, N.C.: McFarland, 1997. Discusses fourteen films from *Stagecoach* (1939) to *Unforgiven* (1992).

Bach, Steven. *Final Cut: Dreams and Disasters in the Making of* Heaven's Gate. New York: William Morrow, 1985. How *Heaven's Gate* (1980) destroyed United Artists.

Behlmer, Rudy. *America's Favorite Movies: Behind the Scenes*. New York: Frederick Unger, 1982. Includes chapters on the making of *Stagecoach* (1939) and *High Noon* (1952).

Blake, Michael F. *Code of Honor: The Making of Three Great American Westerns*. New York: Taylor, 2003. Describes the production of *High Noon* (1952), *Shane* (1953), and *The Searchers* (1956).

Blottner, Gene. *Universal-International Westerns, 1947–1963: The Complete Filmography*. Jefferson, N.C.: McFarland, 2000.

Jane Fonda as the New Woman in *Cat Ballou*.

———. *Universal Sound Westerns, 1929–1946: The Complete Filmography.* Jefferson, N.C.: McFarland, 2003.

Buscombe, Edward. *The Searchers.* London: British Film Institute, 2000. A critical analysis built around the making of the film.

———. *Stagecoach.* London, British Film Institute, 1992.

Clark, Don. *John Wayne's* The Alamo*: The Making of John Wayne's Epic Film.* Secaucus, N.J.: Citadel, 1994.

Costner, Kevin, Michael Blake, Jim Wilson, and Ben Glass. Dances with Wolves: *The Illustrated Story of the Epic Film.* New York: Newmarket Press, 1991. The screenplay and a description of the production.

Countryman, Edward, and Evonne von Huessen-Countryman. *Shane.* London: British Film Institute, 1999.

Drummond, Philip. *High Noon.* London: British Film Institute, 1997. The making of the film and controversies about its meaning.

Eckstein, Arthur, and Peter Lehman, eds. The Searchers*: Essays and Reflections on John Ford's Classic Western.* Detroit, Mich.: Wayne State University Press, 2004. Academic analyses.

Fagan, Herb. *The Encyclopedia of Westerns.* New York: Facts on File, 2003. Details about more than thirty-five hundred, mostly sound, Westerns.

Garfield, Brian. *Western Films: A Complete Guide.* New York: Rawson, 1982. Personal opinions on more than two thousand Westerns.

Gifford, Barry. *Brando Rides Alone: A Reconsideration of the Film* One-Eyed Jacks. Berkeley: North Atlantic Books, 2003.

Grant, Barry Keith, ed. *John Ford's* Stagecoach. Cambridge: Cambridge University Press, 2003. Six academic essays about the film and selected film reviews.

Hardy, Phil. *The Western.* New York: William Morrow, 1983. Reprinted as *The Encyclopedia of Western Movies.* Minneapolis, Minn.: Woodbury Press, 1984. A critical filmography of eighteen hundred Westerns.

Hayes, R. M. *The Republic Chapterplays: A Complete Filmography of the Serials Released by Republic Pictures Corporation, 1934–1955.* 1992. Jefferson, N.C.: McFarland, 2000.

Kasdan, Lawrence, Jake Kasdan, and Ben Glass. Wyatt Earp: *The Film and the Filmmakers.* New York: Newmarket Press, 1994. The screenplay and a description of the production.

Liandrat-Guigues, Suzanne. *Red River.* London: British Film Institute, 2001.

Lyons, Robert, ed. My Darling Clementine. *John Ford, Director.* New Brunswick, N.J.: Rutgers University Press, 1984. The script, interviews, and reviews.

Neibaur, James L. *The RKO Features: A Complete Filmography of the Feature Films Released or Produced by RKO Radio Pictures, 1929–1960.* Jefferson, N.C.: McFarland, 1994.

Nugent, Frank, and Patrick Ford. *Wagonmaster.* New York: Ungar, 1986. The screenplay.

Parish, James Robert. *The Great Western Pictures II.* Lanham, Md.: Rowman and Littlefield, 1988. Describes four hundred films since 1976 plus earlier materials not discussed in the 1976 volume.

Pitts, Michael R. *Western Movies: A TV and Video Guide to 4200 Genre Films.* Jefferson, N.C.: McFarland, 1986. Credits and brief plot summaries.

Prince, Stephen, ed. *Sam Peckinpah's* The Wild Bunch. Cambridge: Cambridge University Press, 1998. Scholarly essays.

Rainey, Buck. *The Shoot-Em-Ups Ride Again.* Lanham, Md.: Scarecrow, 1990. Supplements the original book by Adams and Rainey and also corrects earlier errors.

Rosenbaum, Jonathan. *Dead Man.* London: British Film Institute, 2001.

Sennett, Ted. *Great Hollywood Westerns.* New York: Abrams, 1992. A discussion of Westerns according to their types.

Thomas, Tony. *The West That Never Was: Hollywood's Vision of the Cowboys and Gunfighters.* Secaucus, N.J.: Citadel, 1989. Brief discussions of forty Westerns, with photos.

Variety *Western Movies: Illustrated Reviews of the Classic Films.* London: Hamlyn, 1993.

Weisser, Thomas. *Spaghetti Westerns—the Good, the Bad, and the Violent: A Comprehensive Illustrated Filmography of 558 Eurowesterns and Their Personnel.* Jefferson, N.C.: McFarland, 1992.

Lorne Greene (1915–1987), TV empire builder, portrayed
Ben Cartwright in the long-running NBC series *Bonanza*.

Wood, Robin. *Rio Bravo*. London: British Film Institute, 2003. Explores the film
as a classic Hollywood movie.

FILM DIRECTORS

Anderson, Lindsay. *About John Ford*. New York: McGraw-Hill, 1981.
Bliss, Michael. *Justified Lives: Morality and Narrative in the Films of Sam Peckinpah*.
Carbondale: South Illinois University Press, 1993.
Brill, Lesley. *John Huston's Filmmaking*. Cambridge: Cambridge University Press,
1997. Analysis of his life and films.
Cumbow, Robert C. *Once upon a Time: The Films of Sergio Leone*. Lanham, Md.:
Rowman and Littlefield, 1987. A film-by-film analysis.
Darby, William. *John Ford's Westerns: A Thematic Analysis with a Filmography*.
Jefferson, N.C.: McFarland, 1996.

David, Ronald L. *John Ford: Hollywood's Old Master*. Norman: University of Oklahoma Press, 1995. A brief biography.

Eyman, Scott. *Print the Legend: The Life and Times of John Ford*. New York: Simon and Schuster, 1999.

Fraser, Harry L., and Wheeler W. Dixon. *I Went That-a-Way*. Lanham, Md.: Rowman and Littlefield, 1990. The autobiography of a B Western director.

Frayling, Christopher. *Sergio Leone: Something to Do with Death*. New York: Faber and Faber, 2000. A critical biography.

Fulwood, Neil. *The Films of Sam Peckinpah*. New York: Sterling, 2002. Examines Peckinpah's TV work as well as all his films.

Gallagher, Tag. *John Ford: The Man and His Films*. Berkeley: University of California Press, 1986. A biography with detailed film analyses.

Hillier, Jim, and Peter Wollen, eds. *Howard Hawks: American Artist*. London: British Film Institute, 1997. An anthology of scholarly essays.

Hoffman, Henryk. *"A" Western Filmmakers: A Biographical Dictionary of Writers, Directors, Cinematographers, Composers, Actors, and Actresses*. Jefferson, N.C.: McFarland, 2000.

Kennedy, Burt. *Hollywood Trail Boss: Behind the Scenes of the Wild, Wild Western*. New York: Boulevard, 1997. An anecdotal autobiography of both a director and writer of notable Westerns.

Kern, Sharon. *William Wyler: A Guide to References and Resources*. Boston: Hall, 1984.

Levy, Bill. *John Ford: A Bio-Bibliography*. Westport, Conn.: Greenwood Press, 1998.

Lewis, Jack C. *White Horse, Black Hat: A Quarter Century on Hollywood's Poverty Row*. Lanham, Md.: Rowman and Littlefield, 2002. An autobiography of a B movie screenwriter.

Mast, Gerald. *Howard Hawks, Storyteller*. New York: Oxford University Press, 1982. Academic film analyses.

McBride, Joseph. *Searching for John Ford: A Life*. New York: St. Martin's Press, 2001. The fullest biography.

McCarthy, Todd. *Howard Hawks: The Grey Fox of Hollywood*. New York: Grove, 2002. The fullest biography.

Mesce, Bill, Jr. *Peckinpah's Women: A Reappraisal of the Portrayal of Women in the Period Westerns of Sam Peckinpah*. Lanham, Md.: Scarecrow, 2001.

Murray, Gabrielle. *This Wounded Cinema, This Wounded Life: Violence and Utopia in the Films of Sam Peckinpah*. Westport, Conn.: Praeger, 2004.

Nevins, Francis M., Jr. *Joseph H. Lewis: Overview, Interview, and Filmography*. Lanham, Md.: Rowman and Littlefield, 1998.

Poague, Leland A. *Howard Hawks*. Boston: Twayne, 1984. Film analyses.

Roth, Lane. *Film Semiotics, Metz, and Leone's Trilogy*. New York: Garland, 1983.

Seydor, Paul. *Peckinpah: The Western Films—A Reconsideration*. Urbana: University of Illinois Press, 1997. An updating of his insightful 1980 book.

Siegel, Don. *A Siegel Film: An Autobiography*. London: Farber and Farber, 1993.

America's West in the 1950s.

Simmons, Garner. *Peckinpah: A Portrait in Montage.* Rev. ed. New York: Limelight, 1998. A biography by a man who worked with the director on several of his films.

Spittles, Brian. *John Ford.* London: Pearson Education, 2002. Discusses themes and techniques in Ford's films.

Studlar, Gaylyn, and Matthew Bernstein, eds. *John Ford Made Westerns: Filming the Legend in the Sound Era.* Bloomington: Indiana University Press, 2001. Nine scholarly essays.

Weddle, David. *"If They Move . . . Kill 'Em!" The Life and Times of Sam Peckinpah.* New York: Grove, 1994. The fullest biography.

Witney, William. *In a Door, Into a Fight, Out a Door, Into a Chase: Moviemaking Remembered by a Guy at the Door.* Jefferson, N.C.: McFarland, 1995. An autobiography by the director of numerous B Westerns, Western serials, and TV Western episodes.

Zinnemann, Fred. *A Life in the Movies: An Autobiography.* New York: Scribner's Sons, 1992. Includes a chapter on *High Noon* (1952).

PERFORMERS

Allen, Rex. *My Life from Sunrise to Sunset.* Scottsdale, Ariz.: RexGarRus Press, 1989. An autobiography of the last singing cowboy.

Andreychuk, Ed. *Burt Lancaster: A Filmography and Biography.* Jefferson, N.C.: McFarland, 2000.

Bingham, Dennis. *Acting Male: Masculinities in the Films of James Stewart, Jack Nicholson and Clint Eastwood.* New Brunswick, N.J.: Rutgers University Press, 1994.

Birchard, Robert S. *King Cowboy: Tom Mix and the Movies.* Burbank, Calif.: Riverwood Press, 1993.

Buford, Kate. *Burt Lancaster: An American Life.* New York: Da Capo, 2001.

Carey, Harry, Jr. *Company of Heroes: My Life as an Actor in the John Ford Stock Company.* New York: Madison, 1994. An autobiography with emphasis on the Westerns Carey made with Ford.

Copeland, Bobby J. *The Bob Baker Story.* Oak Ridge, Tenn.: Bojo Enterprises, 1998.

———. *B-Western Boot Hill.* Madison, N.C.: Empire, 1999. Obituaries of B Western performers.

———. *Charlie King: We Called Him "Blackie."* Madison, N.C.: Empire, 2003. A biography and filmography of a notable B Western bad guy.

———. *Five Heroes.* Oak Ridge, Tenn.: Bojo Enterprises, 2000. Profiles of Russell Hayden, Eddie Dean, George Houston, John "Dusty" King, and Tom Keene.

———. *Roy Barcroft: King of the Badmen.* Madison, N.C.: Empire, 2000. Includes interviews, biography, and filmography.

———. *Silent Hoofbeats.* Madison, N.C.: Empire, 2001. The horses of B Western heroes.

———. *The Whip Wilson Story.* Oak Ridge, Tenn.: Bojo Enterprises, 1999.

Crow, Jefferson Brim, III. *Randolph Scott: A Film Biography.* Madison, N.C.: Empire, 1994. A fan's notes.

Davis, Ronald L. *Duke: The Life and Image of John Wayne.* Norman: University of Oklahoma Press, 2001.

———. *William S. Hart: Projecting the American West.* Norman: University of Oklahoma Press, 2003. The first full-length biography of Hart.

Dickens, Homer. *The Films of Barbara Stanwyck.* Secaucus, N.J.: Citadel, 1984. An extensive filmography with numerous photos.

Diorio, Al. *Barbara Stanwyck: A Biography.* New York: Coward, 1984.

Douglas, Kirk. *The Ragman's Son.* New York: Simon and Schuster, 1988. An autobiography.

Etulain, Richard, and Glenda Riley, eds. *The Hollywood West: Lives of Film Legends Who Shaped It.* Golden, Colo.: Fulcrum, 2001. Ten biographical essays on Western stars and director John Ford.

Fagen, Herb. *White Hats and Silver Spurs: Interviews with 24 Stars of Film and Television Westerns of the Thirties through the Sixties.* Jefferson, N.C.: McFarland, 1996.

Fishgall, Gary. *Against Type: The Biography of Burt Lancaster.* New York: Scribner, 1995.

———. *Gregory Peck: A Biography.* New York: Scribner, 2002.

———. *Pieces of Time: The Life of James Stewart.* New York: Scribner, 1997.

Fitzgerald, Michael G., and Boyd Magers. *Ladies of the Western: Interviews with Fifty-one More Actresses of the Silent Screen to Television Westerns of the 1950s and 1960s.* Jefferson, N.C.: McFarland, 2002. A continuation of *Westerns' Women.*

Graham, Don. *No Name on the Bullet: A Biography of Audie Murphy.* New York: Viking, 1990. The most detailed biography of Murphy.

Griggs, John. *The Films of Gregory Peck.* Secaucus, N.J.: Citadel, 1984. A detailed filmography with numerous photos, including Peck's eleven Westerns.

Guerif, François. *Clint Eastwood: The Man and His Films.* New York: St. Martin's Press, 1986. An English translation.

Henry, Marilyn, and Ron De Soundis. *The Films of Alan Ladd.* Secaucus, N.J.: Citadel, 1981. A detailed filmography with numerous photos.

Holland, Ted. *B Western Actors Encyclopedia: Facts, Photos, and Filmographies for More Than 2500 Familiar Faces.* Jefferson, N.C.: McFarland, 1997.

Horner, William R. *Bad at the Bijou.* 1982. Jefferson, N.C.: McFarland, 2000. Interviews with ten Western bad guys.

Johnstone, Iain. *The Man with No Name.* New York: Morrow Quill, 1981. An early biography of Clint Eastwood, much of it based on an interview.

Kaminsky, Stuart. *Coop: The Life and Legend of Gary Cooper.* New York: St. Martin's Press, 1980.

Katchner, George A. *A Biographical Dictionary of Silent Film Western Actors and Actresses.* Jefferson, N.C.: McFarland, 2002. Brief career profiles of more than one thousand performers.

Key, Donald R., ed. *The Round-Up: A Pictorial History of Western Movie and Television Stars Through the Years.* Madison, N.C.: Empire, 1995.

Kozarski, Diane Kaiser. *The Complete Films of William S. Hart: A Pictorial Record.* New York: Dover, 1980. Mostly photos with some substantive commentary.

Larkins, Bob, and Boyd Magers. *The Films of Audie Murphy.* Jefferson, N.C.: McFarland, 2004. Discusses all forty-nine of Murphy's films.

Lentz, Robert J. *Lee Marvin: His Films and Career.* Jefferson, N.C.: McFarland, 2000. Includes materials on Marvin's film, TV, and stage work and a biography.

Levy, Emmanuel. *John Wayne: Prophet of the American Way of Life.* Metuchen, N.J.: Scarecrow, 1988. A thematic study of the John Wayne screen persona.

Logsdon, Guy, William Jacobson, and Mary Rogers. *Saddle Serenaders*. Salt Lake City, Utah: Gibbs City, 1995.

Love, Damien. *Robert Mitchum: Solid, Dad, Crazy*. New York: Sterling, 2003.

Magers, Boyd, and Michael G. Fitzgerald. *Westerns' Women: Interviews with Fifty Leading Ladies of Movie and Television Westerns from the 1930s to the 1960s*. Jefferson, N.C.: McFarland, 1999.

Malloy, Mike. *Lee Van Cleef: A Biographical Film and Television Reference*. Jefferson, N.C.: McFarland, 1998.

Matthews, Leonard. *The History of Western Movies*. New York: Crescent, 1984. A pictorial guide to individual Western stars.

McCord, Merrill T. *Brothers of the West: The Lives and Films of Robert Livingston and Jack Randall*. Bethesda, Md.: Alhambra, 2003.

McDonald, Archie P. *Shooting Stars: Heroes and Heroines of Western Film*. Bloomington: Indiana University Press, 1987. Twelve essays on specific performers.

McGhee, Richard D. *John Wayne: Actor, Artist, Hero*. 1990. Jefferson, N.C.: McFarland, 1999.

McGilligan, Patrick. *Clint: The Life and Legend*. New York. St. Martin's Press, 2002. A detailed biography of Clint Eastwood.

McKinney, Grange B. *Art Accord and the Movies: A Biography and Filmography*. Raleigh, N.C.: Wyatt Classics, 1999.

Meyers, Jeffrey. *Gary Cooper: An American Hero*. Lanham, Md.: Rowman and Littlefield, 2001. A biography.

Mix, Paul E. *Tom Mix: A Heavily Illustrated Biography of the Western Star, with a Filmography*. Jefferson, N.C.: McFarland, 2001.

Molyneaux, Gerard. *James Stewart: A Bio-Bibliography*. Westport, Conn.: Greenwood Press, 1992.

Morris, Georgia, and Mark Pollard. *Roy Rogers, King of the Cowboys*. San Francisco: Collins, 1994. Mainly glossy photos.

Nareau, Bob. *Kid Kowboys: Juveniles in Western Films*. Madison, N.C.: Empire, 2003. Details about more than seventy juvenile actors.

———. *The Real Bob Steele and a Man Called Brad*. Mesa, Ariz.: Da-Kine, 1991.

Nevins, Francis M., Jr. *The Films of Hopalong Cassidy*. Waynesville, N.C.: World of Yesterday, 1988. Details about all sixty-six Hoppy films.

———. *The Films of the Cisco Kid*. Waynesville, N.C.: World of Yesterday, 1998.

Nichols, John H. *Tom Mix, Riding Up to Glory*. Oklahoma City: Persimmon Hill, 1980. A fan's pictorial tribute.

Norris, Merl G. *The Tom Mix Book*. Waynesville, N.C.: World of Yesterday, 1989.

Nott, Robert. *The Films of Randolph Scott*. Jefferson, N.C.: McFarland, 2004.

———. *Last of the Cowboy Heroes: The Westerns of Randolph Scott, Joel McCrea, and Audie Murphy*. Jefferson, N.C.: McFarland, 2000. Career profiles.

Nye, Douglas. *Those Six-Gun Heroes: 25 Great Movie Cowboys*. Spartanburg, S.C.: ETV Endowment of South Carolina, 1982.

JAMES JOHN STEWART·WAYNE

ᴵⁿ ᴬ **JOHN FORD** PRODUCTION

The Man Who Shot Liberty Valance

VERA MILES·LEE MARVIN·EDMOND O'BRIEN   ANDY DEVINE · KEN MURRAY

Print the myth: Who shot Liberty Valance?

O'Brien, Daniel. *Clint Eastwood, Film-Maker.* London: Batsford, 1996.

O'Hara, Maureen, with John Nicoletti. *'Tis Herself: A Memoir.* New York: Simon and Schuster, 2004.

O'Neal, Bill. *Reel Cowboys: Western Movie Stars Who Thrilled Young Fans and Helped Them Grow Up Decent and Strong.* Austin, Tex.: Eakin, 2000.

———. *Tex Ritter: America's Beloved Cowboy.* Austin, Tex.: Eakin, 1998.

O'Neal, Bill, and Fred Goodwin. *The Sons of the Pioneers.* Austin, Tex.: Eakin, 2001.

Pattie, Jane. *John Wayne . . . There Rode a Legend: A Western Tribute.* Austin, Tex.: Greenleaf Book Group, 2001. A coffee-table book mainly for fans.

Phillips, Robert. *Roy Rogers: A Biography, Radio History, Television Career Chronicle, Discography, Filmography, Comicography, Merchandising and Advertising History, Collectibles Description, Bibliography and Index.* Jefferson, N.C.: McFarland, 1995.

———. *Singing Cowboy Stars.* Salt Lake City, Utah: Gibbs Smith, 1994.

Pitts, Michael R. *Charles Bronson: The 95 Films and 156 Television Appearances.* 1999. Jefferson, N.C.: McFarland, 2003.

Rainey, Buck. *Heroes of the Range: Yesterday's Saturday Matinee Movie Cowboys.* Lanham, Md.: Rowman and Littlefield, 1997.

————. *The Life and Films of Buck Jones: The Silent Era.* Waynesville, N.C.: World of Yesterday, 1988. A fan's biography and filmography.

————. *The Life and Films of Buck Jones: The Sound Era.* Waynesville, N.C.: World of Yesterday, 1991. A chronological continuation of the first volume.

————. *Saddle Aces of the Cinema.* San Diego: Barnes, 1980. Career overviews of fifteen Western stars.

————. *The Strong Silent Type: Over 100 Screen Cowboys, 1903–1930.* Jefferson, N.C.: McFarland, 2003. Biographical information and filmographies.

————. *Sweethearts of the Sage: Biographies and Filmographies of 258 Actresses Appearing in Western Movies.* Jefferson, N.C.: McFarland, 1992.

Riggin, Judith M. *John Wayne: A Bio-Bibliography.* Westport, Conn.: Greenwood Press, 1992.

Roberson, "Bad Chuck," with Bodie Thoene. *The Fall Guy.* North Vancouver, B. C.: Hancock House, 1980. The memoirs of a premier stuntman.

Roberts, Allen, and Max Goldstein. *Henry Fonda: A Biography.* Jefferson, N.C.: McFarland, 1984.

Roberts, Randy, and James S. Olson. *John Wayne: American.* Lincoln: University of Nebraska Press, 1995. A biography with emphasis on the development of Wayne's symbolic screen persona.

Rogers, Roy, Jr., and Karen Ann Wojahn. *Growing Up with Roy and Dale.* Ventura, Calif.: Regal Books, 1986.

Rothel, David. *The Gene Autry Book.* Rev. ed. Madison, N.C.: Empire, 1988. Mainly for fans.

————. *The Roy Rogers Book.* Madison, N.C.: Empire, 1987. Mainly for fans.

————. *Those Great Cowboy Sidekicks.* Metuchen, N.J.: Scarecrow, 1984. Profiles of thirty-nine Western movie sidekicks.

————. *Tim Holt.* Madison, N.C.: Empire, 1994.

Rutherford, John A. *From Pigskin to Saddle Leather: The Films of Johnny Mack Brown.* Waynesville, N.C.: World of Yesterday Press, 1996.

Rutherford, John A., and Richard B. Smith. *Cowboy Shooting Stars* and *More Cowboy Shooting Stars.* Madison, N.C.: Empire, 1988, 1993. Brief credits of 240 Western performers.

Sandford, Christopher. *McQueen: The Biography.* New York: HarperCollins, 2001. A biography of Steve McQueen.

Schickel, Richard. *Clint Eastwood: A Biography.* New York: Knopf, 1996.

Scott, C. H. *Whatever Happened to Randolph Scott?* Madison, N.C.: Empire, 1994. A biographical tribute to a father by his son.

Server, Lee. *Robert Mitchum: "Baby, I Don't Care."* New York: St. Martin's Press, 2002. A biography.

St. Charnez, Casey. *The Films of Steve McQueen.* Secaucus, N.J.: Citadel, 1984. A detailed filmography with numerous photos.

Strode, Woody, and Sam Young. *Goal Dust: The Warm and Candid Memoirs of a Pioneer Black Athlete and Actor.* Lanham, Md.: Madison Books, 1990.

Sweeney, Kevin. *Henry Fonda: A Bio-Bibliography.* Westport, Conn.: Greenwood Press, 1992.

Swindel, Larry. *The Last Hero: A Biography of Gary Cooper.* Garden City, N.Y.: Doubleday, 1980. An anecdotal biography.

Terrill, Marshall. *Steve McQueen: Portrait of an American Rebel.* Medford, N.J.: Plexus, 2001.

Thomas, Tony. *The Films of Henry Fonda.* Secaucus, N.J.: Citadel, 1983. A detailed filmography with numerous photos.

———. *The Films of Ronald Reagan.* Secaucus, N.J.: Citadel, 1980. A detailed filmography with numerous photos, including Reagan's six Westerns.

———. *Wonderful Life: The Films and Career of James Stewart.* Secaucus, N.J.: Citadel, 1997.

Thorton, Chuck, and David Rothel. *Allan "Rocky" Lane: Republic's Action Ace.* Madison, N.C.: Empire, 1990.

———. *Lash LaRue: The King of the Bullwhip.* Madison, N.C.: Empire, 2003.

Wakely, Linda Lee. *See Ya Up There, Baby: The Jimmy Wakely Story.* Canoga Park, Calif.: Shasta Records, 1992.

Wills, Gary. *John Wayne's America: The Politics of Celebrity.* New York: Simon and Schuster, 1997. Detailed critique of Wayne's symbolic persona.

Yoggy, Gary A., ed. *Back in the Saddle: Essays on Western Film and Television Actors.* Jefferson, N.C.: McFarland, 1998. Ten essays.

Zmijewsky, Boris, and Lee Pfeiffer. *The Films of Clint Eastwood, 1955–1993.* Rev. ed. Collingdale, Pa.: DIANE, 1993.

Westerns in Other Media

Some entries in this section include biographies of performers who have appeared in both television and films but whose main reputations come from TV Westerns.

Aaker, Everett. *Television Western Players of the Fifties: A Biographical Encyclopedia of All Regular Cast Members in Western Series, 1949–1959.* Jefferson, N.C.: McFarland, 1997.

Arness, James, with James E. Wise Jr. *James Arness: An Autobiography.* Jefferson, N.C.: McFarland, 2001.

Barabas, SuzAnne, and Gabor Barabas. *Gunsmoke: A Complete History and Analysis of the Legendary Broadcast Series with a Comprehensive Episode-by-Episode Guide to Both the Radio and Television Programs.* Jefferson, N.C.: McFarland, 1990.

Cusic, Don. *It's the Cowboy Way! The Amazing True Adventures of Riders in the Sky.* Lexington: University Press of Kentucky, 2003. A biography of a group best known for radio comedy and an appreciation for the singing cowboy tradition.

Grossman, Gary H. *Saturday Morning TV.* New York: Arlington House, 1991. Contains information on 1950s and 1960s Western TV series aimed at children.

Fillbiger, Lee. *Collector's Reference and Value Guide to* The Lone Ranger. Paducah, Ky.: Collector Books, 1997.

Fury, David. *Chuck Connors: The Man behind the Rifle.* Minneapolis, Minn.: Artists Press, 1999. An authorized biography.

Grams, Martin, and Les Rayburn. *The* Have Gun: Will Travel *Companion.* Delta, Pa.: OTR Publishing, 2000. A comprehensive guide.

Heide, Robert, and John Gillman. *Box-Office Buckaroos: The Cowboy Hero from the Wild West Show to the Silver Screen.* New York: Abbeville Press, 1990.

Holland, Dave. *From Out of the Past: A Pictorial History of* The Lone Ranger. Granada Hills, Calif.: Holland House, 1988. An in-depth history with many color photos.

Jackson, Ronald. *Classic TV Westerns.* Secaucus, N.J.: Citadel, 1994. Information and photos.

Lasiuta, Tim. *Collecting Western Memorabilia.* Jefferson, N.C.: McFarland, 2004. Memorabilia from movies, TV, radio, and comics.

Leiby, Bruce R., and Linda F. Leiby. *A Reference Guide to Television's* Bonanza: *Episodes, Personnel and Broadcast History.* Jefferson, N.C.: McFarland, 2001.

Lentz, Harris M., III. *Television Westerns Episode Guide: All United States Series, 1949–1996.* Jefferson, N.C.: McFarland, 1997. A reference guide to one hundred TV series.

MacDonald, J. Fred. *Who Shot the Sheriff? The Rise and Fall of the Television Western.* New York: Praeger, 1987.

Moore, Clayton, with Frank Thompson. *I Was That Masked Man.* Dallas: Taylor, 1998. An autobiography of the most famous Lone Ranger.

Robertson, Ed. Maverick: *Legend of the West.* Los Angeles: Pomegranate Press, 1994. Discusses the production of the show.

Rothel, David. *Richard Boone: A Knight without Armor in a Savage Land.* Madison, N.C.: Empire, 2001. A biography of the actor who played Paladin in *Have Gun, Will Travel.*

———. *Who Was That Masked Man?* Rev. ed. New York: Barnes, 1981. The Lone Ranger in all media.

Stern, Jane, and Michael Stern. *Way Out West.* New York: HarperCollins, 1999. Heavily illustrated guide to various aspects of cowboy culture.

West, Richard. *Television Westerns: Major and Minor Series 1946–1978.* 1987. Jefferson, N.C.: McFarland, 1998.

Yenne, Bill. *The Legend of Zorro.* Greenville, Conn.: Mallard Press, 1991. A pictorial history of Zorro in print, movies, and television.

Yoggy, Gary A. *Riding the Video Range: The Rise and Fall of the Western on Television.* Jefferson, N.C.: McFarland, 1995. An essential resource.

Contributors

Monique James Baxter received her B.A. in communications—radio, TV, and film—and her M.A. in history from the University of Texas–Pan American. After relocating to Oklahoma in 1999, she pursued a Ph.D. in American history at Oklahoma State University in Stillwater, Oklahoma, and is currently employed at the Oklahoma School of Science and Mathematics in Oklahoma City. Her research interests include film, popular culture, women, and the Southwest borderlands. Uniting many of these interests, her master's thesis was titled "The Hispanic Image Reflected in Post-War Texas Films: From Jennifer Jones to Jennifer Lopez." Although she plans to continue studying and writing about Hollywood and its films, her dissertation research focuses on country music's female artists.

Matthew J. Costello is Professor of political science at Saint Xavier University in Chicago. His early work treated governance and development in Africa and Asia. More recently he has focused on transformations in American culture during the cold war as seen in film. These works may be found in *American Studies, Film & History,* and the *Journal of American Culture.* He is currently exploring what superhero comic books reveal about the political culture of the cold war and what they suggest about the cultural consumption of the war on terror.

Joanna Hearne is Assistant Professor of English at the University of Missouri–Columbia, where she teaches and writes on topics in film studies, Native American studies, and folklore. She has contributed articles and reviews to the *Journal of Popular Film and Television, Film & History, Paradoxa, Western*

American Literature, and *Red Ink* and is currently at work on a book-length study of the intertextual relationships between North American indigenous media, ethnographic film, and the Western.

WINONA HOWE is Professor of English at La Sierra University, where she currently chairs the Department of English and Communication; she teaches classes in Victorian literature, children's and young adult literature, and Southwest literature. She received her B.A. from Pacific Union College, her M.A. from Loma Linda University, and her Ph.D. from the University of California, Riverside. Her scholarship includes articles on Charles Dickens and Wilkie Collins, folktales, and the Australian author Arthur Upfield, as well as papers on Alfred Hitchcock, Harry Potter, Victorian culture, and a number of Victorian authors.

ALEXANDRA KELLER is Assistant Professor of film studies at Smith College. Her work on Westerns, James Cameron and blockbuster film and culture, and avant-garde and experimental film and radiophony has appeared in *The Drama Review, Lusitania, Film & History,* and a number of anthologies, including *Westerns: Films through History, Cinema and the Invention of Modern Life,* and Titanic: *Anatomy of a Blockbuster.* She has curated film and lecture series on the American hero, homeland insecurity, and Virginia Woolf and serves on the editorial board of the *American Studies Journal.* She is currently completing two books. *Re-imagining the Frontier: American Westerns since the Reagan Era* examines the effect of President Reagan's political rhetoric on Westerns, describing the unexpected paucity of Westerns during his administration and their equally unexpected reappearance in the 1990s. *James Cameron* is a critical film guide to the films of a major living director.

JOHN SHELTON LAWRENCE of Berkeley, California, is Professor Emeritus, Morningside College, and currently Senior Fellow in Conservation at the Sierra Club in San Francisco. He was a chapter author and filmographer for the *Hollywood's White House* volume (2003) edited by Rollins and O'Connor. His book *The Myth of the American Superhero* (Eerdmans, 2002), coauthored with Robert Jewett, received the John Cawelti Award of the American Culture Association for the Best Book of 2002 and the Mythopoeic Society Scholarship Award in Myth and Fantasy Studies (2004).

KATHLEEN A. MCDONOUGH, an award-winning documentary filmmaker, has a B.A. in history from UC Berkeley, an M.A. in history from UCLA, and an M.F.A. in film production from San Francisco State University. Her film about medieval book production, *A World Inscribed*, received the John E. O'Connor film award from the American Historical Association in 1997. She is an Assistant Professor in the Department of Communication at the State University of New York, Fredonia, teaching documentary production, multimedia design, and applied aesthetics. Her interest in Westerns began when she was a young child watching old movies on television with her father. It was reignited by her five-year stint as a historian and archivist at Levi Strauss & Co., the "cowboy's tailor." McDonough is currently producing a documentary about the bicycle craze of the 1890s.

RAY MERLOCK is Professor of communications at the University of South Carolina Upstate, where he teaches courses in media production, theory, and history and coordinates internships. He received his B.A. from Duquesne University and his M.A. and Ph.D. from Ohio University. A collector of motion picture memorabilia, he has also provided weekly film reviews for radio, television, and newspapers. A longtime member of the Popular Culture Association and the American Culture Association and a member of the advisory board of the *Journal of American Culture*, he has produced scholarship on various aspects of the Western, on other genres, and on *Casablanca*.

CYNTHIA J. MILLER is a cultural anthropologist, specializing in urban studies and popular culture. She is a faculty member in the Institute for Liberal Arts and Interdisciplinary Studies at Emerson College, in Boston, and has taught numerous courses on media history and theory, urban studies, and the rise and fall of early urban entertainment. Her research has included studies of the social impact of film and television on rural communities in the Yucatán and South India, as well as explorations of immigrant communities' uses of cinema to re-create homelands and maintain cultural identity. Her writing has appeared in *Women's Studies Quarterly, Human Organization, ISLE*, and *Anthropologica*, as well as in two volumes in the *Culture and Power* series *Unofficial Knowledges* (Peter Lang, 2003) and *Phobias* (Silva Editorial, 2004). Her current project is an examination of the life and works of Poverty Row producer Jed Buell.

JACK NACHBAR is Professor Emeritus of popular culture at Bowling Green State University in Ohio. He was the cofounder and longtime coeditor of the *Journal of Popular Film and Television*. He is the author or editor of more than a dozen books, including *Focus on the Western* and a two-volume bibliography of books and articles on Western movies. In 2002, he received the American Culture Association's Governing Board Award, a lifetime achievement award for scholarship.

JOHN E. O'CONNOR is Professor of history at New Jersey Institute of Technology (NJIT) and a member of the federated department of history of NJIT and Rutgers University, Newark. He is cofounder of the Historians Film Committee and was editor/coeditor of its journal, *Film & History*, from 1972 until 1991. Also, with Peter C. Rollins, he coedited *Hollywood's World War I* (1997), *Hollywood's Indian* (1988), and The West Wing: *The American Presidency as Television Drama* (2003). He is author/editor of *Images as Artifact: The Historical Analysis of Film and Television*, compiler of the 120-minute *Image as Artifact* video compilation, and author of *Teaching History with Film and Television*, all published or copublished by the American Historical Association in 1990. In 1991, the American Historical Association honored him with the creation of its annual John E. O'Connor Award for the best historical film and video production.

DAVID PIERSON is an Assistant Professor of media studies at the University of Southern Maine in Portland, Maine. His research interests include the rhetorical and discursive dimensions of broadcast and cable TV network programming. His research has appeared in journals such as *Film & History* and the *Journal of Popular Culture*. He has also completed a book chapter, "American Situation Comedies and the Modern Comedy of Manners," for *America Viewed and Skewed: Television Situation Comedies*, edited by Mary Dalton and Laura Linders, to be published by the State University of New York Press.

PETER C. ROLLINS is Regents Professor of English and American/film studies at Oklahoma State University. He edits *Film & History: An Interdisciplinary Journal of Film and Television Studies*, and is coeditor of *Hollywood's Indian* (University Press of Kentucky, 1999), *Television Histories: Shaping Collective*

Memory in the Media Age (University Press of Kentucky, 2001), *Hollywood's White House* (University Press of Kentucky, 2003), and *Television's* The West Wing (University of Syracuse Press, 2003). His *Columbia Companion to American History on Film* (Columbia University Press, 2003) updates and synthesizes the findings in its sector of cultural studies. His films, including *Will Rogers' 1920s: A Cowboy's Guide to the Times* (1976), *Television's Vietnam: The Real Story* (SONY, 1985), and *Television's Vietnam: The Impact of Media* (1986), are available on one cassette for home and classroom use after PBS and WTBS broadcasts. He was given a Lifetime Achievement Award by the National Popular Culture Association and the American Culture Association in 2002 and has been awarded the Ray and Pat Browne Award for best book in American culture on two occasions.

J. E. Smyth is a lecturer in the history department at the University of Warwick. Smyth's articles and reviews on the Hollywood cinema have appeared in the *Historical Journal of Film, Radio, and Television, Film Quarterly, Rethinking History, The Moving Image,* and *Film & History.* She is currently editing a collection of essays on John Ford's *Young Mr. Lincoln* (1939).

John Parris Springer is an Assistant Professor of English and the Director of film studies at the University of Central Oklahoma. He is the author of *Hollywood Fictions: The Dream Factory in American Popular Literature* (University of Oklahoma Press, 2000) and has published in such journals as *Genre, Iris,* and *Literature/Film Quarterly.* His principal areas of research are early cinema and the studio period, within which he is interested in the multiple intersections between print and visual culture. He is currently editing a collection of essays that examine the relationship between documentary and narrative film practices (*Docufictions: Essays on the Intersection of Documentary and Fictional Filmmaking,* forthcoming from McFarland Press).

Kimberly Sultze is an Associate Professor in the Department of Journalism and Mass Communication at St. Michael's College in Colchester, Vermont, where she teaches courses in media criticism, global communication, and digital design for new media. She received her B.A. from Carleton College and her M.A. and Ph.D. from New York University's Department of Culture and Communication, Program in Media Ecology. Her research interests include the analysis, criticism, theory, and history of film and photography, as well as the production and interpretation of visual media across cultures. She is a former head of the Visual Communication Division of the Association for Education in Journalism and Mass Communication, and is working on a book focusing on interdisciplinary approaches to international film. Her article "Women, Power, and Photography in *The New York Times Magazine*" appeared in the July 2003 issue of the *Journal of Communication Inquiry*.

MATTHEW R. TURNER received a B.A. in English and a B.A. in communications from Virginia Polytechnic Institute and State University. After working as a video producer and editor, he received an M.A. in telecommunications from Ohio University and recently completed his doctorate in the School of Interdisciplinary Arts at Ohio University. His research interests include film, theater, visual arts, and philosophy, specifically as seen through the lens of comedy. His dissertation focuses on a semiotic approach to studying comedy in the arts, which also incorporates aesthetic and philosophical theories of comedy.

INDEX

Illustrations are indicated by italicized page numbers.